Diversifying Learner Experience

Caroline Koh

Editor

Diversifying Learner Experience

A kaleidoscope of instructional approaches
and strategies

 Springer

Editor
Caroline Koh
National Institute of Education
Nanyang Technological University
Singapore, Singapore

ISBN 978-981-15-9860-9   ISBN 978-981-15-9861-6 (eBook)
https://doi.org/10.1007/978-981-15-9861-6

This Springer imprint is published by the registered company Springer Nature Singapore Pte Ltd.
The registered company address is: 152 Beach Road, #21-01/04 Gateway East, Singapore 189721, Singapore

Contents

Chapter 1
Introduction: Diversifying Learner Experiences to Promote Engagement and Performance

Caroline Koh

Abstract The purpose of this book is to present a repertoire of strategies and approaches used by educators to engage learners in diverse educational contexts. It aims to explore the ways in which learner experiences can be diversified in order to meet their needs in an environment that is constantly changing. For instance, the reader is introduced to new technologies used in the conceptualization and implementation of innovative strategies that lead to novel learning experiences. Furthermore, in situations that pose serious challenges to learning, there is a need for educators to deviate from conventional modes of instruction to provide contextualized learning experiences.

1.1 Diversification, Differentiation and Development

> All mammals undergo a certain degree of diversification. Darwin knew that. When he drew a family tree, it had many branches on it.
>
> (Donald Johanson, n.d.)

For too long, classroom instruction and practice have been driven by the so-called "one-size-fits-all" model, based on the premise that all students respond equally well to the prescribed pedagogy and curriculum structure. However, the individuals within the classroom form a microcosm of the world outside and reflect its diversity in every aspect of the word. In its simplest form, "diversity" can be defined as variation within a population, but many authors, such as Zepke (2005), would profess that it is a complex, multifaceted and context-dependent term that may imply differences (e.g. physical, moral, cognitive, affective, spiritual) between individuals or between groups (e.g. gender, ethnic, age, sociocultural). Broadly speaking, diversity describes the variety arising in any society or within any individual, as a result of differences in opinion, perceptions, values, preferences, dispositions and personal

C. Koh (✉)
National Institute of Education, Nanyang Technological University, Singapore, Singapore
e-mail: caroline.koh@nie.edu.sg

© Springer Nature Singapore Pte Ltd. 2020
C. Koh (ed.), *Diversifying Learner Experience*,
https://doi.org/10.1007/978-981-15-9861-6_1

1

attributes, among many other factors. Since this book is primarily about learners and learning, the definition of diversity posted by the University of Rhode Island (2020) seems particularly apt. In this instance, diversity is conceptualized as the understanding that "each student brings unique experiences, strengths, and ideas to our classroom," and the process of diversification is thus the "exploration and incorporation of these differences to enrich learning and in our classrooms." Hence, diversifying learner experience involves being cognizant of learner differences and, on the basis of these, designing and creating resources, teaching strategies, learning modes and opportunities that would engage learners and enrich their experiences.

With improved transportation, international migration rates have risen steadily over the years (He, Phillion, Chan, & Xu, 2008). This, together with improved communication systems arising from the internet and the use of new technologies, have led to the current wave of neoliberal globalization whereby countries around the world have experienced cultural and linguistic diversification at unprecedented levels. Societies have had to grapple with fast-pace changes that they struggle to keep up with, and likewise, educational institutions struggle to keep abreast with a rapidly evolving landscape, while staying relevant in the preparation of the future work-force. As such, many educators have questioned the relevance of the "one-size-fits-all" approach currently adopted in many educational systems. For instance, Murray, Shea, Shea and Harlin (2004) observed that the traditional "universal" curriculum structure forces teachers to teach to the test, at the expense of what students need and what they really want to learn and are interested in. As such, with regard to student achievement, those at the lower end of the spectrum sadly fall behind the broadband of average performers, while those at the higher end feel bored and are unable to fulfill their true potential. Students' motivation to learn may decrease, while they remain ill-prepared for the demands of the fluid environment in which they live. An earlier study by Kalchman and Case (1999) highlighted the need of high-ability learners to be provided with a wide spectrum of learning experiences, given the diversity in the group. These authors found that when students were given the opportunity to explore different kinds of functions independently, they performed better than those who went through the conventional, text-based program.

Thus, one of the main shortfalls of the "one-size-fits-all" approach lies in its failure to recognize the *diversity* of individuals within and outside the classroom, the need to *differentiate* between their varied needs, and finally, the imperative to *develop* diverse tools and approaches to instructional design and delivery. The idea of diversifying learning opportunities arose in the 70s, when Baker and his colleagues (1974) investigated student preferences in terms of three different modalities of instruction: conventional mass lecture, small groups and independent study. These authors found that the majority of students still preferred the conventional lecture style, followed by small group learning whereas independent study was generally not favored. It is easy to understand why students *and* educators subscribed to the "one for all" mode of delivery despite its shortfalls—a decade or so ago, it would have been highly impractical to design different modes of instruction and/or curricula for different groups of students within the school/educational institution, let alone within the classroom.

However, the emergence of IT and new technologies have altered the educational landscape and opened up a multitude of opportunities for the proliferation of diverse modes of instruction catering to the diverse student populations. Educators have been emboldened to explore new online resources and students are no longer reliant on the traditional classroom as their sole learning platform. In Darwin's words, and later Johanson's, the tree of learning was able to "branch out," with the emergence of new and hybrid forms of education. This was, in a sense, timely, as educators in both developing and developed countries came to the realization that reforms were needed to cope with twenty-first century challenges. As Klaus Schwab (2016), founder and executive chairman of the World Economic Forum, wrote:

> We stand on the brink of a technological revolution that will fundamentally alter the way we live, work, and relate to one another. In its scale, scope, and complexity, the transformation will be unlike anything humankind has experienced before. We do not yet know just how it will unfold, but one thing is clear: the response to it must be integrated and comprehensive, involving all stakeholders of the global polity, from the public and private sectors to academia and civil society.

He was, of course, referring to what is now known as the Fourth Industrial Revolution or Industry 4.0 (I4.0). The term originates from an initiative by the German government to promote computerization in their high-tech manufacturing industry, as part of the country's investment in research and development (Almada-Lobo, 2015). Conceptually, it describes the emergence and adoption of automation and digitalization in manufacturing technologies, with profound implications on all aspects of life in the twenty-first century. In Schwab's view, the term "revolution" involves an "abrupt and radical change," a change that is not only sudden but shows a clear demarcation from the status quo (Bonciu, 2017, p. 9; Schwab, 2016, p. 11). While Schwab rightly concedes that Industry 4.0 is an emerging phenomenon and as yet, ill-defined and fluid in nature, some of its characteristics are already in place and include transformative technologies such as cyber physical systems, the internet of things, cloud computing, artificial intelligence, mobile devices, 3D printing, and Big Data analytics. As such, one can foresee that the use of robotics will be pervasive in multiple and diverse sectors such as business, health care, education, entertainment, civil defense and law enforcement. In spite of the rise in populism and nationalism in recent years, the pervasiveness of the Internet of Things (IoT) has only consolidated and strengthened the global network through the interconnectedness of more and more devices and their users across business, social, political, cultural and technological domains. Likewise, cloud computing and Big Data analytics will enable the collection and processing of data in quantities that would have been beyond the scope of human ability. The increased automation and digitalization characterizing I4.0 would undoubtedly bring about fast disruptive changes that in turn, require fast adaptation (Eberhard et al., 2017).

In their study on the future of employment, Frey and Osborne (2013) predicted that close to 50% of the existing jobs in advanced economies are at risk of becoming redundant due to automation in the decades to come, while the World Economic Forum (2016) predicts that two-thirds of children starting elementary school will be taking up jobs that are not yet in existence. It is likely, however, that jobs with low risks of being automated are those requiring high levels of cognitive functioning, such as problem-solving, creativity and design, social and affective intelligence. Educational institutions and educators have been urged to respond to the recent trends, and to adapt the way they teach to prepare and equip students with the necessary skills for economy and employability 4.0. The impetus is to prepare a workforce with the knowledge and skills to function not just in only one industry but in a number of different industries (Eberhard et al., 2017). This requires the setting up of multinational offices, with staff hailing from diverse countries and cultural backgrounds, with different working habits and beliefs, and communicating in different languages. As Torres (2001) commented, the preparation of students for work in I4.0 environments will entail the diversification and expansion of educational opportunities, as well as innovating, exploring, trialing and synergizing different modes of education and learning. The more diverse the students' learning experiences, the better are they able to thrive in a work environment that is in constant flux.

In this respect, authors such as Virtanen and colleagues (2012) explored the use of alternative teaching methods and tools and assessed their effectiveness. Their findings suggested that students were generally supportive of the use of nontraditional tools for teaching, such as Prezi for teaching and content organization, Twitter for interaction within class, and an inquiry-based learning method. Although it is tacitly known that educators have been constantly creating and adopting new pedagogies and instructional approaches, many of these have remained within the confines of the classroom and have not been shared with the wider community.

1.2   About This Book

The aim of this book is to bring together and present a repertoire of strategies and innovations that educators from diverse educational contexts have conceptualized and/or implemented in order to cater to the diverse needs of their students/learners. It aims to provide answers to the following questions: In what ways are the students/learners diverse in the context of their study? What are the strategies/approaches/pedagogies used to cater to their diverse needs? How are new technologies used in the conceptualization/implementation of these approaches/innovations? In what ways do the innovative strategies diversify learner experiences?

What seems to be lacking in the literature are evidence-based reports of innovative strategies/approaches that have offered a diversity of experiences to learners. This book attempts to bridge this gap by bringing together a team of international authors who offer perspectives that are grounded in educational research and written in a style that is manageable for practitioners, researchers and administrators. Whereas some chapters describe empirical studies on interventions that lead to diversifying learner experiences, others provide reviews of the literature on specific domains of diversity in learners and learning experiences. The focal strength of the chapters is to present diverse instructional strategies, implemented in different sociocultural settings, such that readers may be convinced that irrespective of their contexts, they should be cognizant of learner diversity, be open to differentiating between learner needs and be willing to take concrete action toward improvement.

The chapters in this book are arranged in three parts, based on their related themes:

Part 1—Diversifying learner experiences within the classroom (Chaps. 2–6)
Part 2—Diversifying learner experiences beyond the classroom (Chaps. 7–10)
Part 3—Diversifying experiences for learners with special needs (Chaps. 11–14)

1.3 Part 1—Diversifying Learner Experiences Within the Classroom

In this section, the authors discuss the principles and methods that lead to a diversification of learner experiences in traditional classroom contexts. These involve simple extension of the existing strategies to other contexts (e.g., Chap. 4) as well as innovative pedagogies made possible through the use of modern technologies (e.g., Chap. 2).

Introducing Part 1 on diversifying experiences within the classroom, *Michael Hast* in Chap. 2 discusses the use of tacit knowledge assessment in primary science learning. The chapter explores recent research based on classroom interventions and from a developmental psychology perspective. The author infers that making use of learners' preconceived understanding in combination with technology-based pedagogy enables differentiated approaches and supports engagement amidst learner diversity.

Whereas the previous author deals with diversification of learner experiences from a cognitive perspective, *Kah Loong Chue*'s Chap. 3 approaches the issue from an affective angle, with the use of Team-Based Learning as an approach to diversify students' learning experiences. The paper presents the findings on the effect of Team-Based Learning on students' activity emotions such as enjoyment, boredom and anger. In addition, the study investigates the moderating effect (if any) of student personality based on the HEXACO model on the effect of TBL on activity emotions.

In Chap. 4, *Nasyita Mohtar* begins by presenting a review of extant research on students' school conduct, peer acceptance and subjective well-being. In lieu of traditional methods such as the use of incentives and deterrents, she explores how these factors could be improved and students' school experiences diversified through a positive psychology intervention whereby students write Peer Praise Notes to their classmates.

In Chap. 5, *Hester Oh* follows up on the previous discourse with a review of the literature on the effect of collaborative learning on student motivation and perceived psychological needs satisfaction. She also explores the feasibility of diversifying learner experiences in an art class by taking a collaborative approach to art-making, thus improving student motivation in the domain.

Chapter 6 presents a review of recent literature on processes and practices aimed at providing gifted and high-ability learners with diverse learning experiences that would allow them to grow to their fullest potential. These experiences centered around three main areas, namely in terms of ability clustering and curriculum suitability, learner motivation and socioemotional needs, and the impact of new technologies on learning.

1.4 Part 2—Diversifying Learner Experiences Beyond the Classroom

The UNESCO report, "The Hidden Crisis" (2011, p. 126), describes challenges faced by learners in exceptional contexts:

> Whether they are in conflict zones, displaced within their own countries or refugees, parents, teachers and children affected by conflict have at least one thing in common: the extraordinary level of ambition, innovation and courage they demonstrate in trying to maintain access to education. Parents understand that education can provide children with a sense of normality and that it is an asset—sometimes the only asset—that they can carry with them if they are displaced.

The next few chapters of this book describe the "ambition, innovation and courage" that have led to the diversification of learner experiences beyond the classroom and/or amidst challenging circumstances.

Introducing Part 2, *David Bell and Jeffrey Smith*, in Chap. 7, describe how the Virtual Excursion online visitation experience at the Museum of New Zealand Te Papa Tongarewa offered a unique opportunity for students to learn in an innovative and engaging manner that the classroom is unable to provide. Learners who took part in the program lauded its combination of personal contact and inclusivity in learning.

In Chap. 8, *Isabelle Ong* proposes yet another innovative approach to learning in her article on "play-flow-ness." In it, she suggests a framework focused on play as a medium for adult learners to attain a state of "flow" in their learning, as well as the conditions for the right balance between the player's positive and negative emotions. This article is unique in that it deals with adult learners rather than child or youth learners. The interest in andragogy (processes and practice of adult teaching) has been on the rise over the years as more adults go back-to-school for re-training or upgrading skills.

In Chap. 9, *Steven Sexton and Sandra Williamson-Leadley* present a different take of the "one-size-fits-all" concept of education. As in the previous chapter, these authors report on adult learners, student teachers embarking on a Master of Teaching and Learning program. Rather than advocating a diversity of courses to cater to the needs of diverse learners, they report on the design of a single higher degree program that is sufficiently diverse to support the multifarious community of student teachers deployed to teach the diverse population of school-aged students in New Zealand.

In Chap. 10, *Syazlin Sazali, Alicia Franklin, Rhonda G. Craven and Alexander S. Yeung* describe how the diversification of learner experiences through the application of IT and use of virtual platforms, enabled education to be made accessible to disadvantaged students living in remote and isolated locations of Australia.

1.5 Part 3—Diversifying Experiences for Learners with Special Needs

Introducing Part 3, Diversifying experiences for learners with special needs, *Miriam Mason, David Galloway and Andrew Joyce-Gibbons* in Chap. 11, describe how three schools run by EducAid strive to provide education to marginalized children in war-torn Sierra Leone. Although the context of this study is highly exceptional, the article provides an interesting insight into how learning experiences can be diversified to cater to the varied needs of children in highly disadvantaged contexts, some of whom suffered trauma, tragedy, violence and deprivation.

In Chap. 12, *Minglee Yong* and *Boon Ooi Lee* describe strategies and approaches to support students with emotional and behavioral disorders (EBD). The chapter provides an overview of extant research findings, with the aim to inform on possible directions for future research and application. More specifically, the authors propose to diversify an EBD student's experiences with the use of a multitier system of support (MTSS) that provides a continuum of interventions that support the student through the various stages of rehabilitation.

Adeline Yeong and *Anuradha Dutt*, in Chap. 13, report on diversifying the learning experiences of youths with Autism Spectrum Disorder with the use of video modeling. Their study focuses on the use of the iPad as a device for self-instructed video modeling that would enable individuals with ASD to acquire daily-living skills.

As a closure to this section, Chap. 14 discusses how the experiences of learners with visual, auditory and mobility impairments can be diversified and supported with the use of serious (digital) games. On the whole, the participants were generally receptive to the use of serious games in learning and rehabilitation. Likewise, controlled trials have revealed improvements in learner achievement motivation and performance.

The book concludes with the editor's final discussion, in Epilogue, of the major findings from the chapters. It draws together the main ideas from each of the three sections, with the aim of producing a workable framework for diversifying learner experiences in an era of constant change and evolution.

1.6 Conclusion

The 14 chapters in this book are a reflection of the scholarly work on diversification of learner experiences in different contexts. In Part 1, the authors present examples of how learners' classroom experiences can be diversified through differentiated approaches based on learners' tacit knowledge in combination with technology-based pedagogy, the use of Team-Based Learning to improve students' activity emotions, the use of Peer Praise Notes to promote positive school conduct, peer acceptance and subjective well-being, processes and practices aimed at diversifying high-ability learners' learning experiences as well as collaborative approaches in art-making.

In Part 2, the reader is given the opportunity to explore examples of diversification of learner experiences beyond the classroom and/or amidst challenging circumstances. The chapters describe how learner experiences are diversified through an online virtual excursion museum visitation, a framework on play as a medium for adult learners, a single higher degree program that is sufficiently diverse to support a multifarious cohort of student teachers, and the use of IT and virtual platforms to make education accessible to disadvantaged students in remote and isolated locations.

Finally, Part 3 considers ways in which the experiences of special needs learners can be diversified through the use of a multitier system of support (MTSS) for the rehabilitation of students with emotional and behavioral disorders, self-instructed video modeling that enables individuals with ASD to acquire daily-living skills, and the use of serious games to instruct and rehabilitate learners with sensory and mobility impairments.

The authors generally recognize how neoliberal globalization and the advent of the internet have brought profound changes and diversity to the educational landscape. Their goal is to initiate ideas and strategies that would be in synch with the needs of present and future generations of students. This book thus provides an anthology of reviews of extant research and strategies that enabled learner experiences to be diversified across contexts.

References

Almada-Lobo, F. (2015). The Industry 4.0 revolution and the future of manufacturing execution systems (MES). *Journal of Innovation Management, 3*(4), 16–21.

Baker, P. J., Bakshis, R., & Tolone, W. (1974). Diversifying learning opportunities: A response to the problems of mass education. *Research in Higher Education, 2*(3), 251–263.

Bonciu, F. (2017). Evaluation of the Impact of the 4th industrial revolution on the labor market. *Romanian Economic and Business Review, 12*(2), 7–16.

Eberhard, B., Podio, M., Alonso, A. P., Radovica, E., Avotina, L., Peiseniece, L., … Solé-Pla, J. (2017). Smart work: The transformation of the labour market due to the fourth industrial revolution (I4. 0). *International Journal of Business & Economic Sciences Applied Research, 10*(3).

Frey, C. B., & Osborne, M. A. (2013). *The future of employment: How susceptible are jobs to computerisation?*. University of Oxford. https://www.oxfordmartin.ox.ac.uk/downloads/academic/The_Future_of_Employment.pdf.

He, M. F., Phillion, J. O. A. N. N., Chan, E., & Xu, S. (2008). Immigrant students' experience of curriculum. *The Sage handbook of curriculum and instruction,* 176–197.

Johanson, D. (n.d.). *BrainyQuote.com.* Retrieved from BrainyQuote.com Web site: https://www.brainyquote.com/quotes/donald_johanson_675984.

Kalchman, M., & Case, R. (1999). Diversifying the Curriculum in a Mathematics Classroom Streamed for High-Ability Learners: A Necessity Unassumed. *School Science and Mathematics, 99*(6), 320–329.

Murray, R., Shea, M., Shea, B., & Harlin, R. (2004). Issues in education: Avoiding the one-size-fits-all curriculum: Textsets, inquiry, and differentiating instruction. *Childhood education, 81*(1), 33–35.

Schwab, K. (2016). The 4th industrial revolution. In *World economic forum.* New York: Crown Business. Retrieved from https://www.weforum.org/agenda/2016/01/the-fourth-industrial-revolution-what-it-means-and-how-to-respond.

Torres, R. M. (2001, October). Amplifying and diversifying learning: Formal, non-formal and informal education revisited. In *ADEA Biennial Meeting*, Arusha, Tanzania.

UNESCO. (2011). EFA global monitoring report. In *The hidden crisis: Armed conflict and education*. Paris: UNESCO.

University of Rhode Island. (2020). *Diversity and Inclusion in the classroom—Introduction*. Retrieved from https://web.uri.edu/teach/multicultural/.

Virtanen, P., Myllärniemi, J., & Wallander, H. (2012). Diversifying higher education: Innovative tools to facilitate different ways of learning. In *Proceedings of the 12th International Conference on Information Communication Technologies in Education (ICICTE) 2012* (pp. 105–116).

Zepke, N. (2005). Diversity, adult education and the future: A tentative exploration. *International Journal of Lifelong Education, 24*(2), 165–178.

Part I
Diversifying Learner Experiences Within the Classroom

Chapter 2
"It is There but You Need to Dig a Little Deeper for It to Become Evident to Them": Tacit Knowledge Assessment in the Primary Science Classroom

Michael Hast

Abstract In response to the volume's overall rationale, the chapter contributes to the critique of a 'one-size-fits-all' model of teaching. It does so through a discussion of the particular use of tacit knowledge assessment within the specific educational context of primary science learning. The chapter initially introduces a core challenge in science teaching—the rise of misconceptions and their resistance to conceptual change through instruction. It continues by exploring an alternative approach to classic conceptual change approaches. Specifically, it reviews recent research in the field of tacit knowledge assessment, taking into account evidence from both the developmental psychology approach and from specific classroom interventions. It argues for a continuation of underlying knowledge constructs beyond infancy into childhood, and that tapping into such knowledge constructs can be made use of in educational practice. The broad conclusion from the insight gained by this review demonstrates how drawing on individual levels of preconceived understanding of science and making use of a 'self-collaboration' approach through the incorporation of technology-based pedagogy can lead to successful conceptual change in the primary science classroom. In doing so, it also highlights how this approach lends itself to differentiation approaches and how it acknowledges diverse learner (and teacher) experiences.

Keywords Primary science education · Conceptual change · Tacit knowledge · Developmental psychology

2.1 Introduction

Repeatedly, individual research papers and reviews of studies, both in the domain of educational research and in the domain of developmental psychology, have reported on a common matter: the many different ideas that children hold about a wide range of topics even before they have been part of any formal pedagogy around those

M. Hast (✉)

National Institute of Education, Nanyang Technological University, Singapore, Singapore

e-mail: michael.hast@nie.edu.sg

C. Koh (ed.), *Diversifying Learner Experience*,
https://doi.org/10.1007/978-981-15-9861-6_2

13

topics. Currently, the frequency of discussion of this matter has almost turned into a classic issue in the context of classroom-based education. In the particular field of science education alone, there exist thousands of studies to illustrate this point (cf. Duit, 2009). Even Duit's exemplary collection of these studies is now already a decade old, and so there are, without a doubt, numerous other examples to consider.

In short, children enter the classroom with a wide range of preconceived scientific ideas about how the world around them works, many of which are formulated through experiences and discourses in everyday contexts (Allen, 2014; Carey, 2009; Hast, 2014a). This is made all the more difficult through the fact that every child has unique experiences of those everyday contexts, and as a result the preconceived ideas also vary widely, in terms of both content and degree of understanding. Yet the science classroom is not a setting of unstructured everyday activities, but of organised knowledge (Kambouri, 2016). The instructor's role, therefore, is to organise that wide range of conceptions within a shared setting. However, such organisation must also remain effective in its guidance through instruction so that preconceived knowledge is reformulated in appropriate ways (Kambouri, Briggs, & Cassidy, 2011).

This chapter aims to address the issue of supporting science learning in the classroom, particularly in view of the general pedagogical challenges posed by children's preconceived understanding of the world, the availability of technology as a potential solution to these challenges, and how such an approach may benefit differentiation in particular. This chapter does so by drawing together literature and findings from cognitive development research as well as from the fields of science education and general classroom pedagogy. In contributing to the bridge that spans these disciplines, the chapter highlights diverse learner and teacher experiences that challenge the notion of a 'one-size-fits-all' model of teaching in science, while at the same time acknowledging a common foundation of understanding that can be tapped into.

2.2   Concepts in the Early Science Classroom

Understanding conceptions in the science classroom has far-reaching implications. Not only is it crucial for practitioners to understand how the extensive everyday world experiences give rise to the beliefs children bring with them (Bliss, 2008; Eshach, 2007), it is also necessary to understand that these early life-world experiences seem to act as a major factor in children's choice to pursue science education at later educational stages (DeWitt et al., 2013). Their interest in and attitudes towards school-based science are already well established in adolescence (DeWitt, Archer, & Osborne, 2014; Symonds & Hargreaves, 2016) but children's positive attitudes towards science are already in decline from as early as 7 years of age and continue to do so over time (Said, Summers, Abd-El-Khalick, & Wang, 2016). Because future economies are predicted to rely increasingly on a workforce that is science and technology literate (e.g. Hazelkorn et al., 2015), it is pivotal to provide opportunities to develop interest in science as early as possible.

For a long time, the perception was that scientific thinking was not really possible until children reached adolescence, but more current positions are in agreement that in fact the thinking processes observed in adolescence and beyond are the result of structured, scaffolded building upon the rudimentary scientific concepts and thought processes evident in children (Zimmerman, 2007) and possibly even in preverbal infants (Heintz, 2014). In order to support children's learning processes in meaningful ways, it is, therefore, necessary to first understand what children's scientific ideas look like, as successful instructional approaches can only be designed with insight into this preconceived knowledge (Duschl, Schweingruber, & Shouse, 2006). Teachers are not ignorant of recognising that children do indeed bring many ideas from their informal experiences into formal learning settings, which are based on knowledge systems with interrelated ideas used to make sense of the world and the experiences within that world (Gomez-Zwiep, 2008; Hast, 2017).

One particular concept that raises concern for pedagogy in the context of science instruction is the role of object weight in object motion. Once again, the initial problem of a range of ideas is evident, with children within single age groups drawing on a number of explanations for the shared phenomenon being discussed, such as trying to explain why certain objects might roll faster along a horizontal surface than others (Hast & Howe, 2012). The most prominent explanation provided in object motion predictions, however, is based on how heavy or light objects are in relation to each other. Consistently, in this respect, across the primary school age range, children believe heavy objects will fall faster than lighter objects because of their perceived weight, and that conversely lighter objects will roll faster along horizontal surfaces due to their lightness. With regard to rolling down slopes, on the other hand, expressed understanding changes with age—younger children are more likely to suggest the lighter of two objects will roll down faster, and older children declare the opposite (Hast, 2014b, 2016, 2018a; Hast & Howe, 2013a). Their understanding of speed change, too, is affected by such conceptions of object weight (Hast & Howe, 2013b).

As a result of such findings, it is clear that children's constructions of common-sense theories of object motion begin early, that these theories have a significant degree of robustness to them, and that they outline an understanding of the laws of the physical world that is incommensurate with accepted scientific views. This is, as such, not surprising since our engagement with the everyday world begins on the first day that we are in that world. The formation of such early theories is thus argued to be based on a combination of innate representations, empirical observations of specific events and culturally transmitted beliefs (Shtulman & Young, 2020). In fact, more recent studies with toddlers argue that the aforementioned weight-related misconceptions may begin to emerge before children reach their third birthday (Hast, 2018b, 2019). These studies argue that the susceptibility to the relative weight of objects, prompted by experience of two balls of differing weights, may lead to biased search behaviours broadly in line with the findings from slightly older children's verbally expressed beliefs. It is perhaps not all too surprising, then, that even in 5-year-old children, ideas about weight-related object motion are well established. Since a core purpose of science education is to engage with and, where necessary, challenge the knowledge that children bring into the classroom, what are the implications of these findings for relevant pedagogy?

2.3 Conceptual Change in the Science Classroom

Conceptual change is arguably a main challenge for instructors in the science classroom. For one, the established beliefs that children bring into formal learning settings not only vary widely in their content but they are frequently incommensurate with the accepted scientific views that are due to be taught. More problematic, however, is that such preconceived ideas are so deeply entrenched in children's thinking that they are often highly resistant to change through instruction (Duit, Treagust, & Widodo, 2013). This then has wider reaching implications, since lower level understanding typically underpins higher level concepts that are taught at later stages, so appropriate preparatory revision would be necessary (Wiser & Smith, 2008). While an understanding of anticipated motion patterns, for instance, generally does seem to improve with age through appropriate instruction (Howe, 2017), the already aforementioned emerging behaviour patterns in 3-year-olds when it comes to weight and object motion, and the consistent verbally expressed predictions across middle childhood may lead to maintained beliefs in adulthood and impact-related concepts around force and motion if not addressed through appropriate conceptual change opportunities (Harris, George, Hirsch-Pasek, & Newcombe, 2018; Venkadasalam & Ganea, 2018).

But it is not just the learners and their conceptions that pose a challenge in successful instruction. Teachers do recognise that children bring with them a wide range of ideas (Gomez-Zwiep, 2008). They also note the challenge of changing such ideas; one teacher who was interviewed on her views of such challenges (Hast, 2017) commented that "*it's very difficult when they've got an idea in their heads to then mould a new one … they found it very difficult to change their view*". However, it is also necessary to consider the interaction of knowledge, skills and confidence that generalist primary teachers themselves frequently seem to lack when it comes to teaching science (Hast, 2017; Howitt, 2007; Pedretti, Bencze, Hewitt, Romkey, & Jivraj, 2008; van Aalderen-Smeets, Walma van der Molen, & Asma, 2012). The implications of such a lack must not be underestimated as they act as a key barrier in being able to successfully promote children's relevant educational achievement (Cremin, Glauert, Craft, Compton, & Stylianidou, 2015). As a result, the question that remains is how both resistance to conceptual change and challenges based on instructors can be tackled in ways that lead to an enhanced educational experience.

Research and pedagogy alike have given significant attention to a common goal—to understand the processes of conceptual change and how to foster it through instruction (see, e.g. Kendeou, Butterfuss, Kim, & Van Boekel, 2019). A very widely cited key theoretical approach to conceptual change in science education was formulated by Posner, Strike, Hewson, and Gertzog (1982). Their approach has been posited as a translation of Piaget's (1978, 1985) classic concepts of assimilation, accommodation and equilibration in the growth of children's thinking and understanding. Here, children can interpret new experiences based on existing schemata by assimilation and thereby find themselves in equilibrium, or they have to reshape existing schemata through accommodation because newly encountered situations cannot be sufficiently explained by what is already known, experiencing disequilibrium. Through equilibration—moving from disequilibrium to equilibrium—schemata become more effective and as a result, children become more sophisticated in their interpretation of the world. Cognitive conflict experienced through disequilibrium can therefore be seen as desirable for pedagogy.

In their specific approach, Posner and colleagues (1982) thus outline four necessary conditions for successful change to be able to occur by drawing on such cognitive conflict. First, the learner must experience dissatisfaction with existing conceptions. Second, a new and intelligible conception must be available. Third, this new conception must appear plausible to the learner. And fourth, it should open up to new fruitful research. However, the first two conditions are not always being met in a sufficiently effective manner. For example, when carrying out scientific experiments, students may not always reformulate their original conceptions if these contradict the outcome of the said experiment and instead, blame for not confirming their conceptions is sought in other variables such as the experimental setup (Howe, 2012). So, in light of the many challenges posed by students and teachers alike, are there perhaps alternative ways to meet the conditions outlined by Posner et al.?

2.4 Tacit Knowledge of the Physical World

Since the resistance to change towards scientific instruction appears to be based on entrenched conceptions of the physical world that make an appearance early in the developmental trajectory, it is worth examining what even earlier beliefs look like. These observations allow us to turn towards another notion in developmental psychology—that humans are naturally endowed with a core set of knowledge that provides an extremely rudimentary foundation of the physical and psychological laws of the world around us. This rudimentary set of principles is seen to allow young infants to make sense of their concrete experiences, and these in turn also enhance this knowledge over time, but without altering the core (Baillargeon & Carey, 2012; Heintz, 2014). It is thus argued that these initial rudimentary beliefs also stand at the centre of older children's and even adults' understanding (Carey, 2009).

How can we be certain that old concepts are still present rather than have been replaced through the acquisition of new knowledge? Research with adults—those much further along the developmental trajectory beyond infancy than school children—can deliver such insight. For one, studies with adults who are cognitively impaired through, for instance, dementia have revealed that across a wide range of scientific domains, intuitive understanding very similar to that expected of young children re-emerges in later life (Shtulman & Valcarcel, 2012; Zaitchik & Solomon, 2008). When cognitively healthy adults have to judge the accuracy of scientific statements under speeded conditions, they are more likely to respond in ways that children would (Babai, Sekal, & Stavy, 2010; Goldberg & Thompson-Schill, 2009; Kelemen, Rottman, & Seston, 2013; Shtulman & Harrington, 2016). Such findings also appear to be consistent across different cultures (Shtulman & Young, 2020) and are argued to be a result of 'explanatory coexistence' (Shtulman & Lombrozo, 2016) whereby non-scientific theories persist even when scientific ones have been learnt; they do not replace earlier ones. Instead, people move between the two based on task or context.

It is, therefore, reasonable to assume that intuitive knowledge representations are also held in early childhood and are perhaps even more readily accessible as in later life, not having been subjected to as many embellishments through experiences. These intuitive representations may in certain instances even prove advantageous. Professional baseball players, for instance, have been shown to be highly capable of knowing where to be positioned to catch a ball and what kind of trajectory that ball will follow, having to make such decisions very quickly. Yet these same players seem unable to explain this knowledge and they perform poorly on related pencil-and-paper tasks (Reed, McLeod, & Dienes, 2010).

The expressions of conceptual understanding that draw on verbalised expressions of predictions on why one object will fall faster than another, or on planning the motion trajectories of balls require conscious effort through deliberation and reflection, as well as translation into language or other symbolic representations (Plessner & Czenna, 2008). On the other hand, the rudimentary beliefs of preverbal infants or the catching abilities of professional ball players are considered to be tacit in nature—knowledge structures that are set to provide quick responses without conscious awareness, by eliciting feelings of familiarity with events (Collins, 2010). It is argued that while verbalised predictions—considered to be explicit forms of knowledge—are subject to conceptual change (Carey, 2015) the underlying tacit structures remain stable (Hast & Howe, 2017; Heintz, 2014).

2.5   Tacit Knowledge Assessment: The Evidence

In view of the challenges encountered within the primary science classroom, it may be possible to consider, as part of the pre-assessment process, that children's various expressed beliefs about different phenomena may not actually reflect the full extent of their knowledge. Explicit representations are necessary for the context of discussing, explaining and justifying, but like the professional ball players, there is perhaps more to the knowledge constructs. Indeed, it is widely accepted that "a great deal of our common-sense knowledge ... is tacit" (Bliss, 2008, p. 123; also see Brock, 2015). If this knowledge still exists, where is it and how can it be accessed? Over recent years, a number of studies with primary school age children have attempted to address this issue by using computer-based tasks to tap into tacit knowledge about object motion, in an effort to exemplify how this tacit knowledge is a largely more accurate representation than explicit predictions might imply.

In one of these studies by Hast and Howe (2015), children between the ages of 5 and 11 years took part in two computer-based tasks. One task required the children to make predictions by choosing one of three statements about the possible outcome of two balls, one heavy and one light, being dropped from the same height at the same time. They could either decide that the heavy ball would fall faster than the light ball, that the light ball would fall faster, or that both would reach the ground simultaneously. No reference was actually made to the balls' weights, but the children were given opportunities to handle the balls before making a decision. Across the age groups, almost all children decided that the heavy ball would fall faster. While they had not been asked to justify their selection, this was actually an outcome that very clearly mapped onto predictions made in similar questioning-based studies that used the same two balls (Hast, 2014b; Hast & Howe, 2013a).

The second task in Hast and Howe's (2015) study required the same children to observe a number of events. Some of these were true representations of object fall where both balls fell at very similar speeds. The other events were simulated modifications of the true events, with one of the two balls falling much faster than the other. While watching the various scenarios the children were simply required to decide as quickly as possible whether they thought the scenario looked right or not. In contrast to the prediction task, the results of the recognition task demonstrated high agreement with the true representations and high rejection of both of the simulated events. Similar dichotomies between deliberated predictions and quick recognition were also noted in other studies investigating object motion, including along horizontal surfaces and down slopes (Hast & Howe, 2017; Howe, Taylor Tavares, & Devine, 2012, 2014). Such evidence of tacit knowledge that differs from verbalised understanding of scientific phenomena can have important implications for conceptual change pedagogy, as is outlined next.

2.6 Tacit Knowledge Assessment as Pedagogical Tool

In two studies that considered the use of tacit knowledge assessment, Howe and colleagues were able to demonstrate that tapping into underlying conceptions about object motion can allow children to revise their own understanding (Howe, Devine, & Taylor Tavares, 2013; Howe, Taylor Tavares, & Devine, 2016). By making similar use of the two processes of prediction and recognition of events as demonstrated by Hast and Howe's (2015) study above, but tying them together into a feedback-and-revision process, a pedagogical tool was developed. An initial paper-based pre-test demonstrated that between them, 8- to 12-year-olds generally demonstrated similar levels of predictive knowledge about object motion events. In both studies, some children then worked with a computer programme where they were required to make predictions, observe the predicted outcomes—whether scientifically accurate or not—and then judge them for accuracy. The remaining children were not exposed to the intervention. The same initial paper assessment was given as a post-test several weeks later, with the outcomes showing that the tacit knowledge assessment children had made significant progress in their conceptual understanding while the control group's results mostly remained static.

Because tacit knowledge assessment provides an opportunity for cognitive conflict, children are able to reformulate conceptions, leading the learner back to a state of equilibrium in their schemata. Revisiting the four conditions for conceptual change outlined by Posner et al. (1982), can tacit knowledge assessment be considered a successful pedagogical approach? While it would be worthwhile to further consider whether the learning outcomes are maintained or even continue to improve through delayed learning effects (cf. Howe, McWilliam, & Cross, 2005; Larrain et al., 2018), it is certainly possible to conclude that, at least on a short-term basis, tacit knowledge assessment works. First, tacit knowledge assessment elicits personal dissatisfaction with existing concepts, since ultimately the children rejected incorrect scenarios even when these had first been predicted. Second, new conceptions were available. These were considered plausible, evident in the children's acceptance of true events even when they had not been predicted, thereby also meeting the third condition. The fourth condition may not be reflected by the assessment process as such, but it can serve as a pre-assessment tool that opens up opportunities for new research in the learning process. Here we come to an important step in challenging the notion of a 'one-size-fits-all' model of teaching in science. Although underlying knowledge possessed by children appears to vary little, the starting points in such tasks—the explicit representations of concepts—come in a wide range and degree of understanding. This suggests children may require different degrees of involvement with such assessment approaches, including whether they work on their own or with a partner, which has shown to impact the experience of the pedagogical tool in Howe and colleagues' studies. Other issues to consider might be the amount of support that children might require depending on their learning needs. The short answer of the pedagogical value of tacit knowledge assessment might be that such assessment is beneficial to the learner, but that a more nuanced implementation in the classroom may actually be required.

2.7 Tacit Knowledge Assessment and Teacher-Student Responsibility

While tacit knowledge assessment seems to be capable of inducing conceptual change, thereby addressing one key challenge in the science classroom, how does this approach chime with the issue of teacher knowledge and confidence? Ronen (2017), for instance, suggests that in the context of conceptual change instruction, it may be necessary to consider the status of a teacher and how much a teacher is really needed, which may also reflect a further benefit of tacit knowledge assessment. Teachers recognise the importance of including their pupils in the processes of teaching and learning about science (Hast, 2017) and providing them with opportunities for ownership of their learning. Virtual experimentation, which tacit knowledge assessment makes use of, provides students with control over their learning—students can become their own teachers (Childers & Jones, 2015). This may be an important step in the primary science classroom since, as noted earlier in this chapter, many generalist primary teachers are limited in their knowledge, skills and confidence (Hast, 2017; Howitt, 2007; Pedretti et al., 2008; van Aalderen-Smeets et al., 2012). However, since such levels will again vary depending on the teacher, it suggests that for some classrooms the implementation of tacit knowledge assessment may be of more benefit than for others, once again highlighting a challenge to a 'one-size-fits-all' model of teaching.

But why might tacit knowledge assessment be argued to be particularly effective as a conceptual change tool as opposed to other forms of instruction? Towards this, it is necessary to understand that trust plays an important role in children's general conceptual constructions. By and large, children trust their own experiences of the everyday world (Howe, 2014) and in their development, they move from a default bias to rely on testimony from others towards developing robust self-generated theories (Jaswal, 2010; Jaswal & Pérez-Edgar, 2014) as well as resistance to misleading testimony from others (Jaswal et al., 2014). This adds to the high resistance to conceptual change through instructions when what is to be learnt in the formalised context is in disagreement with the personally held beliefs. However, tacit knowledge assessment allows children to themselves challenge their own beliefs, making them more likely to revise the preconceived notions. This notion of self-collaboration (Hast, 2014a) should be harnessed in pedagogical approaches rather than seeing the issue of trust as resistance that cannot be overcome.

By placing more responsibility of conceptual change on the learner, several issues can be addressed. For one, lack of teacher knowledge and confidence become less of a liability, thereby being less likely to interfere with the development of educational achievement (Cremin et al., 2015; Hast, 2017). In place, allowing children to have greater autonomy in the process will increase the likelihood of them demonstrating higher levels of motivation in their learning (Reeve, 2006) and greater self determination (Deci & Ryan, 2012, 2013). Since, in tacit knowledge assessment, a teacher takes on the role of a facilitator and the student takes on more of the instruction process, inner motivational resources are more likely to be nurtured. In addition, teachers are provided with opportunities to become more self-determined in their own teaching, which is more likely to lead to self-determined student learning (Roth, Assor, Kanat-Maymon, & Kaplan, 2007).

2.8 Tacit Knowledge Assessment as Differentiation Tool

What can be argued to this point is that tacit knowledge assessment offers new technology-based insight into approaching conceptual change, and while the ultimate learning outcomes perhaps remain to be seen, it seems, nonetheless, to indicate promise where more traditional conceptual change approaches have faced more significant challenges. That is not to imply, however, that all primary school science teaching should be replaced by technological methods. Other traditional pedagogical approaches such as active or play-based learning can still maintain their value. It may merely be a matter for practitioners, based on the knowledge they have of individual learners in their classroom, to find out what works best for each child. In this respect, despite its potential as a pedagogical tool and despite the common foundation of understanding that can be tapped into, tacit knowledge assessment should not be considered as reflecting a 'one-size-fits-all' model of teaching in science.

On the contrary; it is worth considering the value that it might play in the role of differentiation, giving attention to the personalised learning needs of students (Cash, 2017). Addressing differentiation is crucial in the context of science education since every child's degree of understanding of particular scientific phenomena may differ from the next, which can lead to pedagogical challenges in trying to address the range of ideas that exist within one classroom (Kambouri et al., 2011; Kambouri, 2016). Teachers who had been interviewed on their perceptions of and attitudes towards tacit knowledge assessment (Hast, 2017) commented that such approaches "*might enable them to access something beyond what is being taught to the masses, as it were, in the classroom*". Heacox (2017) sets out a number of key recommendations for differentiation success. Does tacit knowledge assessment actually meet these criteria for successful differentiation?

First, according to Heacox (2017), pre-assessment is seen as playing a critical role, which may also include the use of technology. This is easily met since children can make predictions of anticipated motion events. These, in turn, allow the learner—and the instructor—to gauge current level of understanding. Second, differentiation tasks should also be practical and doable. As the conceptual change studies by Howe (Howe et al., 2013, 2016) have shown, understanding of concepts improved through tacit knowledge assessment, and this required minimal intervention from instructors. The main limit of this is perhaps when considering younger children whose reading levels are not yet at a sufficient standard to follow on-screen instructions, so some further thought should be given to how tasks are set up. Finally, differentiation should develop student responsibility and independence in their learning processes. By its very nature, it is the learner who dictates the learning process during the tacit knowledge assessment approach.

2.9 Conclusion and Future Developments

What this chapter has demonstrated is that children bring many different ideas to the classroom based on their varied everyday world experiences and these ideas can pose a challenge to learning and instruction. Tacit knowledge assessment, however, affords new insight into children's conceptions that are more accurate reflections of scientific concepts to be taught. One of Hast's (2017) interviewed teachers pointed out that "*I only know so much and so we can't go any further than that*". In crossing the bridge between developmental psychology and education it is possible to see that, even by taking a single approach, it is possible to challenge a 'one-size-fits-all' model of teaching in science and to demonstrate a potential new tool for differentiation that addresses such teacher concerns.

It can be anticipated that in many other knowledge domains, conceptions will generally become more sophisticated with increasing age (Koerber, Mayer, Osterhaus, Schwippert, & Sodian, 2015). However, the issue of how to guide this development through instruction remains, so as not to misdirect the development. Again, tacit knowledge assessment could show promise as an intervention tool. For example, a recent examination of young children's understanding of rainbows and rainbow formation demonstrated not only that across age groups, advanced conceptions increased and naïve ones decreased, but also that particularly in younger groups some ideas were correctly expressed through drawings but were not necessarily a reflection of the same children's verbal explanations of the same phenomena (Hast, 2020). This generally suggests that more research will be needed in order to gain a stronger understanding of the role that tacit knowledge assessment can play in differentiated science instruction, or even in rule-based domains outside of science. For instance, other science areas such as biology (Shtulman & Young, 2020), and other educational domains such as numeracy (Dillon, Kannan, Dean, Spelke, & Duflo, 2017) and second language acquisition (Rebuschat, 2015) all appear to offer similar dichotomies between expressed and underlying concepts, with potential for appropriate conceptual change instruction approaches particularly for children who might benefit from additional differentiated support.

Beyond specific learning gains in science as such, tacit knowledge assessment could also be considered useful in supporting transition experiences when children move from primary to secondary school. This transition experience typically impacts student achievement and attitudes in a range of subjects, including science (Symonds & Galton, 2015; Symonds & Hargreaves, 2016) and is a rather likely contributor to declining levels of interest in science-related careers that are seen as being even more desirable in future economies (Hazelkorn et al., 2015). In particular, there is some suggestion that children from socially and economically disadvantaged backgrounds are more likely to have negative transition experiences and might benefit from additional support (Symonds, 2015). Once again, this challenges a 'one-size-fits-all' model of teaching that can potentially be addressed through the further development of tacit knowledge pedagogy—and the future of it is looking optimistic.

References

Allen, M. (2014). *Misconceptions in primary science*. Maidenhead: Open University Press.

Babai, R., Sekal, R., & Stavy, R. (2010). Persistence of the intuitive conception of living things in adolescence. *Journal of Science Education and Technology, 19*(1), 20–26. https://doi.org/10.1007/s10956-009-9174-2.

Baillargeon, R., & Carey, S. (2012). Core cognition and beyond: The acquisition of physical and numerical knowledge. In S. M. Pauen (Ed.), *Early childhood development and later outcome* (pp. 33–65). Cambridge: Cambridge University Press.

Bliss, J. (2008). Commonsense reasoning about the physical world. *Studies in Science Education, 44*(2), 123–155. https://doi.org/10.1080/03057260802264149.

Brock, R. (2015). Intuition and insight: Two concepts that illuminate the tacit in science education. *Studies in Science Education, 51*(2), 127–167. https://doi.org/10.1080/03057267.2015.1049843.

Carey, S. (2009). *The origin of concepts*. Oxford: Oxford University Press.

Carey, S. (2015). Why theories of concepts should not ignore the problem of acquisition. In E. Margolis & S. Laurence (Eds.), *The conceptual mind: New directions in the study of concepts* (pp. 415–454). Cambridge, MA: MIT Press.

Cash, R. M. (2017). *Advancing differentiation: Thinking and learning for the 21st century*. Minneapolis, MN: Free Spirit Publishing.

Childers, G., & Jones, M. G. (2015). Students as virtual scientists: An exploration of students' and teachers' perceived realness of a remote electron microscopy investigation. *International Journal of Science Education, 37*(15), 2433–2452. https://doi.org/10.1080/09500693.2015.1082043.

Collins, H. (2010). *Tacit and explicit knowledge*. Chicago, IL: University of Chicago Press.

Cremin, T., Glauert, E., Craft, A., Compton, A., & Stylianidou, F. (2015). Creative little scientists: Exploring pedagogical synergies between inquiry-based and creative approaches in early years science. *Education 3–13, 43*(4), 404–419. https://doi.org/10.1080/03004279.2015.1020655.

Deci, E. L., & Ryan, R. M. (2012). Self-determination theory. In P. A. M. Van Lange, A. W. Kruglanski, & E. T. Higgins (Eds.), *The handbook of theories of social psychology: Volume 1* (pp. 416–433). London: SAGE.

Deci, E. L., & Ryan, R. M. (2013). *Handbook of self-determination research*. Rochester, NY: University of Rochester Press.

DeWitt, J., Archer, L., & Osborne, J. (2014). Science-related aspirations across the primary-secondary divide: Evidence from two surveys in England. *International Journal of Science Education, 36*(10), 1609–1629. https://doi.org/10.1080/09500693.2013.871659.

DeWitt, J., Osborne, J., Archer, L., Dillon, J., Willis, B., & Wong, B. (2013). Young children's aspirations in science: The unequivocal, the uncertain and the unthinkable. *International Journal of Science Education, 35*(6), 1037–1063. https://doi.org/10.1080/09500693.2011.608197.

Dillon, M. R., Kannan, H., Dean, J. T., Spelke, E. S., & Duflo, E. (2017). Cognitive science in the field: A preschool intervention durably enhances intuitive but not formal mathematics. *Science, 357*(6346), 47–55. https://doi.org/10.1126/science.aal4724.

Duit, R. (2009). *Bibliography STCE: Students' and teachers' conceptions and science education*. Retrieved January 22, 2019, from https://archiv.ipn.uni-kiel.de/stcse/.

Duit, R., Treagust, D. F., & Widodo, A. (2013). Teaching science for conceptual change: Theory and practice. In S. Vosniadou (Ed.), *International handbook of research on conceptual change* (pp. 487–503). London: Routledge.

Duschl, R. A., Schweingruber, H. A., & Shouse, A. W. (2006). *Taking science to school: Learning and teaching science in grades K-8*. Washington, DC: The National Academies Press.

Eshach, H. (2007). Bridging in-school and out-of-school learning: Formal, non-formal, and informal education. *Journal of Science Education and Technology, 16*(2), 171–190. https://doi.org/10.1007/s10956-006-9027-1.

Goldberg, R. F., & Thompson-Schill, S. L. (2009). Developmental "roots" in mature biological knowledge. *Psychological Science, 20*(4), 480–487. https://doi.org/10.1111/j.1467-9280.2009.02320.x.

Gomez-Zwiep, S. (2008). Elementary teachers' understanding of students' science misconceptions: Implications for practice and teacher education. *Journal of Science Teacher Education, 19*(5), 437–454. https://doi.org/10.1007/s10972-008-9102-y.

Harris, J., George, N. R., Hirsch-Pasek, K., & Newcombe, N. S. (2018). Where will it go? How children and adults reason about force and motion. *Cognitive Development, 45,* 113–124. https://doi.org/10.1016/j.cogdev.2018.01.002.

Hast, M. (2014a). Collaborating with the 'more capable' self: Achieving conceptual change in early science education through underlying knowledge structures. *ReflectED, St Mary's Journal of Education, 3,* 18–25.

Hast, M. (2014b). Exploring the shift in children's incline motion predictions: Fragmentation and integration of knowledge as possible contributors. *Journal of Educational and Developmental Psychology, 4*(2), 74–81. https://doi.org/10.5539/jedp.v4n2p74.

Hast, M. (2016). Children's reasoning about rolling down curves: Arguing the case for a two-component commonsense theory of motion. *Science Education, 100*(5), 837–848. https://doi.org/10.1002/sce.21237.

Hast, M. (2017). Technology and early science education: Examining generalist primary school teachers' views on tacit knowledge assessment tools. *International Education Studies, 10*(11), 135–147. https://doi.org/10.5539/ies.v10n11p135.

Hast, M. (2018a). It's all relative: The role of object weight in toddlers' gravity bias. *Journal of Experimental Child Psychology, 166,* 696–704. https://doi.org/10.1016/j.jecp.2017.09.013.

Hast, M. (2018b). Incline height and object weight: Examining the fluidity of children's commonsense theories of motion. *Eurasia Journal of Mathematics, Science and Technology Education, 14*(4), 1407–1413. https://doi.org/10.29333/ejmste/83678.

Hast, M. (2019). Representational momentum in displacement tasks: Relative object weight matters in toddlers' search behaviour. *International Journal of Behavioral Development, 43*(2), 173–178. https://doi.org/10.1177/0165025418820689.

Hast, M. (2020). Children's understanding of the rainbow: A trajectory of conceptual development across middle childhood. *Eurasia Journal of Mathematics, Science and Technology Education, 16*(6), em1859. https://doi.org/10.29333/ejmste/8230.

Hast, M., & Howe, C. (2012). Understanding the beliefs informing children's commonsense theories of motion: The role of everyday object variables in dynamic event predictions. *Research in Science & Technological Education, 30*(1), 3–15. https://doi.org/10.1080/02635143.2011.653876.

Hast, M., & Howe, C. (2013a). Towards a complete commonsense theory of motion: The interaction of dimensions in children's predictions of natural object motion. *International Journal of Science Education, 35*(10), 1649–1662. https://doi.org/10.1080/09500693.2011.604685.

Hast, M., & Howe, C. (2013b). The development of children's understanding of speed change: A contributing factor towards commonsense theories of motion. *Journal of Science Education and Technology, 22*(3), 337–350. https://doi.org/10.1007/s10956-012-9397-5.

Hast, M., & Howe, C. (2015). Children's predictions and recognition of fall: The role of object mass. *Cognitive Development, 36,* 103–110. https://doi.org/10.1016/j.cogdev.2015.10.002.

Hast, M., & Howe, C. (2017). Changing predictions, stable recognition: Children's representations of downward incline motion. *British Journal of Developmental Psychology, 35*(4), 516–530. https://doi.org/10.1111/bjdp.12191.

Hazelkorn, E., Ryan, C., Beernaert, Y., Constantinou, C. P., Deca, L., Grangeat, M., et al. (2015). *Science education for responsible citizenship.* Brussels: European Commission.

Heacox, D. (2017). *Making differentiation a habit: How to ensure success in academically diverse classrooms.* Minneapolis, MN: Free Spirit Publishing.

Heintz, C. (2014). Scaffolding on core cognition. In L. R. Caporael, J. R. Griesemer, & W. C. Wimsatt (Eds.), *Developing scaffolds in evolution, culture, and cognition* (pp. 209–228). Cambridge, MA: MIT Press.

Howe, C. (2012). Neuroscience and knowledge acquisition in curriculum contexts: Modelling conceptual development in school science. *British Journal of Educational Psychology Monograph Series II, 8,* 83–98. https://doi.org/10.1348/97818543371712X13219598392327.

Howe, C. (2014). "If you've seen it before, then you know": Physical evidence and children's trust in testimony. In E. J. Robinson & S. Einav (Eds.), *Trust and skepticism: Children's selective learning from testimony* (pp. 151–162). Hove: Psychology Press.

Howe, C. (2017). Developing understanding of object fall: Going beyond inhibitory processes. *British Journal of Developmental Psychology, 35*(3), 463–468. https://doi.org/10.1111/bjdp. 12187.

Howe, C., Devine, A., & Taylor Tavares, J. (2013). Supporting conceptual change in school science: A possible role for tacit understanding. *International Journal of Science Education, 35*(5), 864–883. https://doi.org/10.1080/09500693.2011.585353.

Howe, C., McWilliam, D., & Cross, G. (2005). Chance favours only the prepared mind: Incubation and the delayed effects of peer collaboration. *British Journal of Psychology, 96*(1), 67–93. https://doi.org/10.1348/000712604X15527.

Howe, C., Taylor Tavares, J., & Devine, A. (2012). Everyday conceptions of object fall: Explicit and tacit understanding in middle childhood. *Journal of Experimental Child Psychology, 111*(3), 351–366. https://doi.org/10.1016/j.jecp.2011.09.003.

Howe, C., Taylor Tavares, J., & Devine, A. (2014). Children's conceptions of physical events: Explicit and tacit understanding of horizontal motion. *British Journal of Developmental Psychology, 32*(2), 141–162. https://doi.org/10.1111/bjdp.12026.

Howe, C., Taylor Tavares, J., & Devine, A. (2016). Recognition as support for reasoning about horizontal motion: A further resource for school science? *Research in Science & Technological Education, 34*(3), 273–289. https://doi.org/10.1080/02635143.2016.1168393.

Howitt, C. (2007). Pre-service elementary teachers' perceptions of factors in an holistic methods course influencing their confidence in teaching science. *Research in Science Education, 37*(1), 41–58. https://doi.org/10.1007/s11165-006-9015-8.

Jaswal, V. K. (2010). Believing what you're told: Young children's trust in unexpected testimony about the physical world. *Cognitive Psychology, 61*(3), 248–272. https://doi.org/10.1016/j.cogpsych.2010.06.002.

Jaswal, V. K., Pérez-Edgar, K., Kondrad, R. L., Palmquist, C. M., Cole, C. A., & Cole, C. E. (2014). Can't stop believing: Inhibitory control and resistance to misleading testimony. *Developmental Science, 17*(6), 965–976. https://doi.org/10.1111/desc.12187.

Jaswal, V. K., & Pérez-Edgar, K. (2014). Resolving conflicts between observation and testimony: The role of inhibitory control. In E. J. Robinson & S. Einav (Eds.), *Trust and skepticism: Children's selective learning from testimony* (pp. 110–122). Hove: Psychology Press.

Kambouri, M. (2016). Investigating early years teachers' understanding and response to children's preconceptions. *European Early Childhood Education Research Journal, 24*(6), 907–927. https://doi.org/10.1080/1350293X.2014.970857.

Kambouri, M., Briggs, M., & Cassidy, M. (2011). Children's misconceptions and the teaching of early years science: A case study. *Journal of Emergent Science, 2*(2), 7–16.

Kelemen, D., Rottman, J., & Seston, R. (2013). Professional physical scientists display tenacious teleological tendencies: Purpose-based reasoning as a cognitive default. *Journal of Experimental Psychology: General, 142*(4), 1074–1083. https://doi.org/10.1037/a0030399.

Kendeou, P., Butterfuss, R., Kim, J., & Van Boekel, M. (2019). Knowledge revision through the lenses of the three-pronged approach. *Memory & Cognition, 47,* 33–46. https://doi.org/10.3758/s13421-018-0848-y.

Koerber, S., Mayer, D., Osterhaus, C., Schwippert, K., & Sodian, B. (2015). The development of scientific thinking in elementary school: A comprehensive inventory. *Child Development, 86*(1), 327–336. https://doi.org/10.1111/cdev.12298.

Larrain, A., Freire, P., Grau, V., López, P., Salvat, I., Silva, M., et al. (2018). The effect of peer-group argumentative dialogue on delayed gains in scientific content knowledge. *New Directions for Child and Adolescent Development, 2018*(162), 67–87. https://doi.org/10.1002/cad.20263.

Pedretti, E. G., Bencze, L., Hewitt, J., Romkey, L., & Jivraj, A. (2008). Promoting issues-based STSE perspectives in science teacher education: Problems of identity and ideology. *Science & Education, 17*(8–9), 941–960. https://doi.org/10.1007/s11191-006-9060-8.

Piaget, J. (1978). *The development of thought: Equilibration of cognitive structures*. Oxford: Blackwell.

Piaget, J. (1985). *The equilibration of cognitive structures: The central problem of intellectual development*. Chicago, IL: University of Chicago Press.

Plessner, H., & Czenna, S. (2008). The benefits of intuition. In H. Plessner, C. Betsch, & T. Betsch (Eds.), *Intuition in judgement and decision making* (pp. 251–265). New York, NY: Lawrence Erlbaum Associates.

Posner, G. J., Strike, K. A., Hewson, P. W., & Gertzog, W. A. (1982). Accommodation of a scientific conception: Toward a theory of conceptual change. *Science Education, 66*(2), 211–227. https://doi.org/10.1002/sce.3730660207.

Rebuschat, P. (2015). *Implicit and explicit learning of languages*. Amsterdam: John Benjamins.

Reed, N., McLeod, P., & Dienes, Z. (2010). Implicit knowledge and motor skill: What people who know how to catch don't know. *Consciousness and Cognition, 19*(1), 63–76. https://doi.org/10.1016/j.concog.2009.07.006.

Reeve, J. (2006). Teachers as facilitators: What autonomy-supportive teachers do and why their students benefit. *The Elementary School Journal, 106*(3), 225–236. https://doi.org/10.1086/501484.

Ronen, I. (2017). *Misconceptions in science education: Help me understand*. Newcastle upon Tyne: Cambridge Scholars Publishing.

Roth, G., Assor, A., Kanat-Maymon, Y., & Kaplan, H. (2007). Autonomous motivation for teaching: How self-determined teaching may lead to self-determined learning. *Journal of Educational Psychology, 99*(4), 761–774. https://doi.org/10.1037/0022-0663.99.4.761.

Said, Z., Summers, R., Abd-El-Khalick, F., & Wang, S. (2016). Attitudes toward science among grades 3 through 12 Arab students in Qatar: Findings from a cross-sectional national study. *International Journal of Science Education, 38*(4), 621–643. https://doi.org/10.1080/09500693.2016.1156184.

Shtulman, A., & Harrington, K. (2016). Tensions between science and intuition across the lifespan. *Topics in Cognitive Science, 8*(1), 118–137. https://doi.org/10.1111/tops.12174.

Shtulman, A., & Lombrozo, T. (2016). Bundles of contradiction: A coexistence view of conceptual change. In D. Barner & A. Baron (Eds.), *Core knowledge and conceptual change* (pp. 49–67). Oxford: Oxford University Press.

Shtulman, A., & Valcarcel, J. (2012). Scientific knowledge suppresses but does not supplant earlier intuitions. *Cognition, 124*(2), 209–215. https://doi.org/10.1016/j.cognition.2012.04.005.

Shtulman, A., & Young, A. (2020). Why do logically incompatible beliefs seem psychologically compatible? Science, pseudoscience, religion, and superstition. In K. McCain & K. Kampourakis (Eds.), *What is scientific knowledge? An introduction to contemporary epistemology of science* (pp. 163–178). London: Routledge.

Symonds, J. (2015). *Understanding school transition: What happens to children and how to help them*. London: Routledge.

Symonds, J., & Galton, M. (2015). Moving to the next stage of school at age 10–14 years: An international review of psychological development at school transition. *Review of Education, 2*(1), 1–27. https://doi.org/10.1002/rev3.3021.

Symonds, J., & Hargreaves, L. (2016). Emotional and motivational engagement at school transition: A qualitative stage-environment fit study. *The Journal of Early Adolescence, 36*(1), 54–85. https://doi.org/10.1177/0272431614556348.

van Aalderen-Smeets, S. I., Walma van der Molen, J. H., & Asma, L. J. F. (2012). Primary teachers' attitudes toward science: A new theoretical framework. *Science Education, 96*(1), 158–182. https://doi.org/10.1002/sce.20467.

Venkadasalam, V. P., & Ganea, P. A. (2018). Do objects of different weight fall at the same time? Updating naive beliefs about free-falling objects from fictional and informational books in young children. *Journal of Cognition and Development, 19*(2), 165–181. https://doi.org/10.1080/15248372.2018.1436058.

Wiser, M., & Smith, C. L. (2008). Learning and teaching about matter in grades K-8: When should the atomic-molecular theory be introduced? In S. Vosniadou (Ed.), *International handbook of research on conceptual change* (pp. 205–239). London: Routledge.

Zaitchik, D., & Solomon, G. E. A. (2008). Animist thinking in the elderly and in patients with Alzheimer's disease. *Cognitive Neuropsychology, 25*(1), 27–37. https://doi.org/10.1080/026432 90801904059.

Zimmerman, C. (2007). The development of scientific thinking skills in elementary and middle school. *Developmental Review, 27*(2), 172–223. https://doi.org/10.1016/j.dr.2006.12.001.

Chapter 3
Team-Based Learning, Achievement Emotions and Personality Traits

Kah Loong Chue

Abstract Team-based learning (TBL) is a teaching strategy that has infused into classrooms at all levels. It diversifies learners' experience through its various instructional elements that include a flipped classroom as well as cooperative and individual tasks within the lesson. The current study aims to review research pertaining to TBL, achievement emotions and personality traits with the aim of exploring interactions between them. First, the use of a TBL approach in relation to the achievement emotions of enjoyment, boredom and anger will be examined. Enjoyment and boredom are generally thought to influence cognitive resources and attention, information processing, and academic motivation and performance. On the other hand, anger can have variable effects on learning processes and outcomes. Second, any moderated impact of the TBL approach to students' emotions will be explored. The HEXACO model of personality traits that states that individuals differ on six major continuous dimensions, namely, Honesty-Humility, Emotionality, Extraversion, Agreeableness, Conscientiousness and Openness to Experience will be used. Past studies have shown that any new educational interventions may not be suitable for all students because of different personality traits. It is important for educators to be aware of the roles of personality on learning and teaching methods, as this may pre-empt intervention strategies in the implementation of TBL.

Keywords Team-based learning · Achievement emotions · Enjoyment · Boredom · Personality · HEXACO

3.1 Introduction

In the past decade, Team-Based Learning (TBL) has emerged as a pedagogical approach that diversifies learners' experience through its various instructional elements, such as a flipped classroom to cater for individual learning needs as well as cooperative and individual tasks within the lesson (Michaelsen & Sweet, 2008,

K. L. Chue (✉)
National Institute of Education, Nanyang Technological University, Singapore, Singapore
e-mail: kahloong.chue@nie.edu.sg

© Springer Nature Singapore Pte Ltd. 2020
C. Koh (ed.), *Diversifying Learner Experience*,
https://doi.org/10.1007/978-981-15-9861-6_3

2011). The attraction of TBL lies in the promise of satisfying certain demands of modern education, i.e. courses are content heavy and application focused, instructors need to provide feedback to large numbers of students, and the need to integrate soft skills into lessons. In addition, inherent in the approach are opportunities for students to develop important twenty-first-century competencies, notably in the interpersonal domain (Foo-Lam et al., 2014). TBL has now been incorporated by many educators in several fields, including business, medicine, criminal justice, sociology, literature and psychology (Jakobsen & Knetemann, 2017). As such, there have been numerous studies investigating the effectiveness of TBL in academic settings. Most of these studies have concluded that there is an increase in academic performance, engagement and collaborative performance when TBL is applied consistently in lessons (Swanson, McCulley, Osman, Scammacca Lewis, & Solis, 2017). Nevertheless, some questions pertaining to the use of TBL remain relatively unexplored. In what ways do student experiences vary in a TBL lesson? Do students enjoy the process or are they bored or frustrated most of the time? What impact do TBL lessons have on the emotions of students towards the course? Will there be differences in emotions arising due to different student profiles?

This chapter will delve into the above questions by beginning with a brief overview of the various tenets together with the stages of TBL and how it varies from a traditional teaching session. Next, the framework of achievement emotions, as laid out by Pekrun (2006), will be introduced. It will be followed by an analysis the possible impacts of TBL on achievement emotions. Finally, the chapter will conclude with a discussion of personality as a possible moderator of the impacts.

3.2   What is Team-Based Learning?

The primary aim of TBL is to ensure that students attain mastery in course content, yet are provided with ample opportunity in class to collaborate and apply course concepts. To do so requires teachers to integrate several active learning strategies, e.g. frequent formative assessments and engagement in self-regulatory activities. By incorporating sound educational principles, the four essential elements of TBL are

- Properly formed and managed groups
- Student accountability for both individual and group work
- Frequent and timely feedback
- Group assignments that promote learning and team development (Michaelsen & Sweet, 2008)

What then can a student expect to experience in a TBL session? In reality, their initial encounter with TBL would occur prior to the actual lesson. An introduction to the rationale, approach and basic features of TBL before the lesson is necessary to ensure that students have a general understanding of the requirements needed. Groups would also need to be formed. If possible, the teacher would have obtained relevant information such as specific student characteristics (e.g. prior knowledge or language fluency), that would make it easier for group formation. The group should ideally comprise of diverse members who would bring different perspectives to the task. Concurrently, the teacher would also be wary of the possibility of forming coalitions within the group, so it is highly unlikely that a student would be in the same group as his/her close friends. At the end of the introduction, students should have an overview of the TBL process as well as an awareness of their roles in the forthcoming lessons.

Subsequently, each TBL session begins with a Readiness Assurance Process to ensure that students attain a sufficient level of content mastery before attempting the group assignment. Vastly different from conventional teacher-led instruction, the Readiness Assurance Process is the basis for student accountability to both individual and group work. It comprises five components: (i) pre-assigned readings, (ii) an individual readiness assurance test (IRAT), (iii) a team readiness assurance test (TRAT), (iv) team appeals and (v) instructor feedback.

To minimize content coverage in class, students are provided with a set of required readings and/or assignments to complete before the start of each lesson. Although this imposes an additional time constraint on students, most of the research shows that this flipped model enhances student learning outcomes (Cheng, Ritzhaupt, & Antonenko, 2018). In addition, delivering content outside of class caters to students of diverse learning needs, i.e. they could learn at their own pace and manner (He, Holton, Farkas, & Warschauer, 2016; Johnston & Karafotias, 2016).

The IRAT is the first activity of a TBL session. The test usually comprises a set of multiple-choice questions designed to assess their knowledge and understanding of key concepts. The IRAT can be conducted online or using a paper-based format. In either case, the final score of the IRAT should contribute towards the student's individual grades. After the IRAT has concluded, the students move on to take the TRAT. The TRAT contains the exact same questions as the IRAT. However, the students are now allowed to discuss with their group members before submitting the best possible answer as a group. Students can immediately check on their answers using a self-scoring answer sheet. If the students feel that their answers are more valid or accurate than the correct answer, they have the opportunity to build a case to convince the teacher to accredit their answers in the team appeals segment. This gives students a chance to clarify misconceptions either by reviewing the assigned readings or through feedback from the teacher.

The IRAT, TRAT and team appeals serve three important functions in a TBL session. First, these processes give the students impetus to complete their assigned readings. Failure to prepare sufficiently would usually lead to a lower grade in the IRAT. Furthermore, as group discussions during the TRAT are done in a face-to-face format, any adverse interactional impact caused by inadequate preparation is immediate and personal (Michaelsen & Sweet, 2008). Second, the TRAT and team appeals sections provide an opportunity for students to build up group cohesiveness and familiarity, which may lead to higher team outcomes later on (Thompson et al., 2015). Third, the tests provide timely feedback to both the student and the teacher. Students are given feedback at the task level (Hattie & Timperley, 2007) that are self-referential in nature, i.e. whether they have improved over time (Pekrun,

Cusack, Murayama, Elliot, & Thomas, 2014). If several groups have difficulty with a particular concept, the teacher can obtain this information and subsequently address the issue with the whole class in the instructor feedback component. The desired outcome of the Readiness Assurance Process is that all students should have achieved adequate knowledge and understanding of key concepts.

The final activity in a TBL session requires the groups to apply what they have learnt to solve at least one problem. Michaelsen and Sweet (2008) recommend that the problems should satisfy the 4S criteria, namely, Significant problem, Specific choice, Same problem, Simultaneously report. The first criterion requires that problems need to be relevant and authentic. The second criterion suggests that each problem should preferably have a final concise solution as a lengthy outcome report takes time away from collaborative discussion. Both criteria are based on research evidence that authenticity and discourse are essential elements to promote higher level thinking (Abrami et al., 2015). The last two criteria require that each group addresses the exact same problem and reports the solutions concurrently. Doing so has the benefit of fostering learning across groups and preventing answer drift, i.e. the initial response has the strongest impact on the discussion that follows (Michaelsen & Sweet, 2008). Once the application activity is finished, students are required to submit a peer evaluation of their group members to the teacher. The objectives of administering peer evaluations are twofold: to provide formative assessment to the individual students on how to improve their interpersonal skills and to provide summative assessment to the teacher to ensure fairness in grading (Cestone, Levine, & Lane, 2008).

The flow of activities in a TBL session is summarized in Fig. 3.1. As seen in the figure, learners undergo an active learning experience that is vastly different from a traditional didactic session. However, whilst many TBL sessions occur at higher education level, there are relatively fewer TBL lessons conducted at the secondary or high school level. Wanzek et al. (2014) described an experimental study in which TBL was adapted in a high school where lessons occured for approximately one hour and the unit of a topic can stretch for several days. In the study, TBL was implemented in an 11th grade social studies class. Each class period lasted for 50–55 minutes. Prior to implementation, teachers strategically assigned students to teams by considering their background knowledge, general academic achievement, temperament, participation disposition, and motivation or ability to focus on tasks. The IRAT and TRAT, which

Stage 1: Pre-class preparation	Stage 2: Readiness Assurance Process	Stage 3: Application activities
Introduction to TBL Group formation Assigned readings	IRAT TRAT Group appeals Instructor feedback	Problem solving Peer evaluation

Fig. 3.1 Flow of activities in a TBL lesson

comprised of multiple-choice questions, were taken during the same lesson and students had to submit their IRAT before attempting the TRAT in their teams. A scratch-off card for the TRAT was used so that they could obtain immediate feedback on their answers. After scanning through the cards, teachers gave targeted feedback in the following lesson. After three occasions of IRAT/TRAT, students had to complete a knowledge application activity that was spread out across two lessons. Finally, the teachers facilitated a peer evaluation of the team processes. The study found that students with moderate to high prior knowledge benefitted from TBL whereas students with low prior knowledge had no significant benefits (Wanzek et al., 2014).

Another quasi-experimental study conducted by Jeno et al. (2017) examined the effects of TBL on autonomous motivation. In this study, TBL was implemented in the final 4 weeks of a mandatory physiotherapy course. Students in the course completed pre- and post-surveys on motivation, perceived competence and autonomy support. The study concluded that there was an increase in the level of autonomous motivation coupled with a decrease in the level of amotivation of students. These effects may likely have resulted from the increase in the level of perceived competence and autonomy support. The authors surmised that the structure of TBL with its active learning components was the probable underlying factor that caused these results (Jeno et al., 2017).

In general, meta-analytic studies investigating the effectiveness of TBL have indicated higher levels of academic performance and engagement (Liu & Beaujean, 2017; Swanson et al., 2017). The principal mechanisms behind these positive academic outcomes can be traced to active learning strategies that require students to participate actively in their own learning, e.g. frequent assessment (IRAT, TRAT), self-regulated learning and collaborative problem-solving. However, most of the studies in the meta-analysis focused holistically on the TBL approach, even though TBL is multi-component in nature. Thus, it is difficult to isolate the sections that have the greatest impact. Furthermore, few would argue with the notion that other than cognition and motivation, emotions play a vital role in learning as well. Yet, explorations in this area within the confines of the TBL approach have remained scarce. The ensuing sections will, therefore, review the literature concerning emotions in education and discuss the possible impacts that TBL may have on students' emotions.

3.3   Achievement Emotions

Educators have increasingly recognized that emotions have a large influence on the cognitive processes, performance and motivation of students (Goetz, Pekrun, Hall, & Haag, 2006). Throughout their academic journey, students experience a whole range of emotions that are directly linked to the different aspects of learning, e.g. classroom instruction, achievement, assessments. These academic emotions are now synonymous with the term achievement emotions which are defined as "emotions tied directly to achievement activities or achievement outcomes" (Pekrun, 2006, p. 317). This definition integrates two types of emotions that are commonly felt in academic contexts: emotions that are linked to results such as successes and failures, and emotions that are linked to the current activities at hand.

Underlying the framework of achievement emotions is the control-value theory that posits that achievement emotions are necessarily induced by (1) subjective control over achievement activities and (2) subjective value of the achievement activity (Pekrun, 2006). Subjective control pertains to the perceived controllability of the achievement outcomes and activities. For example, students may feel that if they put in sufficient effort, they will get a good grade (high control) or conversely, they may feel that regardless of effort, a bad grade is unavoidable (low control). Subjective value pertains to the perceived importance of the achievement-related outcomes and activities. An apathetic student is not likely to experience any form of achievement emotion.

The control-value theory also postulates that the various combinations of control and value constitute the appraisal antecedents to three groups of emotions: prospective outcome, retrospective outcome and activity based emotions. Depending on the source and intensity of the control antecedent as well as the valence of the value antecedent, different emotions are subsequently aroused.

Prospective outcome emotions are linked to the possibility of future success/failure. In this group, value refers to the attached importance of attaining success or avoiding failure, and control refers to the perceived probability of success or failure. For example, a student could be focused on obtaining a distinction for an exam (attaining success). If there is a perceived good chance of success (high control), anticipatory joy would be felt. If there is a perceived low chance of success (low control), hopelessness would be felt. Retrospective outcome emotions are linked to prior successes/failures. In this group, value refers to the occurrence or non-occurrence of past successes or failures, and control refers to the perception of whether the outcome was caused by the self, other persons or external circumstances. For example, suppose a student has obtained distinctions for several assessments in a particular subject (prior success). If the student feels that this was due to his/her own effort (self), pride would be felt. Alternatively, if the student feels that the teacher played an essential role in helping his/her development (other), gratitude towards the teacher would be felt.

Activity-based emotions are linked to the actions involved in the activity. In this group, both control and values refer to the actions themselves. Value refers to the overall valence of the activity and may include evaluations of importance, liking and benefits. Control refers to the subjective internal control of the student. For example, suppose a student is tasked to solve math problems in a lesson and this activity is positively valued. If the math problems are within his/her ability level (high control), enjoyment would be felt, whereas the student's attempt to solve math problems beyond his/her ability level (low control) would lead to frustration. On the other hand, another student could be disinclined to solve math problems and hence value the activity negatively. If the student is able to solve the math problems (high control), he/she may feel that it is a waste of time and thus experience anger. If the problems are beyond the student's ability (low control), frustration is felt. Finally, math problems that are too easy or have no relevance (no value) would likely lead to boredom.

Positive activity-based emotions such as enjoyment are generally perceived to promote intrinsic motivation and academic performance whereas negative activity-based emotions such as boredom undermine motivation and academic performance (Pekrun, Lichtenfeld, Marsh, Murayama, & Goetz, 2017; Tze, Daniels, & Klassen, 2016). Tze et al. (2016) found that boredom experienced in class had a greater negative impact on academic motivation and performance than boredom experienced whilst studying. In addition, these emotions were shown to have an effect on social and cognitive collaborative problem-solving, i.e. increasing enjoyment and lowering boredom in the classroom promotes a more effective performance in collaborative problem-solving (Camacho-Morles, Slemp, Oades, Morrish, & Scoular, 2019). Lastly, the consequences of the two emotions of anger and frustration are complex and shown to be dependent on other factors (Kozłowska, 2014; Meindl et al., 2018).

In line with the control-value theory, some implications for educators include (1) matching task demands with students' cognition, (2) foster academic engagement in all students, (3) supporting autonomy and cooperative learning, (4) providing feedback as an opportunity to learn (Paoloni, 2014). Many of these suggestions are line with the underlying principles of TBL and it can be surmised that the TBL approach should increase enjoyment and lower boredom, anger and frustration in students. However, there is scant literature relating the pedagogical approach of TBL to achievement emotions. Rather, as working in groups is a major component of TBL, we can examine this issue based on previous studies involving group work.

3.4 Team-Based Learning and Emotions

Through the various stages of TBL, students are naturally inclined towards specific forms of emotional states. In the pre-class preparation stage, prospective outcome emotions are more prominent and, depending on the appropriateness of task demands, the corresponding emotions (joy, hope, relief, anxiety) would likely be experienced. In the subsequent stages, activity-based emotions (enjoyment, frustration, boredom) will naturally arise as most of the activities take place within the classroom. For example, during the IRAT, students may feel joy from being able to respond to the questions correctly or they may feel frustration at their inability to answer the questions. Following the IRAT, successive activities will require the formation and effective functioning of groups. Thus, the next section will examine extant literature on group work and emotions.

As a construct, group work is multi-faceted, comprising dimensions of cognition, motivation, assessment, interpersonal relationship and management (Volet, 2001). These various facets and some related variables are presented in Table 3.1. When students participate in group work, they would appraise these dimensions and their corresponding variables accordingly. For example, in terms of cognition, a student may evaluate the learning opportunities from peers in the group as well as the

Table 3.1 A list of the
dimensions of group work
and some related variables

Dimension	Variables
Cognition	Peer learning opportunities Task demands Task difficulty
Motivation	Engagement of group members Motivation of self
Assessment	Allocation of marks Comparisons between individual and group for the task
Interpersonal	Conducive group atmosphere Communication within group Conflict within group
Management	Workload allocation Time management

demands of the group task, and determine whether he or she is likely to benefit cognitively. However, the same student may evaluate the assessment facet of the same task and come to the conclusion that marks are not allocated fairly. As the dimensions are distinct from each other, the combination of appraisals may lead to a multitude of emotions.

To disentangle any systemic relations between group work dimensions and emotions, Zschocke, Wosnitza, and Burger (2016) conducted an empirical research study on a sample of pre-service teachers in a real-life group work context. The group sizes were between three to six. All participants responded to a questionnaire that measured their appraisals of the group assignment (pre- and post-task) as well as their emotional experiences (post-task). Their findings indicated that positive emotions, e.g. enjoyment, are associated predominantly with the learning process whereas negative emotions, e.g. anger or boredom, are associated mainly with group processes and task characteristics. In other words, cognitive benefits are the main sources of enjoyment whilst a fair workload and assessment lessens anger and boredom. Furthermore, as expected, a favourable development of management and interpersonal dimensions from pre- to post-task has significantly positive effects on positive emotions and negative effects on negative emotions (Zschocke et al., 2016).

What does the current research on group work and emotions suggest about TBL? In TBL, the TRAT and problem-solving application activity are specifically designed to benefit students' cognition in a group setting. Presumably, with reference to Bloom's taxonomy, the TRAT assesses knowledge and comprehension whilst the application activity assesses higher order thinking skills. Furthermore, self-referential feedback is provided after the group activities, enhancing students' appraisal of the learning process (positive value). In terms of control, both group activities are highly dependent on students' preparedness level and interactions (high control). Taken together, the end result is likely to be an increase in positive emotions, i.e. enjoyment.

At the same time, the manner in which TBL is implemented addresses the assessment, management and interpersonal aspects of group work. Assessment-wise, TBL assesses students at both the individual and group levels to reduce the "unfair" practice of every student obtaining the same marks regardless of effort. To ensure equity in grading, assessment is also supplemented by a peer evaluation at the end of the session. Management-wise, workload allocation issues are diminished substantially as group activities focus chiefly on collaborative discussions and are meant to be completed during class time. In particular, the intention of having a concise solution to the problem-solving activities provides a perceived lighter workload, when compared to traditional group activities, e.g. report writing, presentation. With regards to interpersonal relationships, whilst there is no guarantee that the groups will function cohesively, TBL does provide the time and opportunity needed for organizational group structures to form. Specifically, the team appeals component of TBL could be seen as a chance to unite the group as students appeal for credit as a team.

A major issue that hinders group work is the occurrence of free-riders who are students who do not carry out their fair share of work. In line with the control-value theory of achievement emotions, students often feel that they are unable to control the occurrence and behaviour of these free-riders. This often leads to negative emotions (Linnenbrink-Garcia, Rogat, & Koskey, 2011) and frustration on the part of the other group members (Hall & Buzwell, 2013). However, the underlying reason for free-riding may not be student apathy. Rather, there could be a host of other reasons that include differing work styles and lack of knowledge (Hall & Buzwell, 2013). TBL tackles this issue with a two-pronged approach: (1) the assessment process, as stated above, does not give free-riders the same grade as other members, and (2) the readiness assurance process addresses the difficulties of free-riding students who have insufficient knowledge.

Overall, TBL appears to be a teaching strategy that increases positive emotions and decreases negative emotions in students through its unique implementation of group work. However, it is well known that any form of educational approach may not be effective for all students. In this instance, there could be students who are inherently averse to group work or they may feel that there is too much work involved. These fundamentally innate individual differences may be attributed to the different personalities of the students. The final section will discuss certain personality traits as possible moderator variables in the relation between TBL and emotions.

3.5 Personality Traits as a Moderator

Almost all personality researchers today agree that personality consists of several continuous dimensions that are independent of each other. Nonetheless, there still remains some disagreements over the exact number of dimensions that are required to fully describe a person's personality. Whilst the model with five factors (the Big Five) has emerged at the forefront since the past century, recent studies have indicated the existence of six factors (HEXACO model) that are able to accommodate more personality constructs than the Big Five (Ashton & Lee, 2007). The HEXACO model is represented by the six factors of Honesty-Humility, Emotionality, Extraversion,

Table 3.2 The HEXACO
model with some descriptors

Factors	Low levels	High levels
Honesty-Humility	Sly, greedy, boastful	Sincere, honest, fair-minded
Emotionality	Tough, self-assured, stable	Emotional, oversensitive, anxious
Extraversion	Shy, reserved, introverted	Outgoing, sociable, active
Agreeableness	Quarrelsome, stubborn, ill-tempered	Tolerant, peaceful, agreeable
Conscientiousness	Sloppy, negligent, lazy	Organized, diligent, disciplined
Openness to experience	Shallow, unimaginative, conventional	Intellectual, creative, unconventional

Agreeableness, Conscientiousness and Openness to experience. Table 3.2 shows the factors with some descriptors for the various levels.

Any associations between personality and achievement emotions in an educational setting remain relatively unexplored. A plausible reason could be due to the variation of teaching approaches in the classroom. For example, a student high in openness may enjoy an inquiry-based lesson but may experience boredom in a traditional lecture. The converse may be true for students low in conscientiousness. In a study conducted in a high school, the researchers concluded that students who were less agreeable, conscientious and emotionally stable, experienced more unhappiness and anger during lessons (Sorić, Penezić, & Burić, 2013). However, the researchers did not state the instructional method used during the lessons and it is uncertain if a group-based approach was used.

Personality has been shown to have an effect on an individual's level of cognition, motivation and affect. In turn, these individual effects ultimately play a role in shaping group level information processing and cohesiveness in group settings (Moynihan & Peterson, 2004). Empirical studies have indicated that extraverted, agreeable, conscientious and emotionally stable students enjoy working in groups and contribute to group cohesiveness (Forrester & Tashchian, 2010). By adding an appraisal element, the impact of personality traits on achievement emotions can be examined through the lens of control-value theory. For example, a student's perception of internal control may be influenced by the Emotionality trait. This is supported by studies that have either concluded that an increase in anxiety is associated with an external locus of control (Carden, Bryant, & Moss, 2004) or postulated that high anxiety students have difficulties coping with autonomy (Chue, 2015). Thus, when a student is easily anxious, he or she would be more prone to attributing consequences to external control, and subsequently altering the level of the aroused emotion.

The various personality traits are likely to influence students' appraisal of TBL processes from the value perspective. Students high in experience of Openness are more inclined to appraise the cognition dimension of group work positively. This is reflected in their disposition to actively seek out new and varied experiences (McCrae & Costa, 1997). They would welcome the opportunity to have an intellectual discussion with their peers and the autonomy to resolve issues within the problem-solving activity. Students who vary in the trait Emotionality may appraise the assessment dimension of TBL differently. Temperamental students may perceive the different manner in which marks are allocated as personally threatening and consequently self-induce an intense negative emotional reaction (Spielberger, Anton, & Bedell, 2015).

Students high in Extraversion are more likely to appraise the interpersonal dimension positively. These students are willing to communicate with others and enjoy engaging in discussions with other students (Murphy, Eduljee, Croteau, & Parkman, 2017). On the other hand, students low in Agreeableness would be more prone to appraise the same dimension negatively. Wilful and intolerant individuals would not view working with others as desirable as they are more liable to engage in conflicts within the group. In the same vein, students who are low in Honesty-Humility may not like to work in groups as they do not view other students positively. Finally, students who are low in Conscientiousness may appraise the management aspect differently. They may baulk at the idea of having to prepare for the class beforehand or they may welcome the idea that the workload can now be divided amongst other group members.

3.6   Conclusion

The premise of this chapter was to describe student experiences in a TBL lesson, to explore the impact on students' emotions and to examine any possible moderating effects of personality traits. The TBL structure, with its active learning principles, has generally resulted in a higher level of academic outcomes—both cognitive and behavioural. Yet, the affective domain, i.e. emotional states of students, remains largely unexplored. Using the framework of achievement emotions, it can be surmised that students mainly experience activity-based emotions of joy, frustration, anger or boredom. As empirical literature is scarce on this subject, the impact of TBL on emotions was explored through the construct of group work (Volet, 2001) and the control-value theory (Pekrun, 2006). It is hypothesized that both the structure and the implementation process of TBL are likely to contribute to an increase in the positive emotion of joy and a decrease in the negative emotions of boredom, anger and frustration. At the same time, personality differences may also moderate students' appraisal of TBL in terms of their perceived locus of control and the value placed on the structured activities. The HEXACO model of personality was adopted to analyse these possible moderating influences.

In summary, the success of a teaching pedagogy depends largely on its ability to produce positive cognitive, behavioural and affective outcomes simultaneously. TBL appears to have satisfied two of these three outcomes. As an emerging instructional approach catered for a progressive education, it only remains for future research to investigate these relations comprehensively.

References

Abrami, P. C., Bernard, R. M., Borokhovski, E., Waddington, D. I., Wade, C. A., & Persson, T. (2015). Strategies for teaching students to think critically: A meta-analysis. *Review of Educational Research, 85*(2), 275–314.

Ashton, M. C., & Lee, K. (2007). Empirical, theoretical, and practical advantages of the HEXACO model of personality structure. *Personality and Social Psychology Review, 11*(2), 150–166.

Camacho-Morles, J., Slemp, G. R., Oades, L. G., Morrish, L., & Scoular, C. (2019). The role of achievement emotions in the collaborative problem-solving performance of adolescents. *Learning and Individual Differences, 70,* 169–181.

Carden, R., Bryant, C., & Moss, R. (2004). Locus of control, test anxiety, academic procrastination, and achievement among college students. *Psychological Reports, 95*(2), 581–582.

Cestone, C. M., Levine, R. E., & Lane, D. R. (2008). Peer assessment and evaluation in team-based learning. *New Directions for Teaching and Learning, 2008*(116), 69–78.

Cheng, L., Ritzhaupt, A. D., & Antonenko, P. (2018). Effects of the flipped classroom instructional strategy on students' learning outcomes: A meta-analysis. *Educational Technology Research and Development, 1*–32.

Chue, K. L. (2015). Examining the influence of the big five personality traits on the relationship between autonomy, motivation and academic achievement in the twenty-first-century learner. In *Motivation, leadership and curriculum design* (pp. 37–52). Springer.

Foo-Lam, W. K., Soh, Y. P., Widodo, F., Chia, W. J. A., Heng, K. J., Nah, W. K., ... Toh, Q. K. (2014). An approach to holistic education: Cultivating 21st century competencies using team-based learning (TBL) in the teaching of Higher 2 (H2) Biology. In Y.-J. Lee, N. T.-L. Lim, K. S. Tan, H. E. Chu, P. Y. Lim, Y. H. Lim, & I. Tan (Eds.), *Proceedings of the International Science Education Conference 2014* (pp. 509–574). Singapore: National Institute of Education.

Forrester, W. R., & Tashchian, A. (2010). Effects of personality on attitudes toward academic group work. *American Journal of Business Education, 3*(3), 39–46.

Goetz, T., Pekrun, R., Hall, N., & Haag, L. (2006). Academic emotions from a social-cognitive perspective: Antecedents and domain specificity of students' affect in the context of Latin instruction. *British Journal of Educational Psychology, 76*(2), 289–308.

Hall, D., & Buzwell, S. (2013). The problem of free-riding in group projects: Looking beyond social loafing as reason for non-contribution. *Active Learning in Higher Education, 14*(1), 37–49.

Hattie, J., & Timperley, H. (2007). The power of feedback. *Review of Educational Research, 77*(1), 81–112.

He, W., Holton, A., Farkas, G., & Warschauer, M. (2016). The effects of flipped instruction on out-of-class study time, exam performance, and student perceptions. *Learning and Instruction, 45,* 61–71.

Jakobsen, K. V., & Knetemann, M. (2017). Putting structure to flipped classrooms using team-based learning. *International Journal of Teaching and Learning in Higher Education, 29*(1), 177–185.

Jeno, L. M., Raaheim, A., Kristensen, S. M., Kristensen, K. D., Hole, T. N., Haugland, M. J., & Mæland, S. (2017). The relative effect of team-based learning on motivation and learning: a self-determination theory perspective. *CBE—Life Sciences Education, 16*(4), ar59.

Johnston, N., & Karafotias, T. (2016). Flipping the classroom to meet the diverse learning needs of library and information studies (LIS) students. *Journal of Education for Library and Information Science, 57*(3), 226–238.

Kozłowska, A. (2014). Anger in the context of learning. *Studia Psychologiczne, 52*(4), 32–38.

Linnenbrink-Garcia, L., Rogat, T. K., & Koskey, K. L. (2011). Affect and engagement during small group instruction. *Contemporary Educational Psychology, 36*(1), 13–24.

Liu, S.-N.C., & Beaujean, A. A. (2017). The effectiveness of team-based learning on academic outcomes: A meta-analysis. *Scholarship of Teaching and Learning in Psychology, 3*(1), 1.

McCrae, R. R., & Costa, P. T. (1997). Conceptions and correlates of openness to experience. In *Handbook of personality psychology* (pp. 825–847). Elsevier.

Meindl, P., Yu, A., Galla, B. M., Quirk, A., Haeck, C., Goyer, J. P., … Duckworth, A. L. (2018). A brief behavioral measure of frustration tolerance predicts academic achievement immediately and two years later. *Emotion (Washington, DC)*.

Michaelsen, L. K., & Sweet, M. (2008). The essential elements of team-based learning. *New Directions for Teaching and Learning, 2008*(116), 7–27.

Michaelsen, L. K., & Sweet, M. (2011). Team-based learning. *New Directions for Teaching and Learning, 2011*(128), 41–51.

Moynihan, L. M., & Peterson, R. S. (2004). The role of personality in group processes. *Personality and Organizations*, 317–345.

Murphy, L., Eduljee, N. B., Croteau, K., & Parkman, S. (2017). Extraversion and introversion personality type and preferred teaching and classroom participation: A pilot study. *Journal of Psychosocial Research, 12*(2), 437–450.

Paoloni, P. V. (2014). Emotions in academic contexts. Theoretical perspectives and implications for educational practice in college.

Pekrun, R. (2006). The control-value theory of achievement emotions: Assumptions, corollaries, and implications for educational research and practice. *Educational Psychology Review, 18*(4), 315–341.

Pekrun, R., Cusack, A., Murayama, K., Elliot, A. J., & Thomas, K. (2014). The power of anticipated feedback: Effects on students' achievement goals and achievement emotions. *Learning and Instruction, 29*, 115–124.

Pekrun, R., Lichtenfeld, S., Marsh, H. W., Murayama, K., & Goetz, T. (2017). Achievement emotions and academic performance: Longitudinal models of reciprocal effects. *Child Development, 88*(5), 1653–1670.

Sorić, I., Penezić, Z., & Burić, I. (2013). Big Five personality traits, cognitive appraisals and emotion regulation strategies as predictors of achievement emotions. *Psihologijske Teme, 22*(2), 325–349.

Spielberger, C. D., Anton, W. D., & Bedell, J. (2015). The nature and treatment of test anxiety. In *Emotions and anxiety: New concepts, methods, and applications* (pp. 317–344).

Swanson, E., McCulley, L. V., Osman, D. J., Scammacca Lewis, N., & Solis, M. (2017). The effect of team-based learning on content knowledge: A meta-analysis. *Active Learning in Higher Education*, 1469787417731201.

Thompson, B. M., Haidet, P., Borges, N. J., Carchedi, L. R., Roman, B. J., Townsend, M. H., … Levine, R. E. (2015). Team cohesiveness, team size and team performance in team-based learning teams. *Medical Education, 49*(4), 379–385.

Tze, V. M., Daniels, L. M., & Klassen, R. M. (2016). Evaluating the relationship between boredom and academic outcomes: A meta-analysis. *Educational Psychology Review, 28*(1), 119–144.

Volet, S. (2001). Significance of cultural and motivation variables on students' attitudes towards group work. In *Student motivation* (pp. 309–333). Springer.

Wanzek, J., Vaughn, S., Kent, S. C., Swanson, E. A., Roberts, G., Haynes, M., … Solis, M. (2014). The effects of team-based learning on social studies knowledge acquisition in high school. *Journal of Research on Educational Effectiveness, 7*(2), 183–204.

Zschocke, K., Wosnitza, M., & Bürger, K. (2016). Emotions in group work: Insights from an appraisal-oriented perspective. *European Journal of Psychology of Education, 31*(3), 359–384.

Chapter 4
The Effects of Positive Psychology Interventions on School Conduct, Peer Acceptance and Subjective Well-Being

Nasyita Mohtar

Abstract The primary purpose of this chapter is to examine a positive psychology approach to improving the school conduct, peer acceptance and subjective well-being of young adolescents. It works on the assumption that adolescents need to have frequent opportunities to learn and practise interpersonal skills and good behaviour. They may also need constant reassurance that they are well-accepted and appreciated by their peers. Hence, a simple activity to provide students with the opportunity to do so on a more regular basis is deemed necessary. Thus, the chapter begins with a review of the theoretical framework and research findings relevant to school conduct, peer acceptance, subjective well-being and Positive Psychology Interventions, such as Positive Peer Reporting/Notes (PPR/PPN). The Broaden-and-Build Theory of Positive Emotions is presented, followed by an overview of positive psychology interventions (PPI) and characteristics of effective school-based interventions. A review of positive psychology interventions (PPI) focusing on those involving gratitude and character strengths is presented.

Keywords Adolescents · Peer acceptance · Conduct problems · Pro-social behaviour · Classroom engagement · Classroom misbehaviours · School conduct · Subjective well-being · Positive psychology · Positive activities · Positive peer reporting

4.1 Introduction

The increased complexity of the world today has affected the mental health of young people (Waters, 2011). Over the past century, there has been an increase in mental disorders and a decrease in subjective well-being in high-income countries (Twenge, 2011). Subjective well-being (SWB) refers to the extent to which a person feels or experiences pleasure (Diener, Suh, Lucas, & Smith, 1999) and it involves "a person's cognitive and affective evaluation of his or her life" (Diener, Lucas, & Oishi, 2002,

N. Mohtar (✉)
National Institute of Education, Nanyang Technological University, Singapore, Singapore
e-mail: nasyita_mohtar@hotmail.com

© Springer Nature Singapore Pte Ltd. 2020
C. Koh (ed.), *Diversifying Learner Experience*,
https://doi.org/10.1007/978-981-15-9861-6_4

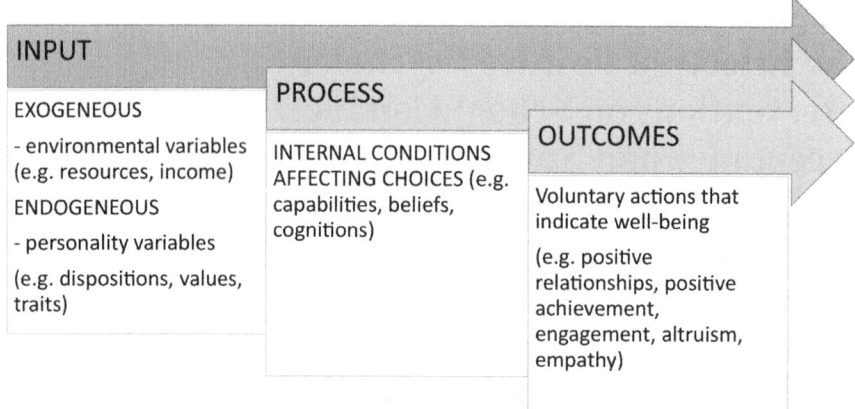

Fig. 4.1 The Engine Model of well-being

p. 63). The cognitive aspect refers to one's evaluation of his or her life satisfaction (e.g., relationship and school). The affective aspect refers to the state of one's moods and feelings (positive affect and negative affect). The Engine Model, an integrative framework proposed by Jayawickreme, Forgeard, and Seligman (2012), outlines the 'chain of causality' leading to an enhancement of well-being. These authors postulate that the variables that influence well-being can be categorised into three classes: inputs, processes and outcomes. The Engine Model posits that interventions to promote well-being could occur at each of these three levels. Thus, input interventions could involve improving the availability of resources and personal dispositions, whereas process interventions involve internal states influencing personal choices, and outcome interventions involve behaviours characterising well-being such as improved relationships and personal accomplishments. The components of the Engine Model are illustrated in Fig. 4.1.

While resources, funding and environmental support would positively impact well-being, other input variables such as physiological changes, academic and social pressures, in addition to process variables such as the need for adjustment from primary to secondary school during early adolescence, could lead to an increase in undesirable outcome variables, such as misbehaviour, as students move up the grade (Arbuckle & Little, 2004). Ong and colleagues (2000) revealed that, in Singapore, one of the most common problem behaviours cited by the students was school-related, non-complying behaviours such as coming to school late, breaking school rules and disobeying teachers. Problem behaviours during adolescence is a cause for concern. A study by McGue, Elkins, Walden, and Iacono (2005) showed that problem behaviours during adolescence were significantly related to adult psychopathology. The longitudinal study in the US, which involved data collection from a sample of 1252 adolescents at age 17 years and again at age 20 (three years later), showed that teenagers with problem behaviours tended to grow into adults with depressive tendencies. In addition, the study also revealed that the risk of being diagnosed as having depressive disorders during adulthood was higher when individuals engage in problem behaviours earlier in life, that is, before the age of 15.

The study by Shum-Cheung and colleagues (2008) also found that although most of the children in their study, who were between the ages 8 and 12, did not have difficulties making friends, 6.4% of them, unfortunately, did. This small percentage, when extrapolated nationally, would translate to a large number in absolute terms (Shum-Cheung et al., 2008). This could be a concern because these students may find difficulty adjusting to secondary school life. In Singapore, students generally attend primary school from the age of 7. At the end of their sixth year (Primary 6), they leave their primary schools to attend secondary schools. For most children, this would mean finding themselves immersed in a totally new setting (e.g., classrooms, teachers and classmates). Therefore, students with existing negative peer experiences in primary school could find it challenging to adjust to their new secondary school life, which may further lead to internalising symptoms and lower academic performance (Bellmore, 2011).

This chapter explores the theoretical framework and research findings relevant to positive affect, positive psychology and Positive Peer Reporting as process variables, as well as school conduct, peer acceptance, subjective well-being as outcome variables. The Broaden-and-Build Theory of Positive Emotions is presented followed by an overview of positive psychology interventions (PPI) and characteristics of effective school-based interventions. The concepts of peer acceptance, school conduct and subjective well-being are then discussed, elaborating on the implications of misbehaviour and lack of peer acceptance amongst adolescents, and how the various concepts of peer acceptance, school conduct and subjective well-being are related to one another within the context of adolescent students. Such a review of the literature paves the way for a study on how a simple class-wide positive activity could diversify students' classroom experiences and in so doing, bring about improvements in their behaviour, social acceptance and subjective well-being.

4.2 Desired Outcomes

4.2.1 Peer Acceptance

Peers play a powerful role in young people's development and schooling (Wentzel & Muenks, 2016, cited in Santrock, 2018, p. 82). This is a widely acknowledged fact by both parents and teachers (Leung & Silberling, 2006). As an individual grows from childhood to adulthood, the focus of their relationships turns from family to friends and likewise, they turn to their peers rather than their families for support (Levitt et al., 2005). As peer relationships become more influential during early adolescence, young adults develop their self-concept partly based on how others view them (Kim, Rapee, Oh, & Moon, 2008). According to Steinberg (2005), early adolescence is a phase marked by a need for autonomy, whereby children focus more on social acceptance and move away from parental influence. Peer acceptance, the extent to which children or adolescents are socially accepted and liked by their peers (Oberle & Schonert-Reichl, 2013), is perceived to be a core indicator for academic success and social and emotional well-being of children and adolescents (De Rosier & Lloyd, 2011, cited in Gallardo, Barassa, & Guevera-Viejo, 2016, p. 1638). Being accepted by peers is an important factor for positive growth in the school setting (Gallardo et al., 2016). For example, peer acceptance was found to be positively linked to academic achievement and higher intelligence levels during adolescence (Gallardo et al., 2016), as well as more pro-social behaviour (Claes & Simard, 1993). Although there are other measures of interpersonal outcome such as relatedness, social popularity and connectedness, this paper focuses on peer acceptance since one has to be accepted by others first before a sense of connectedness, relatedness or popularity could be established.

4.2.2 Factors Affecting Peer Acceptance

Young people who lack peer acceptance do not enjoy positive peer relationships (Nelson, Caldarella, Young, & Webb, 2008). There are various reasons why some children and adolescents lack peer acceptance. For example, in the study by Nelson and colleagues (2008), the lack of peer acceptance was due to the socially withdrawn behaviour of the target adolescents themselves. According to Kim et al. (2008), adolescents display socially withdrawn behaviour due to their shyness or unsociability. Coplan, Girardi, Findlay, and Frohlick (2007) found that children as young as kindergarteners were able to distinguish between the different types of socially withdrawn behaviour, specifically between shyness and unsociability. In their study, they found that shy children were likely to be more peer accepted than the unsociable ones.

Other reasons for the lack of peer acceptance include one or more of the following: (1) higher level of disruptiveness or aggressiveness, (2) immature behaviour and (3) avoidant behaviour (Knack, Tsar, Vaillancourt, Hymel, & Mc Dougall, 2012). Avoidant behaviour could be due to either shyness or preference for solitary activities (e.g., Coplan, Prakash, O'Neil, & Armer, 2004). Not all students who are aggressive are socially rejected. Vaillancourt and Hymel (2006) found that aggressive youth who were high on peer-valued characteristics such as physical attractiveness, athletic competence and special talents were less disliked. However, both aggressive and non-aggressive youths who displayed non-behavioural traits such as physical unattractiveness, low socio-economic status, low academic ability and low athletic ability, were more prone to peer isolation (see Knack et al., 2012, for a review). In her literature review on non-aggressive, peer-isolated children and adolescents, Margolin (2001) cited these children and adolescents as having one or more of the following characteristics: extreme shyness, low academic achievement, athletic incompetence or physical weakness, unattractiveness and lacking stylishness, submissiveness when scorned, social anxiety, immaturity and lack of social competence. Some youngsters might have known how to behave in a socially competent manner, but they were unable to demonstrate it (Wichmann, Coplan, & Daniels, 2004), which could have been the reason for the lack of peer acceptance. Then, there were those who were ignored by their peers but were neither treated poorly nor treated well (Newcomb, Bukowski, & Patee, 1993).

Adolescents with higher peer acceptance displayed greater pro-social behaviours such as co-operating and sharing with others (Badaly, Schwartz, & Gorman, 2012). In a longitudinal study involving sixth-grade students, Wentzel, Barry, and Caldwell (2004) found that students who did not have a friend, displayed less prosocial behaviour, attained lower academic grades and were more emotionally distressed compared to peers who had at least one friend. Two years later, these students who were without a friend in sixth grade were found to have even higher levels of emotional distress. A study conducted by Buchanan and Bowen (2008) involving about 14 000 middle school students showed that peer support played an important role in the psychological well-being of adolescents, especially in the presence of adult supports. Peer support in the study was defined as social support in terms of emotional (e.g., listening), informative (e.g., providing advice) or instrumental (e.g., providing help) and psychological well-being, and was measured in terms of levels of self-esteem, happiness and personal adjustment. Lack of peer acceptance has also been linked to absenteeism, lower academic achievement and early school dropout (Buhs & Ladd, 2001; Parker & Asher, 1987). There are many reasons for dropping out. Parker and Asher (1987) suggested that this might be due to low academic achievement because of missed opportunities to study with friends or simply due to the unpleasant experience of not having friends at school, and hence the lack of motivation to continue schooling. In this respect, the Self-determination theory (SDT) emphasizes the importance of social relations in the classroom and school (Schunk, Meece, & Pintrich, 2014, p. 351).

4.3   School Conduct

A student's school conduct refers to his/her overall behaviour towards authority and peers (Stright & Yeo, 2014). It encompasses his/her behaviour within, as well as outside, the classroom. The following paragraphs aim to discuss school conduct (classroom misbehaviours, conduct problems, pro-social behaviour and classroom engagement) and its implications.

4.3.1   Decreasing Classroom Misbehaviour

Managing student misbehaviour is one of the challenges faced by many classroom teachers (Anderson & Kincaid, 2005). Stewart and colleagues (1998) defined student misconduct as breaking school rules (tardiness, vandalism and stealing). However,

Sun and Shek (2012) argued that misbehaviour or misconduct is a behaviour that is inappropriate though not necessarily rule-breaking. A review of studies from around the world showed that classroom behaviours, deemed problematic to teachers, were mild but constant in nature (Beaman, Wheldall, & Kemp, 2007). Examples of such behaviours were: talking out of turn, inattention, out of seat, lack of motivation and inappropriate banter (Haroun & O'Hanlon, 1997). These behaviours, although not serious in nature, significantly disrupted a student's own learning, interrupted another student's learning and also interfered with the teacher's planned teaching (Merrett & Wheldall, 1984). The review by Beaman and colleagues (2007) pointed out that serious misbehaviours such as stealing and drug abuse also caused difficulties to teachers. However, it was argued that the frequent daily occurrence of the trivial disruptive classroom behaviours, though not serious, were responsible for teaching-related stress.

Why do students misbehave in the classroom? Traditionally, a teacher's lack of classroom management skills and/or a student's personal characteristics had often been cited as the reasons for classroom misbehaviour (Kaplan, Gheen, & Midley, 2002). Lasley (1979) categorised classroom behaviour as either challenging or coping, after spending two months observing classroom behaviour in two schools. Challenging behaviours were defined as misbehaviours with the intention of disrupting lessons, such as attacking the teacher with a non-verbal gesture or aggressive comments, 'smarting-off' with the intention of causing loss of face to the teacher as well as ignoring the teacher. According to Lasley (1979), students might display challenging behaviour due to frustration caused by unfair treatment by the teacher or meaningless classroom activities. Coping behaviours, on the other hand, were perceived as having no intent to cause disruption but were behaviours aimed to make school more bearable. They might be considered by teachers as inappropriate but were perceived as acceptable by fellow classmates. For example, a student might misbehave in the classroom in order to gain social acceptability by peers. Social acceptability in this case depended largely on the class culture. Another reason suggested for student misbehaviour was to relieve boredom and to meet the need for some stimulation. Hence, in both cases, the reason for misbehaviour was generally for self-enhancement and self-satisfaction (Lasley, 1979).

Kaplan and colleagues (2002) posited that classroom goal structure could also play a role in the prevalence of classroom misbehaviour. In their study, they found that students tended to misbehave in performance-oriented classrooms where the emphasis was on doing well relative to others, rather than improving over one's own past performance. Misbehaving publicly allowed students to use misbehaviour as a reason for their failure in school rather than their lack of ability (Baumeister, 1997). Students in performance-oriented classrooms had concerns over their lack of ability and might adopt performance-avoidance goals (Kaplan et al., 2002). They might thus engage in disruptive behaviours as a strategy to protect their self-worth as performance-avoidance goal orientation had been known to be correlated to anxiety (Middleton & Midgley, 1997). In contrast, in mastery-oriented classrooms where the focus was on learning and improving, Kaplan and colleagues (2002) found that there were fewer instances of disruptive behaviour. Hence, they concluded that it was essential to create a classroom culture where the focus was on learning, improving and valuing personal as well as social development rather than emphasising on ability.

Research has shown that teachers tended to lend less support to disruptive students, paying more attention to their misbehaviour instead (Fry, 1983, cited in Infantino & Little, 2005, p. 494). Disruptive behaviour was shown to be negatively related to academic performance (Pullis, 1991). A student who displayed classroom misbehaviours might be actively rejected by his/her peers, which in turn could limit his/her opportunity to take part in social and academic interactions (Beaman & Wheldall, 1997). Hence, it may be necessary to develop strategies targeting minor classroom misbehaviours before these behaviours become more serious (Infantino & Little, 2005). Reducing classroom misbehaviours could increase the opportunity for students to perform better academically (Infantino & Little, 2005).

4.3.2 Decreasing Conduct Problems

According to Frick and McMahon (2008), conduct problems consist of a wide spectrum of 'acting out' behaviours ranging from minor antagonistic behaviours (e.g., temper tantrums) to more serious forms (e.g., physical violence). The authors recommended giving additional attention to two forms of conduct problems: aggression and non-compliance. These two forms of conduct problems are discussed in greater detail below.

Aggression is an important dimension of conduct problems as the act itself causes harm to another person (Crick & Dodge, 1996, as cited in Frick & McMahon, 2008, p. 42). Classroom teachers may not consider aggression as one of their immediate concerns as aggression may occur outside the classroom such as during break time. Aggression was also found to be a conduct problem that was often displayed by students in Singapore schools (Ong, Tan, & Cheng, 2000). In most schools in Singapore, this form of conduct problem outside of the classroom is often handled by the higher authorities of the school such as the head in charge of disciplinary matters and this may not affect classroom teachers directly. However, it is important to acknowledge that childhood aggression predicts conduct problems later in life (Fite, Raine, Stouthamer-Loeber, Loeber, & Padini, 2010). Aggression can be divided into two types: reactive aggression (RA) and passive aggression (PA). According to researchers, the RA person is often impulsive (Raine et al., 2006) and possesses poor emotional regulation skills (Hubbard et al., 2002). Hence, the RA person tends to get easily frustrated and angry when provoked (Pang, Ang, Kom, Tan, & Chiang, 2013). On the other hand, the PA individual expects a positive outcome from an aggressive act (Pang et al., 2013).

A study by Pang and colleagues (2013) involving a large sample of students from four average ranking secondary schools in Singapore showed that aggressive adolescents, regardless of whether they had RA or PA characteristics, tended to have attentional, depressed, anxiety and somatic problems, besides demonstrating rule-breaking and delinquent behaviours. However, adolescents possessing a combined

RA/PA profile showed a greater display of the above problems. According to the authors, adolescents from homes with permissive and authoritarian parenting styles tended to demonstrate greater aggression and for the RA/PA individuals, their parents tended to show a combination of high permissiveness and high authoritarianism.

Aggressive behaviour is classified as physical bullying if it is intended to harm. Victims of physical bullying as well as other forms of bullying could also potentially develop emotional maladjustment. For example, the majority of victims in Singapore secondary schools reported feeling angry and sad (Singapore Children Society, 2008). Victims also claimed that they had difficulty sleeping at night, had trouble concentrating during lessons and some of them resorted to truancy or school absences. Young adults who were bullied in schools tended to possess lower self-esteem and were more depressed than those who did not experience bullying during their school days (Singapore Children Society, 2010).

Another form of conduct problem which deserves attention is non-compliance, such as disobeying adults and defying rules (Frick & McMahon, 2008). Non-compliance appears to play an important role in subsequent academic and social problems displayed by children with conduct problems (Frick & McMahon, 2008, p. 42). Tardiness is one example of non-complying school conduct. In the school context, tardiness can be broadly defined as arriving in school or for class later than the specified time. Participants in the study by Ong and colleagues (2000) also cited tardiness as the second most frequently occurring conduct problems of students.

An approach towards decreasing the incidence of deviant behaviour is to encourage, recognise and model desirable behaviour, in the form of an act of self-lessness targeted at the betterment of others. This so-called pro-social behaviour can be defined as one that benefits other people or society at large, but not necessarily of any advantage to self. Pro-social behaviour and kindness are often taken to be interchangeable, but this paper posits that kindness is the state or disposition of being good-natured and benevolent. Kindness can be demonstrated in the form of pro-social behaviour, whereby one does something for the sole purpose of benefitting another, or society (Ryon, 2013, cited in Caldwell, 2017, p. 3; Helliwell, Aknin, Shiplett, Huang, & Wang, 2017) Thus, authors such as Ryon (2013, cited in Caldwell, 2017, p. 3) defined an act of kindness as doing something for the sole purpose of benefitting another, without any motive of meeting social expectations. On the other hand, pro-social behaviour is defined as behaviour that benefits others or society (Cherry, 2014; Helliwell et al., 2017). In the classroom context, it includes attentiveness, active participation in class activities or having empathy for classmates.

4.3.3 Promoting Pro-social Behaviour

Pro-social behaviour can be classified as either relational or overt (Bergin, Talley, & Hamer, 2003). Some examples of relational pro-social behaviours include providing emotional support, complimenting and showing encouragement towards others as well as not hurting the feelings of others. Overt pro-social behaviours are those that help others through physical means, such as helping others to develop skills and providing community service. A focus group study by Bergin and colleagues (2003) revealed that female adolescents demonstrated relational pro-social behaviour more frequently while male adolescents exhibited overt ones more frequently.

Nevertheless, the authors acknowledged that pro-social behaviours, be it relational or overt, enhanced peer relationships. In early adolescence, peers play an important part in the development of pro-social behaviour. When peers displayed pro-social behaviours towards one another, they were most likely to engage in a cycle of pro-social exchanges (Bukowski & Sippola, 1996, cited in Carlo, Fabes, Laible, & Kupanoff, 1999, p. 137). Students who carried out acts of kindness tended to have greater peer acceptance (Layous, Nelson, Oberle, Schonert-Reichl, & Lyubomirsky, 2012). Guo, Zhou, and Feng (2018) found that students who were peer-rated high on pro-social behaviour experienced greater peer acceptance and academic achievement. The authors suggested that well-accepted students were more likely to have greater school engagement and to receive academic assistance from peers, which could further contribute to their academic success (Guo et al., 2018).

Kidron and Fleishman (2006) suggested that teachers could also have a huge influence on their students' social growth by creating a school-wide culture in which the students have the chance to observe pro-social behaviours modelled by their peers or other adults. School-wide approaches such as Positive Behavioural Interventions and Support had been used in US schools to encourage pro-social behaviour not only for all students in the school, but also for the staff. Teachers in Singapore schools suggested preventive measures to decrease negative behaviour such as raising students' self-esteem and public acknowledgment of good behaviour (Tan & Cheng, 1999).

4.4 Subjective Well-Being

Research on well-being has been on the rise in recent decades. However, there is, to date, a lack of consensus with regards to defining the term 'well-being' (Dodge, Daly, Huyton, & Sanders, 2012). There are no clear-cut distinctions between the various types of well-being. For example, life satisfaction or positive feelings are taken as measures of psychological well-being (Keyes, 1998), just as Watson and colleagues (1988) considered the prevalence of positive feelings over negative ones as indications of emotional well-being. In this chapter, the discussion centres predominantly on Subjective Well-Being (SWB), which refers to how people perceive the quality of their lives in relation to their emotional responses and their assessment of life satisfaction (Diener et al., 1999). There are several reasons for the focus on SWB. Firstly, it is a factor that is most often measured in the field of positive psychology. Secondly, the variables used in assessing SWB provide an indication of emotional health (Keyes, 2007).

A widely accepted SWB model, frequently used in the positive psychology literature, is the tripartite model proposed by Diener and colleagues (1999) which comprises three distinct components: (1) Positive Affect, (2) Negative Affect and (3) Overall Life Satisfaction. Positive and negative affects make up the affective component of SWB while life satisfaction makes up the cognitive aspect of it. Positive and negative affects refer to the frequency of positive and negative emotions experienced by an individual, respectively. Positive affect and negative affect were found to be independent constructs (Lent, 2004). Negative affect, for example, was shown to be associated with anxiety and depression while positive affect was negatively correlated to depression but not anxiety (Long, Hubner, & Wedell, 2012).

Life satisfaction refers to one's cognitive appraisal of the overall quality of life, usually with respect to global life satisfaction or to specific contexts, such as school experiences. Hence, a person who experiences frequent positive affect, infrequent negative affect and a high level of overall or domain-specific life satisfaction is said to have high subjective well-being (Long et al., 2012).

The tripartite model of SWB works on the assumption that people are capable of making meaningful judgements about their own lives and experiences (Tov & Diener, 2013). How people regard their SWB depends, to a certain extent, on their cultural background. However, certain factors have been found to be universally related to SWB (Tov & Diener, 2013). For example, the satisfaction of basic needs, such as food, shelter and supportive relationships as well as psychological needs such as competence and personal freedom, has been found to be associated with a higher level of SWB across cultures in different parts of the world (e.g., Tay & Diener, 2011). On the other hand, some factors were more strongly related to SWB in certain cultures as compared to others. For example, in individualistic societies such as those in Western Europe and North America, personal freedom and self-esteem were found to be strongly associated with life satisfaction (Diener & Diener, 1995). On the contrary, in collectivist cultures such as Asian, African and Latin American cultures, having harmonious social relationships was significantly correlated to life satisfaction and positive emotions (e.g., Oishi, Diener, Scollon, & BiswasDiene, 2004).

Past research indicated positive outcomes of SWB in adults. A review by Diener (2012) concluded that SWB affected one's future health and the quality of social life. People high in SWB tended to demonstrate pro-social and good citizenship behaviours such as donating money or blood for charity. They were also more likely to experience success at the workplace (see review by Diener, 2012). Although there is a smaller body of literature on SWB involving children and adolescents, evidence suggests that SWB is linked to educational functioning. For example, a longitudinal study by Suldo and colleagues (2011) demonstrated that high SWB amongst early adolescents predicted higher academic grades and better school attendance. Another study conducted by Gilman and Huebner (2006) showed that youth with high global life satisfaction reported having more positive academic experience, higher GPAs, more positive relationships with others and less anxiety. SWB was found to play an important role in young adolescents' adjustment to middle school academically, socially and emotionally (Shoshani & Slone, 2013).

4.5 Positive Psychology and Theories of Well-Being

Sheldon and King (2001) defined positive psychology as the scientific study of ordinary human strengths and virtues with the intent of discovering what works and what is improving in the average person. At the subjective level, positive psychology is about subjective experiences such as happiness, joy, well-being and satisfaction. At the individual level, positive psychology aims to enhance positive personality traits such as perseverance, interpersonal skills and courage. At the group level, it is about virtues that drive individuals towards better work ethics, responsibility and citizenship (Seligman & Csikszenmihalyi, 2000). The study of positive psychology therefore enables a deeper understanding of well-being, as well as how it can be enhanced.

One of the theories developed to better understand how positive outcomes, such as well-being, can be acquired is the *Broaden-and-Build Theory* of Positive Emotions. This theory was developed by Barbara Fredrickson (Fredrickson, 1998) to study the effects of positive emotions such as joy and interest. Based on earlier theorists who suggested that positive affect (the extent to which an individual experiences positive emotions) promoted approach behaviour or continued action, Fredrickson (2001) posited that experiences of positive affect would motivate people to interact with their environment and engage in activities. She argued that, as emotion is a subset of the wider spectrum of affective phenomena, positive emotions, too, operate as internal indicators to approach or continuity. Hence, the *Broaden-and-Build Theory* states that positive emotions broaden the span of one's action, attention and cognitive capacity, that is, increase one's thought-action repertoires, as well as build intellectual, social and physical resources (Fredrickson, 2001). Based on earlier findings which showed that resilient individuals displayed an optimistic view to life and were open to new experiences (e.g., Klohnen, 1996, as cited in Rahimi & Bigdeli, 2014, p. 798), Fredrickson (2001) posited that positive emotions could also optimise subjective well-being and psychological resilience.

Evidence for the Broaden-and-Build Theory could be gathered from various studies (Fredrickson, 2013). For the 'broaden aspect' of the theory, positive emotions have been shown to broaden the span of one's visual attention (Wadlinger & Issacowitz, 2006), develop one's circle of trust (Dunn & Schweitzer, 2005), increase one's empathy and compassion for others from a different cultural background (Nelson, 2009), as well as create social inclusion (Johnson & Fredrickson, 2005). For the 'build' aspect of the theory, positive emotions have been shown to build personal resources. For example, positive affect has been shown to promote sociability (Whelan & Zelenski, 2012) and to motivate one to interact with others, thus taking an initial step towards building supportive bonds. Individuals who experienced or expressed more positive emotions tended to be more psychologically resilient (Fredrickson, Tugade, Waugh, & Larkin, 2003) and resourceful (Lyubomirsky, King, & Diener, 2005). Additionally, positive emotions also built cognitive resources such as mindfulness, social resources such as positive relationships with others as well as physical resources, measured in terms of reduction in self-rated illness symptoms

(Fredrickson, 2013). Broadened cognition which, in turn, builds personal resources, produces more experiences of positive emotions. This results in an upward spiral, which in time will enhance emotional well-being. People who experience more positive emotions have been shown to be more resilient to challenges over time and are able to cope better (Fredrickson & Joiner, 2002). Hence, positive emotions "widen people's outlook in ways that, little by little, reshape who they are" (Fredrickson, Cohn, Coffey, Pek, & Finkel, 2008).

If positive affect is said to enhance well-being, what, then, are the factors that promote positive emotions? The *Positive Activity Model*, proposed by Lyubomirsky and Layous (2013), relates the performance of positive activities to happiness and well-being. The model posits that positive activities enhance well-being by increasing positive thoughts, emotions and behaviours, as well as basic psychological needs. The extent to which positive activities promote well-being is influenced by their dosage and variety and the personal attributes of the individual, such as motivation and effort. Thus, *learner* experiences can be diversified, and their well-being enhanced through the administration of a series of well-designed activities known as Positive Psychology Interventions (PPI).

4.6 Diversifying Learner Experiences Through Positive Psychology Interventions

Positive psychology interventions (PPI) are planned, intentional activities which aim to develop cognition, behaviours and positive emotions. They usually need little or no financial resources (Layous, Chancellor, & Lyubomirsky, 2014). Historically, interventions were targeted at young people who were experiencing a crisis such as dropping out of school, alcohol and drug abuse (Steen, Kachorek, & Peterson, 2003). Positive psychology interventions, however, aim to build strengths and not to fix or remediate what is deficient (Sin & Lyubomirsky, 2009). As such, PPIs are potentially effective as strategies to diversify learner experiences within and beyond the classroom. The positive activities can be in many forms which are discussed in the following paragraphs. According to Layous et al. (2014), positive activities could be behavioural such as carrying out acts of kindness or they could be cognitive such as envisaging one's best possible self.

Class-wide positive psychology interventions, involving the use of peer praise, aim to build strengths, specifically to enhance peer acceptance, pro-social behaviour and subjective well-being of adolescents. Drawing on the tenets of the Broaden-and-Build Theory, these interventions aim to cultivate positive emotions through the use of peer praises, as praise will generally evoke positive emotions such as pride, pleasure and joy in the person who is praised (Markelz & Taylor, 2016). Additionally, peer praises will incorporate elements of gratitude and character strengths as a way to foster these positive emotions. The following sections discuss the effects of various positive psychology interventions in the literature, specifically gratitude-based and strength-based interventions, factors affecting the success of positive interventions and the choice of a peer-mediated intervention known as Positive Peer Reporting/Peer Praise Notes.

4.6.1 Effects of Positive Interventions

Positive interventions involve activities which are relatively simple, brief and non-stigmatising (Layous & Lyubomirsky, 2012), yet these have the potential of diversifying learner experiences in a desirable manner. Layous et al. (2014) proposed that these positive activities could enhance an individual's well-being through increasing positive emotions, positive behaviours and psychological need satisfaction. For example, in a study conducted by Della Porta (2012), participants consisting of university students were required to perform acts of kindness, with support from messages of encouragement from peers. The results of the study revealed that participants reported higher level of happiness, decrease in negative affect, and hence improved subjective well-being.

Participating in positive activities has also been shown to satisfy psychological needs such as autonomy and relatedness. For example, in an intervention study in which participants expressed optimism and gratitude, it was found that these participants reported increased relatedness and autonomy (Boehm et al., 2012 as cited in Lyubomirsky & Layous, 2013, p. 60). In addition, the increase in psychological need satisfaction also led to increased life satisfaction.

Many studies have demonstrated that positive activities could enhance relationships and thus prevent loneliness (Layous et al., 2014). For example, the positive activity in the form of loving-kindness meditation intervention conducted by Fredrickson and colleagues (2008) not only led to increased positive emotions amongst the participants, but these positive emotions were also enhanced when participants interacted with one another. This suggests that positive social interactions were nurtured by the positive intervention in the study. Furthermore, the study also demonstrated that an increase in positive emotions also led to an increase in perceived social support. Practising gratitude and optimism was found to increase connectedness which, in turn, led to an increase in well-being (Boehm et al., 2012, cited in Layous et al., 2014, p. 7). When people were happy, they were more interested in social activities (Cunningham, 1988) and perceived relationships as closer (Waugh & Fredrickson, 2006). Putting all these studies together, Layous et al. (2014) posited that enhanced positive relationships could mitigate risk factors like loneliness either directly (e.g., by decreasing feelings of being unloved) or indirectly (e.g., by increasing well-being which can reduce internal beliefs and conditions that could cause loneliness). This was, in fact, consistent with the Broaden-and-Build Theory (Fredrickson, 2001) whereby positive emotions were induced through positive activities which helped to enhance social relationships and this, in turn, led to increased well-being over time.

4.6.2   Gratitude-Based Interventions

Researchers have also assessed the effects of positive interventions which focused on gratitude and character strengths of participants. The word 'gratitude' originates from the Latin word 'gratia' which means 'grace', 'graciousness' or 'gratefulness' (Emmons & Sheldon, 2002). It is linked to other positive terms such as kindness, generosity, giving and receiving (Emmons & Stern, 2013). Gratitude has been conceptualised in many ways, mainly as either a virtue or an emotional state (Froh, Sefick, & Emmons, 2008). Both constructs have been associated with subjective well-being (Watkins, 2004). Emmons and Sheldon (2002) defined the emotional state of gratitude as a mixture of appreciation, thankfulness and a sense of wonder. Gratitude is also perceived as a feeling that occurs when one receives something beneficial (Froh, Kashdan, Ozimkowski, & Miller, 2009).

Gratitude-based interventions have been shown to have large effects on increasing well-being (Froh et al., 2009). Gratitude-based interventions are intentional, positive activities which focus on the cultivation of gratitude (Norrish & Vella-Broadrick, 2009) or those which utilise expressions of gratitude to enhance well-being (Toepfer & Walker, 2009). Most of the earlier gratitude-based studies had involved adult participants. For example, the positive intervention study by Layous and colleagues (2013) assessed the effect of writing letters of gratitude on the subjective well-being of college students. The study revealed that expressing gratitude to others in writing led to greater gains in subjective well-being of the participants in the experimental group compared to subjects in the control group. In another study, Seligman, Steen, Park, and Peterson (2005) conducted an experiment involving 577 adults recruited from the Internet to determine if positive interventions increased happiness and reduced depressive symptoms. Participants were randomly subjected to each of the five assigned positive interventions, two of which were gratitude-based. They were 'Gratitude Visit' and 'Three Good Things in Life'. In the 'Gratitude Visit' treatment, participants were required to write a letter of gratitude to someone who had shown kindness towards them. They were then expected to deliver the letter personally to the recipient. In 'Three Good Things', participants were required to list down, on a daily basis, three good things that they experienced each day. Results showed that the participants in the 'Gratitude Visit' treatment obtained the largest positive changes compared to the other treatments. However, the 'Three Good Things' treatment had a long-term effect on the happiness level of participants even 6 months later.

Watkins, Woodward, Stone, and Kolts (2003) implemented a gratitude-based intervention to investigate the effect of grateful reflections on positive affect. The study also involved university students who were subjected to four experimental conditions. The control group was required to write about their living room layout. The participants in the gratitude condition group were randomly subdivided into three groups. The first group was asked to think about a living person they felt grateful for. The second group was required to write about the person they felt grateful for. The third group was asked to write a letter to the person they felt grateful for and were told that their letter would be delivered by the researchers. As in the previous experiment, this study also made use of Positive and Negative Affect Schedule (PANAS, Watson, Clark, & Tellegen, 1988) to measure positive affect in the participants. Positive affect was measured before and after the intervention. As expected by the researchers, participants in all three gratitude condition groups obtained increases in positive affect but not those in the control group. Participants in the 'thinking' condition obtained the most increase in positive affect much to the surprise of the researchers as they had predicted that the letter-writing condition would have obtained the greatest increase as it required participants to express gratitude socially. The researchers concluded that the letter writers could be anxious about how the recipients would take to their letters.

In another gratitude-based letter-writing study, Toepfer and Walker (2009) conducted an intervention to investigate the impact of writing which focused on expressions of gratitude on happiness level, life satisfaction and gratitude scores. The participants, divided into experimental and no-treatment control group, were college students with a median age of 23. Participants in the experimental group were students of the primary investigator and those of the control group were from other randomly selected classes. While participants in the control group were blind to the intervention, participants in the experimental group were required to write letters of gratitude to people who had done something significant for which they felt thankful. Participants were not allowed to write about something trivial such as being thankful for receiving a gift. The researcher then mailed the letters to the recipients. Unlike previous studies which required participants to write only one letter, the participants in this study wrote a total of three letters over the course of 8 weeks. Measures of happiness, life satisfaction and gratitude were taken at four time points for both groups of participants. Although there was an increase in happiness level over time for both the experimental and control groups, there was a larger increment in happiness scores of the experimental group. The letter writers in the experimental group who had lower mean scores at the beginning of the intervention ended up with a larger mean score at the end of the experiment compared to the control group. Results also showed that the control group scores on gratitude decreased while those of the experimental group increased. There was no significant change in levels of life satisfaction, but the trend showed improvement over time. The authors concluded that sustained writing of letters of gratitude could lead to a greater increase in happiness and gratitude.

Findings from the study revealed that writing letters of gratitude decreased depressive symptoms over time. Similar to the pilot study, Toepfer and colleagues (2012) demonstrated that writing such letters appeared to increase happiness. However, unlike the pilot study, the latter study showed an increase in life satisfaction for letter writers. It also suggested that using elements of gratitude in writing did not elicit gratitude. The authors concluded that it might, firstly, be due to the fact that the small sample in the pilot study was not representative of the cohort. Secondly, because gratitude is a fixed trait, it is less likely to change. The participants might have written to people they might already have a relationship with and hence, gratitude was not affected. Despite the more rigorous procedure, the study still had its

limitations such as the sample consisting mostly of Caucasian females and the possibility of interactions between the participants in the experimental group and those
in the control group. Nevertheless, the intervention was a promising one and writing
letters of gratitude could help people with depressive symptoms.

While most of the above-mentioned studies have involved adults in university
settings or volunteers recruited from the Internet, a few studies in the literature have
also demonstrated the benefits of promoting gratitude in adolescents. One example
of a gratitude-based study involving children and adolescents is a gratitude letter-
writing study conducted by Froh and colleagues (2009). The study was conducted in
a parochial school and the ages of the 89 participants were in the range of 8–19 years.
Half of the participants were randomly placed in the gratitude condition in which
they were asked to write a gratitude letter to a person they were grateful for while
the other half placed in the control group were required to write a journal about their
daily life. All participants were asked to spend about 15 min each day for a period of
five days to carry out the given activities. Participants in the experimental group were
also asked to read out their letter to the recipient. The PANAS was administered in
this study to assess pre- and post-positive affects, and gratitude was assessed using
the Gratitude Adjective Checklist. It was found that the letter-writing intervention
led to an increase in positive affect and sense of gratitude. In addition, it was also
noted that children and adolescents initially low in positive affect benefitted more
from the intervention as they reported greater gratitude at the end of the treatment.
The authors concluded that similar future studies should involve larger samples and
researchers should also be aware of age as a moderating effect to treatment, due to
developmental differences in a social and emotional capacity.

A review of other studies on gratitude-based interventions with adolescents
showed that gratitude could help youths not only in forming, maintaining and
strengthening relationships, but it could also make one feel valuable and connected
to a community (Froh & Bono, 2011). This lasting effect of gratitude on the psychological and social functioning of youths was proven by the longitudinal study carried
out by Froh, Bono, and Emmons (2010) which involved 700 middle school students.
The researchers found that pro-social behaviour of adolescents at the individual level
predicted social integration, that is, pro-social behaviour at a more macro level. Based
on Fredrickson's *Broaden-and-Build Theory*, Froh and colleagues (2010) revealed
that gratitude triggered upward spirals of social as well as emotional well-being. Gratitude has also been linked to increased social support and the former could also act as
a defence against stress and depression during adolescence (Wood, Maltby, Gillett,
Linley, & Joseph, 2008). In their study on the social functions of emotions, Algoe,
Dwyer, Younge, and Oveis (2020) found that people tend to be more receptive and
affiliative towards others who show gratitude, and they also extend this connectedness
to people who were shown gratitude. Finally, Chang and Algoe (2019) found cultural
differences in the way people express and perceive gratitude. While individuals in
Western, individualist cultures and those in Asian, Confucian contexts both perceive
gratitude through reciprocity, the former tend to express gratitude through physical
contact while the latter would do so through demonstrations of self-improvement.

There are limited gratitude-based studies involving children and adolescents but there is enough evidence to show that fostering gratitude in children and youth could potentially enhance their psychological and social well-being as well as academic progress (Froh & Bono, 2011). Hence, Froh et al. (2010) suggested that adults such as parents and teachers should frequently encourage children and youths to make expressions of gratitude. The authors concluded that it would be a worthy aim to examine gratitude and the factors which promote or inhibit its expression. This would enhance young people's potential to develop into flourishing individuals who would, in turn, enhance the very community they live in (Froh et al., 2010). However, despite the enthusiasm for gratitude-based interventions, a meta-analysis of such studies by Davis et al. (2016) showed weak evidence for the effectiveness of gratitude interventions, suggesting the need for more robust interventions. More recently, on the grounds that Davis and colleagues did not include a number of studies in their analyses, Dickens (2017) conducted a series of meta-analyses to further assess the effectiveness of gratitude interventions, but the findings were equivocal, with some interventions leading to improvement for various outcomes, such as happiness, while others had no such influence.

4.7 Positive Peer Reporting (PPR)

Positive Peer Reporting (PPR) was developed by Ervin, Miller, and Friman (1996) who used it in an intervention study involving a peer-rejected girl in residential care. PPR can be considered as a form of gratitude-based intervention which basically involves setting aside a short period of time during a lesson for students to have the opportunity to receive or give praises to their classmates in the classroom. Peers (the tellers) are solicited to make positive remarks about a target student (the recipient). A token economy system is usually used as a positive reinforcement. The token economy system entails giving tangible rewards (e.g., candy and stickers) to individual tellers for providing descriptive praise to the target students. It may also involve the use of points for every acceptable praise comment provided by classmates for target students. These points are then accumulated and later redeemed for class rewards such as extra free time or class pizza party (Murphy & Zlomke, 2014). PPR thus enables students' classroom experiences to be diversified and enriched.

Peers have long been known to be powerful social influences across all ages but more so during childhood and adolescence (Jones, Young, & Friman, 2000). Peers not only act as models, but they also serve as a source of competence and motivation (Schunk et al., 2014). One of the motives on which peer influence works is the need for peer approval. Students want to be liked and will engage in actions that gain their peers' approval. PPR uses this aspect of peer influence to change the behaviour of a target child or adolescent. Contrary to popular belief, peer pressure often functions in a positive rather than negative manner, whereby friends often discourage negative behaviour and poor academic performance (Berndt & Keefe, 1996, as cited in Schunk et al., 2014, p. 355) Thus, by behaving in a more socially appropriate manner, the child or adolescent in the PPR studies gets the approval of his/her friends, leading the latter to acknowledge the new behaviour. This, in turn, motivates the target student to continue behaving in the same 'peer-approved' manner.

Peer-based interventions are not only effective, they are also of practical application and not time consuming (Lambert, Tingstrom, Sterling, Dufrene, & Lynne, 2015). The PPR could also be considered as a form of social support by peers, considered to be of paramount importance during adolescence. Peer support has been shown to contribute significantly to the psychological well-being of young adolescents, especially in conjunction with adult support (Buchanan & Bowen, 2008). By facilitating the PPR in the classroom, the teacher is eminently providing the adult support.

4.8   Use of PPR as a Form of Remediation for Problem Behaviours

The first study on PPR by Ervin and colleagues (1996) succeeded in increasing the peer acceptance of a 13-year-old girl in a residential setting by soliciting remarks on the positive behaviour of the girl from the other students. This affirmation of positive behaviour led the girl to continue behaving in more socially acceptable ways such as working cooperatively and talking pleasantly, which subsequently led to her being more socially accepted by the other students. Thereafter, the PPR intervention has been employed by other researchers both in residential and school settings to improve social interactions and eliminate peer rejection amongst children and youth.

Bowers, Woods, Carlyon, and Friman (2000), for example, implemented the PPR intervention with four male adolescents residing in separate homes. The four participants were selected because they were socially rejected by the other residents in their respective homes. The PPR was implemented with the aim of improving the social interactions of the target participants. Within each home, the youths would take turns to be the Most Valuable Person (MVP) of the day. Peers would report positive behaviours of the MVP during the daily family meetings and would be given points which could be accumulated and exchanged for privileges in the home. Positive, negative and neutral interactions were observed for 10 min after the daily family meetings. An ABAB multiple baseline design was employed for three of the participants. The investigators established baseline social interactions of participants (A), administered the PPR intervention and measured the social interactions after the PPR intervention (B), withdrew the intervention and determined if the participants' social interactions return to baseline (A), administered the intervention again and measured the participants' social interactions (B). The multiple baseline design in the study by Bowers et al. (2000) required the three participants to receive the treatment at different times. The fourth participant's interactions were analysed using a separate ABAB design. Peer acceptance of the target youths was also investigated using sociometric ratings whereby the non-target youths rated how much they liked to work and play with each of the target youths using an 8-point Likert scale.

All four youths displayed an increase in positive interactions during the intervention phase. The sociometric ratings indicated that three of the target participants became more likeable by peers after the PPR treatment suggesting that positive interactions could reduce social rejection. Limitations of the study included, firstly, the inability to determine if positive interactions were initiated by the target participants or by the other peers who might have been motivated to initiate positive interactions in order to receive the reward points. Secondly, other than the structured daily family meetings, observations of the target participants' behaviours could not be carried out in other unstructured settings.

Nelson and colleagues (2008) modified the PPR by using Peer Praise Notes (PPN) to increase the social involvement of three socially withdrawn students in a junior high school. The students were enrolled in a special class for students at risk of emotional or behavioural problems. They were selected by the class teacher based on the scores on the Systematic Screening for Behavioural Disorders. The initial screening process showed that the three target students experienced internalising symptoms such as anxiety and depression. They were also avoided or teased by their classmates. The study made use of written notes instead of verbal praises used in previous PPR studies as adolescents may be uncomfortable with public verbal praises (Nelson et al., 2008). The PPN intervention showed promising results as all three selected students not only displayed more frequent interactions with their classmates but these interactions were also maintained even after the PPN intervention ceased.

The PPR intervention has been implemented by other researchers not only for the purpose of increasing peer acceptance but also as a strategy to improve classroom behaviour. However, many of the PPR interventions in the literature were carried out with younger children. The first published study on peer reporting of pro-social behaviours was conducted by Grieger, Kaufman, and Grieger (1976). When 90 kindergarten children were asked to report pro-social behaviours of their classmates, it was observed that co-operative play increased and there was decreased aggression. Smith, Simon, and Bramlet (2009) conducted a PPR study to assess the effectiveness of the intervention in increasing peer acceptance and reducing negative behaviour of three kindergarten children who were peer rejected. Although the results of the study seem to suggest that PPR decreased negative behaviour of the three children, the findings were inconclusive due to the excessive variability in behaviour within and across the participants. For example, one of the target students exhibited more negative behaviours when the PPR was withdrawn but none at follow-up while the other exhibited a further decrease of negative behaviours during the withdrawal phase but an increase at follow-up. Furthermore, the single-subject multiple baseline design involving only three target participants did not allow for generalizability of the findings to the other children in the cohort.

PPR studies which aimed to increase pro-social behaviours have also been carried out with older children. For example, Jones et al. (2000) implemented the PPR to decrease the disruptive behaviours of three delinquent young adolescents enrolled in a residential programme. These 13-year-old students were targeted in the study due to their serious behavioural issues such as aggression and being verbally abusive towards teachers and peers. A multiple baseline design was used to assess the effectiveness of the PPR on co-operation during group work. During the intervention phase, target students were 'publicly praised' whereby peers took turns to provide compliments to target students in front of the class. The target students, in turn, praised their peers. Points were awarded by the teacher for every peer praise and accumulated for the class reward. Results of the study showed that there was an increase in co-operative behaviour of the three youths during lessons involving group work.

Bowers, McGinnis, Ervin, and Friman (1999) conducted a PPR study with a 15-year-old peer-rejected male delinquent in a residential programme. The youth was referred for negative interactions with his peers and displaying inappropriate behaviours such as lying and fighting. The PPR intervention was implemented to investigate the effects of the PPR on peer acceptance and quality of social interactions of the youth with his housemates. The boy's peers who lived in the same home reported positive comments about him to the 'family teachers' and if a particular comment was judged to be genuine, the peer who made the report would be rewarded. The study made use of a single-subject design comprising baseline and intervention phase. Data on social interactions of the youth with his peers was collected through observations by his 'family teachers' every 5 min during a specific time of the day. Peer acceptance was assessed by having peers rate, on a Likert scale of 1–8, how much they liked to spend free time with the participant. Peers were given rewards for reporting good behaviours of the target participant. The rewards were in the form of points which they could exchange for privileges in the home. The target youth could also be rewarded with points for reporting their own positive behaviours.

Results of the study showed that there was an increase in positive interactions between the participant and his peers, that is, the participant displayed fewer aggressive verbal and physical behaviours during the intervention phase. Problem behaviours of the youth which were found to be within the clinical range during baseline were reduced to below the clinical range during the PPR intervention phase. In addition, the results also showed that peer acceptance of the youth increased, which suggested that his peers were more accepting of him due to his improved behaviour.

The study by Bowers et al. (2000) was also able to demonstrate the ability of the PPR treatment in reducing instances of inappropriate behaviours of the target participants. However, as all the above studies with adolescent participants had only involved one or a few participants in a home setting, findings could not be generalised to other youths in other settings.

An issue which may be of concern was the use of a reward system as a form of positive reinforcement for peers to give positive comments or initiate positive interactions to target students. As indicated by Bowers and colleagues (2000), peers could have interacted positively with target students just so they could obtain the rewards. Cashwell, Skinner, and Smith (2001) also noted that there was a decrease in praise reports after the class received a reward and an increase when the accumulated reward points neared the target class goal. As the token economy system appeared to be consistent with a fixed ratio schedule reinforcement, Murphy and Zlomke (2014) suggested that it might be necessary to manipulate the access to the reward in order to encourage a higher number of peer praise reports when the novelty of the intervention began to wear off. Murphy and Zlomke (2014) also suggested that the provision of extrinsic rewards should be gradually faded and be substituted with more intrinsic reinforcements such as those that come from positive behaviour experiences, the enjoyment of teamwork and gaining friendships. Nevertheless, results of the above studies suggested that providing peer praise reports, whether spoken or written, is a promising intervention which could be implemented in other settings such as the classroom, to add to the diversity of positive activities which could be used to improve behaviour and peer relationships of socially rejected children and youth.

4.9 PPR as a Form of School-Wide Positive Behaviour Support

Teerlink, Caldarella, Anderson, Richardson, and Guzman (2017) implemented the written version of PPR, better known as Peer Praise Notes (PPNs), as part of a School-Wide Positive Behaviour Support (SWPBS) programme to improve the behaviour of students during recess and to reduce the frequency of Office Discipline Referrals (ODRs). Selected students were given the role of 'peer praisers' to look out for good behaviour of peers, indicate the good behaviour in writing on the designated cards and distribute these cards (PPNs) to the peers. Duplicates of these PPNs were given to the teachers and principal. Students who received the PPNs stood a chance of winning prizes via a 'lucky draw' system which took place once a week. The 'peer praisers' were also rewarded with candies after carrying out their duties. Results of the study showed that there was a reduction in the number of discipline referral cases. The authors posited that the presence of the 'peer praisers' might have reminded the other students on the expected behaviours at recess. Additionally, as a handful of the 'peer praisers' were students who were at risk of misbehaving, the duty of distributing the PPNs could have either kept them too busy to misbehave or their experiences as 'peer praisers' might have primed them to follow rules and remember the expected behaviours (Teerlink et al., 2017). The study was, however, carried out in an elementary school setting and results could not be generalised due to the single-case reversal design of the study. The 'peer praisers' also had the tendency to distribute the PPNs only to their friends. Nevertheless, the authors concluded that the study demonstrated the effectiveness of the PPNs in improving the behaviour of students, increasing positive peer interactions and extending active supervision of good behaviour not only by adults but also by peers. They suggested that the PPNs could also be implemented as part of the SWPBS programmes in secondary and tertiary levels.

One type of PPR that was developed by Skinner and his co-workers (1998) is known as Tootling. The word 'tootling' is an amalgam of the word 'tattling' and the phrase "tooting your own horn" which is the equivalent expression of "singing your own praises". The researchers developed the 'tootling' system after acknowledging the negative side effects of the peer-reporting tattling system used by most schools. The tattling system requires students to report misbehaviours of other students. Ironically, tattling itself is an example of an anti-social behaviour being employed through an inclination to conform to expected values of the school (Cooper & Jacobs, 2011). Skinner et al. (1998) believed that there should be a system to encourage pro-social behaviour rather than relying on punishment methods to stop students from misbehaving. Teachers should, however, take advantage of the 'tattling' phenomenon to encourage students to report on not only misbehaviours but also pro-social behaviours of their peers (Skinner, Cashwell, & Skinner, 2000). Unlike tattling, Tootling is a form of PPR applied on a class-wide basis and is defined as reporting of peers' pro-social behaviour (Skinner et al., 1998). Hence, Tootling enabled the diversification of students' classroom experiences, providing a novel opportunity for students' pro-social behaviours to be identified and recognised, as opposed to the conventional 'tattling' or 'whistle-blowing' method used to 'catch' students' misbehaviour.

In Tootling studies, students report pro-social behaviours of any of their classmates instead of just the target ones. Similar to the PPNs, peer reporting is carried out privately by writing on index cards instead of the publicly verbal method of PPR studies. According to Skinner and colleagues (2000), the PPR programme aims to reinforce pro-social behaviours by getting peers to acknowledge appropriate behaviours publicly. Announcing pro-social behaviours publicly, especially those of the target students, would also change perceptions of the peers towards the target students who are usually those who are ostracised by their peers. The Tootling programme, on the other hand, aims to enhance the classroom environment. This is done by getting students to monitor their classmates' appropriate behaviours which, in turn, increase the chances of having more helping behaviours amongst students. In the process, the students' appreciation as well as their awareness of these behaviours may also increase. Furthermore, as students' behaviours are mostly influenced by their classmates, appropriate school behaviours will most likely be noticed and reinforced (Jones et al., 2000).

Studies on tootling by Skinner et al. (2000) and Cashwell et al. (2001), however, have only investigated the effects of this form of peer reporting by studying the frequency of peer praises. Morrison and Jones (2007) took tootling to the next level by investigating the effects of this form of PPR on class-wide social and emotional behaviours. They implemented the PPR as a class-wide positive behaviour support programme to two third-grade classes in a public school. The aim of the study was not only to investigate the effects of the PPR on the sociometric status but also on the behaviours of all the students in the two classes. A modified form of the Critical Events Index (CEI) was used to record class-wide student behaviour in the classroom while sociometric nominations via interviewing individual students were carried out to measure sociometric status. For both classes, there was generally a decrease in negative behaviours and a decrease in the number of socially isolated children.

The study by Morrison and Jones (2007) did not explore the effects of tootling in the absence of group contingencies. The multiple baseline design, the small number of participants consisting only of young third-grade students, did not allow for findings to be generalised to the whole cohort. The researchers agreed that replication of the tootling study on older students is necessary to establish the validity of the measures.

Lambert and colleagues (2015) attempted to replicate the study by Cihak, Kirk, and Boon (2009) by involving older students in the fourth- and fifth-grade general education classrooms from the same elementary school in the US. The classes were chosen because the school was concerned about the frequent occurrence of disruptive behaviours in both classrooms. Results of the study were consistent with those of Cihak et al. (2009) in that there was a decrease in class-wide disruptive behaviour. Unlike the study by Cihak et al. (2009), this recent study was able to compare effects of Tootling in two classrooms and the researchers found that in both classrooms, Tootling resulted in fewer occurrences of disruptive behaviour. Additionally, Lambert and colleagues (2015) also demonstrated that there was an increase in appropriate classroom behaviours in both classes as a result of the Tootling intervention. Inter-observer agreement was carried out and treatment integrity checklists were completed by the classroom teachers to determine the reliability of the study. Failure to examine the effect of Tootling on disruptive behaviour without the use of contingencies was also recognised as a limitation of this study. Although Tootling appeared to be effective in upper elementary classes, Lambert et al. (2015) acknowledged the need to replicate the study further with students of other developmental stages such as early adolescents from the middle school. The authors also recommended the use of this simple activity even in classes with little or no discipline issues as a preventive classroom management strategy early in the year before classroom misbehaviours become a concern.

In her doctoral dissertation, Sherman (2012) compared the effects of the PPR intervention and PPR combined with Tootling intervention on the behaviours and peer acceptance of target elementary students. In the PPR combined with Tootling condition, students were given the option to publicly praise the target students or privately by Tootling, that is, by writing the tootles on notecards distributed by the teachers. Results of the study showed that both treatments were equally effective. Both treatments were successful in improving the behaviours of target students. Also, the decrease in inappropriate behaviours and the increase in appropriate behaviours of these target students were shown to be generalised across settings.

The lack of observation on peer interactions to measure peer acceptance was cited as a limitation of the study. Data which was based on the classroom teachers' perception of peer status might not have reflected actual peer acceptance. The inappropriate and appropriate behaviours were also summed up instead of being measured individually. Therefore, the study was not able to pinpoint the effect of either treatment on a particular behaviour (e.g., out of seat and inappropriate vocalisation). The internal validity was limited by the inconsistent implementation of the intervention as two of the participating teachers did not comply with the research protocol which required them to allow students to write tootles anytime during the lesson. However, due to the optional writing of tootles, some students were found to play with the notecards instead of writing, which resulted in the teachers having to confiscate the notecards. Nevertheless, all the teachers rated the intervention as acceptable and students reported that they enjoyed getting compliments from their peers.

A study by Lum, Tingstrom, Dufrene, Radley, and Lynne (2017) to investigate the effects of Tootling on disruptive and academically engaged behaviour is the only Tootling study to date to be conducted with high school students. The study involved students from three general education classes which had been identified for having the highest display of disruptive behaviours. Similar to previous studies carried out with younger children, the study by Lum et al. (2017) employed the A-B-A-B withdrawal design. The study also included a secondary dependent measure of class-wide academically engaged student behaviours such as actively attending to independent seatwork. Disruptive behaviour decreased and academically engaged behaviours increased during the intervention phases compared to baseline and withdrawal phases. All three classroom teachers involved in the study indicated acceptable ratings for the Tootling intervention.

The above study by Lum et al. (2017) suffered from a few limitations. Firstly, the results of the study could not be generalised to all high school students as the study was conducted with only three classes in a rural high school. Secondly, the researchers were not able to conclude if the positive effects of Tootling were maintained outside of the classroom period (e.g., during another lesson). Thirdly, the teachers did not continue implementing the intervention during the follow-up phase and thus, disruptive behaviour and academically engaged behaviours were observed to increase and decrease, respectively. Nevertheless, the study showed promise that the writing of positive reports about peers could also work in secondary classrooms.

4.10   Conclusion and Future Developments

Although there is ample support for the *Positive Activity Model*'s claim that positive activity enhances positive emotions, a review of the extant literature on PPR and PPN studies reveals a few gaps. Firstly, most of the mentioned studies on PPR and PPN made use of single-subject or multiple baseline designs which focused on small participant samples. In addition, the participants were often chosen because they demonstrated some form of dysfunctional behaviours, and thus, the PPR/PPN interventions focused on remediation rather than prevention or enhancement. Finally, previous studies investigated the effects of PPR and PPN on students' behaviours, peer status and social interactions, but none have directly investigated their effects on students' subjective well-being. It was assumed in those studies that the increase in peer acceptance and improvement in peer status or social interactions would lead to increased subjective well-being.

Based on the literature reviews on the benefits of positive peer reporting (PPR) and Tootling, future investigations could adopt a similar method to enhance outcomes such as pro-social behaviour, emotional well-being and peer acceptance of adolescents. In line with the *Engine Model*, future interventions could involve *processes* such as writing messages in the form of Peer Praise Notes (PPN), which not only enable diversification of learner classroom experiences, but also lead to *outcomes* such as positive recognition and additional encouragement to the recipient when read out or shared with others (Howell, Caldarella, Korth, & Young, 2014). Other benefits of written praises include decreases in undesired behaviour of students, involving social withdrawal (Nelson et al., 2008), disruptive behaviour (Wheatley et al., 2009), office discipline referrals (Nelson, Young, Young, & Cox, 2009) as well as tardiness (Caldarella, Christensen, Young, & Densley, 2011). The written praises may also be more suitable because adolescents prefer to be praised privately and may find public praising embarrassing (Infantino & Little, 2005).

In prospective PPN interventions, participants could address the praise notes to specific peers chosen for a particular day/session. This would ensure that every student has the opportunity to receive praise notes from his/her classmates. Unlike previous studies on PPR and PPN which focused on praising a peer for good behaviour, prospective PPN interventions could involve writing letters of gratitude, identifying character strengths of peers and praising peers for performing kind acts or displaying pro-social behaviours. Based on the *Broaden-and-Build Theory*, peer praises in the form of expressions of gratitude, recognition of pro-social behaviour and peers' character strengths will induce positive emotions. The proposed framework hypothesises that experiences of positive emotions *broaden* a student's momentary thought-action repertoires such as creating social inclusion, being more engaged in the classroom and displaying pro-social behaviours. These broadened thought-action repertoires foster or *build* personal resources such as social inclusion, gaining new friends, enhancing existing peer relationships and obtaining social support. These increased personal resources predict more experiences of positive emotion hence producing upward spirals towards an enhanced overall life satisfaction which would in turn lead to greater subjective well-being over time.

References

Algoe, S. B., Dwyer, P. C., Younge, A., & Oveis, C. (2020). A new perspective on the social functions of emotions: Gratitude and the witnessing effect. *Journal of Personality and Social Psychology, 119*(1), 40–74. https://doi.org/10.1037/pspi0000202.

Anderson, C. M., & Kincaid, D. (2005). Applying behaviour analysis to school violence and discipline problems: Schoolwide positive behaviour support. *The Behaviour Analyst, 28,* 49–64.

Arbuckle, C., & Little, E. (2004). Teachers' perceptions and management of disruptive classroom behaviour during the middle years (years five to nine). *Australian Journal of Educational & Developmental Psychology, 4,* 59–70.

Badaly, D., Schwartz, D., & Gorman, A. H. (2012). Social status, perceived social reputations, and perceived dyadic relationships in early adolescence. *Social Development, 21*(3), 482–500.

Baumeister, R. F. (1997). Esteem threat, self-regulatory breakdown and emotional distress as factors in self-defeating behaviours. *Review of General Psychology, 1,* 145–174.

Beaman, R., & Wheldall, K. (1997). Teacher perceptions of troublesome classroom behaviour. *Special Education Perspectives, 6*(2), 49–53.

Beaman, R., Wheldall, K., & Kemp, C. (2007). Recent research on troublesome classroom behaviour: A review. *Australasian Journal of Special Education, 31*(1), 45–60.

Bellmore, A. (2011). Peer rejection and unpopularity: Associations with GPAs across the transition to middle school. *Journal of Educational Psychology, 103*(2), 282.

Bergin, C., Talley, S., & Hamer, L. (2003). Prosocial behaviours of young adolescents: A focus group study. *Journal of Adolescence, 26,* 13–32.

Bowers, F. E., McGinnis, J. C., Ervin, R. A., & Friman, P. C. (1999). Merging research and practice: The example of positive peer reporting applied to social rejection. *Education and Treatment of Children, 22*(2), 218–226.

Bowers, F. E., Woods, D. W., Carlyon, W. D., & Friman, P. C. (2000). Using positive peer reporting to improve the social interactions and acceptance of socially isolated adolescents in residential care: A systematic replication. *Journal of Applied Behaviour Analysis, 33*(2), 239–242.

Buchanan, R. L., & Bowen, G. L. (2008). In the context of adult support: The influence of peer support on the psychological well-being of middle-school students. *Child and Adolescent Social Work Journal, 25*(5), 397–407.

Buhs, E. S., & Ladd, G. W. (2001). Peer rejection as an antecedent of young children's school adjustment: An examination of mediating processes. *Developmental Psychology, 37*(4), 550–560.

Caldarella, P., Christensen, L., Young, K. R., & Densley, C. (2011). Decreasing tardiness in elementary school students using teacher-written praise notes. *Intervention in School and Clinic, 47,* 104–112.

Caldwell, C. (2017). Understanding kindness—A moral duty of human resource leaders. *The Journal of Values-Based Leadership, 10*(2), 8.

Carlo, G., Fabes, R. A., Laible, D., & Kupanoff, K. (1999). Early adolescence and prosocial/moral behaviour II: The role of social and contextual influences. *Journal of Early Adolescence, 19*(2), 133–147.

Cashwell, T. H., Skinner, C. H., & Smith, E. S. (2001). Increasing second-grade students' reports of peers' prosocial behaviours via direct instruction, group reinforcement and progress feedback: A replication and extension. *Education and Treatment of Children, 24*(2), 161–175.

Chang, Y. P., & Algoe, S. B. (2019). On thanksgiving: Cultural variation in gratitude demonstrations and perceptions between the United States and Taiwan. *Emotion.* Advance online publication. https://doi.org/10.1037/emo0000662.

Cherry, K. (2014). *What is prosocial behaviour?* Retrieved from About.com website: https://psychology.about.com/od/pindex/g/prosocial-behavior.htm.

Cihak, D. F., Kirk, E. R., & Boon, R. T. (2009). Effects of classwide positive peer "tootling" to reduce the disruptive classroom behaviors of elementary students with and without disabilities. *Journal of Behavioural Education, 18*(4), 267–278.

Claes, M., & Simard, R. (1993). Friendship characteristics of delinquent adolescents. *International Journal of Adolescence & Youth, 3,* 287–301.

Cooper, P., & Jacobs, B. (2011). Pupils making a difference: Enhancing the power of the student peer group to promote positive social, emotional and behavioural outcomes. *Emotional & Behavioural Difficulties, 16*(1), 5–13.

Coplan, R. J., Girardi, A., Findlay, L. C., & Frohlick, S. L. (2007). Understanding solitude: Young children's attitudes and responses toward hypothetical socially withdrawn peers. *Social Development, 16*(3), 390–409.

Coplan, R. J., Prakash, K., O'Neil, K., & Armer, M. (2004). Do you "want" to play? Distinguishing between conflicted shyness and social disinterest in early childhood. *Developmental Psychology, 40*(2), 244–258.

Cunningham, M. R. (1988). Does happiness mean friendliness? Induced mood and heterosexual self-disclosure. *Personality and Social Psychology Bulletin, 14,* 283–297.

Davis, D. E., Choe, E., Meyers, J., Wade, N., Varjas, K., Gifford, A., ... Worthington, E. L., Jr. (2016). Thankful for the little things: A meta-analysis of gratitude interventions. *Journal of Counseling Psychology, 63*(1), 20–31.

Della Porta, M. D. (2012). *Enhancing the effects of happiness-boosting activities: The role of autonomy support in an experimental longitudinal intervention.* ProQuest, UMI Dissertations Publishing.

Dickens, L. R. (2017). Using gratitude to promote positive change: A series of meta-analyses investigating the effectiveness of gratitude interventions. *Basic and Applied Social Psychology, 39*(4), 193–208.

Diener, E. (2012). New findings and future directions for subjective well-being research. *American Psychological Association, 67*(8), 590–597.

Diener, E., & Diener, M. (1995). Cross-cultural correlates of life satisfaction and self-esteem. *Journal of Personality and Social Psychology, 68*(4), 653–663.

Diener, E., Lucas, R. E., & Oishi, S. (2002). Subjective well-being: The science of happiness and life satisfaction. *Handbook of Positive Psychology, 2*, 63–73.

Diener, E., Suh, E. M., Lucas, R. E., & Smith, H. L. (1999). Subjective well-being: Three decades of progress. *Psychological Bulletin, 125*(2), 276–302.

Dodge, R., Daly, A., Huyton, J., & Sanders, L. (2012). The challenge of defining wellbeing. *International Journal of Well-Being, 2*(3), 222–235.

Dunn, J. R., & Schweitzer, M. E. (2005). Feeling and believing: The influence of emotion on trust. *Journal of Personality and Social Psychology, 88*(5), 736.

Emmons, R. A., & Sheldon, C. S. (2002). Gratitude and the science of positive psychology. In C. R. Snyder & S. J. Lopez (Eds.), *Handbook of positive psychology*. New York: Oxford University Press.

Emmons, R. A., & Stern, R. (2013). Gratitude as psychotherapeutic intervention. *Journal of Clinical Psychology, 69*(8), 846–855.

Ervin, R. A., Miller, P. M., & Friman, P. C. (1996). Feed the hungry bee: Using positive peer reports to improve social interactions and acceptance of a socially rejected girl in residential care. *Journal of Applied Behavior Analysis, 29*(2), 251–253.

Fite, P. J., Raine, A., Stouthamer-Loeber, M., Loeber, R., & Pardini, D. A. (2010). Reactive and proactive aggression in adolescent males: Examining differential outcomes 10 years later in early adulthood. *Criminal Justice and Behaviour, 37*, 141–157.

Fredrickson, B. L. (1998). What good are positive emotions? *Review of General Psychology, 2*(3), 300–319.

Fredrickson, B. L. (2001). The role of positive emotions in positive psychology: The Broaden-and-Build Theory of positive emotions. *American Psychologist, 56*(3), 218–226.

Fredrickson, B. L. (2013). Positive emotions broaden and build. *Advances in Experimental Social Psychology, 47*, 3–46.

Fredrickson, B. L., Cohn, M. A., Coffey, K. A., Pek, J., & Finkel, S. M. (2008). Open hearts build lives: Positive emotions, induced through loving-kindness meditation, build consequential personal resources. *Journal of Personal and Social Psychology, 95*(5), 1045–1062.

Fredrickson, B. L., & Joiner, T. (2002). Positive emotions trigger upward spirals toward emotional well-being. *Psychological Science, 13*(2), 172–175.

Fredrickson, B. L., Tugade, M. M., Waugh, C. E., & Larkin, G. R. (2003). What good are positive emotions in crises? A prospective study of resilience and emotions following the terrorist attacks on the united states on September 11th, 2001. *Journal of Personality and Social Psychology, 84*(2), 365–376.

Frick, P. J., & McMahon, R. J. (2008). Child and adolescent conduct problems. In J. Hunsley & E. J. Mash (Eds.), *Oxford series in clinical psychology. A guide to assessments that work* (pp. 41–66). Retrieved from https://labs.uno.edu/developmental-psychopathology/articles/Hunsley-conduct_problems_chapter.pdf.

Froh, J. J., & Bono, G. (2011). Gratitude in youth: A review of gratitude interventions and some ideas for applications. *Communique, 39*(5), 1.

Froh, J. J., Bono, G., & Emmons, R. (2010). Being grateful is beyond good manners: Gratitude and motivation to contribute to society among early adolescents. *Motivation and Emotion, 34*(2), 144–157.

Froh, J. J., Kashdan, T. B., Ozimkowski, K. M., & Miller, N. (2009). Who benefits the most from a gratitude intervention in children and adolescents? Examining positive affect as a moderator. *The Journal of Positive Psychology, 4*, 213–233.

Froh, J. J., Sefick, W. J., & Emmons, R. A. (2008). Counting blessings in early adolescents: An experimental study of gratitude and subjective well-being. *Journal of School Psychology, 46*(2), 213–233.

Gallardo, L. O., Barrasa, A., & Guevera-Viejo, F. (2016). Positive peer relationships and academic achievement across early and midadolescence. *Social Behavior & Personality: An International Journal, 44*(10), 1637–1648.

Gilman, R., & Huebner, E. S. (2006). Characteristics of adolescents who report very high life satisfaction. *Journal of Youth and Adolescence, 35*(3), 293–301.

Grieger, T., Kauffman, J. M., & Grieger, R. M. (1976). Effects of peer reporting on cooperative play and aggression of kindergarten children. *Journal of School Psychology, 14,* 307–312.

Guo, Q., Zhou, J., & Feng, L. (2018). Pro-social behavior is predictive of academic success via peer acceptance: A study of Chinese primary school children. *Learning and Individual Differences, 65,* 187–194.

Haroun, R., & O'Hanlon, C. (1997). Teachers' perceptions of discipline problems in a Jordanian secondary school. *Pastoral Care in Education, 15*(2), 29–36.

Helliwell, J. F., Aknin, L. B., Shiplett, H., Huang, H., & Wang, S. (2017). *Social capital and prosocial behaviour as sources of well-being* (No. w23761). National Bureau of Economic Research.

Howell, A., Caldarella, P., Korth, B. B., & Young, K. R. (2014). Exploring the social validity of teacher praise notes in elementary school. *Journal of Classroom Interaction, 49*(2), 22–32.

Hubbard, J. A., Smithmyer, C. M., Ramsden, S. R., Flanagan, K. D., Relyea, N., & Simons, R. F. (2002). Observational, physiological, and self-report measures of children's anger: Relations to reactive versus proactive aggression. *Child Development, 73,* 1101–1118.

Infantino, J., & Little, E. (2005). Students' perceptions of classroom behaviour problems and the effectiveness of different disciplinary methods. *Educational Psychology, 25*(5), 491–508.

Jayawickreme, E., Forgeard, M. J., & Seligman, M. E. (2012). The engine of well-being. *Review of General Psychology, 16*(4), 327–342.

Johnson, K. J., & Fredrickson, B. L. (2005). "We all look the same to me": Positive emotions eliminate the own-race bias in face recognition. *Psychological Science, 16*(11), 875–881.

Jones, K. M., Young, M. M., & Friman, P. C. (2000). Increasing peer praise of socially rejected delinquent youth: Effects on cooperation and acceptance. *School Psychology Quarterly, 15*(1), 30–39.

Kaplan, A., Gheen, M., & Midgley, C. (2002). Classroom goal structure and student disruptive behaviour. *The British Journal of Educational Psychology, 72*(Pt 2), 191.

Keyes, C. L. M. (1998). Social well-being. *Social Psychology Quarterly, 61*(2), 121–140.

Keyes, C. L. M. (2007). Promoting and protecting mental health as flourishing: A complementary strategy for improving national mental health. *American Psychologist, 62,* 95–108.

Kidron, Y., & Fleishman, S. (2006). Promoting adolescents pro-social behaviour. *Educational Leadership, 63*(7), 90–91.

Kim, J., Rapee, R. M., Oh, K. J., & Moon, H. S. (2008). Retrospective report of social withdrawal during adolescence and current maladjustment in young adulthood: Cross-cultural comparisons between Australian and South Korean students. *Journal of Adolescence, 31*(5), 545–563.

Knack, J. M., Tsar, V., Vaillancourt, T., Hymel, S., & McDougall, P. (2012). What protects rejected adolescents from also being bullied by their peers? The moderating role of Peer-Valued characteristics. *Journal of Research on Adolescence, 22*(3), 467–479.

Lambert, A. M., Tingstrom, D. H., Sterling, H. E., Dufrene, B. A., & Lynne, S. (2015). Effects of tootling on classwide disruptive and appropriate behavior of upper-elementary students. *Behavior Modification, 39*(3), 413–430.

Lasley, T. J. (1979). Misbehavior: Challenging, coping with the classroom system. *NASSP Bulletin, 63*(428), 48–51. https://doi.org/10.1177/019263657906342808.

Layous, K., Chancellor, J., & Lyubomirsky, S. (2014). Positive activities as protective factors against mental health conditions. *Journal of Abnormal Psychology, 123*(1), 3–12. https://doi.org/10.1037/a0034709.

Layous, K., Lee, H., Choi, I., & Lyubomirsky, S. (2013). Culture matters when designing a successful happiness-increasing activity: A comparison of the United States and South Korea. *Journal of Cross Cultural Psychology, 44*(8), 1294–1303.

Layous, K., & Lyubomirsky, S. (2012). The how, why, what, when, and who of happiness: Mechanisms underlying the success of positive interventions. To appear in J. Gruber & J. Moscowitz (Eds.), *The light and dark side of positive emotions*. New York: Oxford University Press.

Layous, K., Nelson, S. K., Oberle, E., Schonert-Reichl, K. A., & Lyubomirsky, S. (2012). Kindness counts: Prompting prosocial behavior in preadolescents boosts peer acceptance and well-being. *PLoS ONE, 7*(12), 1–3. https://doi.org/10.1371/journal.pone.0051380.

Lent, R. W. (2004). Toward a unifying theoretical and practical perspective on well-being and psychosocial adjustment. *Journal of Counselling Psychology, 51*(4), 482–509.

Leung, B. P., & Silberling, J. (2006). Using sociograms to identify social status in the classroom. *California School Psychologist, 11*, 57–61.

Levitt, M. J., Levitt, J., Bustos, G. L., Crooks, N. A., Santos, J. D., & Telan, P. (2005). Patterns of social support in the middle childhood to early adolescent transition: Implication for adjustment. *Social Development, 14*, 398–420.

Long, R. F., Huebner, E. S., & Wedell, D. H. (2012). Measuring school-related subjective well-being in adolescents. *American Journal of Orthopsychiatry, 82*(1), 50.

Lum, J. K., Tingstrom, D. H., Dufrene, B. A., Radley, K. C., & Lynne, S. (2017). Effects of tootling on classwide disruptive band academically engaged behaviour of general education high school students. *Psychology in the Schools, 54*(4), 370–384.

Lyubomirsky, S., King, L., & Diener, E. (2005). The benefits of frequent positive affect: Does happiness lead to success? *Psychological Bulletin, 131*(6), 803–855.

Lyubomirsky, S., & Layous, K. (2013). How do simple positive activities increase well-being? *Current Directions in Psychological Science, 22*(1), 57–62.

Margolin, S. (2001). Interventions for nonaggressive peer-rejected children and adolescents: A review of the literature. *Children & Schools, 23*(3), 143–159.

Markelz, A. M., & Taylor, J. C. (2016). Effects of teacher praise on attending behaviours and academic achievement of students with emotional and behavioural disabilities. *Journal of Special Education Apprenticeship, 5*(1).

McGue, M., Elkins, I., Walden, B., & Iacono, W. G. (2005). Perceptions of the parent-adolescent relationship: A longitudinal investigation. *Developmental Psychology, 41*(6), 971.

Merrett, F., & Wheldall, K. (1984). Classroom behaviour problems which junior primary school teachers find the most troublesome. *Educational Studies, 10*, 87–92.

Middleton, M. J., & Midgley, C. (1997). Avoiding the demonstration of lack of ability. An under-explored aspect of goal theory. *Journal of Educational Psychology, 89*, 710–718.

Morrison, J. Q., & Jones, K. M. (2007). The effects of positive peer reporting as a class-wide positive behaviour support. *Journal of Behavioural Education, 16*(2), 111–124.

Murphy, J., & Zlomke, K. (2014). Positive peer reporting in the classroom: A review of intervention procedures. *Behaviour Analysis in Practice, 7*(2), 126–137.

Nelson, D. W. (2009). Feeling good and open-minded: The impact of positive affect on cross-cultural empathic responding. *The Journal of Positive Psychology, 4*(1), 53–63.

Nelson, J. A. P., Caldarella, P., Young, K. R., & Webb, N. (2008). Using peer praise notes to increase the social involvement of withdrawn adolescents. *Teaching Exceptional Children, 41*, 6–13.

Nelson, J. A. P., Young, B. J., Young, E. L., & Cox, G. (2009). Using teacher-written praise notes to promote a positive environment in a middle school. *Preventing School Failure: Alternative Education for Children and Youth, 54*, 119–125.

Newcomb, A. F., Bukowski, W. M., & Pattee, L. (1993). Children's peer relations: A meta-analytic review of popular, rejected, neglected, controversial, and average sociometric status. *Psychological Bulletin, 113*, 99–128.

Norrish, J. M., & Vella-Brodrick, D. A. (2009). Positive psychology and adolescents: Where are we now? Where to from here? *Australian Psychologist, 44*(4), 270–278.

Oberle, E., & Schonert-Reichl, K. A. (2013). Relations among peer acceptance, inhibitory control and math achievement in early adolescence. *Journal of Applied Developmental Psychology, 34,* 45–51.

Oishi, S., Diener, E., Scollon, C. N., & BiswasDiene, R. (2004). Cross-situational consistency of affective experiences across cultures. *Journal of Personality and Social Psychology, 86,* 460–472.

Ong, A. C., Tan, E., & Cheng, Y. S. (2000, September). *Problem behaviours of Singapore youth.* Paper presented at the Proceedings of the ERA-Ame-Amic Joint Conference, Singapore.

Pang, J. S., Ang, R. P., Kom, D. M. Y., Tan, S. H., & Chiang, A. Q. M. (2013). Patterns of reactive and proactive aggression in young adolescents in Singapore. *Social Development, 22*(4), 794–812.

Parker, J. G., & Asher, S. R. (1987). Peer relations and later personal adjustment: Are low-accepted children at risk? *Psychological Bulletin, 102*(3), 357–389.

Pullis, M. (1991). Practical considerations of excluding conduct disordered students: An empirical analysis. *Behavioral Disorders, 17,* 9–22.

Rahimi, A., & Bigdeli, R. A. (2014). The Broaden-and-Build Theory of positive emotions in second language learning. *Procedia—Social and Behavioral Sciences, 159,* 795–801.

Raine, A., Dodge, K., Loeber, R., Gatzke-Kopp, L., Lynam, D., & Reynolds, C. (2006). The reactive-proactive aggression questionnaire: Differential correlates of reactive and proactive aggression in adolescent boys. *Aggressive Behaviour, 32,* 159–171.

Santrock, J. W. (2018). *Educational psychology.* New York: McGraw-Hill Education.

Schunk, D. H., Meece, J. L., & Pintrich, P. R. (2014). *Motivation in education: Theory, research and applications* (4th ed.). USA: Pearson Education.

Seligman, M. E. P., & Csikszentmihalyi, M. (2000). Positive psychology: An introduction. *American Psychologist, 55*(1), 5–14.

Seligman, M. E. P., Steen, T. A., Park, N., & Peterson, C. (2005). Positive psychology progress: Empirical validation of interventions. *American Psychologist, 60*(5), 410–421.

Sheldon, K. M., & King, L. (2001). Why positive psychology is necessary. *The American Psychologist, 56*(3), 216–217.

Sherman, J. C. (2012). *Positive peer reporting and positive peer reporting combined with tootling: A comparison of interventions* (Doctoral dissertation, The University of Southern Mississippi). Retrieved from https://aquila.usm.edu/cgi/viewcontent.cgi?article=1881&context=dissertations.

Shoshani, A., & Slone, M. (2013). Middle school transition from the strengths perspective: Young adolescents' character strengths, subjective well-being and school adjustment. *Journal of Happiness Studies, 14,* 1163–1181.

Shum-Cheung, H. S., Tan, A., Chua, Y. S., Hawkins, R., Lee, A. K. B., Shiu, M., & Fung, D. (2008). *Children's social and emotional well-being in Singapore.* Research Monograph, 7. Singapore: Singapore Children's Society.

Sin, N. L., & Lyubomirsky, S. (2009). Enhancing well-being and alleviating depressive symptoms with positive psychology interventions: A practice-friendly meta-analysis. *Journal of Clinical Psychology, 65*(5), 467–487.

Singapore Children Society. (2008). *Bullying in Singapore schools.* Retrieved, May 17, 2015, from https://www.childrensociety.org.sg/resources/front/template/scs/files/bullying.pdf.

Singapore Children Society. (2010). Young adults' recall of school bullying. Retrieved, July 14, 2018, from https://www.childrensociety.org.sg/resources/front/template/scs/files/monograph9.pdf.

Skinner, C. H., Cashwell, T. H., & Skinner, A. L. (2000). Increasing Tootling: The effects of a peer-monitored group contingency program on students' reports of peers' prosocial behaviours. *Psychology in the Schools, 37,* 263–270.

Skinner, C. H., Skinner, A. L., & Cashwell, T. H. (1998). *Tootling, not tattling.* Paper presented at the twenty-sixth annual meeting of the Mid-South Educational Research Association, New Orleans, LA.

Smith, S. M., Simon, J., & Bramlett, R. K. (2009). Effects of positive peer reporting (PPR) on social acceptance and negative behaviours among peer-rejected preschool children. *Journal of Applied School Psychology, 25,* 323–341.

Steen, T. A., Kachorek, L. V., & Peterson, C. (2003). Character strengths among youth. *Journal of Youth and Adolescence, 32*(1), 5–16.

Steinberg, L. (2005). Cognitive and affective development in adolescence. *Trends in Cognitive Sciences, 9*(2), 69–74.

Stewart, S. M., Bond, M. H., McBride-Chang, C., Fielding, R., Deeds, O., & Westrick, J. (1998). Parent and adolescent contributors to teenage misconduct in Western and Asian high school students in Hong Kong. *International Journal of Behavioural Development, 22*(4), 847–869.

Stright, A. D., & Yeo, K. L. (2014). Maternal parenting styles, school involvement, and children's school achievement and conduct in Singapore. *Journal of Educational Psychology, 106*(1), 301–314.

Suldo, S., Thalji, A., & Ferron, J. (2011). Longitudinal academic outcomes predicted by early adolescents' subjective well-being, psychopathology and mental health status yielded from a dual-factor model. *The Journal of Positive Psychology, 6*(1), 17–30.

Sun, R. C. F., & Shek, D. T. L. (2012). Student classroom misbehaviour: An exploratory study based on teachers' perceptions. *The Scientific World Journal, 2012*(Article ID 208907).

Tan, E., & Cheng, Y. (1999). Discipline problems in schools: Teachers' perceptions. *Teaching and Learning, 19*(2), 1–12.

Tay, L., & Diener, E. (2011). Needs and subjective well-being around the world. *Journal of Personality and Social Psychology, 101*(2), 354–365.

Teerlink, E., Caldarella, P., Anderson, D. H., Richardson, M. J., & Guzman, E. G. (2017). Addressing problem behaviour at recess using peer praise notes. *Journal of Positive Behaviour Interventions, 19*(2), 115–126.

Toepfer, S. M., Cichy, K., & Peters, P. (2012). Letters of gratitude: Further evidence for author benefits. *Journal of Happiness Studies, 13*(1), 187–201.

Toepfer, S. M., & Walker, K. (2009). Letters of gratitude: Improving well-being through expressive writing. *Journal of Writing Research, 1*(3), 181–198.

Tov, W., & Diener, E. (2013). *Subjective well-being.* Retrieved, September 8, 2015 from https://ink.library.smu.edu.sg/soss_research/1395.

Twenge, J. M. (2011). Generational differences in mental health: Are children and adolescents suffering more, or less? *American Journal of Orthopsychiatry, 81,* 469–472. https://doi.org/10.1111/j.1939-0025.2011.01115.x.

Vaillancourt, T., & Hymel, S. (2006). Aggression and social status: The moderating roles of sex and peer-valued characteristics. *Aggressive Behaviour, 32*(4), 396–408.

Wadlinger, H. A., & Isaacowitz, D. M. (2006). Positive mood broadens visual attention to positive stimuli. *Motivation and Emotion, 30*(1), 87–99.

Waters, L. (2011). A review of school-based positive psychology interventions. *The Australian Educational and Developmental Psychologist, 28*(2), 75 90. https://doi.org/10.1375/aedp.28.2.75.

Watkins, P. C. (2004). Gratitude and subjective well-being. In R. A. Emmons & M. E. McCullough (Eds.), *Series in affective science. The psychology of gratitude* (pp. 167–192). New York, NY, US: Oxford University Press.

Watkins, P. C., Woodward, K., Stone, T., & Kolts, R. L. (2003). Gratitude and happiness: Development of a measure of gratitude, and relationships with subjective well-being. *Social Behavior and Personality: An International Journal, 31*(5), 431–451.

Watson, D., Clark, L. A., & Tellegen, A. (1988). Development and validation of brief measures of positive and negative affect: The PANAS scales. *Journal of Personality and Social Psychology, 54*(6), 1063.

Waugh, C. E., & Fredrickson, B. L. (2006). Nice to know you: Positive emotions, self-other overlap, and complex understanding in the formation of new relationships. *The Journal of Positive Psychology, 1,* 93–106.

Wentzel, K. R., Barry, C. M., & Caldwell, K. A. (2004). Friendships in middle school: Influences on motivation and school adjustment. *Journal of Educational Psychology, 96,* 195–203.

Wheatley, R. K., West, R. P., Charlton, C. T., Sanders, R. B., Smith, T. G., & Taylor, J. (2009). Improving behaviour through differential reinforcement: A praise note system for elementary school students. *Education and Treatment of Children, 32,* 551–571.

Whelan, D. C., & Zelenski, J. M. (2012). Experimental evidence that positive moods cause sociability. *Social Psychology and Personality Science, 3*(4), 430–437.

Wichmann, C., Coplan, R. J., & Daniels, T. (2004). The social cognitions of socially withdrawn children. *Social Development, 13*(3), 377–392.

Wood, A. M., Maltby, J., Gillett, R., Linley, P. A., & Joseph, S. (2008). The role of gratitude in the development of social support, stress, and depression: Two longitudinal studies. *Journal of Research in Personality, 42*(4), 854–871.

Chapter 5
The Role of Collaborative Art Class in Promoting Motivation: A Self-Determination Theory Perspective

Hester Oh

Abstract This chapter provides a comprehensive overview of the theoretical constructs and research pertaining to the nature of self-determination and the satisfaction of basic psychological needs from the Self Determination Theory (SDT) perspective, with the objective of exploring whether diversifying learner experiences using collaborative learning promotes the motivation of students in art class, specifically in relation to the context of Singapore. In terms of theoretical underpinnings, SDT points to three needs that are considered universal to the human condition. The theory postulates that there are three basic innate psychological needs that underline behaviour: competence, autonomy, and relatedness. The need for competence is the need for individuals to feel competent and capable in their interactions with others, and in the tasks and activities they undertake. The need for autonomy refers to the need to feel a sense of control, agency, or volition in interactions within the environment, or a perceived internal locus of causality from an attribution point of view. Relatedness refers to the sense of belonging to a group. The satisfaction of these three needs is considered essential for ensuring optimal personal growth and integration. This article thus explores students' motivational regulation in an art class and whether they perceive their innate psychological needs for competence, autonomy, and relatedness to be satisfied in a collaborative learning environment.

Keywords Self-determination theory · Art class · Collaborative learning · Psychological needs · Intrinsic motivation

5.1 Introduction

The contemporary goal in education is to foster learners with a new mindset that embraces "a spirit of continual improvement, a lifelong habit of learning and an enterprising spirit in undertakings" (Wee, 1998, p. 2). At the individual level, personal efficacy and personal development of students is expected to arise through greater

H. Oh (✉)
National Institute of Education, Nanyang Technological University, Singapore, Singapore
e-mail: oh_bee_leng_hester@schools.gov.sg

© Springer Nature Singapore Pte Ltd. 2020
C. Koh (ed.), *Diversifying Learner Experience*,
https://doi.org/10.1007/978-981-15-9861-6_5

resilience and flexible adaptation. Learners are to assume greater interdependence, self-direction, and initiative in the learning process. This not only allows the individual to draw on personal motivational resources to manage and perform, but also reinstates one's control over learning and life processes, thereby reinforcing antecedents of personal agency (Skinner, Welborn, & Connell, 1990).

To ensure optimal benefits from school for adolescents, educators should take the necessary measures to provide a learning context in which they are motivated to engage actively in learning activities (Stipek, 1998). According to Legault, Green-Demers, and Pelletier (2006), one of the major academic problems faced by many adolescents today is the lack of motivation towards academic activities. Over the years, many high school students find themselves disengaged from the academic tasks that are required of them in school. Many factors can contribute to students' lack of motivation. For example, schoolwork can be too difficult or boring, teachers can be too demanding, and non-academic activities may be preferred. This lack of motivation and interest is reflected in students neglecting their studies. Research over the last two decades has indicated that adolescents' academic motivation declines over time (e.g. Anderman and Maehr, 1994; Harter, 1981). Studies show that as children get older, their interests and attitudes towards school in general, and towards specific subject areas such as mathematics, arts, and science, tend to deteriorate (Eccles & Wigfield, 1992; Eccles, Wigfield, & Schiefele, 1998; Haladyna & Thomas, 1979; Hoffmann & Haussler, 1998).

An increasing number of studies have advocated shifting the responsibility back to individuals to allow them to take control over their own learning to reinforce the antecedents of personal agency (Skinner, Welborn, & Connell, 1990). In other words, students need to be intrinsically motivated in order to fully engage in their own learning. In the field of education, the Self-Determination Theory/SDT (Deci & Ryan, 1985, 1991) is largely concerned with students' interest in learning, their value orientation towards education, and their level of confidence towards their own capacities and attributes. These outcomes are manifestations of their intrinsic motivation and internalization of values and regulatory processes. The challenge, therefore, is to help all students develop intrinsic motivation to enable them to deal with their specific learning needs.

5.2   Art Education

Lately, there has been much talk about promoting art education in Singapore, with the aim to develop students who are visually literate and able to appreciate art, through which they develop the motivation in their academic and non-academic endeavours. There are those who believe that a robust arts education builds on individuals' strengths and provides developmental opportunities to bring about positive academic and non-academic outcomes (Benson & Saito, 2000; Lerner, 2005; Witt, 2002). According to Martin et al. (2013), arts participation was correlated with academic outcomes such as motivation, engagement and non-academic outcomes such as self-esteem and life satisfaction.

One of the key objectives of a well-planned art lesson today is to allow for students to create art works and to be able to share their ideas, thoughts, and feelings. In recent years, the art curriculum of Singapore has begun to focus on the processes of solving art problems and the need to provide opportunities for students to engage in collaborative activities when making art. Such an approach asserts that problem-solving involves interaction amongst individuals. This shift in approach has led, since the implementation of the revised art syllabus in 2009, to the emphasis on collaborative efforts in making art and solving art problems (Ministry of Education, n.d.).

To better understand this paradigm change, the focus of researchers in education has shifted from studies on individual cognition to those pertaining to the social mind, from personal understanding to shared understanding, and from individual to group or collaborative projects. The learning sciences have also embarked on a review of methodologies to cater for in situ naturalistic and social interactions in learning (Barab & Kirshner, 2001). All these occurred with the realization that individuals can learn better when working together in social contexts that involve communities of practices (Wenger, 1998). According to Deci and Ryan (2000a), social contexts catalyse both the within- and the between-person differences in one's motivation and personal growth, resulting in people becoming more self-motivated and energized.

5.3   Intrinsic Motivation in the Classroom

Many assume that inherent in human nature is the propensity to be curious about one's environment, the interest in learning and developing one's knowledge. The views of de Charms (1968), Rotter (1966), White (1959), and Harter (1978) stress that motivation is derived in part from the belief that individuals can exert control over their environment. A related perspective, which has been advanced by Deci and Ryan (1985), Connell (1990), Skinner (1995), amongst others, postulates that humans have a need to be autonomous and to engage in activities because they want to. Thus, the SDT (Deci & Ryan, 1985) distinguishes between the various types of motivational orientations, between intrinsic motivation (motivation based on the inherent satisfaction derived from the activity) and extrinsic motivation (motivation based on instrumentalities). The SDT does not embrace a simple intrinsic/extrinsic dichotomy, but, instead, suggests a differentiated spectrum of motives that have both different antecedents and consequences and are associated with different subjective experiences.

Intrinsic motivation refers to the innate tendency to explore, take interest in novelty and challenges, and stretch one's capacities. When intrinsically motivated, individuals engage in activities for their inherent satisfaction (Deci, 1971). Intrinsic motivation plays a primary role in development (Elkind, 1971; Harter, 1978, Krapp, Renninger, & Hoffmann, 1998). Through spontaneous interest, playful engagement, and exploration of one's environment, one's capacities are stretched, new skills are acquired and mastered, and knowledge is expanded. As such, intrinsic motivation is an important process underlying cognitive, affective, and motor development, as well as the exploration of interest towards identity formation.

On the other hand, extrinsic motivation comprises a continuous spectrum of motivational regulations (Ryan and Deci, 2000). The type of motivation that is the least identifiable with autonomous behaviour is called external regulation. These external motivational forces are usually in the form of tangible rewards, punishments, demands, and threats or fear of admonition. The second form of extrinsic motivation is referred to as introjected regulation, characterized by a desire to avoid guilt and shame or to achieve ego enhancement. The third, more autonomous form of extrinsic motivation, is known as identified regulation. Individuals who demonstrate identified regulation genuinely value a particular behaviour and consider it as personally important. They do not, however, genuinely enjoy the task or action they have to undertake. Finally, the last and the most self-determined type of extrinsic motivation is called integrated regulation. Here, the actions are fully integrated into the self and reflect the participants' own beliefs and needs. Yet, even this motivational regulation is not fully intrinsic, because it is still outcome-oriented: the learner is not involved in the educational process solely because of enjoyment or need for stimulation (Ryan & Deci, 2000).

Research has also clearly demonstrated the importance of intrinsic motivation on engagement and success in school. Researchers have linked intrinsic motivation for schoolwork with more interest, curiosity, independence, and desire for a challenge in the classroom (Boggiano & Katz, 1991; Harter, 1978), as well as with better cognitive performance at complex tasks (Benware & Deci, 1984; Grolnick & Ryan, 1987). For example, Ryan, Connell, Plant, Robinson, and Evans (1984) asked students to read a passage and rate their interest and enjoyment of the materials. Students' interest and enjoyment of the materials were associated with both their self-reported comprehension and their actual recall of the materials.

Although the study conducted by Ryan et al. (1984) had shown significantly positive relationships between intrinsic motivation and reading comprehension and recall of materials, their findings needed to be further explored. Thus, Grolnick and Ryan (1984) employed an internalization measure in a process study of learning, in order to explore how both individual differences in internalization and situational conditions affected learning and motivation. They asked 91 fifth graders to read a typical social studies passage drawn from a grade-level text. Some children read the passage under non-controlled conditions—that is, to see what they could learn from it without external rewards or incentives. The second group read the passage under a controlled setting: they were told that later they would be graded on their learning. The third group was assigned to a spontaneous learning condition, in which they were exposed to the material without being prompted to learn it and without mention of a subsequent test. In addition, each child had been independently assessed both in terms of verbal intelligence and self-regulatory style. Of interest was how the conditions and self-regulatory styles affected immediate learning and their subjective experience concerning the learning task. Furthermore, at a 10-day follow-up, children were unexpectedly tested by another experimenter to see what knowledge they had retained over time as it related to these variables.

It was predicted that children who learned the passages under extrinsic conditions would experience more pressure and tension during the learning process and would rate the material as less interesting and enjoyable than children in either intrinsic or spontaneous learning sets. These predictions were substantially confirmed. Furthermore, subjects in spontaneous and intrinsic conditions did not differ from each other in their interest, enjoyment, or feelings of pressure and tension. These findings are in accord with previous studies of intrinsic versus extrinsic circumstances, in which rewards, controls, and other pressures towards particular outcomes have been shown to reduce subsequent intrinsic motivation and interest, as well as to produce feelings of tension and pressure (Ryan, 1982; Ryan, Mims & Koestner, 1983).

Also as predicted, children who learned under either extrinsic or intrinsic conditions, both of which were intentional learning sets, had higher rote recall than those who learned under the spontaneous (incidental) set. However, extrinsic conditions resulted in significantly lower conceptual learning levels than either intrinsic or spontaneous conditions. Thus, while extrinsic pressures did not interfere with the acquisition of the isolated facts, it is negatively related to children's grasp of the main point of the passage. Grolnick and Ryan (1984) suggested that the conceptual integration is an active accomplishment on the part of the learner, and thus is more likely to occur under conditions that foster self-determination. Grolnick and Ryan's (1984) study was useful in conceptualizing research in arts education as it would be of benefit to find out whether a skill-based task, such as art making, would yield similar results.

A recent article by Ryan and Deci (2020) provided an updated review of research from SDT that supported the view that intrinsic motivation and autonomous forms of extrinsic motivation positively predict several desirable outcomes across cultural and educational contexts. In it, the authors recognized the possibility for intentional behaviours to be more nuanced and to show elements of multiple motivational regulations, for example, a person can be simultaneously identified and intrinsically motivated. Thus, a student may appreciate the aesthetic value of a work of art and derive enjoyment in creating it. Over the years, educators have paid a great deal of attention to intrinsic motivation as it results in high-quality learning and creativity (Ryan & Stiller, 1991). According to Deci (1971) when individuals are intrinsically motivated, they will be actively engaged in the tasks. These activities provide their own rewards, and no external rewards are required to get individuals to participate in them.

In what is now known as the Basic Psychological Need Theory (BPNT), Deci and his colleague (Ryan & Deci, 2000) argued that one's psychological needs for competence, autonomy, and relatedness must be met in order to foster the emergence of intrinsic motivation. This eventually helps to develop one's talent and creativity in the field of art, the focus of this research. In a recent publication, Vansteenkiste, Ryan, and Soenens (2020) reviewed several advancements and trends in contemporary research on BPNT, including possible extensions of the shortlist of basic psychological needs, the effect of psychological need frustration on the tendency towards maladaptation, the interlink between psychological and physical needs, new findings on what constitute need-supportive and need-thwarting practices, and the generalizability of the outcomes of need support and satisfaction across contexts.

In an investigation on the development of motivation that occured in Japanese elementary school students over the course of a school year, Oga-Baldwin, Nakata, Parker, and Ryan (2017) found a positive relationship between students' perceptions of the learning environment, engagement, and motivation. This translates into teachers creating a learning environment that is well-structured, optimally paced, and able to engage and generate interest. In such a milieu, students personally invest in their learning as they feel a sense of efficacy and affiliation with their peers.

Since perceived satisfaction for competence, autonomy, and relatedness is important, it is observed that increasingly, more communicative and collaborative environments (Jonassen, 2000) are designed and incorporated in learning and teaching, with the aim to satisfy students' perceived needs in these aspects. This is aligned with the belief that communication and collaboration are inherently social processes. Students can communicate and solve problems with each other through a collaborative environment. Hence, this chapter explores how collaborative learning strategies can be applied in art lessons, with the objective of promoting students' perceived satisfaction of competence, autonomy, and relatedness.

5.4   Perceived Satisfaction of Need for Competence

The need for competence refers to individuals' inherent desire to feel effective in interacting with the environment (Deci & Ryan, 2000a; White, 1959). The desire for competence is evident in an individual's propensity to explore and manipulate the environment and to engage in challenging tasks and extend one's skills. For example, students perceive themselves to be competent when they feel they are able to meet the challenges of their schoolwork.

Competence satisfaction allows individuals to adapt to complex and changing environments, whereas competence frustration is likely to result in helplessness and a lack of motivation (Deci & Ryan, 2000a). Likewise, children blessed with abundant athletic skills, musical or artistic talents are particularly likely to encounter feelings of efficacy and pride early and often. These success experiences and their accompanying effects are thought to satisfy their need for competence and keep them motivated (Deci, 1980; Harter, 1981). Failure experiences can foster the need for competence to the extent that they are construed as challenges to be overcome, but a higher number of successes as compared to failures is certainly desirable (Deci & Ryan, 1985).

Empirical evidence based on SDT suggests that an individual's sense of competence plays a crucial role in student behaviour and motivation. Individuals who lack a sense of competence lack the understanding and mastery of skills necessary to feel intrinsically motivated towards a given task (Deci, 1980). In a classroom environment, students who perceive themselves as incompetent are more likely to become disruptive in their behaviour. In their investigation on students with behaviour and social problem profiles, Olivier, Archambault, and Dupéré (2020) reported that both boys and girls with externalizing problems and student-teacher conflicts reported a lower sense of competence. However, while girls showed lower behavioural, emotional, and cognitive engagement in both Math and Language Arts, boys showed lower behavioural and emotional engagement only in Language Arts. Girls who showed internalizing problems and peer isolation/social problems perceived lower satisfaction of competence and lower emotional and cognitive engagement. On the other hand, boys with externalizing/internalizing/social problems reported lower perceived competence and lower emotional engagement in Math compared to those who are well-adjusted. Pennington (2017) developed and validated an instrument to assess the relationship between student motivation, perceived needs support, and classroom practices in language arts. Her preliminary findings showed that classroom instructional practices may be associated with student-perceived competence and motivation in the task or activity.

5.4.1   Competence and the Artistic Process

The practice of art making is exciting to a child. It is active and constructive, real and concrete, and for students, it is work that they can claim as their own. Indeed, it is difficult to convey in words the sense of purpose and energy to be found in a well-run art room. According to Richmond (1998), for many individuals, art making is valuable for the experience of the process itself (exploring, executing, inventing, and manipulating), and for the challenge in finding precisely the right way to give form, shape, and presence to an idea or subject. According to Csikszentmihalyi (1997), art making involves discipline, close concentration, and persistence. To work at art is to be engaged in living one's life at a level of intense interest and effort that is sometimes rewarded by a successful aesthetic outcome. To be able to achieve this level of intense interest and effort, individuals need to be competent in the various skills and techniques in order for them to produce the art works. Students are motivated and interested in making art if the programme is authentic, such that practical work in art is more a stream of attempts than the regular outcropping of finished masterpieces (Blocker, 2005). According to Blocker (2005), the motivation in the making of art, successful or not, is not just the outcome of successful techniques. It is the process and experience of engaging in the art-making process. To examine the practice of arts facilitation through the lens of the SDT, Swindells et al. (2016) conducted a series of interviews with artists leading projects for older adults. They found that participants' need for competence could be satisfied by identifying and nurturing their skills and aptitudes, and removing their negative self-beliefs through the provision of meaningful and optimally challenging activities.

To be initiated into a world of art practice—be it in drawing, painting, sculpture, clay work, photography, printmaking, or any other art form—is to acquire skills and techniques, to become familiar with certain standards, values, and be compelled to make an almost endless series of decisions and interpretations throughout the creative process. In the latter, nothing is fixed and sequential. Picasso, for example, gave Cezanne some very detailed and unequivocal advice about which colours to use, how to develop light-dark contrasts, painting only what he saw in nature, covering the whole canvas at once with paint, and so forth, which Cezanne went on to adopt to great advantage. Being a less competent painter at that time, Cezanne was not any less motivated in creating his paintings. He immersed himself in the process, experimenting and exploring the media and the subject that he was painting, and was able to grow as a painter over the years. This example shows that satisfying an individual's psychological need for competence is necessary for one to feel motivated in the process of completing the task and hence allows for personal growth. In addition, it is not just the outcome of the task that is important, rather, what is much valued is the process of art making itself.

In working at their own art, students get an insider's view on how art is brought into being, how it is structured, what the material difficulties are, what works best in certain situations, what intent and possibility are, what is excellent technically, etc. They experience the inherent satisfactions and frustrations of art making and in the process, gain an appreciation of and respect for the achievements of artists generally. Satisfying students' psychological need for competence should not be restricted to just teaching the relevant technical skills of art making to them, but rather, it involves equipping them with the capacity to be engaged in the art-making process and to encourage them to further discover their styles and strengths in the art form and develop their own identities as artists.

5.5   Perceived Satisfaction of Need for Autonomy

Another key factor promoting intrinsic motivation is the perceived satisfaction of the need for autonomy. Studies have also shown that children become more intrinsically motivated when brought up by autonomy-supportive parents as compared to controlling parents (Grolnick, Deci, & Ryan, 1997). Additionally, other studies have shown that students of autonomy-supportive teachers display more curiosity, greater mastery of the subject, and higher levels of self-esteem than students of control-orientated teachers (Grolnick, Deci, & Ryan, 1997; Grolnick & Ryan, 1987).

Support for autonomy can be manifested in the classroom in at least three ways: procedurally (encouraging student ownership of form, e.g. allowing students to select the media in which to present ideas), organizationally (encouraging student ownership of the environment, e.g. letting student select due dates for assignments), and cognitively (encouraging student ownership of learning, e.g. asking students to generate their own paths to a solution) (Stefanou, Perencevich, DiCinto, & Turner, 2004).

A large pool of empirical evidence based on the SDT suggests that perceived autonomy-supportive teaching is conducive to engagement and optimal learning in educational contexts (Deci & Ryan, 2000b; Reeve, 2012; Su & Reeve, 2011). Providing students with a rationale to explain why a rule exists or why an apparent uninteresting activity is truly worth students' attention is an autonomy-supportive strategy because it allows students' sense of valuing to guide their classroom activity and consequently to build academic self-efficacy. Likewise, asking students what they want (e.g. asking for their input for the lesson plan) is an autonomy-supportive behaviour because the teacher seeks to identify students' needs so as to integrate them into the day's lesson and this develops students' perception of autonomy support and improves their academic self-efficacy (Reeve & Jang, 2006). Overall, autonomy support revolves around finding ways to support and increase students' inner endorsement of their classroom activities (Reeve, 2009; Reeve, Deci, & Ryan, 2004). When students perceive their teachers to be autonomy supportive (Rigby, Deci, Patrick, & Ryan, 1992), they report high levels of self-determination (Vallerand, Fortier, & Guay, 1997). Autonomy supportive strategies, when endorsed and nurtured in the classroom, provide students with the motivational foundation they need to become highly engaged in school and committed to graduating (Hardre & Reeve, 2003; Vallerand et al., 1997). Compared to students who perceive their environment to be controlling, students with greater perceived satisfaction of autonomy experience a wide range of educationally and developmentally important benefits. These benefits include not only greater psychological need satisfaction during learning activities but also greater persistence in school tasks and higher academic achievement (Black & Deci, 2000; Reeve, 2009; Reeve, Jang, Carrell, Barch, & Jeon, 2004).

5.5.1   Autonomy-Supportive Contexts

Providing choices to individuals satisfies their perceived needs for autonomy, leading to enhanced intrinsic motivation. Environments can facilitate the perception of an internal locus of causality under predictable conditions. The most important is the degree to which the individual experiences choice or the opportunity for self-determination. This was documented in a study by Zukerman, Porac, Lathin, and Deci (1978), in which subjects were offered the opportunity to select which three to six puzzles they would work on and to apportion a total of 30 min of puzzle solving time to the three puzzles. Through a matching procedure, they ensured that the puzzle solving in a no-choice control group would be comparable, so the only difference between the two groups of subjects was that one group had a greater opportunity for self-determination. The results showed that, in a subsequent period, those subjects who had been given choice were more intrinsically motivated in puzzle solving than those who had no choice, as demonstrated by their continued engagement with the puzzles in a free-choice period that followed the experimental period.

In a related series of studies, Perlmutter and Monty (1977) investigated the effects of providing choice on subjects' performance on various learning activities. Choice, of course, provides subjects with the opportunity for self-determination and as was observed in the Zuckerman et al. (1978) study, it enhances their intrinsic motivation. Therefore, exploring the effects of choice on learning can provide evidence about the link between activity or intrinsic motivation and the quality of learning. The

Perlmutter and Monty studies, which manipulated choice in a variety of ways showed repeatedly that choice improved subjects' learning. When subjects were told what to learn, even if it was the same material that they would have chosen to learn, their learning tended to be hindered.

In one of their recent publications, Ryan and Deci (2020) reiterated that the specific ingredients of needs-supportive environments reside in the teacher's provision of autonomy support, which ultimately promotes both the satisfaction of autonomy, relatedness and, in conjunction with structure, competence as well.

5.5.2   Informational Versus Controlling Environment

Although it is evident that choice improves students' learning in these studies, it is important to point out that allowing choice in self-determination is not equivalent to what is commonly labelled "permissiveness". Permissiveness means removing all constraints and structure—for example, letting children do whatever they want. This is not autonomy, but rather neglect. The result is usually chaos for adults and excess anxiety for children. Providing structure implies providing information and guidance to help develop and channel a child's growing capacities and abundant energies. But, like other exchanges between teacher (or parent) and child, guidance can be either informational—that is, autonomy supportive—or controlling.

According to Downing and Watson (2004), many research studies in art focus on free-for-all art tasks as one of the common art practices in autonomous art classrooms. However, the focus of this chapter is on autonomy support in the classroom and not on "permissiveness". It is thus necessary for teachers to continuously be in a position of setting limits on students' behaviour. Teachers need to work with the students and together create some sense of order and "neatness" for an environment conducive to learning to be maintained. However, the problem is how to ensure order and set limits in a manner that is not excessively controlling, such that it does not threaten students' self-respect or undermine their sense of autonomy. Setting limits inherently means getting students to do something they do not want to do, or to refrain from doing something they do want to do. Is it possible to be informational in this context? A study by Koestner, Ryan, Bernieri, and Holt (1984) explored this question.

These researchers began by suggesting that a limited setting can be either informational or controlling in its functional significance to the student, just as other interpersonal (environmental) events can be either. They had first- and second-grade students paint pictures, but they set limits on the students' neatness while performing this messy task. They then constructed three types of situations: controlling limits, informational limits, and no-limits condition, so they could assess the impact of these varying styles on subsequent intrinsic motivation. Informational limits, they suggested, provide as much choice as possible, but without excessive control, and at the same time provide the relevant feedback when necessary. This situation also acknowledges the potential conflict between the student's wishes and the limits being set. The students were reminded that certain behaviours may be appropriate and useful even when he or she feels like doing something different. This point is similar to that made often by Ginott (1972), who emphasized the importance of keeping the student's emotional well-being and self-esteem free from particular behavioural contingencies. Controlling limits in this experiment provided the same constraints on neatness, but without acknowledging the inherent conflicts of interest, and without minimizing the threat to self-determination. They made salient the external control involved.

Koestner et al. (1984) found that when limits were set in a controlling manner, they undermined intrinsic motivation to a greater degree, compared to informationally communicated limits, as measured by both a self-report of enjoyment and a free-choice measure. The conditions of informational limits did not affect intrinsic motivation differently from that of no limits. Similar results were obtained for a measure of creativity at the task, as measured by Amabile's (1983) consensual assessment method. It appears, therefore, that informative structures are reasonable, perhaps even desirable, for helping students learn to accommodate to various aspects of the environment. So long as they are not communicated in a way that unduly pressures the child to conform, they may not be deleterious to the child's self-esteem, autonomy, or creativity.

Nonetheless, some researchers perceive that there are cross-cultural variations in teachers' receptiveness to the notion of control versus autonomy support. In a multinational study, Reeve et al. (2014) investigated the relationship between teacher beliefs and their motivational style or orientation towards control or autonomy. They found that cultural norms such as collectivism/individualism predicted teachers' self-described motivational styles, with those in collectivist societies adopting a more controlling style than those in individualistic nations. Furthermore, in a collectivist context, teachers espoused a controlling style because they viewed control as culturally normative and acceptable.

5.5.3 Art Learning in Autonomy-Supportive Classroom

When learning requires conceptual and creative processing, like in the making of art, students who are taught within a more controlling environment not only lose the initiative in exploring artistic solutions, but they also learn less effectively (Amabile, 1996; Grolnick & Ryan, 1987; Utman, 1997). Other social-psychological literature on intrinsic motivation indicates that an important phenomenon in intrinsic motivation is experiential involvement. Intrinsically motivated individuals perceive that interesting and pleasurable activities are ends in themselves. This suggests that intrinsic motivation is enhanced with the presence of experiential involvement. Deci and Ryan's (1985) Self-Determination Theory further reinforces that intrinsic motivation is facilitated when individuals are given autonomy and their behaviours are freely chosen. Recent research findings report that students are motivated in making art when given the opportunities for a free-to-create, self-initiated form of art making (Grube, 2009; Rufo, 2011, 2012).

However, these earlier studies revolve around free-to-create, student-initiated art making in the elementary classroom. Research by Downing and Watson (2004) found that most of the art practices in the art classrooms were still very much skill-based and when choices were given, they were usually free-for-all types of art-making tasks. Furthermore, they claimed that there was little importance given to developing critical skills in students in the art classrooms, and critical skills are important as they directly inform art practices. Practices that provide students with the opportunities to explore issues of culture or identity through engaging with contemporary art practice help to create autonomy-supported classroom environments where students take the conceptual approach to art making, to freely explore social or cultural issues which motivates them towards self-regulation in the making of their own art works (Hyde, 2007). Likewise, Swindells et al. (2016) found that participants' need for autonomy could be satisfied through the recognition of their uniqueness and creativity and by empowering them to be self-directed in their work.

5.6 Satisfying the Perceived Need for Relatedness

Relatedness refers to the feelings of connection with others and belongingness to a group or community. The experience of belonging or being intimately connected with others provides the requisite emotional security to actively venture out into the task and explore (Baumeister & Leary, 1995; Deci & Ryan, 2000a). Deci and Ryan (1985, 1991) attempted to explain the motivational processes whereby an individual seeks autonomy and self-expression within the context of social relationships, i.e. child with parents, student with teacher, and employees with their superiors. These researchers argue that an individual needs to establish close, stable, nurturing, and protective relationships with their parents or caregivers to experience security, and to establish a base to allow them to freely explore their environment, motivating them to strive to achieve (Blatt, 1995, 1998; Blatt & Zuroff, 1992).

5.6.1 Relatedness and Intrinsic Motivation

Studies conducted on mothers and infants showed that infants who experience both security and maternal autonomy support are more exploratory in their behaviour (e.g. Frodi, Bridges, and Grolnick, 1985). This sense of security and relatedness is reflected in the claim by the SDT that in all interpersonal settings over one's lifespan, intrinsic motivation is more likely to flourish when one is able to feel related to others. A study carried out by Anderson, Manoogian, and Reznick (1976) showed that children experience a low level of intrinsic motivation when working on an interesting task in the presence of an adult stranger who ignores and fails to respond to their initiations. Ryan and Grolnick (1987) also observed lower intrinsic motivation in students whose teachers were perceived to be cold and uncaring. Research also revealed that if authorities fail to forge good relationships and take into account the views of those in the lower power positions, then intrinsic motivation will fail to develop. There will be no internalization of values and individuals will fail to find any benefits to their well-being from their experiences within the social context (Deci, Koestner, & Ryan, 1999).

In addition, in some academic studies, there is evidence that suggests that relatedness could indeed play an important role in children's motivation (e.g. Furrer & Skinner, 2003; Grolnick, Ryan, & Deci, 1991; Moss & St-Laurent, 2001; Ryan, Stiller, & Lynch, 1994; Skinner & Belmont, 1993; Stipek, Salmon, Givvin, & Kazemi, 1998; Wentzel, 1997). Early relationships have also been found to have a stable positive influence on later cognitive and motivational outcomes (Moss & St-Laurent, 2001). Parental involvement affects children's academic motivation and the extent of their internalization of the value of schoolwork (Grolnick & Ryan, 1989). In addition, relatedness with parents and teachers makes a unique contribution to students' motivational orientation and academic engagement (Furrer & Skinner, 2003; Wentzel, 1998). It is therefore expected that relatedness may help predict how much freedom of choice matters to the motivation of children (Reeve, Bolt, & Cai, 1999).

In recent years, many studies have been conducted to explore the influence of students' perceived relatedness with peers and teachers. For instance, Oliver et al. (2020) found lower perceived satisfaction of relatedness amongst both boys and girls who had externalizing problems and experienced conflicts with teachers. In a study on the effect of perceived satisfaction of relatedness with teachers and peers amongst Turkish secondary school students in physical education classes, Xiang, Ağbuğa, Liu, and McBride (2017) found that there were no differences between male and female students in terms of their perceived satisfaction of the need for relatedness with teachers and peers. Their findings are in agreement with those of Rutten et al. (2012), Wallhead, Garn, and Vidoni (2013), and Mouratidis, Barkoukis, and Tsorbatzoudis (2015). In addition, Xiang et al. (2017) found no evidence of a relationship between the satisfaction of relatedness and students' intrinsic motivation. However, for female students, behavioural engagement was influenced by perceived relatedness with both teachers and peers, but cognitive and emotional engagements were influenced by relatedness with peers rather than with teachers. For male students, behavioural engagement was influenced by relatedness with teachers rather than peers, while cognitive and emotional engagement were not affected by teachers and peers. While the above studies focused on students' perceived relatedness with teachers and peers, Klassen, Perry, and Frenzel (2012) studied teachers' relatedness with colleagues and students, and how the perception of relatedness influenced teaching engagement and emotional state. Their findings showed that teachers' perceived satisfaction of relatedness with students predicted higher engagement in teaching and positive emotions, than did their relatedness with colleagues. Similarly, to promote the perception of relatedness amongst adult participants in art projects, Swindells et al. (2016) suggested cultivating peer-to-peer social interaction and establishing personal connections with the participants.

The above studies on the need for relatedness focus mostly on the relationship between adults and children. There is, in fact, a genuine need for children and adolescents to develop relationships with their peers and feel connected to them. Hence, one can predict that relationships amongst the students in the art classroom and how art students interact and collaborate with their peers would affect their innate psychological need for relatedness when they were involved in collaborative art tasks. This in turn could affect art students' motivation towards the subject.

5.6.2 Solitude and the Creative Encounter in Art

In the earlier section, the need to foster relatedness in individuals to promote intrinsic motivation in whatever an individual does was discussed. However, in the field of the arts, there are dissenting views with regards to this. According to Francoise Gilot (2001), artistic creation is a solitary vocation, usually not forced upon the artist, but chosen and even cultivated. In his "Letters to a young poet", Rilke (1934) advised Franz Kapus to foster solitude first and foremost: "What is necessary, after all, is only this: solitude, vast inner solitude" (p. 54). Indeed, the artist eschews social intercourse to engage the work anew through acts of imagination. He also claimed that, of course, this is true not only for artists but also for anyone undertaking an intricate, creative task. Scientists, scholars, and all manner of thinkers and planners may retreat from others to bring their ideas into being. However, it is especially true for an artist who may spend the greater part of his life in the solitary pursuit of creation. Furthermore, the work of most thinkers and planners unavoidably brings them into relationships with others for the purpose of verification, validation, and collaboration as they work on their creations.

Although it seems to appear that artists prefer to engage in solitary pursuit of creation, it is in fact not entirely true that they always work solo. Many times in the process of art making, artists turn to other artists for inspiration. In addition, once the work is completed, and ready for judgement, the art community will come together to critique the works of art. For an artist to openly embrace the feedback given by other members of the community, strong bonds have to be built between the artist and the art community in order to accept feedback when the works are critically appraised. Such communities eventually form strong group identities and bring up many known art movements, where artists begin to make art in similar styles.

The perceived need for relatedness must first be satisfied before the artist can be intrinsically motivated to work on the feedback and comments given to improve their creations (Abra & Abra, 1999; Purser & Montuori, 1999). This is in fact in line with what SDT advocates about satisfying the perceived need for relatedness to bring about intrinsic motivation.

5.7 Concepts of Collaboration

What does collaboration mean? To put it simply, "collaboration" refers to any activity that a pair of individuals, or a group of people, perform together. Amongst researchers, however, including those in academic fields, the term "collaboration" is understood rather differently. Within learning sciences, common to the different definitions of collaboration is the emphasis on the idea of co-construction of knowledge and mutual engagement of participants. In this sense, collaboration can be considered as a special form of interaction. Roschelle (1992), for instance, stressed the role of shared understanding, and wrote that collaboration is "a coordinated, synchronous activity that is the result of a continued attempt to construct and maintain a shared conception of a problem" (p. 70).

According to Crook (1998), one of the key features of interaction that is central to successful collaboration is intimacy amongst participants. Further, Engestrom (1992) has elaborated on a developmental form of interaction consisting of three levels which are: coordination, cooperation, and reflective communication. At the level of coordination, each participant concentrates and performs his/her own role and actions, which are scripted or predetermined. In "collaborative" interactions, says Engestrom, actors focus on a shared problem, trying to find mutually acceptable ways to conceptualize it. This level corresponds to the definition of collaboration (although Engestrom uses the concept, "cooperation"), given earlier, from Roschelle and Teasley (1995). The third form of interaction elaborated by Engestrom is reflective communication, in which the actors focus on reconceptualizing their own interaction system in relation to their shared objects of activity. Both the objects and the scripts are reconceptualized. Only through this expansive cycle, is the interaction system transformed, and new motives and objects for collaborative activity created. These three phases are a natural cycle of any genuine collaborative learning activity.

There also exist broader definitions of collaboration, other than those focused on the mutual engagement of the parties. In fact, Engestrom's third reflective communication could be considered as "participating in activity system", and thus, representing a broader definition of collaboration rather than focused on mutual engagement. Collaboration is defined as a process of participating in knowledge communities (Brufee, 1993). As pointed out by Brufee (1993), collaboration is "a reculturative process that helps students become members of knowledge communities whose common property is different from the common property of the knowledge communities they already belong to" (p. 3). Scardamalia and Bereiter (1994) speak about knowledge-building communities, whereby knowledge building is a special form of collaborative activity oriented towards the development of conceptual artefacts, and towards the development of collective understanding.

In a community of learners, as proposed by Brown and Campione (1994), the core activity is participation in the collaborative process of sharing and distributing expertise. As stated by Brown (1994), "Learning and teaching depend on creating, sustaining and expanding a community of research practice. Members of the community are critically dependent on each other. No one is an island; no one knows it all"; "collaborative learning is not just nice, it is necessary for survival" (p. 10). The idea of collaboration as a basic form of human activity, essential for cultural development, has been emphasized by many writers throughout the history of psychology (Bruner, 1996; Engestrom, 1987; Mead, 1934; Vygotsky, 1962). Such knowledge on the development of culture is crucial when art students work together on collaborative art tasks, making art works collaboratively.

5.7.1 The Effectiveness of Collaborative Learning

In a study on collaborative writing by Ede and Lunsford (1985), the researchers observed that learning always occurred as part of an interaction between learning and the environment or between learning and peers. This is in line with findings by other researchers such as Abercrombie (1960) and Bruffee (1978) who studied the collaborative learning process in detail. Their studies confirm that students often learn both skills (such as writing) and content material more effectively and efficiently when they do so as part of a group. These researchers have shown that collaborative pedagogies have positive effects. Students in classrooms which use collaborative methods do seem to develop certain skills and learn certain content "more effectively and efficiently" than with other methods. However, whether these improved skills result in better writing is open to question. The studies most often cited by collaborative theorists demonstrate not improved writing but the enhancement of certain skills which we might call "precursors" to good writing.

Similarly, Bruffee (1978) found that students' work tended to improve when they got help from peers. In the research, Bruffee did mention that students working with peer tutors demonstrated an increased ability to think through problems and to relate the concrete and the specific in their writing, but he offered only the most general of illustrations in support of his assertion. He also found that students in the Brooklyn peer tutoring program developed an increased amount of self-esteem when they learn collaboratively through the peer-group tutoring programme.

A separate study which analysed the effects of collaboration on skills, such as writing, yielded results that were ambiguous. O'Donnell (1985) found that pairs of writers working together with few guidelines could produce instructions that were more "communicative" than writers working alone. For instance, the instructions given by the pairs included a statement of purpose, used illustrations, used and enumerated the steps of the process, and correctly ordered the steps. However, in a later study conducted in 1987, O' Donnell et al. found that neither paired writers nor individual writers who rewrote a set of instructions used this experience to improve their performance on a later assignment. When revisiting, not only did the pairs of writers produce more complete instructions than the individual writers, but they also focused on different levels of information: the pairs of writers used more "descriptive information", while the individual writers used more "procedural information" in their revisions. The advantages of group writing in this series were therefore not clear-cut.

With such differing views surfacing, one can only speculate whether collaborative learning does have an effect on students' learning in the art classroom. Since the above research is related to writing, it seemed important to ascertain whether the findings were generalizable to an art classroom. In addition, it was important for the current research to study whether the learning of art-making skills (apart from attitude, self-esteem, etc.) could be enhanced through collaborative learning, as this essentially provides information on whether art students' perceived need for competence is satisfied.

5.8   Diversifying Learner Experiences Through Collaborative Learning in Art Class

Collaborative learning groups have been shown to be effective in increasing academic achievement when managed properly (Johnson & Johnson, 1989; Slavin, 1990). There are several reasons for assuming that collaboration influences student motivation. Slavin (1984) argued that one factor influencing the success of such group instructions is the positive motivational effect of peer support for learning. Collaborative learning provides small groups of students the opportunity to work jointly to accomplish learning objectives. When peers recognize that their rewards are dependent on the success of their teammates, they are more likely to provide emotional and tutorial support for learning. As Slavin (1984) pointed out, such support for learning is not typical of many traditional classrooms. Empirical evidence indicates that collaborative learning brings about an increase in intrinsic motivation, whereby students derive enjoyment in learning for its own sake. Several studies (Ames & Archer, 1988; Meece, Blumenfeld, & Hoyle, 1988; Miller, Behrens, Green, & Newman, 1993) have indicated a positive relationship between students working collaboratively together and their intrinsic motivation, and an increase in their perceived satisfaction for relatedness.

In a study that explored students' motivational regulation and their perceived need satisfaction in Singapore (Oh, 2018), the effect of collaborative learning was investigated with regards to students' perceptions of satisfaction of these three psychological needs, and how the satisfaction of these psychological needs affected their motivation towards art as a subject they offered in school. To promote motivation amongst students and to diversify their learning experiences, the art unit in the school revised its upper secondary art curriculum to enable the use of collaborative learning with a focus on open-ended art tasks in the classrooms. This involved the students engaging in an 8-month art programme which was designed to allow for collaborative learning to occur during most of the lessons. The new curriculum showed how art, a subject in which individuals frequently engage in solo work, may create conditions for individuals to work together and hence satisfying students' perceived need for relatedness. The students attended two weekly 1.5 h sessions, during which drawing and painting skills, conceptualizing ideas, art history, and art critique were taught. The collaborative tasks included activities such as "think-pair-share", "circle of artists", and "revolving gallery" which required students to play different roles and work together to achieve common goals. The tasks also required the students to communicate their ideas and creations to their peers, and be receptive to feedback in order to work on improving their works. Such work required the students' perceived need for relatedness to first be satisfied before fruitful discussions could take place.

In addition, the open-ended art tasks that the students carried out took on a thematic approach, allowing their experiences to be further diversified. The students were required to complete six different themes in the academic year. For example, some of the themes that the students worked on were "self-discovery", "heritage and culture", and "popcorn". The students were given the autonomy to interpret the themes in any way they deemed fit. As the tasks were open-ended, the given themes served only as a guide when the students started to explore and interpret them. Each theme-based, open-ended art task lasted for about three to four weeks. Students started by researching the theme, interpreting it, gathering ideas based on their own interpretations, developing their ideas, and finally presenting their final ideas in an art form of their choice. Aside from the open-ended tasks, the students were given free choice in the use of materials for their art tasks. During the first term of the academic year, the students were taught how to handle different media such as colour pencils, acrylic paints, watercolour, and pencils, to ensure that they were competent in managing all of them. In addition, working with diverse materials allowed them to extend and deepen their understanding of nature and the potential of the media.

The art teachers in the art unit envisioned that by engaging students in collaborative learning, the students' psychological need for relatedness would be satisfied as they developed trusting relationships with their classmates when they worked together. In addition, the use of open-ended art tasks aimed to satisfy the students' psychological need for autonomy. Lastly, training students in different drawing and painting techniques during the first term of the academic year would satisfy the students' need for competence. Additionally, it was observed that when collaborating with their classmates on art projects, students became more confident in their art-making skills and this satisfied their need for competence. With these approaches, the teachers hoped to improve the students' self-determined motivation in art.

5.9   Conclusion

Well-designed art lessons which are interesting and challenge students at an optimal level, together with an autonomy-supportive learning environment in which students feel secure, are factors that help students become more motivated in their learning. As an art teacher myself, I was able to apply teaching strategies supporting competence, autonomy, and relatedness to amotivated students. At the end of the course, I understood that even the most unmotivated students, who seem immutable in their motivation and attitude towards learning, can change dramatically if adequate support is provided. These amotivated students eventually developed more self-determined regulation and demonstrated high performance in learning.

References

Abercrombie, M. L. J. (1960). *The anatomy of judgement*. London: Hutchinson.

Abra, J., & Abra, G. (1999). Collaboration and competition. In M. A. Runco & S. R. Pritzker (Eds.), *Encyclopedia of creativity* (pp. 283–293). San Diego: Academic Press.

Amabile, T. M. (1983). The social psychology of creativity: A componential conceptualization. *Journal of Personality and Social Psychology, 45*(2), 357.

Amabile, T. M. (1996). *Creativity in context*. Boulder, CO: Westview Press.

Ames, C., & Archer, J. (1988). Achievement goals in the classroom: Students' learning strategies and motivation processes. *Journal of Educational Psychology, 80*(3), 260.

Anderson, R., Manoogian, S. T., & Reznick, J. S. (1976). The undermining and enhancing of intrinsic motivation in preschool children. *Journal of Personality and Social Psychology, 34,* 915–922.

Anderman, E. M., & Maehr, M. L. (1994). Motivation and schooling in the middle grades. *Review of Educational Research, 64,* 287–309.

Barab, S. A., & Kirshner, D. (2001). Methodologies for capturing learner practices occurring as part of dynamic learning environments. *Journal of the Learning Sciences, 10*(1–2), 5–16.

Baumeister, R., & Leary, M. R. (1995). The need to belong: Desire for interpersonal attachments as a fundamental human motivation. *Psychological Bulletin, 117,* 497–529.

Benson, P. L., & Saito, R. N. (2000). *The scientific foundations of youth development*. Minneapolis, MN: Search Institute.

Benware, C. A., & Deci, E. L. (1984). Quality of learning with an active versus passive motivational set. *American Educational Research Journal, 21*(4), 755–765.

Black, A. E., & Deci, E. L. (2000). The effects of instructors' autonomy support and students' autonomous motivation on learning organic chemistry: A self-determination theory perspective. *Science Education, 84*(6), 740–756.

Blatt, S. J. (1995). The destructiveness of perfectionism: Implications for the treatment of depression. *American Psychologist, 50,* 1003–1020.

Blatt, S. J. (1998). Contributions of psychoanalysis to the understanding and treatment of depression. *Journal of the American Psychoanalytic Association, 46,* 723–752.

Blatt, S. J., & Zuroff, D. C. (1992). Interpersonal relatedness and self-definition: Two prototypes for depression. *Clinical Psychology Review, 12,* 527–562.

Blocker, H. G. (2005). Kant for kids. *Arts Education Policy Review, 107,* 31–33.

Boggiano, A. K., & Katz, P. (1991). Maladaptive achievement patterns in students: The role of teachers' controlling strategies. *Journal of Social issues, 47*(4), 35–51.

Brown, A. L. (1994). The advancement of learning. *Educational Research, 23,* 24–12.

Brown, A. L., & Campione, J. C. (1994). Guided discovery in a community of learners. In K. McGilly (Ed.), *Classroom lessons: Integrating cognitive theory and classroom practice* (pp. 229–270). Cambridge, MA: MIT Press.

Brufee, K. (1993). *Collaborative learning*. Baltimore: John Hopkins University Press.

Bruffee, K. A. (1978). The Brooklyn Plan: Attaining intellectual growth through peer-group tutoring. *Liberal Education, 64*, 447–468.

Bruner, J. S. (1996). *Culture of education*. Cambridge, MA: Harvard University Press.

Connell, J. P. (1990). Context, self, and action: A motivational analysis of self-system processes across the life-span. In D. Cicchetti & M. Beeghly (Eds.), *The self in transition: From infancy to childhood* (pp. 61–97). Chicago: University of Chicago Press. Connell, J. P., & Wellborn, J. G. (1991). Competence, autonomy and related.

Crook, C. (1998). Children as computer users: The case of collaborative learning. *Computers & Education, 30*, 237–247.

Csikszentmihalyi, M. (1997). *Finding flow*. New York: Basic Books.

deCharms, R. (1968). *Personal causation*. New York: Academic Press.

Deci, E. L. (1971). Effects of externally mediated rewards on intrinsic motivation. *Journal of Personality and Social Psychology, 18*, 105–115.

Deci, E. L. (1980). *The psychology of self-determination*. Free Press.

Deci, E. L., Koestner, R., & Ryan, R. M. (1999). A meta-analytic review of experiments examining the effects of extrinsic rewards on intrinsic motivation. *Psychological Bulletin, 125*, 627–668.

Deci, E. L., & Ryan, R. M. (2000a). The darker and brighter side of human existences: Basic psychological needs as unifying concept. *Psychological Inquiry, 11*, 319–338.

Deci, E. L., & Ryan, R. M. (2000b). The what and why of goal pursuits: Human needs and the self-determination of behavior. *Psychological Inquiry, 11*, 227–268.

Deci, E. L., & Ryan, R. M. (1991). A motivational approach to self: Integration in personality. In R. Dienstbier (Ed.), *Nebraska symposium on motivation: Vil. 38, Perspectives on motivation* (pp. 237–288). Lincoln, NE: University of Nebraska Press.

Deci, E. L., & Ryan, R. M. (1985). *Intrinsic motivation and self-determination in human behaviour*. New York: Plenum Press.

Downing, D., & Watson, R. (2004). *School art: What's in it? Exploring visual arts in secondary schools*. London: National Foundation for Educational Research/Arts Council for England/Tate.

Eccles, J. S., & Wigfield, A. (1992). The development of achievement-task values: A theoretical analysis. *Developmental Review, 12*, 265–310.

Eccles, J. S., Widfield, A., & Schiefele, U. (1998). Motivation to succeed. In N. Eisenberg (Ed.), *Social emotional, and personality development in handbook of child psychology* (Vol. 3, pp. 1017–1096). New York, NY: Wiley.

Ede, L., & Lunsford, A. (1985). Research into collaborative writing. *Technical Communication, 32*(4), 69–70.

Elkind, D. (1971). Cognitive growth cycles in mental development. In *Nebraska symposium on motivation*. University of Nebraska Press.

Engestrom, Y. (1992). *Interactive expertise. Studies in distributed working intelligence*. In *Research Bulletin*, Vol. 83, Department of Education, University of Helsinki.

Engestrom, Y. (1987). *Learning by expanding. An activity-theoretical approach in developmental research*. Helsinki: Orienta-Konsultit Oy.

Frodi, A., Bridges, L., & Grolnick, W. S. (1985). Correlates of mastery related behaviour: A short-term longitudinal study of infants in their second year. *Child Development, 56*, 1291–1298.

Furrer, C., & Skinner, E. (2003). Sense of relatedness as a factor in children's academic engagement and performance. *Journal of Educational Psychology, 95*, 148–162.

Gilot, F. (2001). A painter's perspective. In K. H. Pfenninger & V. Shubik (Eds.), *The origins of creativity* (pp. 163–176). New York, NY: Oxford University Press.

Ginott, H. (1972). I am angry! I am appalled! I am furious! *Today's Education, 61*(8), 23–4.

Grolnick, W. S., Deci, E. L., & Ryan, R. M. (1997). Internalization within the family: The self-determination perspective. In J. E. Grusec & L. Kuczynski (Eds.), *Parenting and children's internalisation of values: A handbook of contemporary theory* (pp. 135–161).

Grolnick, W. S., & Ryan, R. M. (1984). *Self-regulation and motivation in children's learning: An experimental investigation.* Unpublished manuscript. University of Rochester, Rochester, NY.

Grolnick, W. S., & Ryan, R. M. (1987). Autonomy in children's learning: An experimental and individual difference investigation. *Journal of Personality and Social Psychology, 52,* 890–898.

Grolnick, W. S., & Ryan, R. M. (1989). Parent styles associated with children's self-regulation and competence in school. *Journal of Educational Psychology, 81,* 143–154.

Grolnick, W. S., Ryan, R. M., & Deci, E. L. (1991). Inner resources for school achievement: Motivational mediators of children's perceptions of their parents. *Journal of Educational Psychology, 83*(4), 508.

Grube, V. (2009). Admitting their worlds: Reflections of a teacher/researcher on the self-initiated art making of children. *International Journal of Education & the Arts, 19*(7). Retrieved from www.ijea.org/v10n7.

Haladyna, T., & Thomas, G. (1979). The attitudes of elementary school children toward school and subject matters. *Journal of Experimental Education, 48,* 18–23.

Hardre, P. L., & Reeve, J. (2003). A motivational model of rural students' intentions to persist in, versus drop out of, high school. *Journal of Educational Psychology, 95*(2), 347.

Harter, S. (1978). Effectance motivation reconsidered: Toward a developmental model. *Human Development, 21,* 34–64.

Harter, S. (1981). A new self-report scale of intrinsic versus extrinsic orientation in the classroom: Motivational and informational components. *Developmental Psychology, 17.*

Hoffmann, L., & Haussler, P. (1998). An intervention project promoting girls' and boys' interest in physics. In L. Hoffmann, A. Krapp, K. Renninger, & J. Baumert (Eds.), *Interest and learning: Proceedings of the see on conference on interest and grader* (pp. 301–316). Kiel, Germany: IPN.

Hyde, W. (2007). A stitch in time: Gender issues explored through contemporary textiles practice in a sixth from college. *Journal of Art and Design Education, 26*(3), 296–306.

Johnson, D. W., & Johnson, R. (1989). *Cooperation and competition: Theory and research.* Edina, MN: International Book Company.

Jonassen, D. H. (2000). Toward a design theory of problem solving. *Educational Technology Research and Development, 48*(4), 63–85.

Klassen, R. M., Perry, N. E., & Frenzel, A. C. (2012). Teachers' relatedness with students: An underemphasized component of teachers' basic psychological needs. *Journal of Educational Psychology, 104*(1), 150.

Krapp, A., Renninger, K. A., & Hoffmann, L. (1998). Some thoughts about the development of a unifying framework for the study of individual interest. In *Interest and learning. Proceedings of the Seeon-conference on interest and gender* (pp. 455–468).

Koestner, R., Ryan, R. M., Bernieri, F., & Holt, K. (1984). Setting limits on children's behavior: The differential effects of controlling versus informational styles on intrinsic motivation and creativity. *Journal of Personality, 52,* 233–248.

Legault, L., Green-Demers, I., & Pelletier, L. (2006). Why do high school students lack motivation in the classroom? Toward an understanding of academic amotivation and the role of social support. *Journal of Educational Psychology, 98*(3), 567–582.

Lerner, R. M. (2005, September) *Promoting positive youth development: Theoretical and empirical bases.* White paper prepared for Workshop on the Science of Adolescent Health and Development, National Research Council, Washington, DC.

Martin, A. J., Mansour, M., Anderson, M., Gibson, R., Liem, G. A. D., & Sudmalis, D. (2013). The role of arts participation in students' academic and non-academic outcomes: A longitudinal study of school, home, and community factors. *Journal of Educational Psychology, 105*(3), 709–727.

Mead, G. H. (1934). *Mind, self and society.* Chicago: University Chicago Press.

Meece, J. L., Blumenfeld, P. C., & Hoyle, R. H. (1988). Students' goal orientations and cognitive engagement in classroom activities. *Journal of Educational Psychology, 80*(4), 514.

Miller, R. B., Behrens, J. T., Greene, B. A., & Newman, D. E. (1993). Goals and perceived ability: Impact on student valuing, self-regulation, and persistence. *Contemporary Educational Psychology, 18*(1), 2–14.

Ministry of Education (n.d.). *Arts education.* Retrieved from, https://www.moe.gov.sg/education/syllabuses/arts-education.

Mouratidis, A., Barkoukis, V., & Tsorbatzoudis, C. (2015). The relation between balanced need satisfaction and adolescents' motivation in physical education. *European Physical Education Review, 21,* 421–431.

Moss, E., & St-Laurent, D. (2001). Attachment at school age and academic performance. *Developmental Psychology, 37,* 863–874.

O'Donnell, A. M. (1985). Cooperative writing: Direct effects and transfer. *Communication, 2,* 307–315.

O'Donnell, A. M., Dansereau, D. F., Hall, R. H., & Rocklin, T. R. (1987). Cognitive, social/affective, and metacognitive outcomes of scripted cooperative learning. *Journal of Educational Psychology, 79*(4), 431.

Oga-Baldwin, W. Q., Nakata, Y., Parker, P., & Ryan, R. M. (2017). Motivating young language learners: A longitudinal model of self-determined motivation in elementary school foreign language classes. *Contemporary Educational Psychology, 49,* 140–150.

Oh, B. L. H. (2018). *On satisfying the need for competence, autonomy and relatedness: Examining motivation in a secondary school art classroom from a self-determination theory perspective.* Unpublished thesis, National Institute of Education, Nanyang Technological University, Singapore.

Olivier, E., Archambault, I., & Dupéré, V. (2020). Do needs for competence and relatedness mediate the risk of low engagement of students with behavior and social problem profiles? *Learning and Individual Differences, 78,* 101842.

Pennington, S. E. (2017). Motivation, needs support, and language arts classroom practices: creation and validation of a measure of young adolescents' perceptions. *RMLE Online, 40*(9), 1–19.

Perlmuter, L. C., & Monty, R. A. (1977). The importance of perceived control: Fact or fantasy? Experiments with both humans and animals indicate that the mere illusion of control significantly improves performance in a variety of situations. *American Scientist, 65*(6), 759–765.

Purser, R. E., & Montuori, A. (Eds.). (1999). *Social creativity.* Cresskill, NJ: Hampton Press.

Reeve, J., Bolt, E., & Cai, Y. (1999). Autonomy supportive teachers: How they teach and motivate students. *Journal of Education Psychology, 91,* 537–548.

Reeve, J., Deci, E. L., & Ryan, R. M. (2004a). Self-determination theory: A dialectical framework for understanding socio-cultural influences on student motivation. *Big theories revisited, 4,* 31–60.

Reeve, J., Jang, H., Carrell, D., Jeon, S., & Barch, J. (2004b). Enhancing students' engagement by increasing teachers' autonomy support. *Motivation and emotion, 28*(2), 147–169.

Reeve, J., & Jang, H. (2006). What teachers say and do to support students' autonomy during a learning activity. *Journal of Educational Psychology, 98*(1), 209.

Reeve, J. (2009). Why teachers adopt a controlling motivating style toward students and how they can become more autonomy supportive. *Educational Psychologist, 44*(3), 159–175.

Reeve, J. (2012). A self-determination theory perspective on student engagement. In *Handbook of research on student engagement* (pp. 149–172). Boston, MA: Springer.

Reeve, J., Vansteenkiste, M., Assor, A., Ahmad, I., Cheon, S. H., Jang, H., …, Wang, C. J. (2014). The beliefs that underlie autonomy-supportive and controlling teaching: A multinational investigation. *Motivation and Emotion, 38*(1), 93–110.

Richmond, S. (1998). In praise of practice: A defense of art making in education. *Journal of Aesthetics Education, 32*(2), 11–20.

Rigby, C. S., Deci, E. L., Patrick, B. C., & Ryan, R. M. (1992). Beyond the intrinsic-extrinsic dichotomy: Self-determination in motivation and learning. *Motivation and emotion, 16*(3), 165–185.

Rike, R. M. (1992). *Letters to a young poet* (J. M. Burnham, Trans,). San Rafael, CA: New World Library (Original work published 1934).

Rilke, R. M. (1934). *Letters to a young peot*. W. W. Norton, Incorporated.

Roschelle, J. (1992). Learning by collaborating: convergent conceptual change. *The Journal of the Learning Sciences, 2*, 235–276.

Roschelle, J., & Teasley, S. D. (1995). The construction of shared knowledge in collaborative problem solving. In *Computer supported collaborative learning* (pp. 69–97). Berlin, Heidelberg: Springer.

Rotter, J. B. (1966). Generalized expectancies for internal verusu external control of reinforcement. *Psychological Monographs, 80* (1, Whole No. 609).

Rufo, D. (2012). Building forts and drawing on walls: Fostering student-initiated creativity inside and outside the elementary classroom. *Art Education*, May, 40–47.

Rufo, D. (2011). Allowing artistic agency in the elementary classroom. *Art Education*, May, 18–23.

Rutten, C., Boen, F., & Seghers, J. (2012). How school social and physical environments related to autonomous motivation in physical education: The mediating role of need satisfaction. *Journal of Teaching in Physical Education, 31*, 216–230. https://doi.org/10.1123/jtpe.31.3.216.

Ryan, R. M. (1982). Control and information in the intrapersonal sphere: An extension of cognitive evaluation theory. *Journal of Personality and Social Psychology, 43*, 450–461.

Ryan, R. M., & Deci, E. L. (2000). Self-determination theory and the facilitation of intrinsic motivation, social development, and well-being. *American Psychologist, 55*(1), 68–78.

Ryan, R. M., & Deci, E. L. (2020). Intrinsic and extrinsic motivation from a self-determination theory perspective: Definitions, theory, practices, and future directions. *Contemporary Educational Psychology*. https://doi.org/10.1016/j.cedpsych.2020.101860.

Ryan, R. M., Connell, J. P., Plant, R., Robinson, D., & Evans, S. (1984). *The influence of emotions on spontaneous learning*. Unpublished manuscript, University of Rochester, Rochester, NY.

Ryan, R. M., & Grolnick, W. S. (1987). Origins and pawns in the classrooms: Self-report and projective assessments of individual differences in children's perceptions. *Journal of Personality and Social Psychology, 50*, 550–558.

Ryan, R. M., Mims, V., & Koestner, R. (1983). The relationship of reward contingency and interpersonal context to intrinsic motivation: A review and test using cognitive evaluation theory. *Journal of Personality and Social Psychology, 45*, 736–750.

Ryan, R. M., & Stiller, J. (1991). The social contexts of internalization: parents and teacher influences on autonomy, motivation and learning. In P. R. Pintrich & M. L. Maehr (EDs.), *Advances in motivation and achievement* (Vol. 7, pp. 115–149). Greenwich, CT: JAI Press.

Ryan, R. M., Stiller, J. D., & Lynch, H. J. (1994). Representations of relationships to teachers, parents, and friends as predictors of academic motivation and self-esteem. *Journal of Early Adolescence, 14*, 226–249.

Scardamalia, M., & Bereiter, C. (1994). Computer support for knowledge-building communities. *The Journal of the Learning Sciences, 3*, 265 283.

Skinner, E. A., & Belmont, M. J. (1993). Motivation in the classroom: Reciprocal effects of teacher behavior and student engagement across the school year. *Journal of Educational Psychology, 85*, 571–581.

Skinner, E. A., Wellborn, J. G., & Connel, J. P. (1990). What it takes to do well in school and whether I've got it: a process model of perceived control and children's engagement and achievement in school. *Journal of Educational Psychology, 82*, 22–32.

Skinner, E. A. (1995). *Perceived control, motivation and coping*. Newbury Park, CA: Sage.

Slavin, R. (1984). Students motivating students to excel: Cooperative incentives, cooperative tasks, and student achievement. *Elementary School Journal, 85*(1), 53–63.

Slavin, R. (1990). *Cooperative learning: theory, research and practice*. Englewood Cliffs, NJ: Prentice-Hall.

Stefanou, C. R., Perencevich, K. C., DiCintio, M., & Turner, J. C. (2004). Supporting autonomy in the classroom: Ways teachers encourage student decision making and ownership. *Educational psychologist, 39*(2), 97–110.

Stipek, D. (1998). *Motivation to learn: From theory to practice* (3rd ed.). Massachusetts: Allyn & Bacon.

Stipek, D., Salmon, J. M., Givvin, K. B., & Kazemi, E. (1998). The value (and convergence) of practices suggested by motivation research and promoted by mathematics education reformers. *Journal of Research in Mathematics Education, 29,* 465–488.

Su, Y. L., & Reeve, J. (2011). A meta-analysis of the effectiveness of intervention programs designed to support autonomy. *Educational psychology review, 23*(1), 159–188.

Swindells, R., Lawthom, R., Parkinson, C., Clennon, O., Kagan, C., & De Bézenac, C. (2016). 'I'm not a therapist you know… I'm an artist': Facilitating well-being and basic psychological needs satisfaction through community arts participation. *Journal of Applied Arts & Health, 7*(3), 347–367.

Utman, C. H. (1997). Performance effects of motivational state: A meta-analysis. *Personality and Social Psychology Review, 1,* 170–182.

Vallerand, R. J., Fortier, M. S., & Guay, F. (1997). Self-determination and persistence in real-life setting: Towards a motivational model of high school dropout. *Journal of Personality and Social Psychology, 72,* 1161–1176.

Vansteenkiste, M., Ryan, R. M., & Soenens, B. (2020). Basic psychological need theory: Advancements, critical themes, and future directions. *Motivation and Emotion, 44,* 1–31.

Vygotsky, L. S. (1962). *Thoughts and language.* Cambridge, MA: MIT Press.

Wallhead, T., Garn, A., & Vidoni, C. (2013). Sport education and social goals in physical education: Relationships with enjoyment, relatedness, and leisure-time physical activity. *Physical Education and Sport Pedagogy, 18,* 427–441.

Wee, H. T. (1998). *What we do in schools today will shape the future of Singapore.* Singapore: Ministry of Education.

Wenger, E. (1998). Communities of practice: Learning as a social system. *Systems Thinker, 9*(5), 2–3.

Wentzel, K. R. (1998). Social relationships and motivation in middle school: The role of parents, teachers and peers. *Journal of Educational Psychology, 90,* 202–209.

Wentzel, K. R. (1997). Student motivation in middle school: The role of perceived pedagogical caring. *Journal of Educational Psychology, 89,* 411–419.

White, R. W. (1959). Motivation reconsidered: The concept of competence. *Psychological Review, 66,* 297–333.

Witt, P. A. (2002). Youth development: Going to the next level. *Parks and Recreation, 37,* 52–59.

Xiang, P., Ağbuğa, B., Liu, J., & McBride, R. E. (2017). Relatedness need satisfaction, intrinsic motivation, and engagement in secondary school physical education. *Journal of Teaching in Physical Education, 36*(3), 340–352.

Zuckerman, M., Porac, J., Lathin, D., & Deci, E. L. (1978). On the importance of self-determination for intrinsically motivated behavior. *Personality and Social Psychology Bulletin, 4*(3), 443–446.

Chapter 6
Diversifying the Experiences of Gifted and Talented Learners: A Review of Recent Trends and Practices

Caroline Koh

Abstract A review of the recent literature on gifted and high-ability learners shows a focus on three main areas: motivation, curriculum and clustering, and the application of technology. This chapter aims to provide an overview of the research in these three domains and the applications of these findings in actual learning contexts. Some authors investigated the influence of the curriculum on the motivation of gifted students, providing evidence that the extent to which gifted students perceive the curriculum as motivating depends on the alignment of their goals and values with those in their learning. Thus, researchers investigated the effectiveness of cluster grouping on the performance of gifted students and found that those in the cluster grouped classes showed a significantly higher performance than their peers in traditional heterogeneous classrooms. In recent years, there has been a significant increase in the number of studies on the use of Information and Communication Technologies (ICT) to diversify and enrich the experiences of gifted/high-ability learners. Some described how technology can be leveraged to expand academic options for gifted students through distance learning. For instance, high-ability students were able to supplement and enrich their learning through more advanced work in virtual learning environments. This enabled them to interact with peers and instructors from all over the world. Yet others explored the experiences and benefits in the use of various forms of ICT-based technologies with regards to the social and emotional development of gifted students. The review presented in this chapter shows that there is a salient interplay between curriculum, technology and motivation. Crystallizing the outcomes of the studies in these three areas could lead to the delivery of a diverse and enriched program for gifted learners.

Keywords Gifted students · Motivation · Curriculum enhancement · Acceleration · Cluster grouping · ICT · Perfectionism · Gifted underachievers

C. Koh (✉)
National Institute of Education, Nanyang Technological University, Singapore, Singapore
e-mail: caroline.koh@nie.edu.sg

© Springer Nature Singapore Pte Ltd. 2020
C. Koh (ed.), *Diversifying Learner Experience*,
https://doi.org/10.1007/978-981-15-9861-6_6

6.1 Introduction

In a professional development course for teachers offered by the National Institute of Education in Singapore, the instructor showed a snippet from the movie 'Mona Lisa smiles'. In the video, the protagonist, a newly appointed lecturer at the prestigious Wellesley College, was caught off-guard in her first class when she realized that her intelligent and overachieving students had already mastered the entire textbook and syllabus. After watching the video, some of the teachers voiced out that they wished their own students were like the high achievers in the video and envied their colleagues who taught high-ability classes. The latter, however, were somewhat discomfited by the remarks, and sheepishly observed that they didn't have things easy either and that 'smart kids have issues of their own'.

The purpose of this chapter is to examine some of the issues faced by 'gifted' and talented learners, and to identify some of the processes and practices that would diversify high-ability learners' experiences, hence catering to their specific needs. A review of the extant literature on gifted and high-ability learners showed that studies tended to revolve around three main areas: curriculum design and ability grouping, learner motivation and application of technology. The chapter begins with the establishment of a working definition of 'giftedness'. This is followed by an overview of the needs of gifted and talented learners and the challenges they face. The chapter closes with a consideration of how diversification of learning experiences can lead to improved motivation, engagement and achievement in gifted and talented learners.

6.2 Defining 'Gifted' and 'Talented'

One of the main challenges in the identification of 'gifted' and 'talented' learners lies in the disparities in the definitions of 'giftedness' across contexts. Stephens and Karnes (2000) described the evolution of an early definition proposed by the US Congress (1970) which defined 'gifted and talented' learners as persons with 'outstanding intellectual ability or creative talent, the development of which requires special activities or services not ordinarily provided by local education agencies'. Over time, this definition morphed into one given by the U.S. Department of Education (1994), which described 'gifted and talented' youths as those who are able to 'show the potential for performing at remarkably high levels of accomplishment when compared with others of their age, experience, or environment', 'exhibit high performance capability in intellectual, creative, and/or artistic areas, possess an unusual leadership capacity, or excel in specific academic fields', and 'require services or activities not ordinarily provided by the schools'. In addition, Stephens and Karnes analysed the definitions of gifted and talented students from 50 states across the U.S. They found variations in the definitions of 'giftedness' in 29 states across the U.S., although generally, superior intellect was perceived as an attribute of giftedness. Furthermore, almost all the states involved in the study mentioned the gifted/talented learners' needs for special provisions to enable them to develop to their full potential. These included 'services or activities not ordinarily provided by the school', 'special facilities, equipment, or methods', 'special instruction, special ancillary services', 'qualitatively differentiated educational experiences or services', 'differentiated instruction or services beyond those being provided in the regular school program', 'appropriate instruction and educational services commensurate with their abilities and needs', 'differentiated or accelerated education or services', amongst others (Stephens & Karnes, 2000, pp. 225–233). This suggests that there is a general consensus for the need to diversify gifted/talented learners' experiences, beginning with a differentiation in the curriculum, in order to provide them with opportunities to nurture and showcase their special abilities.

Generally, the consensus in the need to differentiate and diversify arose as a result of the many reported cases of underachievement amongst students identified as gifted. Researchers reported that in schools, gifted students were not provided with experiences that were sufficiently challenging for their learning to be enhanced. In addition, it is contended that when gifted learners experience boredom with the regular curriculum, they are prone to feel psychologically distressed and/or indulge in misbehaviour (Gallagher, Harradine, & Coleman, 1997; Rogers, 2007; Little, 2012). Hence, just as it is important to enhance the motivation of low achieving learners, an understanding of the factors influencing the motivation of gifted learners seems to be of equal importance.

6.3   Motivating Gifted Learners

Schunk, Pintrich, and Meece (2008, p. 4) described motivation as 'the process whereby goal-directed activity is instigated and sustained'. The strategies that explain and improve gifted students' motivation to learn can be explored with respect to contemporary motivation theories, which hold the key to understanding why some gifted learners are able to perform at the high level of achievement that is expected of them, whereas others do not. As Clinkenbeard (2012, p. 622) mused: 'One of the most intriguing, and often frustrating, puzzles for those who study individuals with great intellectual and creative promise is why some bright students never reach the level of success of which they seem so capable'. While one would expect gifted learners to be high achievers on account of their exceptional intellect, academic ability or creative capability, researchers have highlighted the issue of 'gifted underachievers', students who have been identified as having the potential of performing 'at remarkably high levels of accomplishment', but who, for one reason or another, fail to perform at the level consistent with their abilities or skills. Reis and McCoach (2000, p. 74) proposed that, generally, a gifted underachiever can be described as someone who shows 'a discrepancy between intellectual potential and academic performance'. In addition, Reis also outlined three main reasons for underachievement amongst gifted students:

(i)   underlying physical, emotional and cognitive issues (such as family, financial resources, mental and physical health),
(ii) personal attributes and self-perception (such as low self-esteem and self-efficacy),
(iii) mismatch between the student and his/her school environment.

Like their peers in Western contexts, gifted students in Asian societies such as Singapore experience similar issues. For instance, Yeo and Pfeiffer (2018) highlighted emotional issues such as fear of disappointing parents and academic stress, in addition to heightened anxiety due to intense competition and high parental and personal expectations (Kwek, 2007). To prevent or reverse underachievement, the factors that play an important role in sustaining motivation and achievement in gifted learners need to be considered. Like their peers in the regular curriculum, gifted learners are motivated by factors pertaining to their basic needs, cognition and affect, although their inclinations and preferences may differ.

6.3.1   Intrinsic Versus Extrinsic Factors

Motivation can be categorized according to whether it is intrinsic, arising from an innate drive or desire, or extrinsic, coming from an external source such as the promise of a reward or fear/avoidance of retribution. In intrinsic motivation, the person does something for his/her own sake, usually out of interest and enjoyment. On the other hand, an extrinsically motivated individual does something as a means to an end. There is evidence that gifted learners are more inclined to be intrinsically motivated than their peers in the regular curriculum (Csikszentmihalyi, Rathunde, & Whalen, 1993; Gottfried & Gottfried, 1996; Clinkenbeard, 2012). However, Csikszentmihalyi (1991) posited that the deep engagement associated with intrinsic motivation can only occur when there is close alignment between the individual's capability and the difficulty level of the task. Hence, a gifted learner's intrinsic motivation can only be sustained if the curriculum offers an optimal level of challenge, the absence of which will result in loss of engagement and interest, and ultimately lead to underachievement. Conversely, boredom sets in when the classroom environment offers inappropriate challenge, such as slow-paced and repetitive lesson delivery. In addition, some researchers suggest that students' cultural heritage must be taken into consideration when crafting the curriculum for gifted learners. Moore, Ford, and Milner (2005) and Ford (1996) reported that African-American gifted students communicated boredom and low interest when the curriculum was culturally irrelevant and they could not relate to the taught content. A multicultural gifted curriculum model would thus enable educators to develop diverse learning experiences that are suitable, relevant and challenging to gifted learners.

6.3.2 Socio-cognitive Factors

Gifted learners' perceptions of self and of causality have a strong impact on their motivation and achievement. Vallerand, Gagné, Senécal, and Pelletier (1994) compared the perceptions of intrinsic motivation and competence of gifted learners with those of students in the regular classes. They found that gifted learners perceived themselves as being more intrinsically motivated and competent than their peers taking the regular curriculum. These researchers also posited that intrinsic motivation was upheld when the gifted learners perceived the locus of causality to be internal and that they had the liberty to make decisions and initiate actions.

The findings of Vallerand et al. corroborate the tenets of the Self-Determination Theory (Ryan & Deci, 2000), which posits that a person's autonomous motivation increases when he/she perceives that his/her basic psychological needs for competence, autonomy and relatedness are satisfied. Thus, a gifted learner's intrinsic motivation is enhanced and sustained, if he/she has ownership of his/her learning, a self-perception of competence and efficacy, and most importantly, support and unconditional positive regard from parents and peers.

6.3.2.1 Autonomy and Ownership of Learning

Emerick (1992) found that variables such as intellectual and creative stimulation, opportunities for advanced and independent study, and acknowledgement of personal agency for success are factors contributing to the reversal of underachievement in gifted learners. Hence, to prevent boredom and sustain intrinsic motivation, teachers should consider processes and strategies to diversify gifted students' classroom experiences. Phillips and Lindsay (2006) suggested a number of ways in which this could be done. These include (i) provision of a wide range of opportunities (such as field trips, research projects, work attachments, amongst others) to explore topics or activities beyond the regular school curriculum; (ii) intellectual independence and choice of their preferred learning pace and style (e.g. adoption of alternative approaches to problem-solving, personal presentation style and learning at one's own pace); (iii) opportunities for greater complexity and depth in curriculum content and task demands; and (iv) use of abstraction and creativity in learning (Kaplan, 2009; Little, 2012; Phillips & Lindsay, 2006; Reis, Burns, & Renzulli, 1992; Rogers, 2007; VanTassel-Baska, 2005; VanTassel-Baska & Stambaugh, 2006). In addition, a number of researchers have emphasized on the importance of ensuring learning opportunities that are not only appropriately challenging, but also meaningful and of perceived value to the gifted learners (Little, 2012; Tomlinson, 2003; VanTassel-Baska, 2005).

6.3.2.2 Competence and Perfectionism

The issue with gifted learners is not with their self-perception of competence or self-efficacy (belief in one's ability to succeed in a task or an endeavour), but rather with their tendency to be perfectionistic. This emotional trait, characterized by the demonstration of excessively high standards or expectations of one's own performance (Burns, 1980; Schuler, 2000), is often associated with and even perceived as a major characteristic of giftedness, although there are, most likely, gifted individuals who are not perfectionists. Even though authors such as Hamachek (1978), Roedell (1984) and Silverman (1990) recognized that perfectionism has both positive and negative aspects, there has been a greater emphasis on the adverse effects of perfectionism on the gifted learners' emotional health. Thus, gifted learners who are neurotic/maladaptive perfectionists have an obsessive and destructive tendency to pursue unattainable goals and are unable to derive pleasure in their effort or enjoyment in their success, due to their perception that their performance or achievements are never good enough (Burns, 1980; Pacht, 1984; Parker & Mills, 1996). Neurotic perfectionism is detrimental to the individual as it is often linked with pathological conditions such as depression, anxiety, panic, suicidal tendency, which hinder achievement (Hewitt & Dyck, 1986; Straub, 1987; Adkins & Parker, 1996; Parker & Mills, 1996). Researchers have also found that gifted students in Asian contexts, such as Hong Kong and Singapore, experience the negative effects of neurotic perfectionism to a deeper level than their Western counterparts (Chan, 2010; Kwan 1992; Yeo & Pfeiffer, 2018). This appears to be related to the collectivistic culture in these Asian societies whereby a high premium is placed on academic excellence and scholarly accomplishment.

Notwithstanding, Hamachek specified that the other type of perfectionism, termed adaptive or 'normal' perfectionism, is in fact desirable because it involves 'having high standards, a desire to achieve, conscientiousness or high levels of responsibility' (Parker & Mills, 1996, p. 194) and in sum, it sets the stage for achievement and the pursuit of excellence. Park and Mills posited that the association between neurotic perfectionism and giftedness may well be syllogistic in nature, and that although gifted individuals tend to be perfectionistic, they may not necessarily be maladaptive neurotic. Hamachek (1978) and Schuler (2000) posited that perfectionism consists of a spectrum of behaviours, ranging from normal/adaptive at one end to neurotic/dysfunctional at the other. These behaviours include depression, guilt and shame, compulsion/obsession, ego protection, shyness and procrastination, and self-deprecation. Most gifted learners show varying degrees of these behaviours, which occur more intensely and for a longer duration with heightened neuroticism.

Researchers reported that the neurotic perfectionists tended to be overly concerned about making mistakes, parental expectations and criticisms, high personal standards, low self-efficacy and self-esteem (Schuler, 2000; Parker, 1997). Adaptive perfectionists, on the other hand, were not afraid of making mistakes, showed high self-confidence and self-efficacy and were not unduly bothered about parental criticisms. In Schuler's study, most of the normal/adaptive perfectionists attributed their perfectionistic tendencies to benefits such as becoming better organized, more hardworking and being better at prioritizing, indicating that they tended to adopt a mastery goal orientation. They further stated that attaining their personal best in whatever they do is more important to them than outcomes such as grades. On the other hand, the neurotic perfectionists attributed their perfectionism to performance-related outcomes, such as improved grades, doing better in projects and sports, attaining higher standards than others and parental approval. They perceived that grades and performance were central to their identity and determined how others value or approve of them. As such, they experienced the dual pressure of having to meet what they perceived as the high expectations from others, as well as having to sustain their high-performance standard.

Hence, there is an impetus to ensure that perfectionism amongst the gifted takes the form of a healthy motivation towards maximizing one's potential, rather than a maladaptive obsession to attain unrealistic goals. For this, the supportive role of parents, peers and teachers plays an important part in providing a safe and secure environment, whereby the gifted learners would perceive their need for relatedness to be satisfied.

6.3.2.3 Relatedness and Unconditional Positive Regard

Schuler (2000) raised the concern that teachers were not able to differentiate between gifted learners with maladaptive, neurotic perfectionism and those with a healthy perfectionistic orientation. Understandably, neurotic perfectionists with their ego-protecting inclinations would tend to hide their problems and flaws, and few would openly seek help from adults or peers. It is therefore important to build an environment of trust and openness, whereby the gifted perfectionist would perceive a sense of relatedness or belongingness to their group, class or community. Only then will they feel sufficiently comfortable to share their issues and begin to work towards overcoming their maladaptive behaviours.

One can begin with an understanding of how the gifted perfectionists perceive the people within their microcosm. Schuler (2000) found that the neurotic perfectionists tended to view their classmates as competitors and hence as contributors to the pressure imposed upon them to perform. Likewise, they perceived that teachers also played a part in contributing to the pressure they felt, through exhorting them to be 'the best', although some of them admitted that their teachers did try to reduce their anxiety by alleviating their concern about making mistakes. The neurotic perfectionists viewed their parents as being more perfectionistic than they were and also blamed their parents for having unrealistic expectations and setting unattainable standards for them, while being painfully critical of their performance. The adaptive/normal perfectionists had views of their entourage that were strikingly different from those of their neurotic counterpart. For instance, they considered the competition with classmates and peers as being 'healthy' and a beneficial motivating factor. The normal perfectionists viewed teacher and parental influence as being positive. They lauded their parents for encouraging them to maximize their potential and to be unafraid of making mistakes.

Perhaps the way forward in helping gifted neurotic perfectionists overcome their dysfunctional orientations is to allow them first and foremost to acknowledge that they have maladaptive issues that need to be addressed and that help-seeking is not a shameful endeavour. Prior to this, parents and teachers should themselves have a greater awareness of the potential difficulties that the gifted perfectionists might be harbouring beneath their flawless façades. The process of healing and turnaround can only take place when teachers and especially parents show unconditional positive regard (Rogers, 1957), acceptance and support of a person regardless of his/her attributes, actions or beliefs towards their charges. Unfortunately, some parents of underachievers were found to be indifferent, disinterested, distant and showed little affection towards their bright kids, while others showed either restrictive authoritarianism or neglectful permissiveness (Reis, 1993). Underachievement could also result from emotional conflicts arising from parents' unrealistic goals or expectations, especially when they are not in alignment with those of the child.

6.3.3   Diversifying Experiences to Motivate Gifted Learners

The role of parental and peer support. Phillips and Lindsay (2006) found that family and peer support are key factors in upholding gifted learners' motivation and achievement. Underachievement was less likely to occur with gifted children coming from a stable home, with family members who encouraged them and were there for them when they had problems. In addition, peers were found to play a significant role in keeping underachievement at bay. Prevention or reversal of underachievement and motivational decline can thus be prevented by providing opportunities for gifted learners to join common interest groups with peers who share similar preferences and inclinations. Reis (1993, p. 81) posited that 'busier adolescents who are involved in clubs, extracurricular activities, sports, and religious activities are less likely to underachieve in school'. The importance of support in promoting gifted learners' motivation and achievement can be observed even in Asian contexts. A study conducted with gifted twice-exceptional (with high ability and one other special need) students in Singapore showed that support from parents, teachers and peers contributed to these students' academic success, through the enhancement of their academic engagement and self-efficacy, and the use of effective learning strategies (Wang & Niehart, 2015).

The role of school support. In Emerick's (1992) study, all participants perceived that a particular teacher played a key role in the reversal of their underachievement, suggesting that the availability of a caring adult (counsellor, coach, teacher or parent) is important in initiating the reversal process. In addition, Emerick's study on the factors contributing to the reversal of academic underachievement revealed that 'when appropriate educational opportunities are present, gifted underachievers can respond positively' (p. 145). Some of these factors include teacher-student relationship, learning opportunities that are meaningful and aligned with learner interest and preferred learning style, and contexts that enable self-regulation and peer-group interaction.

Clickenbeard (2012, p. 626) suggested the TARGET model for 'structuring classroom practices in a way that is designed to promote student motivation'. The aim of the model is to help students develop mastery goal orientations through six practices involving Task, Authority, Recognition, Grouping, Evaluation and Time. The model posits that there must be variety in the tasks assigned and these must be optimally challenging to the gifted learners. In addition, the latter favour having a certain degree of Authority in their learning—they wish for greater autonomy, more opportunities for shared decision-making, as well as opportunities for self-regulation. Further, they want Recognition for their effort and ability, and more specifically for their own improvement and mastery of content and skills, rather than their superiority over others. Like their peers, gifted learners value belonging to a group where they feel accepted and to which they are able to contribute in a meaningful way. The TARGET model advocates a flexible Grouping model, whereby groupings in the classroom could alternate between being heterogeneous (to allow gifted learners to interact with other students and avoid charges of elitism) and homogeneous (to allow gifted learners to be optimally challenged working with peers of similar calibre and interest). Flexible grouping thus allows the diversification of learner experiences since the gifted learners will have the opportunity to work with different team members and in so doing, be exposed to a variety of ideas and perspectives. Likewise, to avoid social comparison, it is recommended that Evaluation of gifted learners' work be criterion-referenced and carried out in private to cater for self-improvement, rather than norm-referenced and public. Finally, the TARGET model recommends that the Time given to gifted students should be adjusted according to the academic ability and disposition of the gifted learner, so that the latter is able to perform optimally to maximize their potential.

Although the TARGET model has its merits, some educators may argue that it may not be generalizable across all contexts. One would argue that the model works best with small groups of students and in well-endowed educational settings that are able to customize programs to individual students. In settings where resources are scarce and teachers have to manage large classes, it is a challenge to adhere to the requisites of the model. Nonetheless, in non-Western contexts such as China, there are already elements of the TARGET model in the practice of gifted education. For instance, optimally challenging Tasks are offered to gifted students in the processes of 'Enrichment' (program extension) and 'Pull-out' (extra-curricular activities), while Advancement allows gifted students to skip grades and accelerate learning at a pace that would be adjusted to their academic ability (Rasmussen, 2019).

6.4   Curriculum Design and Ability Grouping

The need to provide appropriate instruction and educational services commensurate with gifted/talented students' abilities arose from the observation that such students are able to master standard curriculum material in a fraction of the time needed by other students, and hence experience boredom, disengagement, inattentiveness and may even show disruptive behaviour and classroom misconduct.

6.4.1   Curriculum Compacting

In an early study, Reis et al. (1992) suggested curriculum compacting as an approach to resolve the problem and to allow gifted/talented students to 'complete the basics in the least amount of time, thereby sparing themselves the tedium of dwelling on content that they either know already or can absorb in short order' (Tannenbaum, 1986, p. 409). Reis and colleagues adopted the technique developed by Renzulli and Smith (1978), whereby the Curriculum Compactor, an instrument for documenting the compacting process, is used to guide teachers through the three stages of the compacting process: (i) identification of students' areas of strengths, (ii) identification of curriculum content that the student needs to master and procedures to reduce teaching time, and (iii) enrichment or acceleration opportunities that could be offered over and above standard curriculum content. The study revealed that teachers had little difficulty identifying students who would benefit from curriculum compacting. In addition, the teachers were able to eliminate as much as 40–50% of the standard curriculum, deemed redundant for gifted/talented learners. It was also found that content reduction did not have any adverse effect on students' achievement test scores. Most teachers opted to use tasks for enrichment rather than for acceleration, possibly due to school policies that prohibited teaching beyond the students' current grade level.

However, the study revealed that while teachers had no problem eliminating materials from the regular curricula, they had difficulties finding replacement activities for their gifted students. Most teachers considered 'replacement' as giving additional problems to solve, more difficult tasks, more reading tasks or alternative assignments. The 'enrichment' activities or strategies were mostly unrelated to the gifted students' real needs and interests, and hence did not serve as appropriate challenges to the students' intellect or capability. Thus, although curriculum compacting does address some of the issues with engaging gifted/talented students, adequate resources need to be provided to ensure its effectiveness. Students are 'gifted' in different ways and at different levels. Catering to the individual needs of the students requires customizing the compacting process to meet the needs of each student. Curriculum content reduction across the board for all gifted students would only perpetuate the 'one size fits all' approach for which curriculum compacting is supposed to provide a better alternative. Thus, the provision of 'qualitatively differentiated educational experiences or services' should ideally be unique for each and every gifted student if the latter's talent is to be effectively and appropriately nurtured. Unfortunately, it is often not possible to put this into practice in contexts such as Singapore and China, where the gifted learners have to sit for high-stake national examinations that determine university entrance.

6.4.2 Ability Grouping

In reality, most schools would have difficulties finding adequate resources to customize curricula and special programs that are unique for each individual gifted student. Ability grouping, defined as 'a practice that places students into classrooms or small groups based on an initial assessment of their levels of readiness or ability' (Kulik, 1992; Tieso, 2003, p. 29), may thus provide a compromise between a whole class instructional approach and one that prescribes customization of the curriculum to individual needs. In 'between-class' grouping, students from different grades but identified as similar in ability level are placed in the same team. The curriculum is then modified to address the needs of the different groups, with each ability group working with different materials and approaches. Although those in support of between-class grouping have highlighted some of its benefits, such as a closer match between the curriculum and the needs of the group members, this approach is logistically complex and requires adequate manpower and a flexible infrastructure. A second approach to grouping, known as 'within-class' or 'flexible' grouping, requires arranging students into 'smaller groups for specific activities and purposes within the same class' (Kulik & Kulik, 1992, p. 75). The temporary nature of within-class grouping enables students to be reassigned to different groups based on the outcome of their latest assessment (Slavin, 1987). Within-class grouping does not pose the scheduling and logistical problems that are inherent in between-class grouping and, according to Sorensen and Hallinan (1986), enables teachers to better engage students and adapt instructional materials to cater to the ability and needs of the students in their groups.

In recent years, researchers in the field of gifted education have proposed the use of cluster grouping as an approach to deliver differentiated curricula to students within the same class (Gentry, 1999; Rogers, 1991; Winebrenner & Brulles, 2008). In this model, identified gifted students are grouped into classrooms with teachers trained in gifted education. However, the gifted cluster classroom also comprises typical (non-gifted) students. In an action research study involving the comparison of students' achievement in mathematics, Brulles, Saunders, and Cohn (2010) found that gifted students in gifted cluster classrooms showed significantly higher achievement gains as compared to their peers in non-cluster classes. Furthermore, cluster grouping was found to be effective in meeting the needs of both the gifted and typical students, with greater growth in mathematics than in reading (Gentry & MacDougall, 2009; Gentry & Owen, 1999). Likewise, Matthews, Ritchotte, and McBee (2013) found statistically significant increment in the acquisition of skills in mathematics for both gifted and typical students in the years following cluster grouping, but they were unable to establish conclusively whether the benefits to the students were due to cluster grouping or the professional development of the teachers that improved the latter's ability to respond to their students' needs. Earlier studies conducted by Brulles et al. (2010) and Gentry and MacDougall (2009) claimed that teacher professional development is critical to the success of the cluster program model. Undoubtedly, teachers need adequate training to increase their competence in curriculum design, modification and differentiation, hence enabling them to cater to the learning needs of their gifted charges, as well as to engage them in a meaningful way.

In sum, there is a general agreement that student achievement can be significantly improved by diversifying learner experiences with some form of temporary and flexible ability grouping, accompanied by appropriate curriculum modification and/or differentiation to suit the needs of the learners (Tieso, 2003).

6.4.3 Curriculum Differentiation and Modification

Kaplan (2009, p. 107) posited that differentiation should include 'The who—the learner and his or her needs, interests, and abilities; the what—the content and skills of the subject matter to be taught; the how—the pedagogy to be used to teach the content, skills, or both; and the where—the setting, grouping, or both needed to effectively implement the curriculum (the what) to the learner (the who)'. In line with Kaplan's interpretation of the 'who' and 'what' aspects of differentiation, Passow (1962, p. 6) suggested that curriculum differentiation involves 'the recognition of differing learning rates, styles, interests and abilities' of learners and hence the provision of appropriate and meaningful experiences and instructions to suit diverse learner abilities and interests . This is echoed by Sisk (2009, p. 269) who described differentiation as 'changing the pace, level, or type of instruction in response to the gifted student's needs, learning styles, and interests'.

The process of curriculum differentiation for gifted learners should thus start with an assessment of these students' prior knowledge and abilities, to provide the basis for subsequent ability groupings and curriculum design or modification to match the actual needs of the various groups (Renzulli, 1994; Tomlinson, 1995, 1999). The outcomes of the prior-knowledge assessment would guide the process of curriculum modification, whereby the existing curriculum is revised in one or more ways, including (i) identification and removal of redundant/unchallenging/repetitive/inappropriate content, (ii) the application of higher order thinking through enhancement of the existing curriculum components, (iii) inclusion of new curricular content in line with new developments in the relevant disciplines, (iv) use of innovative pedagogies for content delivery and learner engagement, (v) the introduction of an interdisciplinary aspect to the curriculum, and (vi) leveraging new technologies to enhance learner experiences. Erickson (1998, p. 47) suggested that rather than randomly putting together a number of unconnected facts and skills in an attempt to design or revamp a curriculum, teachers should focus on 'essential understandings' which she described as 'foundational ideas on which students build increasing conceptual depth and understanding'. The curricula should thus focus primarily on key constructs and principles in a given discipline (Tieso, 2003), leaving room for the students to explore the details and deepen their understanding. According to Erikson, teachers should adopt a systems approach focusing on four main areas, namely (i) learning outcomes (expected students' knowledge and understanding, skills and abilities), (ii) the foundational knowledge base (key concepts and essential understandings) for the relevant area of study or discipline, (iii) key processes and skill sets for quality performance, and (iv) valid instruments and measures for performance assessment.

6.5 Application of New Technologies in Gifted Education

Siegle (2004, p. 33) professed that 'future education movements to promote students' technology literacy will serve gifted children well since current technology literacy goals are very compatible with many gifted and talented students' learning preferences. Some educators feel that technology is a boon to gifted education as they share the view that 'technology not only allows teachers to provide differentiated instruction for gifted children and adolescents, but also serves as an educational and creative outlet for some of the best and brightest minds in the world' (Periathiruvadi & Rinn, 2012, p. 153).

6.5.1 Diversifying Gifted Learners' Experiences Through Technology Literacy

Burkhardt et al. (2003, p. 15) defined technology literacy as knowledge about the nature of technology, its purposes, how it works and how it can be applied optimally to achieve specific outcomes. Siegle (2004, p. 33) posited that the current emphasis in technology development, data-driven virtual learning, offers ample opportunities for experiences that are attuned to gifted students' learning interests and preferences. Table 6.1 and the ensuing sections show the parallels between the gifted students' learning needs and preferences and the corresponding technology literacy competencies.

Complexity and depth. As discussed earlier, gifted learners experience boredom and disengagement, leading to underachievement if their curricula are not optimally challenging and do not meet their learning preferences and interests. A number of studies attempted to diversify gifted learners' experiences by exploring the use of technology in the gifted curriculum, whereby students had the opportunity to work on complex tasks requiring the use of multiple tools. For instance, in a study on math curriculum by Duda (2011), gifted students worked with graphing calculators and emulator programs to explore new concepts to help them get a deeper understanding

Table 6.1 Technology literacy and gifted learners' preferences

Gifted learners' needs and preferences	Technology literacy competencies
Complexity and depth in the curricula	Demonstration of sound conceptual understanding and proficiency in the use of technology systems Application of technology to identify and provide solutions to complex real-world problems
Flexibility and acceleration	Use of technology tools to increase productivity (by reducing production time)
Thinking critically	Demonstration of the ethical use of technology for the benefit of both society and self Use of technology to assess and evaluate information from a variety of sources
Creative engagement and production	Effective use of technology tools for creative production Use of technology tools to communicate ideas within and beyond the curriculum

of math theories and problems. Dove and Zitkovich (2003) explored gifted students' application of technology to identify and solve real-world problems, in a study in which the gifted students used digital cameras and palm-held computers to learn about environmental issues.

Flexibility and acceleration. Blair (2011) reported that online learning provided flexibility in the choice of courses and pace of learning. For instance, students could learn at their own pace and take courses that were challenging and of interest to them, unlike at school where they had to follow a pre-determined curriculum delivered at a pace that may not optimize their learning. With online learning, students are given the opportunity to accelerate their progress and gain advanced placement. This is facilitated by the availability of Massive Open Online Courses (MOOCs) on sites such as Coursera, Udemy, FutureLearn, amongst many others. Gifted learners are spoilt for choice with the gamut of courses they can explore.

Wallace (2005) described how technology can be leveraged to diversify academic experiences for gifted students through distance learning and virtual environments that serve as their window to the world. He gave the example of a distance education program run by the Center for Talented Youth at John Hopkins University, which offered options for enrichment, acceleration and advancement and garnered high satisfaction from participants. In this instance, courses were developed in different formats to suit the *individual* needs and readiness levels of the high-ability students.

Thinking critically and creatively. It was found that online courses, if organized effectively, could enhance the problem-solving skills of high-ability students (Bohmova & Rostejnska, 2009). Likewise, Siegle (2017) encouraged the introduction of coding in the curriculum as a means of enhancing students' problem-solving and organization skills. He advocates that through the process of troubleshooting coding errors, children will pick up values such as resilience and independent learning. Furthermore, in a separate study, Ng and Nicholas (2010) explored the feasibility of using online courses and online discussion forums as platforms for creating virtual thinking communities, where people have the opportunity to think critically and reflect. There is no shortage of social networking sites for gifted students to showcase their creative ideas or products. Many successful artists launched their careers with posts on Facebook, YouTube and Instagram, while Twitter is well-known as a platform of political discourse. In addition, these sites offer opportunities for the feedback and affirmation that gifted learners often crave for.

Technology and motivation. Housand and Housand (2012, p. 706) posited that students who are considered as digital natives 'utilize technology as an integral part of life, both in work and play, and therefore do not view technology use as an opportunity but, rather, as a fundamental tool for normal day-to-day functioning'. Technology-mediated strategies can thus enhance motivation if, as the Self-Determination Theory posits, the learner perceives the satisfaction of competence, relatedness and autonomy (Ryan & Deci, 2000).

Otto and Tavella (2010) found that high-ability students who have high competence, derive less satisfaction with their learning experience and are less motivated when they perceive the task to be too easy. Teachers and curriculum developers may consider the use of game-based learning (learning through games) and gamification (the application of game-like mechanics), which allow gifted students to level up and move to a more challenging task once they have successfully completed a previous one. This enables students to be optimally challenged throughout the learning experience.

Online discussion platforms and social media sites offer multiple opportunities for gifted students to connect and collaborate with like-minded peers globally. Learning management systems, such as Blackboard Learn, offer various solutions (e.g. Blackboard connect and Blackboard collaborate) that enable communication and collaboration amongst teachers, students and parents, thus catering to the fulfilment of students' needs for relatedness.

As for the satisfaction of autonomy, Reynolds and Caperton (2011), in their study on game development, posit that technology tools may be used to provide a sense of choice and volition in an incremental manner, starting with an impression of choice and progressing towards greater autonomous regulation as the learner acquires greater resilience and self-assurance. Thus, virtual worlds or computer-based simulated environments, such as Second Life, offer ample opportunities for autonomy in the learning experience. For instance, users are able to choose or design their avatars and the environment in which they operate. In education, the virtual world, Whyville, allows users to explore a variety of topics, including science, business, art and geography. Virtual worlds may also be used in conjunction with virtual learning environments for educational purposes, as with the integration of Second Life with the learning management system, Moodle (Livingstone & Kemp, 2008).

6.6　Conclusion

This chapter gives a review of seminal as well as recent publications that offer an introduction to the extant literature on gifted students and their learning. In that respect, the three focus areas identified showed that, contrary to popular belief, not all gifted students are high achievers, and those who underachieve could be motivated to improve if curricula are modified to provide them with novel experiences and optimal challenges, the affordances of which can be found in the new and emerging technologies of this century.

References

Adkins, K. K., & Parker, W. (1996). Perfectionism and suicidal preoccupation. *Journal of Personality, 64*(2), 529–543. Alexandria, VA: Association for Supervision and Curriculum Development.

Blair, R. (2011). Online learning for gifted students from the parents' perspectives. *Gifted Child Today, 34*(3), 28–30.

Böhmová, H., & Roštejnská, M. (2009). Chemistry for gifted and talented: On-line course on talnet. *Problems of Education in the 21st Century, 11*, 14–20.

Brulles, D., Saunders, R., & Cohn, S. J. (2010). Improving performance for gifted students in a cluster grouping model. *Journal for the Education of the Gifted, 34*(2), 327–350.

Burkhardt, G., Monsour, M., Valdez, G., Gunn, C., Dawson, M., Lemke, C., ... Martin, C. (2003). 21st century skills: Literacy in the digital age. Retrieved January, 29, 2008.

Burns, D. D. (1980). The perfectionist script for self-defeat. *Psychology Today*, 34–52.

Chan, D. W. (2010). Perfectionism among Chinese gifted and nongifted students in Hong Kong: The use of the revised almost perfect scale. *Journal for the Education of the Gifted, 34*, 68–98.

Clinkenbeard, P. R. (2012). Motivation and gifted students: Implications of theory and research. Psychology in the Schools, 49(7), 622–630.

Csikszentmihalyi, M. (1991). *Flow: The psychology of optimal experience* (Vol. 41). New York: HarperPerennial.

Csikszentmihalyi, M., Rathunde, K. R., & Whalen, S. (1993). *Talented teenagers: A longitudinal study of their development*. Cambridge University Press.

Dove, M. K., & Zitkovich, J. A. (2003). Technology driven group investigations for gifted elementary students. *Information Technology in Childhood Education Annual, 2003*(1), 223–241.

Duda, J. (2011). Mathematical Creative Activity and the Graphic Calculator. *International Journal for Technology in Mathematics Education, 18*(1).

Emerick, L. J. (1992). Academic underachievement among the gifted: Students' perceptions of factors that reverse the pattern. *Gifted Child Quarterly, 36*(3), 140–146.

Erickson, H. L. (1998). *Concept-based curriculum and instruction: Teaching beyond the facts*. Thousand Oaks, CA: Corwin Press.

Ford, D. Y. (1996). Reversing underachievement among gifted Black students: Promising practices and pro- grams. New York: Teachers College Press.

Gallagher, J. J., Harradine, C. C., & Coleman, M. R. (1997). Challenge or boredom? Gifted students' views on their schooling. *Roeper Review, 19*, 132–136.

Gentry, M. L. (1999). Promoting student achievement and exemplary classroom practices through cluster grouping: A research-based alternative to heterogeneous elementary classrooms.

Gentry, M., & MacDougall, J. (2009). Total school cluster grouping: Model, research, and practice. In J. S. Renzulli, E. J. Gubbins, S. K. McMillen, R. D. Eckert, & C. A. Little (Eds.), *Systems*

& *models for developing programs for the gifted & talented* (2nd ed., pp. 211–234). Mansfield Center, CT: Creative Learning Press.

Gentry, M., & Owen, S. (1999). An investigation of the effects of total school flexible cluster grouping on identification, achievement, and classroom practices. *Gifted Child Quarterly, 43*, 224–243. https://doi.org/10.1177/001698629904300402

Gottfried, A. E., & Gottfried, A. W. (1996). A longitudinal study of academic intrinsic motivation in intellectually gifted children: Childhood through early adolescence. *Gifted Child Quarterly, 40*(4), 179–183.

Hamachek, D. E. (1978). Psychodynamics of normal and neurotic perfectionism. *Psychology: A Journal of Human Behavior*.

Hewitt, P. L., & Dyck, D. G. (1986). Perfectionism, stress, and vulnerability to depression. *Cognitive Therapy and Research, 10*(1), 137–142.

Housand, B. C., & Housand, A. M. (2012). The role of technology in gifted students' motivation. *Psychology in the Schools, 49*(7), 706–715.

Kaplan, S. (2009). Myth 9: There is a single curriculum for the gifted. *Gifted Child Quarterly, 53*(4), 257.

Kulik, J. A. (1992). *An analysis of the research on ability grouping: Historical and contemporary perspectives*. Storrs, CT: National Research Center on the Gifted and Talented.

Kulik, J. A., & Kulik, C.-L.C. (1992). Meta-analytic findings on grouping programs. *Gifted Child Quarterly, 36*(2), 73–77.

Kwan, P. C. K. (1992). On a pedestal: Effects of intellectual-giftedness and some implications. *Educational Psychology, 12*, 37–62.

Kwek, K. (2007). *5 19) High anxiety: An elite affection? The Straits Times* (p. S10). Singapore: Singapore Press.

Little, C. A. (2012). Curriculum as motivation for gifted students. *Psychology in the Schools, 49*(7), 695–705.

Livingstone, D., & Kemp, J. (2008). Integrating web-based and 3D learning environments: Second life meets moodle. *UPGRADE (European Journal for the Informatics Professional), 9*(3), 8–14.

Matthews, M. S., Ritchotte, J. A., & McBee, M. T. (2013). Effects of schoolwide cluster grouping and within-class ability grouping on elementary school students' academic achievement growth. *High Ability Studies, 24*(2), 81–97.

Moore III, J. L., Ford, D. Y., & Milner, H. R. (2005). Recruitment is not enough: Retaining African American students in gifted education. *Gifted Child Quarterly, 49*(1), 51–67.

Ng, W., & Nicholas, H. (2010). A progressive pedagogy for online learning with high-ability secondary school students: A case study. *Gifted Child Quarterly, 54*(3), 239–251.

Otto, M., & Tavella, M. (2010). Motivation and engagement in computer-based learning tasks: Investigating key contributing factors. *World Journal on Educational Technology, 2*(1), 1 15.

Pacht, A. R. (1984). Reflections on Perfection. *American Psychologist, 39*(4), 386.

Parker, W. D. (1997). An empirical typology of perfectionism in academically talented children. *American Educational Research Journal, 34*(3), 545–562.

Parker, W. D., & Mills, C. J. (1996). The incidence of perfectionism in gifted students. *Gifted Child Quarterly, 40*(4), 194–199.

Passow, A. H. (1962). *Differentiated curricula for the gifted/talented*. Ventura, CA: Leadership Training Institute on the Gifted and Talented.

Periathiruvadi, S., & Rinn, A. N. (2012). Technology in gifted education: A review of best practices and empirical research. *Journal of Research on Technology in Education, 45*(2), 153–169.

Phillips, N., & Lindsay, G. (2006). Motivation in gifted students. *High Ability Studies, 17*(1), 57–73.

Rasmussen, A. (2019). Policy intersections in education for the gifted and talented in China and Denmark. In *Nordic-Chinese intersections within education* (pp. 173–193). Cham: Palgrave Macmillan.

Reis, S. M. (1993). *Why not let high ability students start school in January?* (p. 93106). Research Monograph: The Curriculum Compacting Study.

Reis, S. M., Burns, D. E., & Renzulli, J. S. (1992). *Curriculum compacting: A guide for teachers.* National Research Center on the Gifted and Talented.

Reis, S. M., & McCoach, D. B. (2000). The underachievement of gifted students: What do we know and where do we go? *Gifted Child Quarterly, 44*(3), 152–170.

Renzulli, J. S. (1994). *Schools for talent development: A practical plan for total school improvement.* Mansfield, CT: Creative Learning Press.

Renzulli, J. S., & Smith, L. H. (1978). *The compactor.* Mansfield Center, CT: Creative Learning.

Reynolds, R., & Caperton, I. H. (2011). Contrasts in student engagement, meaning-making, dislikes, and challenges in a discovery-based program of game design learning. *Educational Technology Research and Development, 59,* 267–289.

Roedell, W. C. (1984). Vulnerabilities of highly gifted children. *Roeper Review, 6*(3), 127–130.

Rogers, C. R. (1957). The necessary and sufficient conditions of therapeutic personality change. *Journal of Consulting Psychology, 21*(2), 95.

Rogers, K. B. (1991). The relationship of grouping practices to the education of the gifted and talented learner: Research-based decision making series.

Rogers, K. B. (2007). Lessons learned about educating the gifted and talented: A synthesis of the research on educational practice. *Gifted Child Quarterly, 51,* 382–396.

Ryan, R. M., & Deci, E. L. (2000). Self-determination theory and the facilitation of intrinsic motivation, social development, and well-being. *American Psychologist, 55*(1), 68.

Schuler, P. A. (2000). Perfectionism and gifted adolescents. *Journal of Secondary Gifted Education, 11*(4), 183–196.

Schunk, D. H., Pintrich, P. R., & Meece, J., L. (2008). Motivation in education (3rd Ed.). Upper Saddle River, NJ: Pearson Merrill Prentice Hall.

Siegle, D. (2004). The merging of literacy and technology in the 21st century: A bonus for gifted education. *Gifted Child Today, 27*(2), 32–35.

Siegle, D. (2017). Technology: Encouraging creativity and problem solving through coding. *Gifted Child Today, 40*(2), 117–123.

Silverman, L. K. (1990). The crucible of perfectionism. In *Mental health in a changing world* (pp. 39–49).

Sisk, D. (2009). Myth 13: The regular classroom teacher can "go it alone." *Gifted Child Quarterly, 53*(4), 269–271.

Slavin, R. E. (1987). Ability grouping and student achievement in elementary schools: A best-evidence synthesis. *Review of Educational Research, 57*(3), 293–336.

Sorensen, H., & Hallinan, S. (1986). Effects of ability grouping on growth in academic achievement. *American Educational Research Journal, 23*(4), 519–542.

Stephens, K. R., & Karnes, F. A. (2000). State definitions for the gifted and talented revisited. *Exceptional Children, 66*(2), 219–238.

Straub, J. H. (1987). An eclectic counseling approach to the treatment of panics. *Journal of Integrative & Eclectic Psychotherapy, 6*(4), 434–449.

Tannenbaum, A. J. (1986). Giftedness: A psychosocial approach. *Conceptions of Giftedness,* 21–52.

Tieso, C. L. (2003). Ability grouping is not just tracking anymore. *Roeper Review, 26*(1), 29–36.

Tomlinson, C. A. (1995). *How to differentiate instruction in mixed-ability classrooms.* Alexandria, VA: Association for Supervision and Curriculum Development.

Tomlinson, C. A. (1999). *The differentiated classroom: Responding to the needs of all learners.*

Tomlinson, C. A. (2003). *Fulfilling the promise of the differentiated classroom: Strategies and tools for responsive teaching.* Association for Supervision and Curriculum Development.

U.S. Congress, Public Law 91–230, April, 1970.

U.S. Department of Education. (1994). *National excellence: A case for developing America's youth.* Washington, DC: U.S. Government Printing Office.

Vallerand, R. J., Gagné, F., Senécal, C., & Pelletier, L. G. (1994). A comparison of the school intrinsic motivation and perceived competence of gifted and regular students. *Gifted Child Quarterly, 38*(4), 172–175.

VanTassel-Baska, J. (2005). Gifted programs and services: What are the nonnegotiables? *Theory into Practice, 44*(2), 90–97.

VanTassel-Baska, J., & Stambaugh, T. (2006). *Comprehensive curriculum for gifted learners* (3rd ed.). Boston: Allyn & Bacon.

Wallace, P. (2005). Distance education for gifted students: Leveraging technology to expand academic options. *High Ability Studies, 16*(1), 77–86.

Wang, C. W., & Neihart, M. (2015). How do supports from parents, teachers, and peers influence academic achievement of twice-exceptional students. *Gifted Child Today, 38*(3), 148–159. https://doi.org/10.1177/1076217515583742.

Winebrenner, S., & Brulles, D. (2008). *The cluster grouping handbook: A schoolwide model: How to challenge gifted students and improve achievement for all.* Free Spirit Publishing.

Yeo, L. S., & Pfeiffer, S. I. (2018). Counseling gifted children in Singapore: Implications for evidence-based treatment with a multicultural population. *Gifted Education International, 34*(1), 64–75. https://doi.org/10.1177/0261429416642284

Part II
Diversifying Learner Experiences Beyond the Classroom

Chapter 7
Learning Beyond Museum Walls: Virtual Excursions at Te Papa Tongarewa

David Bell and Jeffrey Smith

Abstract Most museums maintain an educational brief. In many, this is achieved through the integration of informal education programmes—guided and self-guided tours, and practical learning activities, often with curriculum-linked learning content—into single-visit class engagements. In the past, museums have supported these one-off, or occasionally repeat, visiting experiences with outreach support. This can take the form of museum educators visiting schools, or resource loan systems. Maintaining an amalgam of educator-implemented school visits and 'physically' exercised outreach programmes is difficult to coordinate and can tax museum resources. Digital media offer opportunities to expand the museum education purview, support (and even replace) on-site visitation and reach more learners, in different ways. This account examines the *Virtual Excursion* online visitation experience offered by The Museum of New Zealand Te Papa Tongarewa. It finds the *Excursion* programmes offer museum experiences for communities that are unable to access the Museum or outreach services in person. It also describes how the interface between technology-enhanced museum facility and school classroom settings accommodates diverse participants, learning dispositions and requirements, and aide-supported, culturally diverse, and collaborative learners.

Keywords Museum education · Outreach · Digital learning media

7.1 Museums and Outreach Education

This account examines the *Virtual Excursion* online visitation experience offered by The Museum of New Zealand Te Papa Tongarewa. It presents the *Excursion* programmes that offer museum experiences for communities unable to access the Museum or outreach services in person. It also describes how the interface between

D. Bell (✉) · J. Smith
University of Otago College of Education, Dunedin, New Zealand
e-mail: david.bell@otago.ac.nz

J. Smith
e-mail: jeffrey.smith@otago.ac.nz

© Springer Nature Singapore Pte Ltd. 2020   121
C. Koh (ed.), *Diversifying Learner Experience*,
https://doi.org/10.1007/978-981-15-9861-6_7

technology-enhanced museum facility and school classroom setting accommodates diverse participants, learning dispositions and requirements, and aide-supported, culturally diverse, and collaborative learners.

This chapter draws on an independent formative evaluation of the *Hinātōre* digital learning laboratory and *Virtual Excursion* programme at Te Papa Tongarewa (Bell & Smith, 2017). Its research employed a qualitative, abductive, inferential methodology. Data were collected from class observations, and interviews with students, class teachers, and Museum educators. Analysis focused on Te Papa's priority key competency areas of collaboration, communication, and cultural engagement, and also noted the impact on competencies of creativity, curiosity and critical thinking. Participant responses confirmed the effectiveness of the Museum's *Virtual Excursions* for providing collaborative, accessible, inclusive and effective learning engagements. They acknowledged the appeal of the combination of personal contact and low-tech requirements for inclusive and classroom-based learning, and confirmed their immediate and retentive learning effectiveness and remarkable potential for scalability. For students, the experience introduced new opportunities for inquiry learning in, and beyond, their own classrooms. The chapter describes how the *Virtual Excursion* operates in practice, evaluates its effectiveness for all participants, and commends the accessibility, flexibility and scalability of this model as an exemplar suitable for application in a range of other museum settings.

Museums and related cultural institutions offer experiences of enjoyment and pleasure, social engagement, contemplation, or cultural enrichment. They also provide rich resources for learning. A commitment to 'the purposes of education, study and enjoyment' (ICOM, 2007) informs policy, curatorial practice and visitor experience in most museums. Visitors value 'the museum experience for its ability to present interesting information…new knowledge and intellectual challenges' (Tinio, Smith, & Smith, 2014, p. 198). School classes visiting these institutions enjoy the cognitive benefits of sensory or somatic learning, and acquire new skills working directly with collection artefacts (Durham University, 2018). Trained museum educators can support students by contextualising learning, fostering critical inquiry, cultivating subjective responses, and fostering social engagements that favour positive learning dispositions (Bell, 2017).

The on-site museum visit model has limitations, however. Not all schools can access museums in person, and successful integration of museum learning into the classroom curriculum can require repeat visits. Many museums respond to these issues by offering outreach visits or object loans: 'bring[ing] the museum to the media center of the school' or public place (Blenz-Clucas, 1993, p. 150). Outreach educators can meet children, prepare them for the on-site experience, introduce visit protocols, share preparatory resources, and establish contexts, questions or activities for the visit. Subsequently, museums can offer teachers further resource and teaching support. Even modest museums can make educators 'available for classroom visits, school assemblies, civic organizations, and other groups' (Oregon Nikkei Endowment Center, 2018). They can arrange school loans of display materials of artefacts, poster or wall displays, together with dedicated guidelines and lesson plans to enhance classroom activities. In some ambitious initiatives, museums forge partnerships between their education teams, schools and practitioners in other institutions (SFMOMA, 2018a). These 'transformative partnerships have been cited as an innovative, effective way for museums, galleries and schools to work together to enrich classroom curricula, support student success, and facilitate the utilisation of available community museum and cultural resources' (Eckhoff, 2011, p. 256).

Outreach services may also tax museum time, staff and budget resources. They may be unable to reach the distant or low-decile schools that are unable to visit the museum itself. Digital media can ameliorate these problems. Museum education websites offer teachers access to age-specific and curriculum-linked resources, including contextual materials, posters, video links, study guides for teachers, artefact discussion questions and fora for teacher discussion (SFMOMA, 2018b). Using online collection links, learners can search, locate, and download quality images of artefacts and documentation to support learning from their own classroom (British Museum, 2018). Some sites allow learners to engage in museum-based research, working collaboratively, while developing their own personally inflected learning experiences through inquiry research pathways (National Park Service, 2018). Using museum archives, students can independently develop skills of observation, inference and critical thinking. Some museums have also initiated 'virtual excursion' facilities through which learners can 'virtually' visit the museum itself. These experiences can extend the purview of museum education teams to embrace international communities of learners into their learning worlds (White Rabbit Gallery, 2018).

7.2 Outreach at the Museum of New Zealand Te Papa Tongarewa

The Museum of New Zealand Te Papa Tongarewa education team offers outreach support in two ways. First, their attractively presented, accessible, online resources aim to 'bring the national museum into your classroom with our free, cross-curricular range of educational resources—including fun, interactive ideas to support students' learning aims' (Te Papa, 2018a). Teachers select materials from seventeen categories to support teaching and learning in culture and language, the arts, sciences, or history. Materials are learner focused; many have been developed from on-site learning activities, and include contributions from children.

Te Papa's second outreach medium is their *Virtual Excursions Ngā Hāerere Mariko* online visit experience (Te Papa, 2018b). Using just a computer with a webcam and microphone in their classroom, teachers can access personalised 60-min *Virtual Excursions* at Te Papa, each led by one of the Museum's educators (and sometimes curatorial or language expert staff; Streeter, 2018). These 'excursions' are suitable for learners aged between three and thirteen, in groups of up to 30, at a total cost of $50 per session. They promise opportunities to

- connect with one of our friendly and knowledgeable educators, using Zoom, to explore a real Te Papa exhibition without leaving the classroom
- talk directly with the educator as they walk through the space with a Steadicam
- ask questions, request close-ups and influence the tour's focus
- discover incredible *taonga* treasures and their stories as though you were here with them (Te Papa, 2018b).

Teachers can negotiate their own class learning levels, special interests or curriculum focus for one of five excursion themes: *Matauranga Māori* (New Zealand Māori culture topics); *Tangata o le Moana: The Story of Pacific people in New Zealand*; *Gallipoli: The Scale of Our War*; bespoke *Explore Te Papa* topics of their choice (including the collection storerooms) and *Toi Art* exhibitions.

Researchers at the University of Otago College of Education conducted an independent evaluation of Te Papa's *Virtual Excursion* programmes and its *Hīnātore* digital learning laboratory in 2017 (Bell & Smith, 2017). This formative study focused on the evaluation of short-term outcomes and their implications for sustained learning. It sought to inform the development of Te Papa programmes, and to contribute to the wider informal education sector. The research focused on Museum priority competencies of collaboration, communication, and cultural engagement, and on links to Te Papa's collections, hands-on activities, and cultivating learner agency. Researchers also noted incidental impacts in competencies of creativity, curiosity and critical thinking, equity of access to the Museum, and Te Papa's ongoing experimentation with new modes of on-site and distance education.

7.3   Methodology, Methods and Procedure

To conduct this independent evaluation of visitor and provider experiences of the *Virtual Excursion* programmes, the researchers adopted a qualitative abductive inference methodology, focusing their research on a pathway through observation, to explanation, into prediction (Walton, 2001). This allowed them to maintain open relationships between premise and conclusion, and to tailor their data gathering opportunities to appropriate instances arising in the education team's arrangements with school class groups. Initial negotiation established a target range between Year 1 and Year 8 generalist primary classes in two schools in the Dunedin education community. Early in the preparatory phase a further group, a Year 11 History class was included to provide a specialist subject class experience to complement the generalist primary class findings. The outcomes of this research pathway established an initial interface, design, trial and evaluation platform that may inform an inclusive, iterative, longitudinal research pathway in the future.

Research methods included the collection of data from observations of classes during the excursion sessions. These were followed by open-question interviews with school classroom teachers, student participant groups and Te Papa educators. Each teacher responded to the Te Papa team's five-item Likert scale evaluation immediately after their excursion. The project thus comprised on-site school classroom observation of the activities as they were being experienced; interviews with participating students and interviews with participating teachers and Te Papa educators. Data were analysed to determine value experiences and short-term impact of Te Papa distance learning experiences, and to establish a foundation for an investigation examining longer-term outcomes. The research was granted University of Otago Category A Ethics Approval and Ngāi Tahu Research Consultation Committee Approval. Data were collected in school term 3 2017, analysis and evaluation and the preparation of the research report were completed through October/November, and the final report was presented in December 2017.

Observation and interview data were compared to Te Papa key competencies of collaboration, communication and cultural engagement; incidental competencies in creativity, curiosity and critical thinking; and broader impact areas in using Te Papa objects and displays, digital technologies, new modes of learning, and providing enhanced equity of access for learners. Conversations with classroom teachers were developed through series of linked open questions: How were you able to negotiate your Te Papa learning experiences to best inform your classroom programme? How did you prepare your children for the *Virtual Excursion* experience? How did the Te Papa experience enhance your own, and your children's competencies in the fields of Collaborative skills; Communication skills; Cultural engagement; in making links with objects in the Te Papa collections? In what other ways did the Te Papa experience inform your class learning experience? How has the Te Papa experience impacted on subsequent teaching and learning engagements in your classroom? In future Te Papa learning experiences, are there any other areas you would like the museum educators to focus on?

Researcher conversations with student participant groups were developed through the following open-ended questions: How would you describe your *Virtual Excursion* at Te Papa? Describe a new discovery you made during your Te Papa visit. What was the most interesting thing you did during your Te Papa experience? How has it helped you with your classwork at school? If your class can come back to Te Papa what is one thing would you like to do again? If you can 'come back to' Te Papa, what is the *new* thing you would you like to find out next? If you could bring your friend or your family to Te Papa outside school time, what is the first thing you would want to share with them?

Te Papa educators were asked: How did you negotiate these experiences with the classroom teachers? How did you relate learning to the class curriculum focus? Explain how you feel you have engaged children in collaborative learning; enhancing communication skills; cultural engagement?

7.4   Summary of Research Findings

Researchers observed each class during their virtual visit, and conducted interviews with teachers, and between six and twelve children selected by the teacher from each class, five weeks after the excursion. Two Year 5/6 classes from a single primary school participated in the research. The students in one class discussed the available themes and selected a *Mountains to Sea* ecological theme. The second teacher chose the *Gallipoli* theme to enhance the class study of ANZAC (Australian and New Zealand Army Corps). The Year 11 History class complemented their recent study of the First World War with a *Gallipoli* tour (Te Papa, 2018c). Four out of the six Year 11 students interviewed had visited the exhibit in person and with their families earlier in the year.

7.4.1   Value Experience Relating to Collaboration, Communication and Cultural Engagement

7.4.1.1   Collaboration

Class teachers were very positive about the collaboration in *Virtual Excursions*. The experiences effectively cultivated collaborations between Te Papa educators, class-room teachers and students. These underpinned the success of pre-visit discussions and the excursions themselves. The successful engagement of all participants was enhanced by the collaborative dispositions of Te Papa educators and the responsive guidance of class teachers.

Te Papa team skills contributed to effective pre-visit negotiations of each excursion experience. Teachers appreciated the contact with educators in setting up the tour. They received clear advice about how sessions worked, and how to access the technical interface between classroom and Museum. School teachers were able to relate learning to class themes, or internal assessments. Procedures viewing, communicating and appointment of a class 'chair' or speaker were clearly established prior to the event. *Google Hangouts* was used for all three excursions.

Te Papa educators were positive and inclusive. They cultivated a sense of 'being there' by greeting learners at the Museum entrance, and using their cameras to guide them upstairs to the displays, pausing to discuss key exhibits—te waharoa, the entrance gateway, or a giant ammonite, for example. Panning camera views allowed children to see where they were, look around and situate themselves. Educators initiated ako-style reciprocal relationships that drew students into the learning conversations. Adept coordination of camera and dialogue enhanced a focus on qualities of spectacle (the peculiarities of the colossal squid, for example) that captured children's imaginations and sustained collaborations between educators and children.

Educators encouraged student collaborations by inviting them to 'chat amongst themselves' around clearly framed questions like 'why do you think he did this?'

These brief intervals gave students time to discuss, think and share ideas. Students discussed these questions vigorously. This enhanced a sense of inclusive participation and 'voice', accommodated subjective responses, and provoked perceptive observations. Te Papa educators informed collaborative investigations beyond the excursion itself. Links were offered to each class to Te Papa visual resources, websites or YouTube links (a carnivorous snail video was extremely popular). This encouraged class collaboration as learners extended their research following the visit. Educators also invited classes to forward questions to them, encouraging opportunities for post-visit collaboration.

While Te Papa educators led excursion narratives, class teachers guided response and collaborations in the classroom. Teachers managed their learners as they organised the classroom, and monitored movement and access to microphones. They repeated questions and responses for clarity, and ensured all children had opportunities to respond. They clarified terms and objects introduced by the Museum educator, noting examples on the whiteboard, or referring to classroom posters. One teacher noted that this learning model required children to work alongside each other, negotiating access to laptops, listening, thinking about what was said and about other children's responses. This established collaborative learning interactions that extended beyond the excursion into subsequent class investigations.

7.4.1.2 Communication

Effective visual and verbal communication underpinned each excursion. Teachers confirmed the positive benefits of the *Virtual Excursion* for enhancing children's communication skills. The experience required the exercise of looking, listening, and speaking skills, and adapting speaking for the microphone. It cultivated confidence in communication, and encouraged children to ask their own questions.

Educators balanced periods of question and response with informative commentaries around display content. The i-Phone/camera provided a key communication device. Being able to see the educators in 'selfie-shots' shared a sense of their own enthusiasm and emotional responses through their questions, gestures and eye contact. Switching between 'selfie' mode, wide-angle, tracking, panning, close-up or zooming shots guided students' scrutiny of displays. Sequences of looking, identifying and interpretative questions invited students into critical thinking events, asking them to contextualise their observations, infer, question different points of view, support responses with evidence or see things in a range of ways. Student evaluations suggested that communication was in some regards richer than in on-site visits.

Educator commentaries developed learning narratives and sustained student interest. Their engaging conversational style supported learner "buy in". They structured conversations through inductive sequences of what? why? where? or how? questions. Visual strategies engaged learner interest by establishing diverse looking skills, from whole display review into scrutiny of detail supported by using the camera to move in on detail areas like the passage of the eye. Conversations developed through identifying questions, into description ('what is happening here?'), into analysis ('how many?' 'when?'), through comparisons ('how was this different from…?') that accommodated different points of view, into interpretation or empathetic questions ('how do you think she felt?' 'how would you feel?' 'so why do you think that?').

These diverse question strategies underpinned effective communication. Using *open questions* early in each experience invited *close scrutiny* and *interpretations* of what learners saw. Thus, with the giant ammonite display, the question 'does anyone know what this creature was?' was extended through *visualising* 'what do you think it looked like?' followed by *descriptions* of its appearance, size and how it operated. These questions encouraged children to share their own knowledge and opinions throughout each excursion. Educators encouraged this with *inquiring questions*— 'what do we know about?'—that asked students to draw on their existing knowledge, and helped to structure a relation between the exhibits, learner knowledge, and the construction of common appreciations of themes and objects. *Inclusive questions inviting multiple responses* accommodated different ways of thinking and responding in response to display themes. Subsequent questions invited children to *speculate* on their observations: '*how do you think* they did this?' Some invited *non-verbal responses*—making the noises of a giant snail devouring a milk worm—or simply to listen to display sound effects in ways that intensified their multi-sensory appreciations of the displays. *What do you think?* questions invited *individually subjective responses.* Questions encouraging *imaginative engagement*—what do you think it was like? What would you do?—encouraged students to imagine how humans or animals might feel or experience events.

Effective communication was supported by reference to museum wall matter, with close-up camera views of labels, tables and illustrative materials. Educators allowed sufficient time for children to explore material, think about it and ask their own questions. Guiding students into the analysis of statistics brought home the magnitude of events—from Gallipoli to the migration of the godwit—in an objective, informative manner. Educators invited students to examine display-matter *as research evidence.* They led them through the examination and interpretation of photographs or contemporary records of historical events. These insights fostered each student's subjective responses. Fostering *empathetic learning*—'how do you think he felt? Why do you think he felt that way?'—was especially effective in displays of death, grief and loss. Students valued this empathetic learning, and in some instances were deeply moved. All educators *invited students to ask their own questions,* and to forward post-visit questions via their class teachers. Students commented that they valued these opportunities, and that the responses expanded on their prior knowledge.

Classroom teachers played key roles in managing effective communication within the class and between students and Te Papa educators. They directed learners' attention to specific details in the projected images, and clarified questions of scale when these arose. They supported museum educators in monitoring classes for 'silent signals' like hands-up gestures. Cultivating more specific mediating roles for classroom teachers might enhance this participation in the future. Conducting tours prior to museum opening time eliminated the distraction of public presence experienced in on-site visits.

7.4.1.3 Cultural Engagement

Opportunities for enhancing cultural engagement varied significantly between excursion themes. The ecology experience embraced te reo Māori language alongside English in discussing names of flora, fauna and place. Learners respected this, and responded in te reo. This also helped students situate learning within Aotearoa New Zealand habitats. Classroom teachers could opt into the *Matauranga Māori* cultural topic in subsequent sessions to develop complementary appreciations of culturally significant practices, rituals or community relationships with the eco-environment. Two Year 5/6 children suggested, assertively, it would be interesting to learn more about Māori cultural perspectives on the human impact on ecosystems and conservation.

Gallipoli excursions introduced themes of cultural difference and similarity—of national identity, for example, and of values and gender roles. In both excursion themes ako reciprocal teaching/learning practices enhanced skills, attitudes and dispositions in te tino uaratanga o aroha, manaakitanga, mana whenua, a mana aotūroa—te ao Māori values of empathy, sharing, respect, inclusion, belonging, and exploration that underpin the vision, values and competencies of the *New Zealand Curriculum* (Ministry, 2007).

7.4.2 Observing Key Competencies in Creativity, Curiosity and Critical Thinking

While the research brief focused on priority competencies of collaboration, communication and cultural engagement, the researchers also maintained a watching brief for instances or potentials of creative curiosities and critical thinking.

7.4.2.1 Creative Curiosities

All educators offered explicit guidance into students own explorations that encouraged the imaginative, empathetic, connection-making, questioning, curiosities that underpin creative learning and practice. They inspired Year 5/6 students especially to extend their excursion learning in new and exciting directions. Children sustained their independent investigations for several weeks after the excursion itself. Year 11 *Gallipoli* tour students demonstrated creative initiatives in independently building positive links between what they learned in the excursion and the cognitive and skill expectations of achievement standard assessments.

7.4.2.2   Cultivating Critical Thinking

All educators encouraged learners, individually, or in groups, to think critically, and to construct meaningful links between museum displays, educator commentaries, and classroom questions. Conversational strategies inviting learners to *look, describe, classify* or *identify, analyse, interpret, compare, inquire, speculate, imagine, empathise,* or *express* themselves cultivated these opportunities.

Class conversations valued multiple responses representing different perspectives. With the *Gallipoli* theme in particular, these multi-view strategies encouraged students to think beyond historical narratives, and appreciate the deprivation and struggle experienced by the soldiers themselves. Te Papa educators maintain an ongoing practice of reflexive self-review. In the year following the research, this has enhanced their critical thinking approaches using the *Visual Thinking Strategies* model (Jones, 2018; Visual Thinking Strategies, 2018).

7.4.3   Identifying Learner Engagement in Broader Te Papa Impact Areas

Researchers recorded the ways educators used objects from the collections, employed digital technologies, experimented with new modes of learning and provided enhanced (national) equity of access to Te Papa learning opportunities.

7.4.3.1   Using Te Papa Objects and Displays

Arranging *Virtual Excursions* in the hour before Te Papa opened to the public allowed participants to concentrate on displays without interruption. Educators made effective use of displays to establish learning narratives, a sense of temporality, or to initiate in-depth commentary or discussion. Teachers noted that viewing collection displays and objects, even via the video link, made learning 'real' to the children, and made ecological connections and human relationships explicit. This was effective learning. History students also appreciated the ways the detailed and informative commentaries were interwoven around engaging displays, revealing significant details several students had not noticed in their personal visits to the exhibit.

Educators employed displays as *evidential sources* to inform learners' interpretative investigations in each theme. Te Papa displays *situated* learning in recognisable settings, affording a sense of *authenticity* or 'bringing things to life' for the learners. This in turn informed *empathetic* learning and subjective, 'felt', experience. Learners appreciated that the visual learning through juxtapositions of photographs and displays, and visual engagement with dioramas enhanced better understandings of material they had studied prior to the excursion. They also acknowledged how the displays provoked in-depth discussion, and balanced appreciations of all sides of a situation. These engagements encouraged an interest in extended learning—students repeatedly stated their desire for return visits to Te Papa with their families.

7.4.3.2 Using Digital Technologies for Effective Distance Learning

Participants were highly effective in using existing technology in the service of learning. These learners were very familiar with the smartphone as a vehicle for communication. The notion of someone somewhere using a smartphone to bring friends or family into a situation at a distance occurs all the time for many of them. Museum educators capitalised on this in their adoptions of digital technologies. The *Google Hangouts* app underpinned the ease of classroom access to the *Virtual Excursions*. Class teachers acknowledged that straightforward connections favoured punctual, trouble-free engagement. Te Papa educators used their low-tech devices very effectively to situate learners in museum spaces, and track their virtual movement through the displays. Participants experienced a sense of moving through the galleries, and engaging with displays. They appreciated the stable and clear camera operation, and the way it was used to guide closer scrutiny than some had experienced in person. Educators' versatile shifts between camera viewpoints conveyed their own enthusiasms, personalised the experience for students, and helped them relate to the educators.

Classroom participants experienced two limitations with these technologies. First, many students struggled to make their own questions heard, and educators were challenged to 'read' non-verbal responses. While teachers repeated questions, and educators were patient, this may have compromised the impetus of the learning narratives. Educators compensated by making their own enthusiasms, attitudes, and curiosities clear verbally and visually. Second, though screen projections were clear, they were smaller than the Museum interiors. Together with the peculiarities of Museum light conditions, this occasionally conditioned student's perceptions of scale or atmosphere.

7.4.3.3 Providing Enhanced Equity of Access for Learners

All school participants found the *Virtual Excursion* accessible and straightforward. The Te Papa reception process was collegial, positive and helpful in identifying excursions appropriate for class learning themes, arranging visitation times, and explaining how the excursions operated. Classes found the technology easy to operate. They particularly appreciated Te Papa educator contributions of resources and online links to inform subsequent class and independent children's learning, and offers to support learners after the visit itself. Class teachers accessed theme-specific Te Papa online resources in the weeks following their excursions.

7.4.3.4   Participant Interview Outcomes and Positive Learning Experiences

Class teachers confirmed their high satisfaction with the *Virtual Excursions*. Year 5/6 teachers indicated that they found this to be a positive and profitable engagement with the Te Papa resources, much enhanced by the educators' skills. They would love to use this again as an igniter—it generated a degree of passion and excitement in the children, capturing their imagination and motivating learning. The secondary teacher also acknowledged the positive impact of the learning, even in a single session. She subsequently rewrote her programme to embrace Te Papa online links and the excursion in the next year.

Analysis of the Te Papa Likert scale questionnaire returns revealed broad approval, but also a differential in learner responses to the visits. While all primary learners (aged 9–10) responded, less than half of the older students (aged 15–16) did so. Primary participants showed overwhelming approval; 70% of Year 11 respondents indicated a 3 judgement on the 5-point scale. This may reflect the timing of the experience within class programmes. Year 11 students noted an earlier virtual experience might better inform their preparation for internally assessed assignments on cause and consequence for national certificate qualifications.

Primary learners were highly engaged during and after the excursions and demonstrated high cognitive retention rates. The clarity and accuracy of interview responses revealed that material had anchored firmly in individual and class memories. Children were able to identify all key examples introduced during the excursion, and explain the significant interests of each in detail. They appreciated the ways the educators had made the experiences vivid, and provided avenues for class extension. They had all capitalised on these in enjoyable independent research projects. Children's interests were especially piqued by quirky or provocative characteristics—glowing milky guts, or donut shaped squid brains—or by the provocation of empathetic responses. The pace of each visit was intense. Children suggested they would have enjoyed longer, slower visits, with pauses for more looking, thinking and discussion. They also expressed some interest in exploring the wider worlds of Te Papa, including its 'store-room', a theme that has subsequently been adopted into the excursion repertoire (Streeter, 2018).

Secondary students also demonstrated high retention rates. Students felt the excursion 'brought learning to life', enhancing 'getting inside' situations and individual experiences. They remembered the subtle details of displays and commentaries—more so than several had retained from in-person visits.

7.5   Conclusion

'Virtual visits' are not unique to Te Papa Tongarewa. Some institutions use non-interactive PowerPoint photo-albums (Portland Japanese Garden, 2018) or 360-degree video display scans (Royal Ontario Museum, 2018). These allow classes to orient themselves to displays, spatial arrangements, and juxtapositions prior to on-site visits to the museums. Others use *Google Street View*-type technology to allow participants to 'walk' through galleries, with link buttons to access text or video narratives about objects (White Rabbit Gallery, 2018). Five qualities distinguish Te Papa's *Virtual Excursions* from these experiences. First, their accessibility and flexibility offer easy use in the classroom. Their technologies are familiar to participants and available in most schools. Teachers appreciated being able to tailor experiences to their own learning, and Te Papa support for post-visit learning. The medium can be adapted quickly and cheaply to a broad range of Te Papa's extensive collections. The medium can accommodate opportunities for rich cultural engagement, in both the bi-cultural focus and multi-cultural dimensions of its exhibits.

Second, learning was effective. Students revealed impressive cognitive retention. In each primary class, students had been inspired to find out more, accessing resources suggested by educators, and developing their own research investigations. Participants acknowledged an effective 'connectedness' between classroom and Museum, and between learning and displays. Like Malaguchi's notion of the environment as the 'third teacher' (Biermeier, 2015), both Museum and class settings fostered further learning around the Te Papa themes. Educators effective synthesis of commentary and guiding the viewer's eye to trace links between objects and sustain learner attentions engendered a sense of 'being there'; viewers were able to accommodate to the fact that they were viewing artefacts in a different medium "and 'look past' the limitations of the medium" to engage a convincing sense of 'facsimile accommodation' (Locher, Smith, & Smith, 1999, p. 128).

Third, the successes of these virtual outreach engagements were enriched by the inclusive dispositions, rich cognitive stock and effective skills of its educators. Researchers acknowledged the reciprocal engagements that enriched both the pedagogic and cultural dimensions of learning. Class teachers acknowledged the care with which Te Papa teams considered their learning environment, class curriculum and thematic focus. The infectious enthusiasms of excursion educators inspired learners to engage eagerly, and extend their learning subsequently. These lively interactions encouraged the exchange of ideas, free flow of questions and sharing of resources. The researchers recognise also the commitment of Te Papa education teams to reflective evaluation, and refining their practices and relationships—evident in post-research programme developments. (Streeter, 2018). One outcome of these dispositions has been a redevelopment of several of the Museum's Hīnātore digital learning laboratory strategies, and the innovation of melded excursion and digital learning experiences in the display areas at the museum. These new practices would be the focus of an extended research study during 2020.

Fourth, the remarkable potentials for transferability and scalability of Te Papa's *Virtual Excursions* have great capacity for engaging a range of national and even international audiences. This was a constructive use of what normally would be downtime for the Museum. If there were a strong commitment to productively using the Museum during this time, multiple tours with highly trained volunteers could bring the excursions to classrooms across the nation, or even internationally, on an ongoing basis. It would be close to a revolutionary idea for museums. Operating outside the usual constraints of public programming, Te Papa's rapidly developing digital visitation interface could be adapted even further to include innovative combinations of onsite and distance learning, offer multiple visits simultaneously, or *Virtual Excursion* broadcasts, or provide professional development opportunities for teachers.

The adaptability of digital excursion programmes like these favours their adoption in many different settings or societies—including those in which the practical constructs of 'school', "classroom' or 'museum', may differ from those of this study. Given access to basic digital technologies, the transferability of excursion narratives and conversational strategies, their inclusive nature, their affordability, and their capacities for forging effective connectedness between museum and classroom offer models of practice for learning in, and between, diverse societies or cultural communities.

Most importantly, the *Virtual Excursions* diversified learners' horizons. They provided entrée into an otherwise inaccessible institution. They gave the 'museum outing', and domestic digital media a new, enlivened, and informed sense of purpose. Students located and used new ways of learning with objects, curatorial constructs, and a wealth of museum resources that could be sustained beyond the excursion itself. The visits drew them into new communities of knowledge they could access in the future, independently or in groups. Importantly, they also cultivated the competencies (communication, collaboration, cultural engagement) and dispositions (creative curiosities, critical faculties and purposeful digital engagement) to inform these engagements. These visits were important because they empowered learners for the skills and social engagements of learning beyond the walls of the classroom.

Te Papa's virtual visits have introduced rich potentials for national access by Te Papa's regional communities. They have stimulated the enthusiasms of children and other participants and stakeholders for the learning activities they foster. Their flexibility and accessibility have significant capacity for transferability and scalability. Most importantly, they serve their Museum education brief, communities and charter responsibilities by cultivating effective learning and accommodating equal access of learners from every part of New Zealand—and beyond.

Acknowledgements We would like to thank the management and education teams at The Museum of New Zealand Te Papa Tongarewa for initiating, funding, and supporting our research there, and also the learning communities who participated. This chapter was completed during University of Otago Research and Study Leave.

References

Bell, D., & Smith, J. (2017). *Evaluation of the Hīnātore learning laboratory and virtual excursion experiences at the Museum of New Zealand Te Papa Tongarewa.* Commissioned report. Dunedin, NZ: University of Otago College of Education.

Bell, D. (2017). Aesthetic encounters and learning in the museum. *Educational Philosophy and Theory, 49*(8), 776–787.

Biermeier, M. A. (2015). Inspired by Reggio Emilia: Emergent curriculum in relationship-driven learning environments. *Young Children, 70*(5). Retrieved from https://www.naeyc.org/resources/pubs/yc/nov2015/emergent-curriculum.

Blenz-Clucas, B. (1993, September). Bring the museum to the media center. *School Library Journal,* 150–153.

British Museum. (2018). *Collections online.* Retrieved from https://www.britishmuseum.org/research/collection_online/search.aspx.

Durham University. (2018). *4schools.* Retrieved from https://www.dur.ac.uk/4schools/.

Eckhoff, A. (2011). Transformative partnerships: Designing school-based visual arts outreach programmes. *The International Journal of Art & Design Education, 30*(2), 256–265.

ICOM (International Council of Museums). (2007). *ICOM statutes.* https://archives.icom.museum/statutes.html#2.

Jones, L. (2018, August 24). Museum of New Zealand Te Papa Tongarewa. Personal Correspondence.

Locher, P., Smith, L., & Smith, J. (1999). Original paintings versus slide and computer reproductions: A comparison of viewer responses. *Empirical Studies of the Arts, 17*(2), 121–129.

National Park Service. (2018). *Questioning artifacts: Teaching with museum collections.* Retrieved from https://www.nps.gov/goga/learn/education/loader.cfm?csModule=security/getfile&PageID=206243.

New Zealand Ministry of Education (Ministry). (2007). *The New Zealand curriculum.* Wellington: Learning Media.

Oregon Nikkei Legacy Center. (2018). *Japanese American history museum.* Retrieved from https://www.oregonnikkei.org/education.htm.

Portland Japanese Garden. (2018). *Portland Japanese garden virtual tour.* Retrieved from https://japanesegarden.org/wp-content/uploads/2017/01/Portland_Japanese_Garden_Virtual_Tour.pdf.

Royal Ontario Museum. (2018). *Learning: Activities and resources.* Retrieved from https://www.rom.on.ca/en/learn/activities.

SFMOMA (San Francisco Museum of Modern Art). (2018a). *Building bridges between schools and art.* Retrieved from https://www.sfmoma.org/educators/school-partnerships-projects/.

SFMOMA (San Francisco Museum of Modern Art). (2018b). *Teacher resources.* Retrieved from https://www.sfmoma.org/teacher-resources/.

Streeter, P. (2018, October 15). Museum of New Zealand Te Papa Tongarewa. Personal communication.

Te Papa Tongarewa. (2018a). *Teaching resources ngā raumi mā te pouako.* Retrieved from https://www.tepapa.govt.nz/learn/for-educators/teaching-resources.

Te Papa Tongarewa. (2018b). *Virtual excursions ngā hāereere mariko.* Retrieved from https://www.tepapa.govt.nz/learn/for-educators/virtual-excursions.

Te Papa Tongarewa. (2018c). *Gallipoli: The scale of our war.* Retrieved from https://gallipoli.tepapa.govt.nz/.

Tinio, P. L., Smith, J. K., & Smith, L. F. (2014). The walls do speak: Psychological aesthetics and the museum experience. In P. L. Tinio & J. K. Smith (Eds.), *The Cambridge handbook of the psychology of aesthetics and art* (pp. 195–218). Cambridge, UK: Cambridge University Press.

Visual Thinking Strategies. (2018). *VTS Visual thinking strategies.* Retrieved from https://vtshome.org/.

Walton, D. (2001). Abductive, presumptive and plausible arguments. *Informed Logic, 21*(2), 141–169.

White Rabbit Gallery. (2018). *The sleeper awakes virtual tour.* Retrieved from https://www.whiterabbitgallerytours.com/.

Chapter 8
Play and Flow: Harnessing Flow Through the Power of Play in Adult Learning

Isabelle Ong

Abstract In the past decade, there has been a surge of interest in adult learning through play. Play is an organic medium of communication and provides a creative interface for humans to experiment with ideas and advance thought complexity. The purported benefits of playing in adult learning encompass psychological and physical health benefits not limited to creativity, stress management and academic performance. Currently, researchers are exploring ways individuals can optimize learning by entering a state of 'flow' where they become fully immersed when engaged in a single task. Despite the strong semblance between flow and play, there are no known research studies examining the intersection between flow, play and adult learning. Driven by this research gap, the key purpose of this article is to delineate the concepts of flow and play and consider their intersection in adult learning based on the developmental continuum of the eight play selves developed by Cook-Greuter (Dissertation Abstracts International 60:3000, 1999). Through the lens of flow theory, the concept of harnessing play to diversify learner experiences and optimize adult learning will be detailed along with suggestions on intentionally incorporating play activities to create the optimal conditions for flow. Implications for practice and research in higher education settings are discussed.

Keywords Flow theory · Play · Optimize adult learning · Play selves · Flow-play intersection

8.1 Introduction

Worldwide, educators are facing a challenge with efficiently providing diverse experiences to learners through the development of innovative practices, and the provision of learning tools and supportive environments (Corbeil, 1999). Historically, educational institutions have been confronted with the long-standing challenge of providing experiences for learners that are both engaging and meaningful (Shernoff

I. Ong (✉)
Isabelle Ong, National Institute of Education, Nanyang Technological University, Singapore, Singapore
e-mail: jennsabelle@gmail.com

© Springer Nature Singapore Pte Ltd. 2020
C. Koh (ed.), *Diversifying Learner Experience*,
https://doi.org/10.1007/978-981-15-9861-6_8

& Csikszentmihalyi, 2009). Despite the focus and energies invested in this issue by major educational stakeholders such as policymakers, researchers and educators, many students remain apathetic towards school (Shernoff & Csikszentmihalyi, 2009). However, what we can be certain of is that learners have multiple intelligences and learn in different ways (Gardner, 1993). Hence, a one size fits all approach is contraindicative to learning. While there are no easy answers to this persistent issue, the author's recent experience of conducting a play therapy course for adult learners sparked her interest in exploring play in adult learning. The possibility of a link between 'play' and 'flow' arose with the exploration into the idea of adults playing when learning. Through an investigation of these two concepts, the author found that play lends itself well to adult learning and may create an environment that can provide learners with opportunities to optimize learning capabilities and create diverse learner experiences. In this chapter, the diversification of learner experiences refers to the intentional provision of unique opportunities that can allow learners' distinct learning needs to be met.

To date, there are no published research studies examining the interaction between flow, play and adult learning. A possible reason for play and adult learning being understudied could be attributed to the challenges of breaking age-old conventions that adults cannot and should not play. Driven by this gap in the extant literature, the key purpose of this article is to propose the advancement of flow through play in adult learning. Through the lens of the flow theory, the concept of harnessing play to optimize adult learning is discussed along with suggestions on intentionally incorporating play activities to create the optimal conditions for flow. This review of the literature will be followed by concrete examples of the applications and implications of the model for adult learning.

8.2 Play

The age-old adage, 'All work and no play make Jack a dull boy' has survived through the ages. Play is a universal experience that has existed since ancient times. Play is an organic and creative medium of communication and provides an interface for humans, both young and old, to experiment with ideas and advance thought complexity. There is substantial research supporting the critical role that play has in the development and learning of children in various fields including mental health and education (Whitebread, Basilio, Kuvalja, & Verma, 2012). In the past decade, there has been a surge of interest in adult learning through play, particularly in gaming. Corbeil (1999) proposed several reasons why play naturally lends itself to adult learning. Firstly, play provides an incentive to learning in the real world as well as the symbolic world (Corbeil, 1999). Secondly, play lends itself to opportunities for learning by exploring and imitating, the two primary activities of learning (Corbeil, 1999). As such, it gives individuals a sense of temporary chaos and pleasure, which are indirectly learning-related (Corbeil, 1999). Thirdly, playing offers safety to those who engage in it without the danger of getting hurt in real-life situations (Corbeil, 1999). Further, in human development, play provides a continuum in the progression of child to adult and naturally facilitates the thought maturation of a human being across the lifespan, although the nature of play needs to be adapted accordingly to sustain adult interest (Corbeil, 1999).

8.2.1 Definition of Play

In a review of the definitions proffered by various theorists, there is a consensus amongst experts that play eludes a clear definition and defies a neat and standard description. Eberle (2014) has suggested that it is challenging to define play, owing to its rich and diverse attributes and the difficulty of expressing its dynamic relationships in words. For the purposes of this paper, we shall consider two definitions of play. One of the most popular definitions of play was suggested by Erikson (1950) who stated that '…play is a function of the ego, an attempt to synchronize the bodily and social processes with the self … It is free from compulsions of a conscience and from impulsions of irrationality' (p. 214). More recently, Eberle (2014) defines play as an "…ancient, voluntary 'emergent' process driven by pleasure that yet strengthens our muscles, instructs our social skills, tempers and deepens our positive emotions, and enables a state of balance that leaves us poised to play some more" (p. 231). Both definitions share the idea that play is an abstract, freeing, rich and boundless process and offers pleasure and multi-dimensional benefits to individuals who engage in it. To tackle the tenuousness of play definitions, most authors have attempted to describe play by characterizing it and explicating its functions.

8.3 The Value of Play

Broadly speaking, play offers varied benefits including cognitive, physiological, emotional and social benefits for individuals across all ages (Eberle, 2014). While the study of play in adults is limited at this time, more research has been conducted on the study of adult playfulness as a personality trait. For example, playfulness in adults is associated with enhanced stress coping (Barnett, 2012; Magnuson & Barnett, 2013), intrinsic motivation and intrinsic life goals (Proyer, 2012).

In Proyer's (2014) research study assessing the self-perceptions of playfulness of 324 adults in their everyday life, participants listed a broad variety of functions of adult playfulness including well-being, humour and laughter, creativity, increased coping and coping strategies, enhanced mastery, and relationship-building. Further, these self-perceptions were studied in relation to five different contexts that included leisure, work, and interpersonal relationships in the collegial, partnership and friendship domains, suggesting that playfulness may be applied in various contexts (Proyer, 2014). Interestingly, participants that rated higher on playfulness levels provided a greater variety of functions of playfulness compared to participants who scored lower on playfulness, suggesting that individuals who considered themselves more playful benefitted more from being playful (Proyer, 2014). Although the findings from Proyer (2014)'s study are based on self-report and lacked representativeness in terms of participants' age, not coincidentally, these perceived functions of playfulness overlap with the potential functions of play. Although the seminal studies on the functions of play have been controversial in terms of their limited validity, contesting claims and lack of conceptual tools to assess them, these researchers, whose research subjects were primarily animals, reported a plethora of play benefits including creativity and the mastery of skills in the cognitive, physiological, and social domains (Burghardt, 2005).

The distinction between play and playfulness has been drawn by some researchers (Magnuson & Barnett, 2013) who propose that play refers to the behaviours one expresses when engaging in play activities while playfulness refers to the individual's proclivity to perceive a situation in ways that allow oneself and/or others to experience light-hearted and positive emotions (Barnett, 2007). While there exists a distinction between the play action of doing and the dispositional trait of playfulness, what we can concur is that play behaviour shares many similarities with playfulness as a personality trait, and the act of playing could foster playfulness, which in turn, can potentially yield benefits for adults who engage in it.

An important implication of the conceptualization of playfulness as a personality trait that is mostly stable over time, is that it limits our ability to productively work with this construct (Magnuson & Barnett, 2013). Rather, conceptualizing playfulness along a developmental continuum ranging from low to high levels (Glynn & Webster, 1992) allows us to adaptively work with the construct and expend on the potential of augmenting it (Magnuson & Barnett, 2013).

8.3.1   Benefits of Adult Play on Learning

Although the extant research on adult play and learning is very limited at this point in time, the few researchers (Maxwell, Reed, Saker, & Story, 2005; Proyer, 2011; Tegano, 1990) who have studied the relationship between adult playfulness and cognitive abilities have indicated the potential of using play to leverage one's cognitive abilities and increase creativity. For example, Proyer (2011) found that playfulness in adults was positively correlated with enhanced academic performance whereby students who were more playful gleaned higher scores in their exams. Interestingly, participants who self-identified as playful expressed a higher desire to engage in additional readings beyond the minimum requirement to pass their exam, suggesting higher motivation and aspirations for academic success (Proyer, 2011). While their findings are not causative and focused only on one facet of intelligence, that is, convergent thinking (Proyer, 2011), and need to be interpreted with care, the study suggests the potential of incorporating play in adult learning.

Maxwell and colleagues (2005) also found that adults who were playful possessed a learning orientation, demonstrated adaptive selling, and augmented job performance. Additionally, an indirect effect of being fun-loving positively impacted job satisfaction through stress reduction as employees were more equipped to handle their stress (Maxwell et al., 2005).

These employees possessed learning orientation characteristics that helped them become resilient to mistakes, and they used these as learning opportunities to be competent, while their flexible thinking allowed them to adapt in new and different ways that augmented their job performance (Maxwell et al., 2005). In short, a playful attitude allows individuals to be intrinsically motivated and experience positive emotions whereby they enjoy learning new approaches by virtue of having fun with learning and being creative (Maxwell et al., 2005). Even when these individuals encountered tough situations, their perception of these challenges as a game helped to reduce their stress (Maxwell et al., 2005).

Likewise, in their review of the role of play in the field of psychiatry, Berger and colleagues (2017) indicated that several researchers reported the positive effects of play interventions in enhancing cognitive function amongst the adults, including individuals with mental health issues, who commonly experienced cognitive difficulties.

8.4 Re-examining Play, Work and Learning

Despite the growing interest in adult play and learning, there is a scarcity of research examining the effects of playing and playfulness in adults. The extant research on adult playfulness is limited (Maxwell et al., 2005; Magnuson & Barnett, 2013; Proyer, 2014) while the literature on children and play is abundant. A reason why we may not be seeing more research undertaken on adults and play, could be the phenomenon of cultural denial whereby adults typically do not engage in play, deeming it a wasteful activity, amidst the hectic demands and fast pace of life (Gol-Guven, 2017). The relationship between play and learning can be a contentious one due to the connotations associated with work, which learning is oftentimes synonymously associated with. According to Burghardt (2005), when play is framed as work that needs to be completed mandatorily and an external objective has to be met, it does not constitute play in the real sense of the word. However, when work or learning is considered play, and the individuals involved consider it playful and a means to an end, work becomes play. Therefore, the distinction between work and play becomes a sort of deception where the lines between the two are blurred, and constitutes a 'modern conceit' in Burghardt's own words (2005, p. 398). In the context of this contentious relationship between adult play and learning, it may be useful to consider what happens when adults do not play.

8.5 Implications of Play Deprivation

Although there is plenty of research supporting the benefits of play amongst children, it naturally follows that children who lack play or are deprived of play will not be able to enjoy the full plethora of potential play benefits. While there are few studies that have investigated the direct impact of play deprivation on children due to ethical reasons (Mrnjaus, 2014; Whitebread et al., 2012), researchers who have studied children in play-deprived environments found that they suffered from significant cognitive, social, emotional and mental health deficits such as depression and aggression compared to their peers in well-adjusted environments (Chugani et al., 2001; Hughes, 2003; Valentino et al., 2011). Not surprisingly, the effects of play deprivation also extended to adults whereby aggressive and criminalized young men demonstrated childhood and adult play deficits in sharp contrast to creative and talented adults who indicated high playfulness levels (Brown, 1998 cited in Lester & Russel, 2010). The idea of play deprivation in adults is best surmised by Corbeil (1999) who stated that '…failure to play is a failure to develop. A healthy adult, full of potential, plays games. An adult who no longer plays is declining, if not in decay' (p. 175). Unfortunately, despite the dismal prospects for play-deprived adults, only one adult developmental model of play currently exists.

8.6 An Adult Developmental Model of Play

An educational researcher, Susanne Cook-Greuter (1999) suggests that play continues to develop across the adult developmental lifespan. This perspective on the child-adult continuity of play has been shared by others such as Corbeil (1999). Based on the theory of post-autonomous ego development, Cook-Greuter (1999) proposed that adult play continues to evolve throughout adulthood in terms of ego development, consciousness and perspective.

8.6.1 Play Selves and Play Forms

According to her model, there are eight different play selves and each of them expresses itself in unique ways and lends itself to a unique perspective of the self, others and the world around them (Cook-Greuter, 1999). Each of these eight play selves was designed based on the adult's developmental level of consciousness and accordingly, the play preferences or forms were mapped onto these play selves (Gordon & Esbjorn-Hargens, 2007). An important caveat to make is that although the examples of the play forms listed are not exclusive to each play-self, they have the greatest appeal to their assigned play-self. It is also important to note that each of the developmental stages strives towards the next stage, but also encompasses play forms well-suited to the previous stages (Gordon & Esbjorn-Hargens, 2007). For example, an ordered player would find it appealing to play competitive sports as well as battle games. Cook-Greuter (1999)'s eight play selves and their preferred play forms are discussed here. Additionally, Cook-Greuter (1999)'s model suggests that play is dynamic in that one's preferences for play form may be transformed and shaped by variables such as the context of play and other individuals' worldviews (Gordon & Esbjorn-Hargens, 2007) such that an individual may adopt a play-self at work while adopting another play-self with family.

8.6.2 Magical Player

At its most basic developmental level, this play-self assumes an egocentric identity, is impulsive in nature and only sees the dichotomy of black and white, good and bad. Their style of playing is typically ritualistic and repetitive and others are considered individuals who need to take care of their needs. They typically experience the world as complicated and chaotic. Examples of play forms that appeal to this player include magic tricks, rituals and fantasy games.

8.6.3 Aggressive Player

Similar to the magical player, this player assumes an egoistic identity and is self-protective. This style of playing is heroic and focused on survival. Others are deemed as competitors for power and material items and aggressive players experience the world as risky and unpredictable. Examples of play forms that are well-suited for aggressive players include battle games, wrestling and survival games.

8.6.4 Ordered Player

An ethnocentric identity is adopted by this play-self and this play is characterized as both structured and rule abiding. This play-self sees the world literally, has a diffuse sense of self and seeks group conformity. Some examples of play forms that appeal to this player include card and board games, games with a cognitive focus, and games focused on rule-adherence.

8.6.5   Status Player

This play-self adopts a socio-centric identity and views play as a competition in and of itself. While this play-self is diligent, its focus is on rationality, winning and losing to compete for status and to gain newfound individuality. Status players also perceive the world as predictable. Play forms that attract status players comprise any competitive play such as video games, competitive sports and games of chance.

8.6.6   Sensitive Player

This self is individualistic yet values interpersonal connections and adopts a world-centric view. Cooperative play is a hallmark of this play-self as one is acutely aware of culture and context and has the capacity to assume others' perspective and empathize with them. Sensitive players see their world coloured with multiple perspectives and truths. Play forms that appeal to them include any team-building games and activities that bond their group members together.

8.6.7   Complex Player

Like the sensitive player, this self is autonomous and adopts a world-centric view. This play-self draws upon chaos to further develop the self and its play style is rapid and unpredictable. Others who have differing views are viewed with tolerance. Play forms that allude to the complex player include improvisation, drama and virtual reality.

8.6.8   Dynamic Player

This play-self is integrative in nature and assumes a kosmocentric identity. Possessing such an identity suggests that one is in the postpersonal developmental stage and experiences a mind-spirit wholeness where awareness, thoughts, behaviour and its implications are united (Brown, 2006). The focus of this play-self is service to humanity and dynamic players seek to transform the self, others and the world. Understanding and non-evaluation towards others is a hallmark feature of this player type. Play forms catering to this self are centred on a connection to the integrative aspects of self, including one's spiritual realm. Some examples of these play forms include meditation, breath work and inquiry.

8.6.9 Unitive Player

This is the rarest play-self and the identity of this self is pneumacentric where the play-self adopts both a transpersonal and ego-aware worldview. Such a play-self can access transpersonal realities and realms and is not bounded by a static identity. Its play style is characterized as creative, spontaneous and innovative. Spontaneity and openness characterize this play-self and others are viewed as a part of the one being that everyone shares. This self seeks to liberate all beings and play form examples for this self, includes identification with the world's play and improvisation in the spiritual and psychic realms.

Based on Cook-Greuter (1999)'s model, there seems to be an underlying assumption that all individuals fit into one or more of the eight play selves. Hence, one could argue that the model limits the possibility that adults can also play without ascribing to a play-self, and may not have a preference for specific play forms.

It is noteworthy that the first four play selves comprise 85% of the population, while the next other four play selves are rarer, comprising only 15% (Cook-Greuter, 1999). Taken together, it is pertinent to explore the perspectives that each play-self adopts in a shared play activity as the agenda, purpose and needs for each are distinct (Gordon & Esbjorn-Hargens, 2007). Returning to the argument that play is central to adult development, it seems exigent to consider the process of play. Burghardt (2005) considers play a kind of deep immersion in an activity wherein an individual is so absorbed in the process that she or he becomes oblivious to the external surroundings, space and time. This deep absorption is also known as flow, a term coined and developed by Csikszentmihalyi (1991).

8.7 Flow

Csikszentmihalyi (1997, 2014a, b) first introduced the concept of flow and defined flow as a complete immersion in a given experience where one is intensely involved, fully attentive towards the task, and is working at the optimal capacity in every moment, oblivious to space, time and other happenings. Flow is a concept that exists within the field of positive psychology; the latter serves to shift the pathological focus and disease model of human functioning to developing conditions that are conducive to the flourishing of individuals and optimizing their well-being by capitalizing on their strengths and virtues (Seligman & Csikszentmihalyi, 2014). At the subjective level of positive psychology, experiences that contribute to this flourishment can be organized over time. For example, well-being and contentment are valued subjective experiences in the past. Hope and optimism are valued subjective experiences in the future, while flow and happiness are subjective experiences situated in the present (Seligman & Csikszentmihalyi, 2014).

Flow theory and research was rooted in a curiosity in understanding the subjective experience of intrinsic motivation where the activity is gratifying and is an end in itself (Nakamura & Csikszentmihalyi, 2014). Flow research has been undertaken during the 1980s and 1990s in varied contexts such as academia, art, business, sports and leisure. The experience of flow was found to be universal across demographics such as age, culture, gender and across various activities such as play and creativity. However, the focus of this paper will be on play.

Characteristics of flow. Three distinguishing characteristics of one who enters flow include first, the emergence between awareness and action, where one loses self-consciousness and becomes consumed into the activity (Csikszentmihalyi, 2014a, b). Secondly, individuals enjoy a sense of control during flow as these flow activities contain the structure necessary for them to feel a sense of accomplishment and enjoyment (Csikszentmihalyi, 2014a, b). During this time, individuals feel capable of reducing errors to a minimum, and anxiety is kept at bay (Csikszentmihalyi, 2014a, b). Thirdly, as mentioned afore, one who enters flow is so fully involved every single moment that time is forgotten and a harmony between one's feelings, thoughts, and wishes ensues (Csikszentmihalyi, 1997, 2014a, b).

Core conditions to enter flow. Csikszentmihalyi (1997, 2014) asserts that there are three core conditions for flow to occur and they include (1) clearly delineated goals that structure the experience and provides direction and purpose, (2) the provision of immediate feedback to indicate one's progress in the activity and informs one on next steps and (3) striking a delicate balance between one's skill level and challenge to where one is fully engaged in the experience. When all these conditions are met, one becomes fully absorbed, fully attuned and focused, to where one's consciousness is devoid of distractions, non-relevant emotions, self-consciousness, time and space (Csikszentmihalyi, 1997). This active state of being is sustained when one continually feels the importance of engaging in the experience and challenges are adaptively increased alongside one's skills (Csikszentmihalyi, 1997).

Apart from the three core conditions, it is also critical that the individual regards it as highly important to perform well in the activity and consider the activity a pleasurable and intrinsically rewarding one (Csikszentmihalyi, 2014a, b). Although flow can also emerge in other lone or social routine activities such as chatting with friends and driving, flow activities are typically active in nature as opposed to passive activities such as watching a movie (Csikszentmihalyi, 1997).

8.8   The Connection Between Flow and Play

A few researchers (Csikszentmihalyi, 1996, 1997; Gol-Guven, 2017; Gray, 2015) have attempted to compare play with flow, most likely because of their semblance and shared attributes. Gray (2015) proposed that all activities that meet and create the conditions of flow are playful to some extent, and apart from the many commonalities they share, one that stands out in particular, is the deep immersion that characterizes the process of this experience. Four commonalities that flow and play share include the following: (1) since play is self-directed and autonomous, similar to flow, one feels a sense of control over the environment, (2) play is rule-based and this structure is consistent with the clarity of goals that flow entails, (3) the imagination involved in play is congruent with the loss of self-consciousness in flow as the self merges with the activity and (4) intrinsic motivation is inherent in both play and flow activities (Gray, 2015). Hence, play and flow may be more similar than we think, although play has taken on a weaker and compromised reputation, possibly resulting in its minimal connections with flow (Gray, 2015).

As noted by Gol-Guven (2017), the concept of flow has largely focused on operationalizing the concept and conditions that are optimal for entering a state of flow. However, there remain gaps in the literature that have not yet been addressed, such as how instructors can set the stage for flow in adult learning, or which considerations and platforms can help to design learning environments conducive to flow. Additionally, questions such as which barriers prevent one from staying in flow and how flow is experienced during play (Gol-Guven, 2017) have not yet been examined. Given the many overlaps between play and flow, there is merit in considering how play can serve as a medium for adult learners to enter a state of flow and jointly harness their potential to not only provide diverse learner experiences, but also optimize learner capabilities.

Despite the similarities shared between play and flow, the two concepts are not synonymous. Although flow is typically experienced during play, there are specific core conditions needed for one to enter flow (Csikszentmihalyi, 2014a, b). In other words, if these conditions are not met in play, one may not experience flow. According to Csikszentmihalyi (2014a, b), flow is a 'conceptually independent process' (p. 137) that may not necessarily accompany play. Hence, one could visualize play as the broader context for engaging in flow.

For example, in flow, one's actions intertwine with one's awareness of the action (Csikszentmihalyi, 2014a, b). When playing a game of Monopoly, the individual's focus is typically on the game strategy and one engages in various actions aligned with that strategy but is not usually conscious of her or himself playing. When the individual is distracted by thoughts of whether one is performing in the game, flow is disrupted (Csikszentmihalyi, 2014a, b). Hence in the broader context of playing the Monopoly game, during the act of playing, one may or may not experience states of flow depending on whether the individual perceives her or his skills to be stretched in the context of playing the game.

To further illustrate the difference between flow and play, one can consider the idea that flow typically involves full immersion in the play activity to an extent where the self fuses with the play activity or world (Csikszentmihalyi, 2014a, b). In a state of flow, one may feel like having lost one's ego while becoming highly attuned to one's internal processes (Csikszentmihalyi, 2014a, b). For example, an individual who is deeply engaged in yoga may experience his/her self becoming one in connection with the yoga poses, thereby attaining a higher level of absorption and focus on the play activity. Hence, flow is a specific state of being that one may experience during play. However, an individual who engages in play may not necessarily experience flow if the specific conditions for flow are not met. In this case, if an individual has various thoughts about whether he/she is doing the yoga poses the right way or is considering transitioning into a different pose, then flow in this play context is less likely to happen.

8.8.1 Potential Outcomes of Play and Flow in Adult Learning

The potential outcomes of play and flow in adult learning are numerous. As there is limited literature on flow and play in academia, we can consider the potential outcomes of intersecting both play and flow by extension of the research findings on flow.

Based on research studies conducted on flow, researchers have suggested that engaging in flow experiences can be particularly helpful for students.

Affective outcomes. In a longitudinal study of high school students who were talented, those who experienced more flow demonstrated greater commitment to their talent and exhibited less anxiety than their counterparts who experienced less flow (Csikszentmihalyi, Rathunde, & Whalen, 1993). Other researchers (Adlai-Gail, 1994) predicted that the greater the time spent in flow, the higher the likelihood one would experience higher levels of self-esteem. Researchers involved in a cross-national study examining traits of happy and less happy individuals found that participants experienced the highest happiness levels when they were experiencing flow (Csikszentmihalyi & Wong, 2014). Specifically, when there was a good fit between their perceived challenge and personal abilities, participants reported being most happy.

Behavioural outcomes. Additionally, in another longitudinal study, students who were talented in Mathematics demonstrated higher achievement if they experienced flow in the second part of the course (Heine, 1996). The study by Rossin, Ro, Klein, and Guo (2009) on assessing the impact of flow on learning outcomes in an online course, found less direct learning outcomes between flow and learning performance. In their study, the researchers found that despite the lack of support for flow and learning performance, there were significant relationships between flow and learners' perceived learning, their perceived skills development and satisfaction levels (Rossin et al., 2009). These perceptions of learning suggest that apart from studying the direct effects of flow on behavioural outcomes, researchers may also benefit from investigating how flow as a psychological construct impacts specific learning processes and motivation. Additionally, in a separate study involving 94 adolescents in Malaysia, Elias, Mustafa, Roslan, and Noah (2010) found significant positive correlations between flow and 6 motivational forces, namely, time reference, need for achievement, learning goals, expectancy values, self-efficacy and self-determination. These outcomes seem to support the idea that the impact of flow on learning outcomes may not always be direct and that there may be utility in understanding how flow interacts with the various motivational factors to influence learning.

Biological outcomes. Researchers also found support for a reduction in adverse physical health risks (Patton, 1999) and reduced rates of delinquency (Schmidt, 2000) when they experienced flow and mastered challenging activities. Maxwell et al. (2005) suggested that presenting a learning activity as play would help to stimulate a playful attitude. While this prospect would benefit from further research, there are more foreseeable benefits than risks in framing learning activities as play to foster a light-hearted, organic and more enjoyable learning environment.

Play is a natural medium for flow to occur in adult learning. There is currently no academic discourse on the intersection between play, flow and adult learning. Although preliminary, it is hoped that this discussion on play and flow will be a start to raising awareness on harnessing the untapped potential of play in learning based on the adult developmental play model by Cook-Greuter (1999). As there are no current guidelines on how play can serve as a platform for adult learners to strive towards a state of flow during learning, the following section will consider ways in which instructors can build play and flow into instruction.

8.9 Recommendations for Adult Learning Instructors

To create diverse learning experiences that can accommodate learners' preferred learning styles and potentially facilitate flow, instructors could consider the following practical recommendations for introducing flow and play in their instruction, respectively.

8.9.1 Conditions for Play

Four core conditions for play need to be present for flow to occur. Firstly, instructors need to be well-acquainted with the various play selves and play forms to apply them effectively. While it may not be necessary to be well-versed in each of the eight play selves, it would be helpful to be familiar with key characteristics of these play selves as well as their associated play forms. This information would be helpful during course design and lesson planning as instructors consider the possibilities when designing play activities.

Secondly, although it is not always possible for play activities to be used naturally, they should be intentionally selected and aligned with the subject matter. For example, in a trauma and counselling course, play forms that lend themselves well to the subject matter include improvisation, movement and drama, breath work, and meditation. Trying to use some of these play forms in a Mathematics course may seem forced, artificial and even pretentious.

The third play condition is the creation of play space and time. Instructors need to be very intentional about carving out space and time for play. While space refers to setting up the play complete with the materials and supplies, as well as clear instructions, timing refers to the positioning of the activity within a single class and course. Time is underscored as essential for play (Gordon & Esbjorn-Hargens, 2007) and rightly so, as positioning a game of Bingo in the first class would have less meaning and utility than having it towards the end of the course to assess students' knowledge and understanding of the content material in a fun and enjoyable way. Other valuable considerations include helping learners by setting up the stage for play and helping learners get energized and ready to transition out of their real-world roles, and into their imaginative role (Gordon & Esbjorn-Hargens, 2007). For example, instructors can invite learners to use props, to step out of reality and enter the play domain. It might also be helpful to gear up and prepare a class of adult learners for a role-play by getting in-role him or herself or playing some soft music in the background.

The fourth condition is to create and provide opportunities for risk-taking during play. Play is a natural medium for players to take risks and make decisions on which boundaries they are comfortable risking (Gordon & Esbjorn-Hargens, 2007). For example, this might take the form of the instructor designing the role-play activity set up where each player may have an obstacle to overcome and needs to step out of their safety zone. Another example would be within the context of a team-building game, where players may need to each take chances and take a stab at tasks that they typically do not perform in real life (Gordon & Esbjorn-Hargens, 2007). In this way, players can assume control of being out of control and as a result, experience both risk and mastery (Gordon & Esbjorn-Hargens, 2007). Although the discussion on transitional play lies beyond the scope of our discussion due to the depth and complexity of the concept, it is important to note that the play forms indicated for the various play selves provide the support needed for players to developmentally transition to the next play-self (Gordon & Esbjorn-Hargens, 2007).

8.9.2   Conditions for Flow

Within the larger context of play, there are three core conditions for flow to occur (Csikszentmihalyi, 1997, 2014a, b) as discussed afore. The first core condition is the establishment of clearly defined learning goals within the play context. For example, in a Master's level counselling theories course for counsellors in-training, a board game (designed to assess students' content knowledge of the various concepts and key terms of various counselling theories) should have its learning objectives clearly stated and delivered to allow players to know what they would be playing, the rationale for the game, and how they can play.

Secondly, the play activity should offer immediate feedback that serves as a guide for the player on how to proceed next. Using the same board game example, a player who provides a wrong answer to a question will receive immediate feedback that the answer is incorrect. He/she would get to use one of the three lifelines to seek help in answering the question or to stay in 'detention' for two turns before attempting to answer another question.

The third flow condition asserts the importance of ensuring that a delicate balance is struck between learners' skill level and the challenges of the play activity. This helps to avoid any frustration that players experience to the extent of disconnecting from their flow and play activity. Again, using the board game example above, if a player has trouble answering level three counselling theory questions, he/she has the option of staying at levels one or two and continue to familiarise with the basic theoretical concepts before venturing to the application-type questions at level three. If only level three questions have been developed for the game, players might end up checking out both literally and psychologically.

Since a flow activity provides a set of unique challenges that get progressively more challenging (Nakamura & Csikszentmihalyi, 2014), instructors need to consider developing learning activities with a spectrum of difficulty levels. Drawing upon Vygotsky's growth principle, instructors could be mindful of the challenge they present to students in that the challenge should adequately stretch one's current skill sets within reasonable limits and result in more sophisticated actions taken to complete the task (Nakamura & Csikszentmihalyi, 2014). Each set of mastery inspires growth and the individual's desire to re-experience flow (Nakamura & Csikszentmihalyi, 2014). However, to be able to determine which challenges are best suited for students, instructors need to have a good grasp of their learners' pre-existing skill level.

To design challenges well-suited for their adult learners, instructors could develop brief assessments such as short quizzes at the start of the course to determine learners' entry-level skills and content knowledge. Making these small adjustments can help instructors be well attuned to their learners' skill level and guide them appropriately throughout the course. Instructors could also develop a checklist of key course competencies and share the list with students so they can monitor their skill mastery progress.

Another way instructors can introduce flow through play is to replicate 'serious play' (p. 255) by teaming up and collaboratively developing activities of varied interests and allowing adult learners to engage in these activities, as was carried out in Indianapolis' key school (Nakamura & Csikszentmihalyi, 2014). In this way, instructors serve as a guide to help learners select activities and identify new challenges as they develop their skills and competencies, in alignment with nurturing the intrinsic motivation inherent in flow and play (Nakamura & Csikszentmihalyi, 2014).

8.10 Future Research Directions

The research implications of this work are many, but one crucial implication would be to explore the interaction between the concepts of 'play', 'flow' and 'adult learning' as well as the confluence between play and flow conditions and their impact on adult learning. Specifically, which play conditions mediate flow in adult learning? Advancing the discussion in this area would strengthen the case for incorporating play in higher education coursework and programmes and enable adult learners to experience flow and optimize their learning capabilities in ways previously not possible in conventional educational settings. Additionally, it would be important for researchers to advance the field of knowledge by studying the mechanisms responsible for the positive correlation between playfulness and academic performance (Proyer, 2011). The potential effects of infusing flow through play are profound and one can only imagine the infinite possibilities that may emerge when adults are given the opportunity to play as part of their learning process.

Currently, play is the most common type of flow experience, and games have been considered the most typical play activity (Csikszentmihalyi, 2014a, b). However, the games studied in previous research are typically leisure activities such as archery, chess, golf and rock-climbing. On the other hand, most academic disciplines do not lend themselves to these types of play activities. Given the wide array of play activities, researchers could explore which types of play activities and games can be applied to diverse educational settings to facilitate flow in adult learners. As adult learners typically comprise individuals who differ in their expertise and comfort with using technology, it may be germane for researchers to identify ways in which play activities and applications can accommodate learners with diverse technological skill sets. The challenge indicated above in developing play activities that can mediate flow in adult learning is further complicated by the challenge of entering a state of flow. According to Csikszentmihalyi (2014a, b), objective challenges or skills do not guarantee that a person will enter a state of flow. Rather, it is the individual's perception of the challenge posed and the skills they possess, based on their personality characteristics, that determine whether they either under or overestimate the challenge and/or the skills they possess to navigate the challenge. Hence, further study is needed to investigate how these subjective personality variables may impact the design of play activities in various contexts, particularly as it applies to adult learning.

8.11 Conclusion

At present, adult learning educators are facing the challenge of efficiently meeting the needs of their diverse adult learners in terms of learning tools and environments (Corbeil, 1999). With the ever-growing advantages and options that technology supplies to higher learning institutions, there are multiple pathways for instructors to address adult learners' diverse learning needs through playing and entering a state of flow, thereby unlocking potential benefits beyond what conventional classroom instruction can offer. Furthermore, instructors can be more cognizant of the key conditions for play and flow that are both relevant and applicable for designing instruction that caters to diverse learner styles and improvement in learner motivation and engagement. At a more fundamental level, the author's hope is that this discussion will pave the way to advocating for adults to continue playing and reap the beneficent gains of playing, while challenging the long-standing stigma and mindset that play is only meant for children and that adults should 'grow up'.

Plato (1988, Laws vii, p. 803) asserted that 'life should be lived as play'. In the spirit of play and life, it is hoped that the dialogue on flow and play in adult learning will strengthen and sustain itself as a tribute to Plato that adults can continue to playfully flow and learn in organic and pleasurable ways that support and promote their developmental trajectory over the course of their life span.

References

Adlai-Gail, W. (1994). *Exploring the autotelic personality*. Unpublished doctoral dissertation, University of Chicago

Barnett, L. A. (2012). Playful people: Fun is in the mind of the beholder. *Imagination, Cognition and Personality, 31*, 169–197.

Berger, P., Bitsch, F., Brohl, H., & Falkenberg, I. (2017). Play and playfulness in psychiatry: A selective review. *International Journal of Play, 1–16*. 10.1080/21594937.2017.1383341.

Brown, B. (2006). *An overview of developmental stages of consciousness*. Retrieved from https://integralwithoutborders.net/sites/default/files/resources/Overview%20of%20Developmental%20Levels.pdf.

Burghardt, G. M. (2005). *The genesis of animal play: Testing the limits*. Massachusetts, MA: MIT Press.

Chugani, H. T., Behen, M. E., Muzik, O., Juhász, C., Nagy, F., & Chugani, D. C. (2001). Local brain functional activity following early deprivation: A Study of Post-institutionalized Romanian Orphans. *NeuroImage, 14*, 1290–1301.

Cook-Greuter, S. (1999). Postautonomous ego development: A study of its nature and measurement. (Doctoral dissertation, Harvard University, 1999). *Dissertation Abstracts International, 60*(06), 3000.

Corbeil, P. (1999). Learning from the children: Practical and theoretical reflections on playing and learning. *Stimulation & Gaming, 30*(2), 163–180.

Csikszentmihalyi, M. (1991). *Flow: The psychology of optimal experience*. New York: Harper-Collins.

Csikszentmihalyi, M. (1996). *Creativity: Flow and the psychology of discovery and invention*. New York: HarperCollins.

Csikszentmihalyi, M. (1997). *Finding flow: The psychology of engagement with everyday life*. New York, NY: Basic Books

Csikszentmihalyi, M. (2014a). *Flow and the foundations of positive psychology: The collected works of Mihaly Csikszentmihalyi*. New York, NY: Springer.

Csikszentmihalyi, M. (2014b). Play and intrinsic rewards. In M. Csikszentmihalyi (Ed.), *Flow and the foundations of positive psychology: The collected works of Mihaly Csikszentmihalyi*. New York, NY: Springer.

Csikszentmihalyi, M., & Wong, M. M.-H. (2014). The situational and personal correlates of happiness. In M. Csikszentmihalyi (Ed.), *Flow and the foundations of positive psychology: The collected works of Mihaly Csikszentmihalyi*. New York, NY: Springer.

Csikszentmihalyi, M., Rathunde, K., & Whalen, S. (1993). *Talented teenagers*. Cambridge: Cambridge University Press.

Eberle, S. G. (2014). The elements of play: Toward a philosophy and a definition of play. *Journal of Play, 6*(2), 214–233.

Elias, H., Mustafa, S. M. S., Roslan, S., & Noah, S. M. (2010). Examining potential relationships between flow and motivational forces in Malaysian secondary school students. *Procedia Social and Behavioral Sciences, 9*, 2042–2046. https://doi.org/10.1016/j.sbspro.2010.12.443.

Erikson, E. H. (1950). *Childhood and society*. New York, NY: Norton.

Gardner, H. (1983; 1993). *Frames of Mind: The theory of multiple intelligences.* London, UK: Fontana Press.

Glynn, M., & Webster, J. (1992). The Adult playfulness scale: An initial assessment. *Psychological Reports, 71*(1), 83–103.

Gol-Guven, M. (2017). Play and flow: Children's culture and adults' role. *Journal of Early Childhood Studies, 1*(2), 247–261. https://doi.org/10.24130/eccd-jecs.196720171230.

Gordon, G., & Esbjorn-Hargens, S. (2007). Are we having fun yet? An exploration of the transformative power of play. *Journal of Humanistic Psychology, 47*(2). https://doi.org/10.1177/002216 7806297034.

Gray, P. (2015). Studying play without calling it that. Humanistic and positive psychology. In J. E. Johnson, S. G. Eberne, T. S Henricks, & D. Kuschner (Eds.), *The handbook of the study of play* (pp. 121–138). London: Rowman & Littlefield.

Heine, C. (1996). *Flow and achievement in mathematics.* Unpublished doctoral dissertation, University of Chicago.

Hughes, B. (2003). Play deprivation, play bias and playwork practice. In Brown, F. (Ed.) *Playwork theory and practice* (pp. 66–80). Open University Press.

Lester, S., & Russell, W. (2010). *Children's right to play: An examination of the importance of play in The lives of children worldwide.* Working Paper No. 57 The Hague, The Netherlands: Bernard van Leer Foundation.

Maguson, C. D., & Barnett, L. A. (2013). The playful advantage: How playfulness enhances coping with stress. *Leisure Sciences, 35,* 129–144. https://doi.org/10.1080/01490400.2013.761905.

Maxwell, S., Reed, G., Saker, J., & Story, V. (2005). The two faces of playfulness: A new tool to select potentially successful sales reps. *Journal of Personal Selling & Sales Management, 25,* 215–229.

Mrnjaus, K. (2014). The child's right to play?! *Croatian Journal of Education, 16*(1), 217–233.

Nakamura, J., & Csikszentmihalyi, M. (2014). The concept of flow. In M. Csikszentmihalyi (2014). *Flow and the foundations of positive psychology: The collected works of Mihaly Csikszentmihalyi.* New York, NY: Springer.

Patton, J. (1999). *Exploring the relative outcomes of interpersonal and intrapersonal factors of order and entropy in adolescence: A longitudinal study.* Unpublished doctoral dissertation, University of Chicago.

Plato. (1988). *The laws of Plato* (T. L. Pangle, Trans.). Chicago: University of Chicago Press.

Proyer, R. T. (2011). Being playful and smart? The relations of adult playfulness with psychometric and self-estimated intelligence and academic performance. *Learning and Individual Differences, 21,* 463–467. https://doi.org/10.1016/j.lindif.2011.02.003.

Proyer, R. T. (2012). Examining playfulness in adults: Testing its correlates with personality, positive psychological functioning, goal aspirations, and multi-methodically assessed ingenuity. *Psychological Test and Assessment Modeling, 54*(2), 103–127.

Proyer, R. T. (2014). Perceived functions of playfulness in adults: Does it mobilize you at work, rest and when being with others? *Revue europeene de psychologie-appliquee, 64,* 241–250. https:// doi.org/10.1016/j.erap.2014.06.001.

Rossin, D., Ro, Y. K., Klein, B. D., & Guo, Y. M. (2009). The effects of flow on learning outcomes in an outline information management course. *Journal of Information Systems Education, 20*(1), 87–98.

Schmidt, J. (2000). Overcoming challenges: The role of opportunity, action, and experience in fostering resilience among adolescents. Manuscript submitted for publication.

Seligman, M. E. P., & Csikszentmihalyi, M. (2014). Positive psychology: An introduction. In M. Csikszentmihalyi (2014). *Flow and the foundations of positive psychology: The collected works of Mihaly Csikszentmihalyi.* New York, NY: Springer.

Shernoff, D. J., & Csikszentmihalyi, M. (2009). Flow in schools: Cultivating engaged learners and optimal learning environments. In R. Gilman, E. S. Hueber, & M. Furlong (Eds.), *Handbook of positive psychology in schools* (pp. 131–145). New York: Routledge.

Tegano (1990). Relationship of tolerance of ambiguity and playfulness to creativity. *Psychological Reports, 66,* 1047–1056.

Valentino, K., Cicchetti, D., Toth, S. L., & Rogosch, F. A. (2011). Mother-child play and maltreatment: A longitudinal analysis of emerging social behaviour from infancy to toddlerhood. *Developmental Psychology, 47,* 1280–1294.

Whitebread, D., Basilio, M., Kuvalja, M., & Verma, M. (2012). *The importance of play: A report on the value of children's play with a series of policy recommendations.* Brussels, Belgium: Toys Industries for Europe.

Chapter 9
Initial Teacher Education in a Neo-liberal System: Making One-Size Fit All

Steven S. Sexton and Sandra Williamson-Leadley

Abstract Initial teacher education (ITE) is designed to prepare students for entity into the teaching profession. Exemplary ITE programmes have an explicit intent to graduate better student teachers than other ITE programmes. Specifically, they include more teaching practice, greater partnerships with schools, integration of theory and practice and have a strong focus on priority learners. This chapter reports on one exemplary master's level ITE programme and how its conceptual framework supported and facilitated the emerging teacher identity of diverse student teachers. Through authentic implementation of its conceptual and theoretical understandings about the role of the teacher, the role of teaching and the role of education, this programme provided a shared vision of teaching and learning guided by those strategies and approaches that allowed these students teachers to be exposed to diverse experiences. Teaching is about learning and its role in shaping children through the curriculum and classroom interactions. As such, teachers and schools must hold themselves responsible for what they do in their classrooms and schools.

Keywords Initial teacher education · Curriculum · Teacher identity · Diverse experiences

S. S. Sexton (✉)
College of Education, University of Otago, Dunedin, New Zealand
e-mail: steven.sexton@otago.ac.nz

S. Williamson-Leadley
Sandra Williamson-Leadley, College of Education, Health & Human Development, University of Canterbury, Christchurch, New Zealand
e-mail: sandra.williamson-leadley@canterbury.co.nz

© Springer Nature Singapore Pte Ltd. 2020
C. Koh (ed.), *Diversifying Learner Experience*,
https://doi.org/10.1007/978-981-15-9861-6_9

9.1   Introduction

There is both Aotearoa[1] New Zealand (Cameron & Baker, 2004; Lind, 2013) and international research (Hattie, 2009; OECD, 2005) on the critical role teachers play in educating children and young people. As a result, in New Zealand, the Ministry of Education, like many governments, has focused on how we prepare teachers for the profession. Specifically, Aotearoa New Zealand has looked closely at the work of teachers (Timperley, Wilson, Barrar, & Fung 2007) and the way we prepare teachers for our educational system (Kane, 2005).

The 2007 curriculum document (Ministry of Education, 2007) is the official policy for all of our English-medium teaching and learning in Years 1–13. Currently, this accounts for 95% of all school-aged students, students aged five through nineteen (Education Counts, 2017a). In addition, our educational system has been operating under a neo-liberalism agenda since 1985. While there have been two complete curriculum rewrites since neo-liberalism began, we operate under a one-size fits all ideology.

The New Zealand Curriculum's (Ministry of Education, 2007) strength is that in its 92 pages, there is not one required piece of content to be covered in any of the thirteen years of schooling. There are guidelines on how to teach but not what to teach. The document's weakness is that one single document is supposed to support over 200 ethnicities (Manning, 2013) in Aotearoa New Zealand, including our *Te Tiriti o Waitangi* (Treaty of Waitangi) *Māori* (indigenous people of Aotearoa) partners. As stated, nearly 95% of all school-aged children attend English-medium schools while 15% of Aotearoa New Zealand's population self-identify as *Māori*. Therefore, the majority of *Māori* children attend English-medium schools.

In 2013, the Ministry of Education invited tertiary providers to design, develop and implement master's degree level initial teacher education (ITE) programmes to raise the status of the teaching profession. Two programmes began in 2014. These programmes were given a ministerial directive to support Aotearoa New Zealand's priority learners, both the student teachers in the programme and those in Aotearoa New Zealand's schools. Priority learners were defined to be those students who have not been served well by the educational system: *Māori*, Pasifika (people with ancestry from neighbouring Pacific Island nations such as Tonga, Samoa and Niue), low socio-economic status (SES) families and those with special needs. These new master's degree level ITE programmes, however, were required to impose a minimum academic entry-level that privileged *Pākehā* (White European descent New Zealanders) applicants.

This chapter reports on one of the two first exemplary Master of Teaching and Learning (MTchgLn) programmes approved. This MTchgLn programme was designed to include not only the exemplary programme characteristics most suitable for Aotearoa New Zealand (Darling-Hammond, 2006; Lind, 2013), but also those

---

[1] Aotearoa is the indigenous name for New Zealand meaning 'the land of the long while cloud' New Zealand recognises Māori as the indigenous people of New Zealand and the unique relationship between Māori and tauiwi (non-Māori).

relevant, useful and meaningful strategies drawn from national and international academic literature on what is effective ITE. As such, this programme was built upon Realistic teacher education (Korthagen, Kessel, Kosters, Lagerwerf, & Wubbels, 2008; Korthagen, Loughran, & Russell, 2006); Reflexive teachers (Cunliffe, 2004; Thompson & Pascal, 2012) and Adaptive expertise (Timperley, 2013).

Between 2014 and 2018, this programme has attracted, supported and graduated into the teaching profession, a range of teachers (see Table 9.1). We present how this programme's conceptual framework's *mana motuhake* (social justice), *ako* (working in partnership), *mātauraka* (evidence-based teaching), *Te Tiriti o Waitangi* (partnership), and *whanaukataka* (community of learners) (see Fig. 9.1) have been implemented through the designing, development, and delivering of a curriculum to support the diverse range of student teachers this programme needs to reflect Aotearoa New Zealand's school-aged students.

It has been reported that 74% of all teachers are *Pākehā*/European, middle-class and middle-aged females (Education Counts, 2017b), which does not reflect the student population as indicated in Table 9.1. Darling-Hammond, Hammerness, Grossman, Rust, and Shulman (2005) noted that strong ITE programmes have clear and coherent connections between professional teaching experience and the programme's coursework. These connections are underpinned by the programme's conceptual and theoretical understandings about the role of the teacher, the role of teaching and the role of education. As such, this MTchgLn programme's conceptual framework not only provides a shared vision of teaching and learning but also guides the strategies and approaches to allow students teachers to be exposed to diverse experiences.

Firstly, in *Māori* tradition children are seen to be inherently competent, capable, complete and gifted no matter what their age or ability. Descended from lines that stretch back to the beginning of time, they are important living links between past, present, and future, and a reflection of their *tīpuna* (ancestors). These ideas are fundamental to how *Māori* understand teaching and learning. *Whakataukī* (poetic forms of *Te Reo Māori* that often merge historical events or holistic perspectives with underlying messages) often highlight how recollections of the past are fine to have but wisdom comes from being able to prepare opportunities for the future. *Whakataukī* are used in a range of contexts in *Māori* such as *whaikōero* (formal speaking) to support the speaker in making a point, a statement, aligning the present with the wisdom of *tīpuna*. *Whakataukī* are metaphors that support critical thinking by allowing the receiver of the *Whakataukī* to consider another way of thinking from a worldview other than their own. To affirm *Whakataukī* is to accept the indigeneity of a *Māori* lens and invite the receiver to align their thought processes to this. This is biculturalism in its truest sense as one worldview interacts with another on the same level. Each *Te Tiriti o Waitangi* partner has equal status, their individual *mana* (self-respect and self-esteem) remains intact and intertwines to co-construct a collective understanding. *Whakataukī* can be used to provoke *kaiako* (teacher) to adopt a cultural lens and be open and reciprocal to learning and teaching. Here, in this context, the *Whakataukī* used to introduce each *EDUC471 Teaching in the New Zealand Context* lesson was a statement to support these student teachers' practice, specifically on

Table 9.1 New Zealand and MTchgLn demographics 2014–2018

	Gender		Sector		Age		Ethnicity					Disability	Low SES[a]
	Female	Male	Primary	Secondary	Age range	Average age	Māori	Asian	Pacifica	New Zealand/Pākehā	Other		
Total applications received	305	165	189	281	18–57	27	42	24	17	296	91		
470													
Percentage	64.9%	35.1%	40.2%	59.8%			8.9%	5.1%	3.6%	63%	19.4%		
Applications accepted	177	83	115	145	19–52	26	25	8	9	202	16	Declared disability	
260												10	
Percentage	68.1%	31.9%	44.2%	55.8%			9.6%	3.1%	3.5%	77.7%	6.2%	3.8%	
New Zealand school age demographics													
800,334 students#	50.2%	49.5%	65%	35%	5–16	11	24%	11.8%	9.8%	50.1%	4.2%	11%	Bottom 11%

[a]SES = Socio-Economic Status #Education Counts School Census (2017a)

Fig. 9.1 MTchgLn conceptual framework

how both the student teacher and the ITE programme can reflect and implement these into our learning spaces. Secondly, this programme requires student teachers in their *EDUC471 Teaching in the New Zealand Context* paper to identify three barriers to their students' learning and how they, as the classroom teachers, will mitigate or address each of these barriers in their classroom. Thirdly, in *EDUC476 Diversity and Inclusion* student teachers work with one student who has not been well-served by the educational system from their professional experience to present a case study of that student's schooling experiences to include a critical analysis of the impact of values, knowledge, and enactment of human rights and educational policy on the student's presence, participation, and achievement at school. Finally, for every teaching professional experience, the student teachers explicitly identify how they are catering for the diverse needs of their students in their programme of teaching.

9.2 New Zealand Educational Context

As stated, New Zealand is a multicultural society representing over 200 ethnicities. While the numeric majority are *Pākehā*/European, there is a significant *Māori* population with recognised customs and traditions, as well as growing Asian and Pacific Island communities (Statistics New Zealand, 2015). However, nearly 74% of all teachers are *Pākehā*/European, middle-class, middle-aged females (Education Counts, 2017b).

New Zealand has had a formal education policy since the 1877 Education Act established free, compulsory, and secular education for all children between the ages of seven and thirteen (Sutherland, Jesson, & Peters, 2001). This act grounded New Zealand education in an ideology of social equity. This ideology has continued through various amendments leading to the current 1989 Education Act that guarantees.

> every person who is not an international student is entitled to free enrolment and free education at any State school or partnership school kura hourua during the period beginning on the person's fifth birthday and ending on 1 January after the person's 19th birthday. (Parliamentary Counsel Office, 2017, para. 1)

It has been argued, however, that since 1877, New Zealand education has only had the appearance of equality and egalitarianism (Sutherland, Jesson, & Peters, 2001) and has disadvantaged working-class, female and *Māori* students (Carpenter & Jaramillo, 2014). While New Zealand education has become more equitable for *Māori*, Pasifika, girls, children in low socio-economic status (SES) families, and those with special needs, Carpenter and Jaramillo highlighted that teachers must be made aware of how inequality, oppression and power operate to contribute to greater social justice. For Carpenter and Jaramillo social justice was about equity, opportunity, the ability to demonstrate reciprocity and tolerance of others. As such, this chapter highlights the importance of teacher diversity to represent the population better (Keddie, 2012).

9.3 Making One-Size Fit All

It is illegal to discriminate in New Zealand based on gender, race, ability and sexual orientation. Student teacher experiences, however, indicated that this has not always been their reality. The following student teachers' examples of how this MTchgLn programme used the concepts from its own conceptual framework to promote, support and facilitate student teachers labelled 'priority learners'.

Kathy had been labelled for most of her life as the 'dyslexic' girl and chose not to disclose this to her ITE colleagues until after they had formed impressions of who she was based on what she does rather than a label assigned to her. She carried this into her primary school setting so that her school would judge her on her teaching ability, not a label. She self-disclosed her dyslexia to her placement class in a teaching moment halfway through her first placement and encountered dissonance when her mentor teacher then raised concerns over her ability to be a teacher. Jacqui, like Kathy, has had the label of dyslexia attached to her since primary school. She, however, did disclose this in her application as this has had an impact on her academic history. As stated, this programme has a directive to enforce an academic entry grade average. Jacqui's application came with outstanding letters of support from two local principals who had been employing her to work with their high school students having difficulty in science. Both noted she was an exceptional teacher already and this MTchgLn programme would benefit significantly from her participation. Finally, Witi was a young *Māori* man who found his first teaching placement, in what he described as a privileged all-boys' secondary school, troubling. Witi grew up in a low SES family where food and clothes were a luxury. He has been in paid employment to support himself financially since he was 14 and working full-time since 16.

9.3.1 Kathy

Kathy entered this programme to become a primary teacher. She presented as a confident and capable 28-year old *Pākehā*/European. In class discussions on how she saw the role of the teacher and student, she became very passionate about equality versus equity. Most of her colleagues answered 'yes' to the question, 'will you treat all your students equally?' She and a few others in the class become vocal around how there was a difference between equality and equity. For most of her colleagues, the New Zealand school system was designed to support them as white, middle-class, *Pākehā*/European students. At this point, Kathy self-disclosed her dyslexia and how she experienced school. Her dyslexia meant she had been labelled and marginalised for most of her schooling. She talked about many of her teachers having minimum expectations of what she could do, and clearly articulated how she felt about those teachers who had no expectations about her. She had deliberately chosen not to disclose her dyslexia as, while they all knew her as Kathy, several will now only see her as 'Dyslexic' Kathy. She made the same decision to withhold her self-disclosure for her school placement.

In this ITE programme, the student teachers are placed in a partner school from the start of the year to see how teachers and schools set up routines and implement teaching programmes. Students are in their schools for the first two weeks of the school year and then return for two-days per week before undertaking a sustained teaching placement. The student teachers are in schools for this early sustained teaching experience not only to see how the year begins, but also to build relationships with both their mentor teacher and students. This is a programme design to support *whanaukataka* (community of learners). Over the course of the first term (New Zealand schools generally operate on a four-term school year, each term approximately 10-weeks long), Kathy worked with both her mentor teacher and Year 2 students (7-year-old students) to take on more and more of the role of the teacher. In Term 2, she was in the middle of her sustained teaching experience when she self-disclosed her dyslexia in a lesson. She had already been in this class for 37 days without incident and was distraught to find out that her mentor teacher had now raised concerns with the school's principal over her ability to be a teacher, now that she knew Kathy was dyslexic.

Kathy sat in tears, in a university mentor's office, questioning if she could go back into the classroom and pointed to a *whakataukī* on the wall, *Whaia to ake ngakanui, i te pono, i te marama* (which can be translated as, 'Know who you are, be who you are') and simply asked, 'how?' This was taken off the wall, she taped it to the front of her folder and her options were discussed. Kathy saw her role as the teacher as being someone to show her students their potential before their peers and society might teach them otherwise. Kathy knows the importance of early intervention for students with learning barriers (Ferrer, Shaywitz, Holahan, Marchione, Michaels, & Shaywitz, 2015). She also knows the importance of teachers seeing dyslexia and other learning 'disabilities', as students who need different learning strategies. It was recommended she be the confident, capable and committed Kathy that she was prior to this incident and trust the relationships she had built in this school.

While her mentor teacher may have had issues with her dyslexia, her principal did not. Her principal had observed Kathy (and every other student teacher in her school) in class and knew she was on track to completing her placement successfully. Her principal also saw this as an opportunity for staff professional development. The school principal and this ITE programme did not make this an issue between mentor teacher and student teacher. It became a learning opportunity for addressing misconceptions around dyslexia and other labels.

This ITE programme's *mana motuhake* (social justice) promotes student teachers to be agents of change, first as student teachers and then classroom teachers. Teachers are instrumental in addressing students' competence beliefs and sense of value (Hattie, 2012). Kathy, working with the school's principal, co-conducted several sessions of staff professional development where the staff were shown how to work with students to develop personal goals for skill mastery, address the notion of their ideal self and their perceptions regarding their abilities. Kathy through her own personal experiences explained how personal goals are prominent in leading students to action for reversal of negative beliefs (Wigfield & Eccles, 2002). Additionally, Kathy highlighted that when students can exercise choice within the appropriate guidance to set goals, they become more engaged and take ownership of their learning. Together Kathy and her principal led the staff through *mātauraka* (a critical analysis) of Urdan and Schoenfelder's (2006) article on classroom motivation. They highlighted how, when students form their own goals and self-evaluate regarding those goals, attitude and self-efficacy can be improved (Urdan & Schoenfelder, 2006). Teachers need to understand that as students move in the present towards future images of themselves, their expectations inform the possible self-images to which they aspire (Carver & Scheier, 2000). Addressing the basic needs of self-worth through competence, and security through relatedness to peers and learning areas are key components of that self-determination process. These professional development sessions culminated in not only the whole school staff, but also Kathy, establishing positive learning experiences and redressing competency beliefs in learning situations (Zimmerman, 2000).

9.3.2 Jacqui

Jacqui was in this ITE programme to be a secondary school science teacher. Jacqui entered this programme after having spent the past five years working very hard to complete her bachelor's degree. To help support herself while studying, she became a tutor. It was her tutoring of high school students having difficulties in chemistry that sparked her desire to be a teacher. She sees student well-being as one of her core responsibilities as a teacher. Jacqui was very aware that research has identified that 11% of school-aged students have learning disabilities (Statistics New Zealand, 2014); she was one of them. Her dyslexia has forced her to think outside the box and find ways to learn what many of her peers take for granted, such as note taking. Her biggest difficulty has always been her ability to express her ideas clearly in written formats. As such, she has found other ways to help her learn.

Several staff members in this MTchgLn questioned her suitability as a secondary teacher as she was unable to meet the academic entry requirement. She was only allowed entry into this programme due to the strong support offered by local principals. Their written testimonials as to her merit and their willingness to place her in their schools for their students' benefit allowed this programme to seek and obtain an exemption from the academic entry requirement for this programme.

As part of all ITE programmes in New Zealand, student teachers are required to pass competency exams in Numeracy, Literacy, and the use of ICT. After her first attempt at the Literacy exam, questions were again raised as to whether letting her remain in this programme was in the best interest of her placement school students. Jacqui was not prepared for this very personal attack by programme lecturers that wanted to end her teaching career after only two weeks in the programme. Not only was Jacqui horrified and justifiably upset by this reaction but also, so were several other members of this programme. This programme's conceptual framework is more than a graphic image. If we as teacher educators would never accept a student teacher telling us that a student, for whatever reason, should not be in their class, then we as teacher educators must role model what we expect.

Jacqui and a university mentor sat down and discussed how she could continue in this programme. Jacqui has spent her entire school life experiencing a neo-liberal educational system that was not designed to support her. Her Bachelor's degree had shown she was capable of tertiary study. So working with the university's Disability Support Services and the systems that were available, Jacqui did demonstrate a passing standard of Literacy.

Like Kathy, she was given a *whakataukī* as a means to help focus her efforts, *Ki te kotahi te kākano ka whati, ki te kāpiua e kore e whati* (can be translated as, 'When we stand alone we are vulnerable, but together we are unbreakable'). Education is founded on relationships and New Zealand is a small 'town' where everyone knows someone in common. Her previous tutoring established a network of chemistry teachers who already knew she was capable of being an effective teacher. Her reputation for being able to explain chemistry to students resulted in her being offered a teaching position while still in her first placement in May.

9.3.3 Witi

Witi was placed into an all-boys' secondary school to support his development as a student teacher. Secondary student teachers in New Zealand are placed in schools that are able to support student teachers in specific subject areas. This school has a strong department in his subjects and these expert teachers would provide him with mentoring in how to bring his subject knowledge into the school system. Witi entered this MTchgLn programme confident in his subject knowledge. He had not only completed his bachelor's degree but also he was a fluent speaker of three languages.

In a class discussion about prior schooling experiences and how student teachers saw the role of the teacher and student, he noted his secondary schooling was not pleasant. He had left at the earliest opportunity when he turned 16 after years of bullying about his second-hand school uniform, lack of food for lunch and his transient home life as he was shunted around family members. He gained entry into his bachelor's degree through an alternative university entry pathway. As he studied subjects of personal interest, his confidence in his own abilities increased and his grades reflected his academic ability. He had learned to believe in himself and his own abilities. He applied for entry into this MTchgLn programme with the intention of making a difference. Witi entered this programme with a strong sense of *mārama* (the understanding of one's own identity, language, and culture). In his interview, he explained in detail how his students were not going to experience the same negative educational environment he experienced.

As part of the foundation paper of their ITE programme, student teachers compare and contrast the pedagogies of *The New Zealand Curriculum* (Ministry of Education, 2007) with traditional *Māori* pedagogies (Hemara, 2000; Pere, 1982). The intent is to provide the student teachers with explicit opportunities to explore bicultural views and reflect on their own beliefs and values. Witi did not need to learn what or how to implement New Zealand's cultural competencies of *ako* (to teach and learn), *whanaungatanga* (relationship building), *tangata whenuatanga* (*Māori* learning as *Māori*), *manaakitanga* (showing respect and care for others) and *wānanga* (communicating with *Māori* to benefit *Māori* learners) (Ministry of Education, 2011). These were concepts he lived and embraced as a young *Māori* man. However, being in what he saw as a privileged all-boys' secondary school at the age of 24 challenged his *mārama*.

Witi requested a different placement school. It took several discussions outside of class between himself and a university mentor to help him work through his apprehensions. His mentor teacher invited him on a tour of his placement school as a chance to familiarise himself with the school. This occurred before any of the students returned for the school year. Witi needed to see himself as a teacher, not as a bullied 15-year old coming to terms with his own family's financial instability. To support his self-as-teacher role identity development, he was given a *whakatauakī* to think about, *Ko au ko au, ko koe ko koe, me haere ngatahi* (which can be translated as, 'I am me, you are you, but we can go on together'). This *whakatauakī* recognises that while people may be different and hold different ideas, values, and beliefs; as a community, they are still able to work together.

Witi needed the confidence to stand in front of a class and feel comfortable being seen as a teacher, not an object of ridicule by other students. One of the programme design features of this ITE programme is that student teachers are welcomed as members of the school staff prior to students returning to school. In this regard, they are given more *mana* (relating to personal status and power) as teaching staff members rather than student teachers. Witi's mentor teacher introduced him to his classes as one of their teachers and then explained how a university mentor would be coming into classes periodically to offer advice and support to both Witi and herself as a means of professional development. This allowed Witi to be himself while being supported, both psychologically and professionally, in learning how to be the teacher he wanted to be.

Witi completed his placement at this school and then transferred to a co-educational school for his second schooling experience. His time at this all-boys' school had more positive moments than negative as he learned that this was his opportunity to develop his own teaching persona. He was not going to be their 'mate' (a New Zealand term forged in World War 1 that goes deeper than being a friend and is based on shared experiences, mutual respect, and unconditional assistance). He was not there to be their 'male' teacher, or 'student' teacher, or '*Māori*' teacher; he was there to learn how to be 'a' teacher.

9.4 Conclusions

In 2013, Lind reported on the characteristics of exemplary ITE programmes in countries similar to Aotearoa New Zealand. Lind noted what other countries like the United States, Finland, Singapore, Netherlands, England, Scotland, and Australia were doing and then reported on the five overarching characteristics from these countries. While these five characteristics are notable and have been included in Aotearoa New Zealand exemplary programmes, what Lind did not include was the unique *Te Tiriti o Waitangi* partnership status Aotearoa New Zealand has between *tangata whenua* (Indigenous New Zealand *Māori*) and *tangata tiriti* (non-*Māori* New Zealanders). The juxtaposition of indigenous knowledge in ITE and neo-liberalism based education is not limited to Aotearoa New Zealand.

There are more than 370 million indigenous people spread across more than 70 countries worldwide. Each of these people practice their own traditions with their own unique social, cultural, economic and political characteristics. Unfortunately for many indigenous people what they have in common is that they 'inhabited a country or a geographical region at the time when people of different cultures or ethnic origins arrived. The new arrivals later became dominant through conquest, occupation, settlement or other means' (United Nations Permanent Forum on Indigenous Issues, n.d., para. 1). Fortunately, Hitchcock, and Koperski (2008) note there are indigenous people who have been able to remain on their ancestors' land. Similarly, McGregor (2004) reports on the *Anishinaabe* and *Haudenosaunee* in Canada, Perry, and Holt (2018) the *Worimi* in Australia, and Sexton (2019) on *Māori* in Aotearoa New Zealand as indigenous people who have retained or reclaimed some of their distinct characteristics.

We argue that neo-liberalism is an unjust and discriminatory system that only allows space for one worldview. Even the very notion that money and profit should be a driving force for change is indicative of a western-centric way of knowing. What is overlooked in this ideology are any other alternative worldviews, such as in Aotearoa New Zealand's *Te Ao Māori* (the *Māori* worldview), which is beginning to carve out a place in the public education system under the guidelines *Our Code Our Standards* (Education Council, 2017).

The New Zealand Curriculum (Ministry of Education, 2007) and *Our Code Our Standards* (Education Council, 2017) set out a vision for a bicultural education system, which allows both *Māori* and *Tauiwi* (non-Māori) students to be themselves and work in partnership. While neoliberalism is the driving force behind many education systems around the world, there are some attempts to address this (Hitchcock & Koperski, 2008; McGregor, 2004; Perry & Holt, 2018; Sexton, 2019). Education must make a difference in all children's lives and social justice demands this, especially for those who have been left behind by neoliberalism.

Loughran, Keast, and Cooper (2016) called for pedagogical reasoning in teacher education. They contended that ITE is not about handing down teaching strategies from a more experience teacher to student teachers. They concluded ITE should be 'teachers' willingness to reframe, reconsider, contextualise, and problematize their practice rather than seek to mimic or replicate the practices of those they observed through their experiences in teacher education' (p. 416). They believed that ITE should be educative, not training, leading to student teachers being better prepared to develop their own vision for their own future teaching. We agree in terms of this programme's conceptual framework for our student teachers, *Rangatira mō āpōpō* (*Rangatira* often refers to our 'young adults', but in this context this whakataukī is best translated as 'Leaders of the future').

Guillén, Gimenes, and Zeichner (2016) noted that 'socially-just education programmes engaged in these movements for justice … just justice, social transformation, or the everyday lived lives of our communities, therefore necessarily begin with the local communities most affected' (p. 247). Education has the ability to make a positive difference in students' lives. Our world is full of diverse individuals and therefore it is crucial that our classrooms provide an environment where everyone is safe, supported, and welcomed. This expectation is for both students and their teachers.

Teachers who embrace diversity in the classroom and do not see it as a hindrance are able to build responsive, reciprocal, and corroborative relationships needed to enrich each individual's education. Teachers should be encouraging difference as a means to learn from one another. The student teachers in this study bring personal strengths, both to this programme and to their placement schools. They challenged not only stereotypes about themselves but also homogenising attitudes, beliefs, and ideas about education.

The purpose of ITE is to prepare student teachers with the skills, knowledge, and behaviours needed to be effective teachers for their students. Rollnick and Mavhunga (2016) highlighted that for many in ITE there is a significant gap between subject matter knowledge and its pedagogy. They then went on to note the value of ITE student teachers linking what they teach with how they teach. The student teachers in this programme have highlighted how we are all unique individuals and should focus on the normalisation of difference. As such, schools need a more sophisticated notion of normality, knowledge, and learning; teachers need to cause intentional social, cultural or behavioural change, i.e. teachers as agents of change. As Ballard (2012) stated in his argument about teachers becoming agents of change, 'a great deal depends on what we think warrants valuing' (p. 72). If as student teachers, they believe they have the ability to go against these messages, then when they become teachers, they are better prepared to be agents of change. Teaching is about learning and its role in shaping children through the curriculum and classroom interactions. As such, teachers and schools must hold themselves responsible for what they do in their classrooms and schools. Teachers must be made aware that their own beliefs and values, which are derived from cultural and social contexts, determine what is and is not important.

References

Ballard, K. (2012). Inclusion and social justice: Teachers as agents of change. In S. Carrington & J. Macarthur (Eds.), *Teaching in inclusive school communities* (pp. 65–87). Milton, Australia: Wiley.

Cameron, M., & Baker, R. (2004). *Research on initial teacher education in New Zealand: 1993– 2004. Literature review and annotated bibliography.* Wellington, New Zealand: Ministry of Education.

Carpenter, V. M., & Jaramillo, N. (2014). Social justice in education. In A. St George, S. Brown, & J. O'Neill (Eds.), *Facing the big questions in teaching: Purpose, power and learning* (2nd ed., pp. 65–72). South Melbourne, Australia: Cengage.

Carver, C., & Scheier, M. (2000). On the structure of behavioral self-regulation. In M. Boerkaerts, P. Pintrich, & M. Zeidner (Eds.), *Handbook of self-regulation* (Vol. 13, pp. 41–48). San Diego, CA: Academic press.

Cunliffe, A. L. (2004). On becoming a critically reflexive practitioner. *Journal of Management Education, 28*(4), 407–426.

Darling-Hammond, L. (2006). *Powerful teacher education: Lessons from exemplary programs* (1st ed.). San Francisco, CA: Jossey-Bass.

Darling-Hammond, L., Hammerness, K., Grossman, P., Rust, F., & Shulman, L. (2005). The design of teacher education programs. In L. Darling-Hammond & J. Bransford (Eds.), *Preparing teachers for a changing world: What teachers should learn and be able to do* (pp. 390–441). San Francisco, CA: Wiley.

Council, E. (2017). *Our code our standards.* Wellington, New Zealand: Education Council.

Education Counts. (2017a). *School rolls.* Retrieved November 14, 2018 from https://www.educat ioncounts.govt.nz/statistics/schooling/student-numbers/6028.

Education Counts. (2017b, February 5). *Teaching staff.* Retrieved November 14, 2018 from https:// www.educationcounts.govt.nz/statistics/schooling/teaching_staff.

Ferrer, E., Shaywitz, B. A., Holahan, J. M., Marchione, K. E., Michaels, R., & Shaywitz, S. E. (2015). Achievement gap in reading is present as early as first grade and persists through adolescence. *The Journal of Pediatrics, 167,* 1121–1125. https://doi.org/10.1016/j.jpeds.2015.07.045.

Guillén, L. I., Gimenes, C. I., & Zeichner, K. M. (2016). Teacher education for educational and social transformation. In J. Loughran & M. L. Hamilton (Eds.), *International handbook of teacher education* (Vol. 2, pp. 239–272). Singapore: Springer Science+Business Media.

Hattie, J. (2009). *Visible learning. A synthesis of over 800 meta-analyses relating to achievement.* London, England: Routledge.

Hattie, J. (2012). *Visible learning for teachers maximizing impact on learning.* New York, NY: Taylor and Francis.

Hemara, W. (2000). *Māori pedagogies: A view from the literature.* Wellington: NZCER.

Hitchcock, R. K., & Koperski, T. L. (2008). Genocide of indigenous peoples. In D. Stone (Ed.), *The historiography of genocide* (pp. 577–617). London: Palgrave Macmillan.

Kane, R. G. (2005). *Initial teacher education policy and practice: Final report.* Retrieved October 11, 2018 from https://ir.canterbury.ac.nz/bitstream/handle/10092/5398/12632441_Itepolicyand practice.pdf;sequence=1.

Keddie, A. (2012). Schooling and social justice through the lenses of Nancy Fraser. *Critical Studies in Education, 53*(3), 263–279.

Korthagen, F. A. J., Kessels, J., Koster, B., Lagerwerf, B., & Wubbels, T. (2008). *Linking practice and theory: The pedagogy of realistic teacher education.* New York, NY: Routledge.

Korthagen, F., Loughran, J., & Russell, T. (2006). Developing fundamental principles for teacher education programs and practices. *Teaching and Teacher Education, 22,* 1020–1041.

Lind, P. (2013). What are the characteristics of exemplary initial teacher education programmes in countries similar to Aotearoa/New Zealand? *Waikato Journal of Education, 18*(1), 87–99.

Loughran, J., Keast, S., & Cooper, R. (2016). Pedagogical reasoning in teacher education. In J. J. Loughran & M. L. Hamilton (Eds.), *International handbook of teacher education* (Vol. 1, pp. 387–421). Singapore: Springer Science+Business Media.

Manning, B. (2013, December 11). Census2013: More ethnicities than the world's countries. *New Zealand Herald.* Retrieved November 14, 2014 from https://www.nzherald.co.nz/news/article. cfm?c_id=1&objectid=11170288.

McGregor, D. (2004). Coming full circle: Indigenous knowledge, environment, and our future. *American Indian Quarterly, 28*(3/4), 385–410.

Ministry of Education. (2007). *The New Zealand Curriculum for English-medium teaching and learning in years 1–13.* Wellington, New Zealand: Learning Media.

Ministry of Education. (2011). *Tātaiako: Cultural competencies for teachers of Māori learners.* Wellington, New Zealand: Learning Media.

OECD. (2005). *Teachers matter: Attracting, developing and retaining effective teachers.* Paris, France: OECD Publishing.

Parliamentary Counsel Office. (2017, February 5). *Education act 1989.* Retrieved November 14, 2018, from https://www.legislation.govt.nz/act/public/1989/0080/latest/DLM177440.html.

Pere, R. R. (1982). *AKO concepts and learning in the Maori tradition.* Monograph. Hamilton, New Zealand: Department of Sociology, University of Waikato.

Perry, L., & Holt, L. (2018). Searching for songlines of Aboriginal education and culture within Australian higher education. *The Australian Educational Researcher, 45*(3), 343–361. https://doi. org/10.1007/s13384-017-0251-x

Rollnick, M., & Mavhunga, E. (2016). The place of subject matter knowledge in teacher education. In J. J. Loughran & M. L. Hamilton (Eds.), *International handbook of teacher education* (Vol. 1, pp. 423–452). Singapore: Springer Science+Business Media.

Sexton, S. S. (2019). Indigenous knowledge. In B. Akpan (Ed.), *Science Education: Visions of the Future* (pp. 447-462). Singapore: Springer.

Statistics New Zealand. (2014). *Disability survey: 2013.* Retrieved November 15, 2018, from https:// archive.stats.govt.nz/browse_for_stats/health/disabilities/DisabilitySurvey_MR 2013.aspx.

Statistics New Zealand. (2015, January 15). *2013 Census—Major ethnic groups in New Zealand.* Retrieved 14 November 2018 from http://archive.stats.govt.nz/Census/2013-census/profile-and-summary-reports/infographic-culture-identity.aspx.

Sutherland, S., Jesson, J., & Peters, H. (2001). Tension and compromise in New Zealand education. In V. Carpenter, H. Dixon, E. Rata, & C. Rawlinson (Eds.), *Theory in practice for educators* (pp. 71–88). Palmerston North, New Zealand: Dunmore Press.

Thompson, N., & Pascal, J. (2012). Developing critically reflective practice. *Reflective Practice, 13*(2), 311–325.

Timperley, H. (2013). *Learning to practise: A paper for discussion.* Wellington, New Zealand: Ministry of Education.

Timperley, H., Wilson, A., Barrar, H., & Fung, I. (2007). *Teacher professional learning and development: Best evidence synthesis iteration.* Wellington, New Zealand: Ministry of Education.

United Nations Permanent Forum on Indigenous Issues. (n.d.). *Who are indigenous peoples?* Retrieved July 14, 2020 from https://www.un.org/esa/socdev/unpfii/documents/5session_factsh eet1.pdf.

Urdan, T., & Schoenfelder, E. (2006). Classroom effects on student motivation: Goal structures, social relationships, and competence beliefs. *Journal of School Psychology, 44,* 331–349. https:// doi.org/10.1016/j.jsp.2006.04.003

Wigfield, A., & Eccles, J. (2002). Development of competence beliefs, expectancies for success, and achievement values from childhood to adolescence. In G. Phye (Ed.), *Development of achievement motivation* (pp. 91–120). San Diego, CA: Academic Press.

Zimmerman, B. (2000). Attaining self-regulation: A social cognitive perspective. In M. Boekaerts, P. Pintrich, & M. Zeidner (Eds.), *Handbook of self-regulation* (Vol. 13, pp. 695–716). San Diego, CA: Academic Press.

Chapter 10
Cultivating Learner Experiences: Using Information and Communication Technology to Counter Locational Disadvantage

Syazlin Sazali, Alicia Franklin, Anthony Dillon, and Alexander S. Yeung

Abstract In contemporary times, there are children who suffer from limited access to resources, even in some developed countries. In Australia, because of its vast landscape, students in rural and remote locations suffer from a variety of disadvantages. Due to limited resources available in their local environment, students in remote locations do not achieve to their best potential. This chapter illustrates how information and communication technology (ICT) may enable educators to engage students in interactive learning activities online. The study is part of a collaborative research project known as *Ngara Wumara* in Aboriginal language, which means "cultivating capabilities" in English, funded by the Australian Research Council (LP140100481). As part of the research project, interviews were conducted with children who worked in a circus, their parents, and other adults, who traveled with the circus from place to place. As their special circumstances prevented them from attending school on a regular basis, the children attended a virtual project-based learning program via Google Classroom. Interview data showed that ICT can expand accessibility to collaborative learning for students who have limited opportunities in a traditional classroom. However, effective virtual classroom environments require adequate technical and infrastructure support, which should be the government's priority in distance education.

Keywords Locational disadvantage · ICT · Interactive online activities · Virtual project-based learning · Google Classroom · Collaborative learning · Distance education

S. Sazali · A. Franklin · A. Dillon · A. S. Yeung (✉)
Australian Catholic University, North Sydney, Australia
e-mail: Alexander.Yeung@acu.edu.au

S. Sazali
e-mail: ssazali@georgeinstitute.org.au

A. Franklin
e-mail: Alicia.Egan@acu.edu.au

A. Dillon
e-mail: Anthony.Dillon@acu.edu.au

10.1 Introduction

In contemporary times, despite an array of technological innovations, there are children in developing countries who continue to suffer from limited access to resources. Due to Australia's vast landscape, students in rural and remote locations suffer from a variety of disadvantages. Limited access to resources and educational opportunities undermines the ability of students in remote locations to achieve their full potential. This pattern is further reflected among gifted and talented students who tend to perform far below their counterparts in urban locations where resources are more readily accessible. Such locational disadvantage may also disproportionately impact on Aboriginal students, who continue to suffer from a broad range of disadvantages resulting from the repercussions of the British colonization over the last two centuries (Mooney, Seaton, Kaur, Marsh, & Yeung, 2016). This chapter illustrates how, in a distance education context, ICT can effectively enable the delivery of project-based learning via Google Classroom to students whose special circumstances may have prevented them from attending school on a regular basis.

Specifically, in this chapter, we attempt to illustrate how student-centered project-based learning (PBL) can be successfully delivered through digital technologies to accommodate the learning potential and diverse interests of students who are disadvantaged in terms of location. Based on the findings, recommendations are provided to assist educators, researchers, and administrators in meeting the diverse needs of learners from disadvantaged backgrounds and environments.

10.2 The Need for Information and Communication Technology

Information and communication technology (ICT) has become an almost indispensable part of our daily life. However, whether ICT is indispensable in all the learning processes of a student may be arbitrary (Pena & Yeung, 2009, 2010). Although there is increasing advocacy for ICT in the classroom, pedagogical and technological approaches may not always align with, and complement each other for the best learning results. For certain student populations, however, ICT may serve as a solution to some basic issues of schooling. A relevant example is the potential of ICT in bringing together students from diverse backgrounds and remote communities hundreds of kilometers apart.

In Australia, 31.5% of the Australian population live outside metropolitan locations, covering the majority of the nation's land area (Australian Bureau of Statistics, 2020). Remoteness is categorized by the Australian Bureau of Statistics as Major Cities, Inner Regional, Outer Regional, Remote Areas, and Very Remote Areas. The classification is based on access to services as measured by the Accessibility and Remoteness Index of Australia (see Australian Government Department of Health, 2011). Of these, 29.3% of students are enrolled in schools outside of major cities

(Halsey, 2018). Such geographical dispersion makes it almost impossible for students in rural and remote locations to engage in collaborative face-to-face PBL activities. This basic issue related to location has disadvantaged rural and remote student populations for many decades.

One potential solution that has received increasing attention in recent years is the use of ICT to support the learning experiences of students in diverse settings including those in rural and remote locations (Nielsen, Miller, & Hoban, 2014). However, innovative ICT provisions do not necessarily align with innovative teaching and learning processes. Learning activities that are essential for building twenty-first-century skills (Moyle, 2010) may not always be effectively delivered through ICT applications. Personal and contextual factors (Goodwin, Low, Ng, Yeung, & Cai, 2015; Lee, Chung, & Yeung, 2019; Lee, Ip, & Yeung, 2016; Lee, Yeung, & Ip, 2017; Yeung, Tay, Hui, Lin, & Low, 2014) may play varying roles in making ICT effective as a tool for program delivery (Yeung, Lim, Tay, Lam-Chiang, & Hui, 2012a; Yeung, Taylor, Hui, Lam-Chiang, & Low, 2012b). How ICT is able to facilitate various pedagogical approaches (e.g., student-centered pedagogies, collaborative learning, individualized instruction, etc.) is yet to be explored. Among personal factors, there may be significant cultural, linguistic, and structural barriers faced by students. For some, however, ICT may be the best, if not the only, solution as their individual circumstances may prevent them from regularly attending school. These include those students who are geographically isolated or whose families may be regularly moving from one place to another. In this chapter, we attempt to illustrate how student-centered PBL can be successfully delivered through digital technologies to accommodate the learning potential and diverse interests of students who are disadvantaged in terms of location.

10.3   Connected Learning for an Effective Educational Program

While ICT has the potential of virtually bringing students together from locations far apart, successful learning ultimately depends on the instructional program and pedagogy. In the present study, the project-based learning (PBL) program implementation was partly guided by the Larmer, Mergendoller, and Boss (2015) Gold Standard PBL model. The model integrates student learning goals, essential project design elements, and project-based teaching practices. In a project-based classroom, students actively participate from the very beginning. Students work together with their teachers to formulate a research question about a topic, followed by processes of planning and researching to create new knowledge. They then reflect on their understandings and improve and present their findings. In our case, Fig. 10.1 illustrates a modified version of this model to demonstrate how technology can be integrated in a connected learning model to support the PBL process. As seen in Fig. 10.1, the learning process is directed and controlled by the student, whereas the teacher serves

Fig. 10.1 Innovative technology application in assisting project-based learning

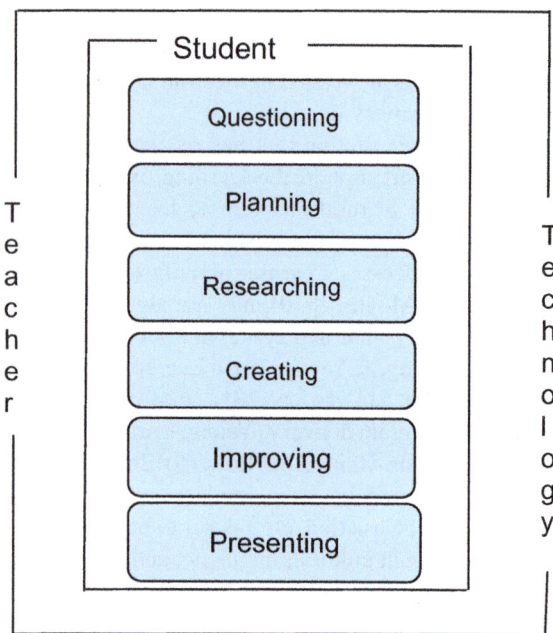

as a facilitator of the learning activities. Technology is used to assist and complement the delivery of PBL.

The benefits of a virtual learning platform to facilitate student learning have been demonstrated by other researchers (e.g., Cheung & Vogel, 2013; Colazzo, Molinari, & Villa, 2013; Davis, Chen, Hauff, & Houben, 2018; Kuo, Chu, & Huang, 2015; Schipke, 2018). Like these previous studies, the benefits for our case would include the opportunity to engage in collaborative learning (Kuo et al., 2015), gains in both social and cognitive outcomes (Schipke, 2018), and networking with others (Colazzo et al., 2013; Davis et al., 2018). Specific to the current approach is the self-directed nature of the learning activities. However, for these students, the acceptance of the virtual learning environment could be a challenge (Cheung & Vogel, 2013).

10.4   Case Study: Google Classroom for Circus Kids

To illustrate the contribution of ICT to facilitate students' engagement in PBL activities, we report a case study on the perceptions of stakeholders, especially students from a special sample—circus children. In Australia, circus communities play an important role in the live performance industry. The industry reported a contribution of $1.41 billion to the Australian economy with significant growth in revenue from the Circus & Physical Theatre category (Live Performance Australia, 2015). Due to the growing number of traveling circus families who spend most of the year on the road, it is challenging to provide quality education for the circus children. This is a major challenge for the nation's education authority as school education is compulsory for children from the age of six until they are at least seventeen (NSW Department of Education, 2018), and yet these children are unable to stay in a regular school setting. In the face of this challenge, the government has promoted distance education as a possible solution. For example, the National School for Traveling Show Children (NSTSC) under the Distance Education program was introduced to cater to the needs of traveling students who are unable to attend regular school for at least one term (i.e., 50 school days or more).

Mostly from rural, and some from very remote, locations, these students who are always on the move do not have a chance to stay in the same school for education. Hence, they need a distance education provision that is of high quality. The online distance learning program described here capitalizes on virtual classroom technology that expands educational access and provides specialized learning opportunities for this special student population. Such an approach is believed to enable students' academic achievement, improve their web-based skills, enhance student satisfaction and consequently course retention, and provide students in remote areas, in particular, with viable educational choices (Barbour & Reeves, 2009; Natale & Cook, 2012; Rice, 2006). In this study, the delivery of PBL via Google Classroom was expected to benefit these children who are disadvantaged in terms of location. To understand the impact of a virtual classroom in project-based learning, we conducted a case study with a sample of such students, along with their teachers and parents.

10.5 Methods

10.5.1 Research Questions

The research questions (RQs) of this study are

RQ1: What are the impacts of project-based learning on students through Google Classroom delivery?

RQ2: What are the barriers (perceived by students, parents, and teachers) that affect the success of the virtual project-based learning?

10.5.2 Participants

This study explores the experiences of three children who travel with a circus, four teachers, and three parents through semi-structured in-depth interviews. The students were enrolled in a distance education program in New South Wales, Australia. They were identified as Aboriginal students (although circus children are not necessarily

Aboriginal) who worked as circus performers alongside their families who were also employed by the circus. The students and their parents were interviewed in separate sessions. Three teachers of the distance education program and a tutor who traveled with the circus were also interviewed.

10.5.3 Processes

The interviews consisted of guiding questions on the stakeholders' perceptions, focusing on the impact and challenges of using Google Classroom in PBL. The participants were also asked to comment on ways to improve the learning experience.

10.5.4 Analysis

Transcripts were coded according to participants' responses to the questions. Thematic analysis was conducted following Braun and Clarke's (2006) framework that includes (1) getting familiar with the data, (2) generating initial codes, (3) identifying themes, (4) reviewing themes, (5) defining themes, and (6) writing up. Qualitative data analysis software NVivo was used to assist in the analysis. The interpretative analysis firstly considered the impact of Google Classroom on student learning experiences. The transcripts were further explored with a focus on the perceptions of participants about any challenges in the uptake of digital education. The response to the challenges gave background themes on the barriers to using Google Classroom to support PBL.

During the data analysis process, meaning units were highlighted and extracted from the participants' responses. Themes emerging across the set of interviews were identified. Initial ideas were discussed, and broader themes were recorded. As we worked through the coding process, meaning units associated with each theme were grouped and repeated revisions were carried out to refine the themes and their grouping. Themes and subthemes were further explored to see if they related to each other. To ensure reliability of the result, the themes and sub-themes were regularly discussed among the project manager, the analyst, and the investigator team. A thematic map that illustrates the themes and subthemes was constructed after the final refinement of the themes.

10.6 Results

Figure 10.2 summarizes the themes elicited from the interviews and the related sub-themes. Overall, Google Classroom was perceived in terms of six themes: (1) learning diversity, (2) personal development, (3) connectedness, (4) adaptability,

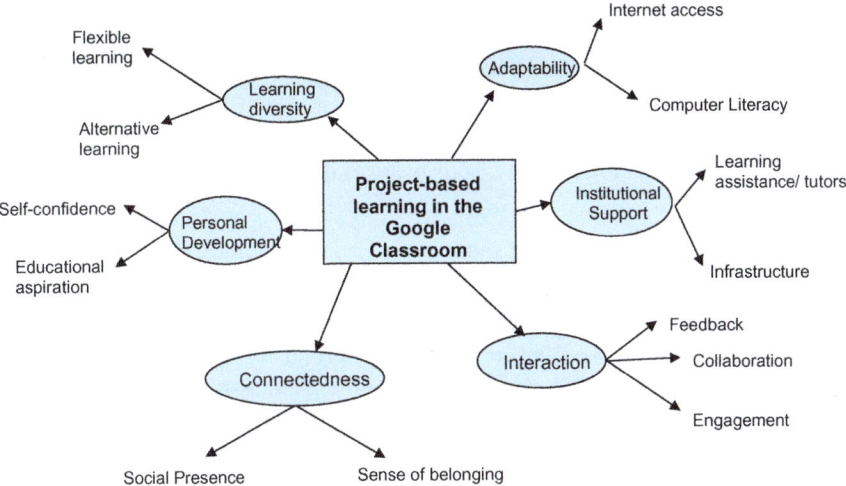

Fig. 10.2 Themes summary from the experience of circus students, teachers, and parents with project-based learning via Google Classroom

(5) institutional support, and (6) interaction. Of these themes, personal development, connectedness, and interaction are directly related to the impact of Google Classroom in the intervention.

10.6.1   Learning Diversity

The Google Classroom experience was perceived as flexible, providing an alternative learning platform that suits the user's adaptability to the new technology and institutional support.

Learning flexibility. Interview participants indicated that virtual learning and Google classroom provided flexibility in terms of the location and schedule of educational delivery. Indeed, students noted that engaging in virtual learning enabled them to remain in remote settings while participating in collaborative learning with other students elsewhere. It has been suggested that for disadvantaged children, virtual classrooms may provide a valuable alternative to mainstream education given the cultural emphasis placed on staying connected with family and community (Lohoar, Butera, & Kennedy, 2014). A real-time virtual classroom would enable remote, disadvantaged students to engage in learning activities and reach their full potential and maintain their collectivist lifestyle and value system. The students in the case study remained with their circus communities and received quality education at the same time, as explained by a parent:

Well so I was born into the circus and my husband has been with the circus for about 20 years. (Name removed) is our eldest child ... she also works in the circus. So, when she's not doing school, she's practicing moves and acts in the show.

Alternative learning. The parents interviewed agreed that Google Classroom is an alternative learning method and they were aware of its future importance, as a parent noted

I think it's the way of the future, that's why you - I can see it, this is the future of learning in schools and I'm surprised we haven't done it earlier actually, to be honest with you. So, it's been good, and the kids are preparing for the future, I see.

Another parent also agreed that one of the benefits of using technology is to search for information, which is not a usual focus in traditional classrooms.

10.6.2 Personal Development

It is evidenced from the analysis that using Google Classroom to complete online projects could foster the ethos of teamwork and help overcome learning barriers. The virtual classroom provides inclusive digital learning which further enhances self-confidence and educational aspiration. A teacher mentioned that "...*because we have constructed our Google Classrooms from a project-based learning format, as in we've challenged the kids with a problem to be solved, it's almost levelled the playing field between our high ability students and [who] are probably lower ability students, because the high ability students just can't answer the question kind of thing. So, they've really got to think about it.*"

Self-confidence. Virtual classroom activities appeared to enhance self-competence beliefs. As the virtual PBL approach encouraged students to work on projects that connected academic learning to what they were passionate about and gave them opportunities to make things relevant to these interests, it resulted in good personal development and increased self-confidence, especially among the Aboriginal students. A teacher commented

Regarding the kids who identify as Indigenous, I have found they're a little bit more reserved at commenting and stuff like that. I'm not exactly sure why with some of my kids... they're a bit nervous about probably being judged by their comments. So, they're a little bit hesitant to kind of put their comments out there and yeah just with the Circus kids it's kind of like taking them a little while to warm up to it.

After enrolling in the program for a year, a parent noticed that her daughter liked doing work on the computer.

Educational aspiration. It was also observed from the parents' feedback that PBL could support young people in remote locations in remaining engaged in education as parents indicated that the Google platform generated interest and in turn ongoing educational aspiration. The virtual PBL approach encouraged students to work on projects that connected academic learning to what they were passionate about, which helped them to relate their education to their lives. A parent noted

> He seems to be trying harder at school… I know that from… we talk to him at home, you know, about to try going to go to school and learning and trying harder and he seems to be like, a bit more… he seems to be more interested. Before he would be like, ooh.

10.6.3 Connectedness

A third theme that emerged from the data is connectedness. Students value relationships and thrive in an active collaborative learning environment (Goss & Sonnemenn, 2017) and interviewees indicated that student engagement in virtual learning enabled greater connectivity and belonging among students.

Social presence. Responses from a teacher highlighted that Google Classroom improved remote students' social presence: "*…to know that they are part of a class. A lot of the time I think they just think they're doing it on their own.*" Students can communicate and view other students' work in the virtual classroom, and there are opportunities for active interaction. "*They can ask for help off each other as well as the teachers and then we use that in the satellite room as well and you can put up everybody's work on the screen at the same time and we can talk about it. So, I think it's another dimension in assisting these children feel less isolated and more like they've got a classroom.*"

Sense of belonging. A strong sense of belonging and feeling of connectedness appeared to improve learning outcomes. Commenting on a student's performance, a teacher said "*He is putting effort and he's more motivated too [than] what he has been.*" Positive effect was also observed by another teacher: "*…this has had a fairly substantial impact on him in the sense that he's getting more involved in things. He's feeling more comfortable as time goes on and having a bit of an input and he's learning.*"

10.6.4 Interaction

Virtual classroom activities enabled the students to communicate and collaborate from any device with an Internet connection. Assignments were created in Google Doc template and were easily accessible in Google Drive. The virtual classroom simplifies the tasks of receiving and returning the students' assignments. Hence, virtual classroom has advantages over traditional classroom in several ways.

Feedback. Teachers can communicate with students and provide assignment feedback "*instantly*" through the platform. Students can also access other G Suite apps such as Slides, Forms, and Gmail to collaborate in a project. The project can be completed online at real-time with peers also helping to provide feedback.

Collaboration. A major contribution of Google Classroom is the facilitation of peer collaboration. As one teacher puts it

> I guess working collaboratively as well with their peers. So, they get to see what - they get to see how their peers are working and the kind of answers that they're giving and that may influence them in a positive way.

Engagement. It was identified from the interviews that students' active engagement in both collaborative and independent learning processes in a virtual classroom was thought to be much alike in many aspects of circus training. The students found the development of skills "...*like a circus tent sometimes*," a reply when asked about his views on using Google Classroom to complete his project. The virtual platform seems to have fostered both collaboration and learning engagement by creating a real-time classroom. A teacher remarked

> So, it was kind of brought it back to the fact like if you're a teacher in the classroom you are moving around the class seeing how kids are going, checking where they're up to, and yeah Google Classroom combined with Google Doc allows us to do that for these kids who are miles away or overseas.

10.6.5 Institutional Support

An important theme that emerged was the need for institutional support. Helping students to adapt with the technology, the program attempts to remove the structural barrier to education. However, technology itself may not solve all problems, and human support may also be crucial. There are students who are not disposed toward virtual PBL and may require more technological assistance.

Learning assistance tutors. The program employs tutors who travel together with the circus. The need for learning assistance tutors seems well justified as the pattern of low literacy levels of the families and the circus community's unique lifestyle mean that many parents are unable to help their children with the school work required through distance education. The need for human support was evidenced in the interviews. Indeed, surfing the multitude of information on the Internet itself can be challenging. Therefore, the role of a face-to-face tutor is essential in providing technical guidance on the spot. Highlighting this essential support, a tutor interviewed discussed the need for greater time and support for students:

> You know, I can't be with them all the time, that's the trouble. I'm not just their tutor, I'm also the tutor of a girl in year nine and a girl in year 10, who have their own sets of problems. So, I've got to be with them sometime too as well. They don't have my full attention.

Infrastructure. In addition to sessions with their tutor to complete their projects, the students attended a weekly satellite lesson for each school subject in a portable classroom caravan. The infrastructure provided by the circus management was apparently limited as students and tutor struggled with limited space due to increasing student enrollment in the program: *"We don't have a lot of room in our classroom."* Evidence points to the need for infrastructure support for the intervention to provide optimal benefits.

10.6.6 Adaptability

Adaptability in this context represents the ability of learners to accept the new learning platform. Despite parents' positive feedback on Google Classroom, adaptability issues kept emerging in the analysis. While Google Classroom helped to connect distance learners and teachers, the application of PBL could be challenging in such a learning environment (Verstegen et al., 2016).

Internet access. Internet access is a major challenge when the circus travels to places with poor Wi-Fi connection. As the students needed to connect to the Internet to complete their projects, lack of digital connectivity hindered their learning progress. An apparent issue is that the approach requires great reliance on stable Internet connections. A parent highlighted that they *"travel around a lot and sometimes we go out into the smaller town,"* where Internet connections are poor.

Computer literacy. Computer illiteracy, if taken as a requirement, could demotivate students from engaging in their learning. When asked about how their children adapted to the new technology at the start of the program, a parent responded *"... they're not used to doing it, that's all."* Obviously, it took time for the children to get used to this learning mode.

On the contrary, it was also observed from the parents' feedback on PBL delivered via Google Classroom that in fact, they saw their children improving in computer literacy at the later stages of the course, and they were happy about it.

10.7 Discussion

Many studies have investigated the impact of ICT on student learning (e.g., Bai, Mo, Zhang, Boswell, & Rozelle, 2016; Skryabin, Zhang, Liu, & Zhang, 2015), and interaction is identified as a central component of an effective collaborative learning process (Rashid & Asghar, 2016). While a project-based approach promotes collaborative learning, the integration of ICT has expanded the accessibility to collaborative learning for students who have limited opportunities of face-to-face interactions in a traditional classroom setting. Careful examination of the data in this study showed that the crucial elements for successful learning, in this case for the special student sample, include interaction during the process of learning, a sense of connectedness encompassing social presence and a sense of belonging, and personal development potentials for building self-confidence and educational aspirations. These findings provide answers to our research questions.

RQ1: "What are the impacts of project-based learning on students through Google Classroom delivery?" Pertaining to geographically disadvantaged students, a sense of connectedness could foster the ability to build personal and interpersonal capabilities. Social presence and a sense of belonging strengthen the connection to the learning process and translate into better self-confidence and educational aspiration. Hence consistent with the report by Alexander et al. (2013), an interactive learning that strongly connects to the learners tends to improve the learning outcomes. However, it is also important for us to understand and address potential barriers to the success of digital education.

RQ2: "Which are the barriers (perceived by students, parents, and teachers) that affect the success of the virtual project-based learning?" The major concerns identified from the analysis were adaptability issues and infrastructure. Internal (e.g., student adaptability/readiness) and external (e.g., tutors, infrastructure) factors are important potential barriers identified from the study. Profiling the digital readiness of circus students and other distance education students, including teachers and parents, is a gap that needs to be addressed. Such a study is lacking and is yet to be conducted in Australian settings.

Particularly relevant to the special sample in our study is the merit of ICT in providing students in a remote location access to an educational opportunity that they would not have enjoyed otherwise. This opportunity enabled them to interact online with other children who are gifted and talented. An amazing finding from this research was that even PBL, which typically requires regular and concentrated interaction among cooperating learners, was effectively conducted online. This illustrates the power of ICT in making a difference to the lives of remote learners who are disadvantaged in various ways (Mooney et al., 2016), and in supporting learning in rural and remote locations (Nielsen et al., 2014). Overall, our findings echo the benefits of a virtual learning platform to facilitate student learning, as demonstrated by other researchers (Cheung & Vogel, 2013; Colazzo et al., 2013; Davis et al., 2018; Kuo et al., 2015; Schipke, 2018). However, while some researchers expect stakeholders' acceptance of virtual learning as a potential challenge (Cheung & Vogel, 2013), the students and families in our sample seemed to happily accept it as a beneficial alternative to conventional schooling. Our findings indicate that online distance learning such as that described here has the potential of expanding educational access and providing specialized learning opportunities for special student populations, such as the circus kids in the present study.

10.8 Recommendations

Based on our findings, we recommend the following:

1. In the context of geographically disadvantaged students, a virtual classroom environment is a possible solution.

2. Project-based learning that requires interactions among learners is viable in a virtual classroom setting.
3. Virtual classroom activities would benefit students in remote locations through the design of projects that focus on helping students develop real-world skills and connect to their daily life.
4. The implementation of virtual classrooms should be strengthened with adequate technical and infrastructure support.
5. A blend of online and on-site provisions will be useful for best program effects. However, having a tutor travel with the circus all the time, looking after a few students may not be cost-effective. Therefore, further research should investigate more cost-effective ways to provide support to students in remote locations.
6. Basic to the success of any ICT application, stable and reliable Internet access and quality should be a prioritized consideration for policy-makers. For ICT to be effectively used to educate geographically disadvantaged students, advanced technological support should be the government's first priority.

10.9 Conclusion

Our findings suggest that ICT, if used appropriately, can provide rich learning opportunities for the most disadvantaged students. The most significant contributions of ICT for circus students who are continually moving from one place to another include interaction, connectedness, and personal development. Educators of special student samples who do not have access to regular classrooms should consider applying ICT to suit instructional purposes and learners' needs. Program developers should consider how best to design programs and pedagogies presented through virtual platforms to effectively cater to learners' needs. Education for disadvantaged students is always a challenge for administrators in schools and teacher education. However, given our finding that even collaborative PBL activities can be facilitated through a virtual classroom, the design of innovative and effective virtual classroom materials and activities remains as an important endeavor for educators and researchers.

References

Alexander, S., Barnett, D., Mann, S., Mackay, A., Selinger, M., & Whitby, G. (2013). *Beyond the classroom: A new digital education for young Australians in the 21st century*. Retrieved from Analysis and Policy Observatory Website: https://apo.org.au/node/34413.
Australian Bureau of Statistics (2020). Regional population. Retrieved from https://www.abs.gov.au/statistics/people/population/regional-population/2018-19#data-download
Australian Government Department of Health. (2011). *Accessibility Remoteness Index of Australia (ARIA)*. Retrieved from https://www1.health.gov.au/internet/publications/publishing.nsf/Content/ARIA-Review-Report-2011~ARIA-Review-Report-2011-2~ARIA-Review-Report-2011-2-2-3.

Bai, Y., Mo, D., Zhang, L., Boswell, M., & Rozelle, S. (2016, 05). The impact of integrating ICT with teaching: Evidence from a randomized controlled trial in rural schools in China. *Computers & Education, 96,* 1–14. https://doi.org/10.1016/j.compedu.2016.02.005.

Barbour, M. K., & Reeves, T. C. (2009, 02). The reality of virtual schools: A review of the literature. *Computers & Education, 52*(2), 402–416. https://doi.org/10.1016/j.compedu.2008.09.009.

Braun, V., & Clarke, V. (2006, 01). Using thematic analysis in psychology. *Qualitative Research in Psychology, 3*(2), 77–101. https://doi.org/10.1191/1478088706qp063oa.

Cheung, R., & Vogel, D. (2013). Predicting user acceptance of collaborative technologies: An extension of the technology acceptance model for e-learning. *Computers & Education, 63,* 160–175.

Colazzo, L., Molinari, A., & Villa, N. (2013). ICT-enabled learning settings: Course, person or community? *International Journal of Distance Education Technologies, 11*(3), 32–46.

Davis, D., Chen, G., Hauff, C., & Houben, G.-J. (2018). Activating learning at scale: A review of innovations in online learning strategies. *Computers & Education, 125,* 327–344.

Goodwin, A. L., Low, E. L., Ng, P. T., Yeung, A. S., & Cai, L. (2015). Enhancing playful teachers' perception of the importance of ICT use in the classroom: The role of risk taking as a mediator. *Australian Journal of Teacher Education, 40*(4).

Goss, P., & Sonnemenn, J. (2017). *Engaging students: Creating classrooms that improve learning.* Grattan Institute.

Halsey, J. (2018). *Independent review into regional, rural and remote education: Final report.* Retrieved from Department of Education and Training website: https://docs.education.gov.au/documents/independent-review-regional-rural-and-remote-education-final-report.

Kuo, Y.-C., Chu, H.-C., & Huang, C.-H. (2015). A learning style-based grouping collaborative learning approach to improve EFL students' performance in English courses. *Journal of Educational Technology & Society, 18*(2), 284–298.

Larmer, J., Mergendoller, J., & Boss, S. (2015). *Setting the standard for project-based learning.* Alexandria, VA: ASCD.

Lee, C., Yeung, A. S., & Cheung, K. W. (2019, 05). Learner perceptions versus technology usage: A study of adolescent English learners in Hong Kong secondary schools. *Computers & Education, 133,* 13–26. https://doi.org/10.1016/j.compedu.2019.01.005.

Lee, C., Ip, T., & Yeung, A. S. (2016). Use of computer technology for English language learning: Do learning styles, gender, and age matter? *Computer Assisted Language Learning, 29*(5), 1033–1049.

Lee, C., Yeung, A. S., & Ip, T. (2017). University English language learners' readiness to use computer technology for self-directed learning. *System, 67,* 99–110.

Live Performance Australia. (2015). *Life performance industry posts $1.41 billion in revenue and 1.83 million in attendance.* Retrieved from https://liveperformance.com.au/news/live_performance_industry_posts_141_billion_revenue_and_1838_million_attendance.

Lohoar, S., Butera, N., & Kennedy, E. (2014). *Strengths of Australian Aboriginal cultural practices in family life and child rearing.* Retrieve from Child Family Community Australia website: https://aifs.gov.au/cfca/publications/strengths-australian-aboriginal-cultural-practices-fam.

Mooney, J., Seaton, M., Kaur, G., Marsh, H. W., & Yeung, A. S. (2016). Cultural perspectives on Indigenous and non-Indigenous Australian students' school motivation and engagement. *Contemporary Educational Psychology, 47,* 11–23.

Moyle, K. (2010). *Building innovation: Learning with technologies.* ACER Press.

Natale, C. F., & Cook, J. (2012, 11). Virtual K–12 learning: New learning frontiers for state education agencies. *Peabody Journal of Education, 87*(5), 535–558. https://doi.org/10.1080/0161956x.2012.723491.

Nielsen, W., Miller, K. A., & Hoban, G. (2014, 10). Science teachers' response to the digital education revolution. *Journal of Science Education and Technology, 24*(4), 417–431. https://doi.org/10.1007/s10956-014-9527-3.

NSW Department of Education. (2018). *Compulsory school attendance.* Retrieved from https://education.nsw.gov.au/student-wellbeing/attendance-behaviour-and-engagement/school-attendance.

Pena, M. I., & Yeung, A. S. (2009). University students' satisfaction with online and face-to-face Spanish learning. *International Journal of Learning, 16,* 637–648.

Pena, M. I., & Yeung, A. S. (2010). Satisfaction with online learning: Does university students' computer competence matter? *International Journal of Technology, Knowledge and Society, 6*(5), 97–108.

Rashid, T., & Asghar, H. M. (2016, 10). Technology use, self-directed learning, student engagement and academic performance: Examining the interrelations. *Computers in Human Behavior, 63,* 604–612. https://doi.org/10.1016/j.chb.2016.05.084.

Rice, K. L. (2006, 06). A comprehensive look at distance education in the K–12 context. *Journal of Research on Technology in Education, 38*(4), 425–448. https://doi.org/10.1080/15391523.2006. 10782468.

Schipke, R. C. (2018). Cooperative learning and Web 20: A social perspective on critical thinking. *Journal of Educational Multimedia and Hypermedia, 27*(2), 193–208.

Skryabin, M., Zhang, J., Liu, L., & Zhang, D. (2015, 07). How the ICT development level and usage influence student achievement in reading, mathematics, and science. *Computers & Education, 85,* 49–58. https://doi.org/10.1016/j.compedu.2015.02.004.

Verstegen, D. M., Jong, N. D., Berlo, J. V., Camp, A., Könings, K. D., Merriënboer, J. J., & Donkers, J. (2016). How e-learning can support PBL groups: A literature review. *Advances in Medical Education Educational Technologies in Medical and Health Sciences Education,* 9–33. https://doi.org/10.1007/978-3-319-08275-2_2.

Yeung, A. S., Lim, K. M., Tay, E. G., Lam-Chiang, A. C., & Hui, C. (2012a). Relating use of digital technology by pre-service teachers to confidence: A Singapore survey. *Australasian Journal of Educational Technology, 28*(8), 1317–1332.

Yeung, A. S., Taylor, P. G., Hui, C., Lam-Chiang, A. C., & Low, E.-L. (2012b). Mandatory use of technology in teaching: Who cares and so what? *British Journal of Educational Technology, 43*(6), 859–887.

Yeung, A. S., Tay, E., Hui, C., Lin, J. H., & Low, E. (2014). Pre-service teachers' motivation in using digital technology. *Australian Journal of Teacher Education, 39*(3), 135–153.

Part III
Diversifying Experiences for Learners with Special Needs

Chapter 11
Catering for Diversity in Psychosocial and Learning Needs in a Low-Income Country

Miriam Mason, David Galloway, and Andrew Joyce-Gibbons

Abstract This chapter reviews the work of three largely residential schools run by EducAid, a small NGO in Sierra Leone. Thousands of children had missed out on schooling following the rebel war (1991–2002). Marginalised children included child soldiers, children whose parents had died in the fighting and children returning from refugee camps. The post-conflict context was one in which many students had been exposed to violence, trauma and tragedy. The challenge was to provide a loving, learning community with appropriate teaching and learning methods for a wide range of ages, educational experience, competence and confidence. Some students have missed years of schooling, but others arrive at EducAid having missed little or none of their education. Consequently, some teenagers are illiterate on admission, with attainments below those of much younger children. EducAid, therefore, devised a personalised learning system that encourages children to take responsibility for their own learning, and to learn with and from peers, supported by teachers. Progression depends on reaching a specified standard in each module. The purpose-written modules cover the content of the national exams but provide opportunities for students to interact with each other in ways that challenge their previous negative and violent experiences. In other words, catering for diversity in learning can not be carried out independently of diversity in psychosocial experiences.

Keywords Marginalised children · Low-income country · Personalised learning · Non-government organisation

M. Mason (✉)
EducAid Sierra Leone & Durham University, Durham, UK
e-mail: miriam@educaid.org.uk

D. Galloway · A. Joyce-Gibbons
Durham University, Durham, UK
e-mail: d.m.galloway@durham.ac.uk

A. Joyce-Gibbons
e-mail: andrew.joyce-gibbons@durham.ac.uk

© Springer Nature Singapore Pte Ltd. 2020
C. Koh (ed.), *Diversifying Learner Experience*,
https://doi.org/10.1007/978-981-15-9861-6_11

11.1 Introduction

This chapter reviews the work of three largely residential schools, two secondary and one primary, run by EducAid, a small NGO in Sierra Leone, West Africa. EducAid's first school opened in 2000, 18 months before the eleven-year war ended in 2002. Thousands of children had missed out on schooling. Marginalised children included child soldiers, children whose parents had died in the fighting and children returning from refugee camps (Katta, 2016). Walter (2011) noted high levels of return to conflict in countries emerging from civil war unless the causes are tackled, and in Sierra Leone, they have arguably not been. While there has been no return to wholesale war, the conditions continue for on-going instability. The post-conflict context was one in which many students had been exposed to violence, trauma and tragedy. The challenge was to provide a loving, learning community with appropriate teaching and learning methods for students with a wide range of ages, educational experience, competence and confidence.

Today, eighteen years after the war ended, Sierra Leone remains an impoverished country, ranking 8th poorest in the 2019 Human Development Index (UNDP, 2019). Nearly 42% of the population are aged below 14 and 60.3% are below 24, yet the government budget for education remained low: 2.9% of GDP until 2019 compared with 6.2% in Ghana, 5.9% in South Africa and 5.6% in the UK (Central Intelligence Agency, 2016; International Monetary Fund, 2018). However, a new government has increased education expenditure to 7% of GDP. Correlating with low levels of development and high levels of poverty is the high level of corruption. Sierra Leone ranks 130th out of 175 countries on a corruption index (Trading Economics, 2017; UNDP, 2018). Unsurprisingly, surveys in 2017 found that 19% of school-aged children were not enrolled at or attending school (Government of Sierra Leone, 2018).

EducAid's admission policy still prioritises the country's most vulnerable children. These include children of former child soldiers, street children, children from families affected by the Ebola crisis in 2014–15 and, more recently, children who lost their homes and families during the 2017 mudslide in Freetown (Relief Web, 2017). There is little correlation between children's previous public exam results and their actual ability when they apply to attend EducAid. It is quite possible for a child to have completed primary school with a pass result from the National Primary School Examination (NPSE) but actually to have no functional literacy or numeracy. This illustrates the low reliability of public exam results and is just one example of the corruption and poor governance relating to basic services. EducAid accordingly has to provide its own assessment of each student on admission.

11.2   Issues in Catering for Diversity in a Low-Income Country

Some children coming into EducAid have had a relatively stable experience of schooling starting at four or five years old but the person(s) paying for them could have fallen ill, lost their jobs or died and their education has been interrupted. Many have lived with relatives other than their parents as '*men pikin*,' an informal system of fostering that can result in serious neglect and abuse in which children often become unpaid labour for the household in return for food and shelter. Others have had a year or so in education followed by a period out of school. Some have not been allowed to start attending school until age eight or nine or more. Across Sierra Leone, girls are the subject of sexual abuse both in their homes and in schools (Mansaray & Johnson, 2013). As a consequence, age ranges, education experiences, and levels of trauma and abuse of those coming to EducAid can vary enormously even within one class. The children come with a huge range of educational attainments irrespective of years apparently spent in school and indeed of age. This diversity is in addition to the range of ability and motivation that occurs within any group of students. The diversity of cases facing EducAid teachers, therefore, encompasses not only a wide range of educational attainments within each class, but also an equally wide range of potentially stressful experiences within their families and communities.

Along with almost all other countries, Sierra Leone is committed to the UN (1989) Convention on the Rights of the Child and the Salamanca Statement and Framework for Action on Special Needs Education (UNESCO, 1994[1989]). High-income countries support schools in catering for students' diverse and exceptional needs with a well-established network of services such as educational psychologists, speech therapists, physiotherapists, school medical services, learning and behaviour support teams. None of these exist in most low income countries. Within schools in high-income countries, it is usual to find a similarly well-established network of services for students with special needs. In the UK, for example, each school nominates a teacher as the Special Educational Needs Coordinator (SENCO) and is expected to maintain a register of students with special needs and disabilities. Most SENCOs have received specialist training, either in-service or in the form of post-graduate qualifications. Schools receive additional resources to support students with severe or complex needs, and these students have an education health and care plan (EHC) which is reviewed at least annually (Department for Education & Department of Health, 2015). None of this support is available in most low-income countries, nor are specialised curricular resources readily available.

Because diversity encompasses such a wide range of educational attainments and of negative experiences outside the school setting, addressing students' educational and psychosocial needs has to be grounded in the most basic principles of teaching and learning: starting at each student's current level of educational attainment and progressing when she or he demonstrates the confidence, knowledge, understanding and skills required for more complex work. It also has to be grounded in recognition that diversity can be a resource, not a problem. That implies creating an environment in which students learn from each other. Consistently, the literature on peer tutoring demonstrates benefits for both tutors and tutees (e.g. Topping, Miller, Thurston, McGavock, & Conlin, 2011) but even when based on school or district-wide initiatives (e.g. Tymms et al., 2011) the research is based mainly on carefully planned and monitored projects. In the context of a resource-impoverished low-income country, the challenge is to create a culture in which students see supporting each other's learning and social development as a normal part of learning and living.

In EducAid's experience, diversity in learning and psychosocial needs are closely related and both academic and social learning have to be guided by a clear set of values. The prioritisation of the values guiding all other activities provides a context and framework for the academic work. The wide range of needs is addressed by building an appreciation of diversity as part of students' growth as citizens.

11.3 Values

In Sierra Leone, educational reform has been limited by two related constraints. First, post-war reconstruction focused largely on the donor-driven Education for All (EFA) programmes (Nishimuko, 2007). The priority was to create sufficient school places by building new schools or upgrading existing ones. Yet in spite of these efforts, the most basic responsibility of universal primary education has not been achieved, with 19% of children out of school (Government of Sierra Leone, 2018). Girls remain particularly vulnerable. Sierra Leone ranks 19th highest in the world for child marriage[1] (Girls Not Brides, 2017) and 'very high' on the Social Institution & Gender Index (OECD, 2017). Of girls and young women aged 15–19, 28% have a child or are pregnant, and 22% have had sex with a man at least ten years older than them. By the age of 15, 13% of girls are married and 39% by age 18 (Save the Children, 2016, pp. 1, 4). Second, pre-occupation with infrastructure has left little time or energy for fundamental questions about the purpose of education and the role of schools in developing a sense of social responsibility and citizenship. As a result, rote learning remains the dominant teaching method and corporal punishment the dominant method of control. School curricula, established before the war, remain content heavy. The West African Examinations Council (WAEC) continue to resist change in the syllabi and exam structure. Dillard, (2012) sees this as a reaction to fears since the Council's inception that adapting a Western curriculum to the needs of Africans would be seen as dumbing down education for Africans. When assessments focus on content, teaching, too, focuses on content (Pritchett, 2013).

In this context, it remains EducAid's view that the social and societal purposes of education must underpin its work and it has spent the last twenty years evolving its curriculum and ways of working to deliver the quality of education that places at least as much importance on raising citizens as on exams. EducAid's vision is summarised

---

[1]Child marriage rate' refers to the percentage of women aged 20–24 years who were first married or in a union before age 18, unless otherwise specified.

Fig. 11.1 EducAid's stated values and vision (EducAid, 2017)

in Fig. 11.1: a dignified, democratic and globally engaged Sierra Leone where poverty is eradicated by educated citizens and six cross-cutting values (EducAid, 2017). Making this vision a reality requires as much attention to what students learn from the culture and climate of the school, and from *how* they are taught—the hidden curriculum—as from the official curriculum. It entails demonstrating that there are alternatives to the corporal punishment and sexual abuse that are rife in government schools and that the violence, trauma, neglect and abuse that many students experienced prior to admission need not define their future. So how are these ideals achieved in practice?

11.4   Values Led Education: Catering for Diversity in Learning and Attainment

In government schools, progression from year to year is often automatic, irrespective of attainment, without addressing the variety of needs within the class. In EducAid, there is a structure that is completely unrelated to how long students have previously attended school, how old they are and indeed how long they have been out of school. Progression is personalised and is based on exactly that: how an individual is progressing through the syllabus.

Some students have missed years of schooling, but others arrive at EducAid having missed little or none of their education. Moreover, some children's previous negative and violent experiences have severely affected their ability to benefit from school, for example, due to problems in concentration. Consequently, some teenagers are illiterate on admission, with attainments below those of much younger children. EducAid, therefore, devised a personalised learning system that encourages children: (i) to take responsibility for their own learning; (ii) to learn with and from peers, supported by teachers. Progression depends on reaching a specified standard in each module. The purpose-written modules cover the content of the national exams but provide opportunities for students to interact with each other in ways that challenge their previous stressful experiences. In other words, catering for diversity in learning cannot be separated from provision for a new set of psychosocial experiences.

11.4.1   Independent and Peer Learning

Once students have reached the required standard in the entry-level classes, they work on their exam subjects, progressing independently through pre-prepared materials. They have to take responsibility for their own progress, negotiating their path through the whole syllabus with their teachers. All those studying a particular sub-topic sit together and become each other's first port of call if one gets stuck. Students become used to supporting each other's learning, strengthening their citizenship, community and leadership abilities while they do it. One student explained:

> By me doing my extra studies and meeting students to assist me, especially where I am lacking, through this process I was able to improve in many subjects and pass unit tests. It has really, really improved me through working hard, concentration, courage and seriousness. And now, I can boast of many things and also assist those that are down there.

He has learned to take responsibility for his own progress and push himself hard to develop. He was helped and now is in a position to help.

No two students will have exactly the same path through the syllabus. The teachers work with each student according to their needs and organise them in different groupings. They work through units in different sequences, dependent on the needs of each individual. Sitting around the same table may be students who will complete a given unit of work within a couple of days and others who will take some weeks. There may be some who are struggling with lack of self-confidence in the subject mixed in with those who are competent and quick in their learning. Students are actively encouraged on a daily basis to make sure they have helped someone and sought help from someone. 'Ubuntu'—a word from southern Africa meaning "I am because we are"—is a watch-word with which staff and students constantly remind each other of their inter-dependence and mutual responsibility to share, care for and support each other. At the end of each school day, the children, nominate each other for Ubuntu stars if they have demonstrated "ubuntu" attitudes and behaviours.

11.4.2 Values-Focused Activities Included in the Pre-prepared Subject Workbooks

The pre-prepared materials cover the full syllabus for each subject. But they also seek consciously to develop critical and creative thinking, to provide opportunities for peer learning and to make the link to the EducAid values. For example, in order to challenge gender stereotypes, in each science unit the life story of a female scientist who works in that field of science is discussed.

11.5 Values-Led Education: Catering for Diversity in Prior Experience and Current Psychosocial Needs

Many of EducAid's students have had stressful and potentially traumatic experiences prior to admission. In fact, one could argue that by virtue of having lived in Sierra Leone through the Ebola crisis, which all but the very youngest remember clearly, all Sierra Leonean youth have been through experiences that would elsewhere clearly class as traumatic. Some education reform programmes, such as the UK Aid supported 'Leh Wi Learn' support to secondary schools (DFID, 2018) have focused entirely on academic support. Other NGOs, such as the (Pikin to Pikin Movement, 2017) work in schools but focus on human rights and psychosocial concerns. EducAid has striven to address both academic and psychosocial needs, recognising the crucial place each play in enabling a young person to achieve hhis/her potential as well as allowing him/her to contribute positively to society more generally. In fact, it is the view of the organisation that one without the other results in a serious underperformance in both.

As argued by Sonuga-Barke (2019), the family environment is probably the most significant factor in ensuring success and resilience of traumatised youth. With this in mind, EducAid has worked purposefully to create a family environment for its pupils as well as pushing for academic excellence. Because of significant scandals in orphanage systems in some countries, there is a real danger of regarding the family as invariably the best place for a child without considering the particular context. For example, UNICEF (2016) have developed a global policy that is so pro-family that it has ended up being opposed to orphanages, almost on principle (Mercer, 2014). Because of the extreme poverty that occurs in so many rural and urban families in Sierra Leone, it is the experience of EducAid that adding another child to some family homes can actually result in significant abuse and neglect. In response, EducAid aims, on the one hand, to provide a positive family experience within the institution but also to facilitate relationships with the blood family that are not relationships of dependence and therefore not so easily open to abuse.

Learning from global standards of children's rights (Global Initiative to End All Corporal Punishment of Children, 2015) and from the recommendations of the Truth & Reconciliation Commission for Sierra Leone (TRC, 2004), EducAid has always had a zero-tolerance approach to corporal punishment, sexual abuse and harassment. However, this is not inconsistent with academic excellence. Students are encouraged to push themselves to be as academically successful as they can, but they are also taught that this is insufficient preparation for life and certainly not enough for them to achieve EducAid's vision. Accordingly, they are provided with a range of opportunities to develop their critical thinking, independence, leadership and citizenship behaviour. Specific strategies include.

- Vertical tutor groups and families
- Community Service
- EVC: A way of working that emphasises that 'Every Voice Counts'
- Restorative Justice Approaches and Peer Mediation
- Gender equality programming
- Leadership learning.

11.5.1 Vertical Tutor Groups and Families

All EducAid schools are divided into vertical tutor groups which are divided into peer-led mixed-age families, each family led by a senior student. The students launder, study outside the classroom, undertake daily chores, eat and often sleep in their families. Every day, the families spend time together discussing issues such as: budget allocation within the school, the planning of upcoming events, and challenges they have identified in the running of the school. The students then provide feedback to the school leadership. By creating a safe environment in which students can share ideas, the family groups aim to teach the importance of relationships. The families are also the first point of contact if there are social or academic issues with an individual—the family is where any student can expect to get their first round of support whatever the issue. This provides opportunity for the development of a safe space in a small enough unit for it to become one's school family. It also provides the opportunity for developing leadership, close and caring relationships and mechanisms for holding each other to account.

11.5.2 Community Service

Each year, all students, from Class 6 in primary school to the top end of secondary school, are required to undertake a two or three-week period of community service. They learn the dignity and empowerment that is to be found in giving. If they have no money to give, they have their time, their skills, knowledge and love. They serve in nearby schools giving assistance to younger children in targeted areas such as reading or maths tuition. They serve by helping in cross-country road repairs particularly during the rainy season when some villages get cut off. They help with cleaning or with other chores in the nearby hospitals or clinics. They learn the principles of "passing it forwards". Having received kindness themselves, they are encouraged to find opportunities to pass some kindness on to others.

11.5.3 EVC: 'Every Voice Counts' (EVC)

EVC includes a range of ways of working that endeavours to engage EducAid students in being upstanders not bystanders when they see an injustice. The peer-led families are a component of EVC where students participate in the decisions on how the school is run. Students learn not just to compete with each other but to collaborate and support each other as well as to hold each other to account for the completion of chores and for doing the right thing. In class, EVC means that all students are responsible for upholding classroom norms and agreed expectations.

EVC systems also require that student representatives attend the morning briefing along with the staff. Equally, students participate in lesson observations and provide feedback to teachers. Staff and students are taught how to give useful feedback with two key rules: 1. Be specific and 2. Don't be mean.

The schools are run with the cooperation and collaboration of the students, with students learning their responsibilities along with their rights. It is made clear that they not only have a right to have their voices heard but also a responsibility, particularly to protect the rights of others or to speak up against an injustice or wrong behaviour. Nothing is just the responsibility of the teacher.

11.5.4 Restorative Justice Approaches and Peer Mediation

In EducAid schools, unlike most other Sierra Leonean schools, corporal and humiliating punishments are banned. Teachers are encouraged to use restorative methods to support students to take responsibility for behaviours that will result in them being able to achieve their academic and social goals. This includes having agreed expectations that govern and guide the behaviour of all, including the teachers, within a given classroom. Students as well as teachers are responsible for upholding these expectations and hold each other to account when things have not gone as they should have done.

Some students are also specifically trained in peer mediation skills. These students are selected by staff and students in each tutor group and are called in if families and classes have been unable to handle an issue, hopefully before it needs to involve the teachers. In line with the creation of a learning environment that learns from the best of family life, the focus for behaviour management is not the suppression of the bad but the celebration of good relationships. When a member of the school community has broken a classroom agreement or failed to show appropriate love and concern to a colleague, they are encouraged to put the relationship right by replacing the bad with a good. For example, if a child has been reprimanded several times for disrupting the class with too much talk, he/she will be asked to choose a task that will in some way serve the class and compensate for the lost teaching and learning time. He/she might offer to fetch the drinking water for the class or sweep the class after school in reparation.

If students want to argue the toss about an issue, peer mediators may spend some time talking to them to help them realise the impact of their behaviours on the class. The teacher can intervene if the mediators are unable to resolve the situation but having one or two peer mediators to support them, away from the public eye, often enables a child to climb down and make a positive decision.

11.5.5   Gender Equality Programming

In Sierra Leonean culture, girls are less likely to attend school than boys (UNESCO-UIS, 2018) and in women aged 15–49, 89.6% are subjected to female genital mutilation (FGM) (Statistics Sierra Leone, 2013). In response to issues relating to gender inequality, EducAid has a dedicated Equality Team that works throughout all the EducAid schools on providing girl-friendly programming, training for male and female staff, materials and workshops for the Girl Power Group[2] and the White Ribbon Campaign[3] clubs to provide an alternative rhetoric and narrative for both the men and boys, and the women and girls. EducAid also has a Girls' Safe House where the resident primary school girls live. The safe house aims to provide an environment that can undermine the societal messages that can disempower girls in the wider community. The norms within the house are respect, safety, strength and possibility.

The Women's Project is an accelerated learning project for secondary age girls with below secondary academic standards. It offers a special access route to help them reach the standard needed for secondary school. It is a girls' only environment where girls can gain the competence and confidence they need to operate with excellence in the mainstream classes. The focus is on numeracy, literacy and self-esteem.

11.5.6   Leadership Learning

The students are given plentiful opportunities to develop their leadership thinking and behaviours. These include.

---

[2]The Girl Power Group is a weekly girls' club that focuses on providing the girls with knowledge about their rights and responsibilities as women as well as role-models of strong and inspirational women that they can emulate.

[3]The White Ribbon Campaign is a weekly boys' club that focuses on providing the boys with knowledge about their role in fighting for equality as well as what it means to be a really strong (i.e. not violent) man and role-models for them to emulate.

Prefects. Prefects are selected by the student council which has representatives selected by the staff and students within each tutor group. Their role is to support staff in the day-to-day running of classroom and school activities. They take responsibility for tasks such as preparing the classroom, distributing and collecting the learning materials, supporting their colleagues in attending punctually after breaks.

Family leaders. Family leaders are selected by the students in each tutor group. They are subsequently trained to be like parents (rather than bosses) in their family groups. They learn to make sure that every family member is looked after, gets their food even if they are doing an activity at meal-time, and is supported by another family member or someone from another family for academic concerns.

Participating in lesson observations and the provision of feedback to teachers. Each teacher is observed by a group of staff and students each term as part of an on-going concern to improve their teaching and the learning environment they provide for their students. Students, selected by their colleagues from within their tutor groups, participate in the teams that undertake these observations. To do this well means that all members of the team have to understand that this is not about witch-hunting or trying to catch somebody out but about us all actively trying to get better. In one piece of feedback, a class four student was able to tell his teacher that his writing on the board was making it hard for him to learn. He was able to say this respectfully and was cited by the teacher concerned, with pride, as an example of the open relationships he had been able to create in his classroom.

Leading whole school assemblies. Whole school assemblies are held daily in the primary schools, and on a weekly basis in the secondary schools. Sections of the assembly are run by students so that they learn to speak in public with confidence in a supportive environment.

Participating in site briefings. Every morning on each school site, the staff and some student representatives, selected from the student body on a rotational basis for one week at a time, meet to discuss the running of the school for the day. The children are responsible for reporting on any student welfare issues and also contribute to other discussions about how things are run.

Sharing the in-class responsibility for upholding the agreed expectations. Every student is expected to hold their colleagues to account for upholding the agreed expectations, such as

- We will treat each other with respect.
- We will be punctual.
- We will protect each other's learning.

It is expected that students will request each other to change behaviour if they see their colleagues failing to live up to the agreed standard.

Participate in the shared leadership teams in which all staff members take part. In line with the EVC spirit, all members of the staff are also members of leadership teams that govern all aspects of the school, for example

- Academic team.
- HR team.
- Finance team.

Student representatives, selected by tutor groups, participate in fortnightly meetings. While acknowledging that confidentiality must be maintained on sensitive issues such as an individual's health, they provide feedback to the student body and also provide them with the opportunity to discuss the relevant issues.

Taking responsibility for reporting breaches of the EducAid Staff Code of Conduct.[4] There is a monthly discussion and review of the Staff Code of Conduct to ensure that every member of the community knows: (i) what behaviour is acceptable and safe and what is unacceptable and unsafe; (ii) how to report breaches and to whom; (iii) that the safety of the informant and potential victim is paramount before discussing how any investigation should proceed.

In monthly leaders' meetings, these strategies are discussed and reviewed to see how the organisation can continue to hold itself to account to achieve its aims. As the need arises, new ideas are piloted, approaches adjusted, practicalities modified. In line with one of its core values of pursuing excellence, through this process of continual improvement, the organisation strives to provide better and more appropriate opportunities for the development of all its student beneficiaries.

11.6 Discussion: Challenges in Implementation and How They Are Overcome

11.6.1 Consistency Between Schools

As an independent NGO, EducAid is not constrained by all the regulations in government schools. EducAid's approach to teaching and learning is nevertheless unusual and it is reasonable to ask how consistency is achieved across the two secondary and one primary school. Consistency is achieved in four ways. First, teachers in all three schools are involved in a wider programme of in-service education for teachers in other schools (Mason, 2019). This requires them to share experiences and agree on underlying values. Second, teachers from each school visit the others and the leaders meet together on a monthly basis for staff training and discussion. Third, each school holds an annual whole staff meeting for one week. During this week all staff engage in activities, discussions and learning that inform the ways all schools will be run for the year. Fourth, an annual monitoring and evaluation exercise takes place and is shared across schools. Each school's and students' performance is evaluated against ten goals:

1. Excellent performance in public exams

---

[4]The EducAid Staff Code of Conduct focuses on issues of child protection and safe-guarding.

2. High levels of literacy and numeracy
3. Improved self-confidence
4. Improved self-discipline
5. A high number/proportion of girls in all EducAid schools
6. Increased concern for others/community spirit/giving back
7. Good communication skills
8. Increased creative thinking
9. Girls achieving as highly as boys
10. High-quality learning materials produced by EducAid.

11.6.2 Staffing

While there have been some very notable exceptions, our experience has been that many teachers from government schools cannot abandon practices common in their previous experience, for example, corporal punishment, late arrival—or non-arrival—at class, and corruption in assessing students' work. To meet this challenge, a majority of teachers in all three schools were themselves former students of EducAid and have bought into the schools' values.

11.6.3 Funding and Priorities

As a small NGO with no government funding, EducAid is under constant financial pressure. Almost alone among schools in Sierra Leone, EducAid students have no official uniform. Larger international NGOs have criticised this policy. EducAid's response is straightforward: uniforms cost money and would mean fewer students. In 2016 EducAid was asked to take over schools that another NGO had built but did not have the educational experience to run. It was an attractive offer but the additional costs would have been unsustainable. Instead EducAid started to provide school improvement programmes based on continuing professional development and learning (CPDL) for teachers in other schools (Mason, 2019; Mason & Galloway, 2020 under review). This extended EducAid's influence and was more sustainable than running more schools.

11.7 Conclusions

11.7.1 Does It Work?

EducAid operates in one of the poorest countries in the world. In every department and at every level, the government is challenged in the delivery of services.

The provision of good data is not an exception in this regard. However, the limited evidence does suggest that EducAid schools have been able to consistently support their students, despite drawing from the most vulnerable sections of the population. In the West African Secondary Schools Certificate Examination EducAid schools are recognised as being among the highest performing in the country (Mason, Galloway, & Joyce-Gibbons, 2018). Equally, EducAid students have been unusual in obtaining international scholarships, not through their connections but based on their public exam results and their ability to perform well in interviews. The former registrar of the University of Makeni says of EducAid students: "EducAid students know their history and their mathematics but also they know how to learn what they don't know. They have been taught how to teach themselves" (EducAid Sierra Leone, 2016).

11.7.2   The Wider Context

In a context of great inequality such as Sierra Leone[5] (Odusola, Cornia, & Bhorat, 2017), it is important to avoid two potentially fatal pitfalls. First, constructive relationships are a crucial requirement for effective learning (even though on their own they are not sufficient). Resources are not the crucial determinant of relationships between teachers, between teachers and students and between students. Relationships are created by individuals, not by resources. Elsewhere, one of us describes his experience as a newly qualified educational psychologist in Sheffield, UK, in the 1970s (Galloway & Goodwin, 1987). By today's UK standards, resources for catering for diversity and SEN were pitifully limited. The choice for educational psychologists was between recommending transfer to a special school (for a tiny minority,) and working with the class teacher (without any additional resources) to support a child's learning and behaviour. Yet some schools succeeded in creating a climate in which children with the most severe learning educational and psychosocial difficulties flourished.

Second, Freire (1970) described education systems that rely on rote learning as "banking," where the learner is not respected as a contributor to the learning process. In such systems, the learner is trained to accept the views of the teacher unquestioningly and, consequently, either learn to support the status quo by taking his place among the oppressed or, occasionally, by being one of the few that transition into the oppressors' camp. Freire maintains that without a participatory system, the education that is provided further dehumanises both sides of a population that has already been dehumanised by inequality and oppression.

---

[5] Sierra Leone is one of only four countries in Africa that has an inequality adjusted Human Development Index (IHDI) value that is more than 40% lower than its Human Development Index (HDI) value (Odusola, Cornia, & Bhorat, 2017). The IHDI is an indication of the impact of unequal distribution of health, education and income in the population. 'Two countries with different distributions of achievements can have the same average HDI value. Under perfect equality the IHDI is equal to the HDI, but falls below the HDI when inequality rises.' (UNDP, 2014).

Catering for diversity in learning and educational attainment, and catering for diversity in prior experiences and current psychosocial needs cannot be separated without having a negative impact on the child's learning and psychosocial outcomes. They must be integrated into the curricular work in and out of the classroom, and also into social life outside the classroom.

References

Department for Education, & Department of Health. (2015). Special educational needs and disability code of practice: 0 to 25 years. In *Goverment policies: Education and health*. London: Crown. DFE-00205-2013.

DFID. (2018). Leh Wi Learn - Sierra Leone secondary education improvement programme—DevTracker Project GB-CHC-220949-P292. Retrieved January 11, 2019, from https://devtracker. dfid.gov.uk/projects/GB-1-205234.

Dillard, M. (2012). Examinations standards, education assessments, and globalising elites: THE case of West African Examinations Council. *The Journal of African American History, 88*(4), 413–428. Retrieved from https://www.jstor.org/stable/3559089.

EducAid. (2017). What we do_EducAid. Retrieved July 13, 2017, from https://www.educaid.org. uk/what-we-do/.

EducAid Sierra Leone. (2016). EducAid—Building a better Sierra Leone—YouTube. Retrieved January 1, 2019, from https://www.youtube.com/watch?v=N3zShMcb6wA.

Freire, P. (1970). *Pedagogy of the oppressed*. New York: Herder and Herder.

Galloway, D., & Goodwin, C. (1987). *The education of disturbing children*. Harlow, England: Longman Group UK ltd.

Girls Not Brides. (2017). Sierra Leone—Child marriage around the world. Retrieved September 22, 2018, from https://www.girlsnotbrides.org/child-marriage/sierra-leone/.

Global Initiative to End All Corporal Punishment of Children (GIEACPC). (2015). *Towards non-violent schools: Prohibiting all corporal punishment—Global report 2015*. London: Global Initiative to End All Corporal Punishment of Children. Retrieved from https://endcorporalpunishment. org/wp-content/uploads/thematic/Schools-report-2015-EN.pdf.

Government of Sierra Leone. (2018). *Sierra Leone multiple indicator cluster survey 2017 (MICS-2)*. Sierra Leone: Freetown.

Katta, M. (2016). Ending corruption in Sierra Leone: An evaluation of the government's response to the TRC Report. Retrieved January 9, 2019, from https://www.carl-sl.org/pres/ending-corrup tion-in-sierra-leone-an-evaluation-of-the-governments-response-to-the-trc-report/.

Mansaray, A., & Johnson, A. O. (2013). A study in sexual abuse of in-school adolescent girls In the eastern province of Sierra Leone. *Scholarly Journal of Education, 2*(March), 27–32.

Mason, M. (2019). *Devising new models for school improvement in developing nations : Sierra Leone, a case study*. Durham University.

Mason, M., Galloway, D., & Joyce-Gibbons, A. (2018). Closing the attainment gap: Collaboration between schools in Sierra Leone. *Education & Child Psychology, 35*(1), 27–39.

Mason, M., & Galloway, D. M. (2020 under review). Knowledge Mobilisation in Sub-Saharan Africa: An impact evaluation of CPDL in improving children's performance. *Journal of Professional Capital and Community*, (Special Issue: Mobilizing Knowledge in Professional Learning Networks).

Mercer, J. (2014). CHILDMYTHS: Orphanages, CHIFF, and UNICEF recommendations—Is there science behind anti-orphanage positions? Retrieved February 9, 2019, from https://childmyths. blogspot.com/2014/01/orphanages-chiff-and-unicef.html.

Nishimuko, M. (2007). Problems behind Education for All (EFA): The case of Sierra Leone. *Educate, 7*(2), 19–29.

Odusola, A., Cornia, G. A., & Bhorat, H. (2017). *Income inequality trends in sub-Saharan Africa.* New York.

OECD. (2017). Sierra Leone_Social institutions & gender index. Retrieved August 27, 2017, from https://www.genderindex.org/country/sierra-leone/.

Pikin to Pikin Movement. (2017). About us—Pikin to pikin movement. Retrieved January 11, 2019, from https://www.pikintopikin.org/sample-page/about-us/.

Pritchett, L. (2013). *The rebirth of education: Why schooling in developing countries is flailing; How the developed world is complicit; and what to do next. Center for Global Development Brief.* Washington.

Relief Web. (2017). Sierra Leone_ Mudslides—Aug 2017_ReliefWeb. Retrieved January 21, 2019, from https://reliefweb.int/disaster/ms-2017-000109-sle.

Save the Children. (2016). Child marriage in Sierra Leone. Retrieved January 19, 2019, from https://www.savethechildren.org.uk/content/dam/global/reports/advocacy/child-marriage-sierra-leone.pdf.

Sonuga-Barke, E. J. S. (2019). Editorial: 'It's a family affair'—The social drivers of child and adolescent resilience. *Journal of Child Psychology and Psychiatry, 60*(1), 1–3. https://doi.org/10.1111/jcpp.13011

Statistics Sierra Leone. (2013). Sierra Leone: Demographic and health survey 2013. https://doi.org/10.4324/9780203403099_Sierra_Leone

Topping, K., Miller, D., Thurston, A., McGavock, K., & Conlin, N. (2011). Peer tutoring in reading in Scotland: Thinking big. *Literacy, 45*(1), 3–9.

TRC. (2004). *Recommendations. Final report of the truth and reconciliation commission for Sierra Leone—Volume II* (Vol. 15). Freetown, Sierra Leone.

Trading Economics. (2017). Corruption Index - Countries - List. https://tradingeconomics.com/country-list/corruption-index

Tymms, P., Merrell, C., Thurston, A., Andor, J., Topping, K., & Miller, D. (2011). Improving attainment across a whole district: school reform through peer tutoring in a randomized controlled trial. *School Effectiveness and School Improvement, 22*(2). https://doi.org/10.1080/09243453.2011.589859.

UNDP. (2014). Inequality-adjusted Human Development Index (IHDI) I human development reports. Retrieved January 19, 2019, from https://hdr.undp.org/en/content/inequality-adjusted-human-development-index-ihdi.

UNDP. (2018). Sierra Leone HDI 2018_human development reports. Retrieved September 18, 2018, from https://hdr.undp.org/en/countries/profiles/SLE.

UNESCO. (1994). The salamanca statement framework. Policy; UNESCO. Retrieved October 28, 2020 from https://doi.org/ED-94/WS/18

UNESCO-UIS. (2018). Sierra Leone data—Education and literacy. Retrieved July 15, 2020, from https://doi.org/10.1017/S002185530000615X.

UNICEF. (2016). *The state of the world's children 2016: A fair chance for every child.* New York. Retrieved July 15, 2020 from https://www.unicef.org/publications/index_91711.html.

Walter, B. F. (2011). *Conflict relapse and the sustainability of post-conflict peace. World development report 2011, World Bank.* Washington DC. Retrieved July 15, 2020 from http://web.worldbank.org/archive/website01306/web/pdf/wdrbackground paper_walter_0.pdf.

Chapter 12
Tier 2 Intervention for Students with Internalizing Symptoms

Minglee Yong and Boon Ooi Lee

Abstract Students in secondary schools face increased vulnerability for developing internalizing symptoms such as feelings of anxiety, sadness, and hopelessness, as well as social withdrawal and somatic complaints. These symptoms are associated with reduced engagement in school, interpersonal problems, and possibly other serious mental health issues. To support students with internalizing symptoms, schools can play an important role in early identification and intervention. The multitier system of support is described as the recommended framework for providing a continuum of services for students with internalizing symptoms. At the Tier 1 level, schools can implement a universal social–emotional learning curriculum to equip all students with foundational skills in emotion regulation, perspective-taking, self-management, and problem-solving. At the Tier 2 level, intervention programmes can provide additional support for students screened to be at-risk of developing more serious internalizing symptoms. These programmes aim to alleviate symptoms and prevent further deterioration of functioning. Tier 2 interventions are currently less widespread. The goals of this chapter are to identify treatment components and features of effective school-based Tier 2 programs for students with internalizing symptoms and to provide specific recommendations for integrating programmes into multitier system of support in schools. The effective implementation of Tier 2 programmes will address diverse needs of students and help them achieve more positive social–emotional outcomes.

Keywords Internalizing symptoms · Multitier system · Tier 2 · Social–emotional learning · School-based intervention · Depression · Anxiety · Mental health · Secondary prevention · Evidence-based · Models of intervention

M. Yong (✉) · B. O. Lee
National Institute of Education, Nanyang Technological University, Singapore, Singapore
e-mail: minglee.yong@nie.edu.sg

B. O. Lee
e-mail: boonooi.lee@nie.edu.sg

© Springer Nature Singapore Pte Ltd. 2020
C. Koh (ed.), *Diversifying Learner Experience*,
https://doi.org/10.1007/978-981-15-9861-6_12

12.1 Introduction

For students in secondary schools, adolescence marks the developmental period of numerous transitional milestones such as the onset of puberty and biological changes, increasing academic demands, shifting affiliative relationships from family to peers, greater reliance on peer opinion and social status, and increasing salience of self-identity and self-esteem issues. Coping with these stressors can increase students' vulnerability for internalizing symptoms. Internalizing symptoms such as feelings of worry, nervousness, sadness and hopelessness, as well as social withdrawal and somatic complaints, indicate internal distress that affects the mood and emotion (Costello, Mustillo, Erkanli, Keeler, & Angold, 2003; Thorpe, Kamphaus, & Reynolds, 2003). Intense and persisting internalizing symptoms often have significant neurobiological components that may include dysfunctional neural circuits associated with emotional processing. Affected individuals may engage in biased information processing and experience dysregulation in the stress response system, leading to difficulties coping with intense and chronic stressors (Hammen, Rudolph, & Abaied, 2014). Internalizing symptoms can also have a significant hereditary component, as evidenced by high hereditary estimates of internalizing symptoms among family members (Hammen et al., 2014).

According to epidemiological studies conducted in the USA, the rates of internalizing symptoms including depressive and anxiety disorders increase rapidly from 1–2% in childhood to about 2–13% in adolescence (Angold & Costello, 1993; Avenevoli, Knight, Kessler, & Merikangas, 2008; Merikangas et al., 2010). By age 18, it is estimated that about 20% of adolescents would have experienced serious internalizing symptoms and 65% would have experienced less severe symptoms (Lewinsohn & Hops, 1993). By adulthood, the lifetime prevalence rate is estimated to be 16.6% (Kessler et al., 2005). In Singapore, the adult lifetime prevalence rate estimate is about 14% (Chong et al., 2012). Prevalence estimates for youth in Singapore are currently unavailable. While prevalence estimates appear to be slightly lower for Asian populations, researchers have attributed the discrepancy to differences in manifestations of symptoms across cultures (Lee, Sagayadevan, Vaingankar, Chong, & Subramaniam, 2015). For example, mainland Chinese psychiatric outpatients with depression tended to present with more somatic symptoms and fewer psychological symptoms than their Euro-Canadian counterparts (Dere et al., 2013). Thus, the prevalence rate of depression in mainland Chinese may appear lower as they are less likely to endorse psychological symptoms. Regardless of slight differences in estimates, a significant number of individuals experience internalizing symptoms during adolescence and adulthood.

The adolescent stage of development is often associated with the first onset of internalizing disorders that may have a recurrent and protracted course (Avenevoli, Swendsen, He, Burstein, & Merikangas, 2015; Fergusson & Woodward, 2002). More than 50% of youth with internalizing symptoms are likely to experience a recurrence in adulthood. Persisting internalizing symptoms may co-occur with other mood or behavioural issues (Angold & Costello, 1999) and these presentations may portend more serious and life-long mood issues (Avenevoli et al., 2008). Youth with internalizing symptoms, even those who may not meet the criteria for diagnoses of psychiatric disorders have been found to experience negative outcomes (Avenevoli et al., 2008; Vander Stoep et al., 2012), such as poor academic engagement and attainment (Huang, 2015; McCarty et al., 2008; Weidman, Augustine, Murayama, & Elliot, 2015), academic failure and incompletion (Quiroga, Janosz, Lyons, & Morin, 2012), and interpersonal problems (Hammen, 2009). Youth with severe internalizing symptoms also report substance abuse, suicidal ideation, planning, or attempts. (Avenevoli et al., 2015; Capaldi & Stoolmiller, 1999). Given the negative trajectory of youth with internalizing symptoms, it is important to provide early identification and intervention services.

12.2 Limited Access and Low Utilization of Services

Unlike externalizing behaviours (non-compliance, hyperactivity, impulsivity, hostility, and aggression), internalizing symptoms are less likely to be observed by parents and teachers and thus, more difficult to detect due to the inwardly directed nature of symptoms (Cook et al., 2011; Dowdy, Doane, Eklund, & Dever, 2013). Youth may express emotional distress through somatic symptoms (e.g., headache, fatigue) (Lee, 2013). Parents and teachers may lack awareness about the risk and severity of internalizing symptoms and their negative impact. Cultural stigma associated with negative emotions and mental health challenges may also impede expressions of internal distress and help-seeking behaviours from youth and their caregivers (Heary, Hennessy, Swords, & Corrigan, 2017; Lee, 2009; Nearchou et al., 2018; Subramaniam et al., 2017). Consequently, youth and parents are less likely to seek appropriate services in a timely manner. In the USA, 80% of youth who would benefit from services for internalizing symptoms do not receive them (Kataoka, Zhang, & Wells, 2002). Hence, despite significant prevalence rates of internalizing symptoms, high probability of future challenges, and associated functional impairment, few students receive early intervention to alleviate internalizing symptoms and their risk factors (Avenevoli et al., 2015).

In Singapore, community mental health services for youth also face similar challenges. In response to the rise of mental health issues, the Singapore government has budgeted S$160 million to increase community mental health services as part of a 5-year Community Mental Health Masterplan from 2017 to 2021 (Choon, Loh, Renjan, Tan, & Fung, 2017). Various community mental health services for youth have been initiated (Choon et al., 2017), including REACH (Response, Early intervention and Assessment in Community Mental Health), which is a mental healthcare service unit that collaborates with schools, voluntary welfare organizations, and general practitioners to help youth with psychosocial issues. The Community Health Assessment Team (CHAT) conducts programmes to promote awareness of mental disorders and provides support to people between 16 and 30 years old. As a community outreach service, CHAT also works closely with students, educators, and counsellors from Institutes of Higher Learning (i.e., polytechnics, universities and vocational institutions) and social service agencies.

Despite the provision of programmes and services, accessibility and mental health services use in Singapore remain low. According to one community mental health survey conducted in Singapore (Ng, Fones, & Kua, 2003), although 19.9% of people aged below 20 years old experience clinically significant emotional distress, only 2.8% of them sought professional help. Youth turn to their social support such as friends and family members for help (Ang & Yeo, 2004; Lee, 2009). However, for significant internalizing problems affecting functioning, informal social support is inadequate and ineffective. When systematic mental health treatment is not provided early, the burden of internalizing symptoms becomes more severe and interferes with normal developmental processes (Hammen et al., 2014), resulting in irreversible functional impairment, such as failure to make age-appropriate academic progress and dropping out of school (Quiroga, Janosz, Bisset, & Morin, 2013).

Another major challenge is the shortage of trained mental health professionals that likely impedes service delivery and effectiveness. In Singapore, there are only about 2.86 child psychiatrists per 100,000 youth, far below the 8.67 child psychiatrists per 100,000 youth population in the USA (Choon, Ong, Chin, & Fung, 2015). Furthermore, psychiatrists comprise only about 6–8% of mental health professionals practising in the USA (Grohol, 2018; Heisler, 2018). The majority of mental health service providers in the US are psychologists (28–41%), mental health counsellors (36%), mental health social workers (25–35%), marriage and family therapists (5–12%), and psychiatric nurses (4%). Despite the importance of psychosocial interventions in mental health treatment (Coplan, Aaronson, Panthangi, & Kim, 2015; Crowe, Beaglehole, Wells, & Porter, 2015; Hausmann et al., 2007; Kolch & Plener, 2016), there is currently no data about the provision of such services by professionals other than psychiatrists in Singapore. The shortage of trained professionals directly impacts accessibility, resulting in long waiting time, lack of appropriate and specialized care, and fragmentation of services in the public health and social service sectors.

12.3   Preventive Role of Schools

Given the limited availability and accessibility of services in the community and the current low public awareness of youth with internalizing symptoms, schools are critically important in providing early identification and intervention services (Thompson, Reinke, Holmes, Danforth, & Herman, 2017; Weist et al., 2017). While schools may not have the expertise to support students with severe needs, they can play an active role in preventive care. Schools are uniquely suited for this role for several reasons. First, schools are able to reach almost the entire youth population, thus reducing disparities in access to services due to socioeconomic status or racial differences (Lyon, Ludwig, Stoep, Gudmundsen, & McCauley, 2013). Through universal screening, schools are able to help with early identification of students at-risk of internalizing symptoms. Second, less stigma is associated with students and families receiving services in schools. Furthermore, support from schools is likely to promote public awareness and understanding of youth with mental health issues. Third, youth can maintain confidentiality and independently self-refer to access school-based services without close involvement of parents. Providing this avenue for self-referral is important given the covert nature of internalizing symptoms that defy detection by parents and teachers. Fourth, preventive programmes for internalizing symptoms can contribute to schools' existing programmes that promote social–emotional learning and resilience in the student population.

12.4 School-Based Models of Intervention

Different models have been proposed to implement school-based programmes for youth with internalizing symptoms (Flaherty & Weist, 1999; Weist et al., 2018). In the School Mental Health model (SMH), community mental health staff are contracted to provide school-based services to students. They typically provide individual and small-group counselling for school-referred students. As these community staff are not part of the school system, they usually work independently of school processes and have limited opportunity to collaborate with school staff. Hence, services may not be well integrated and benefits to students may be difficult to sustain.

When using the School Mental Health model, there may be a separation in the systems that address students' internalizing versus externalizing problems. While teachers tend to feel the responsibility and the urgency to address students' externalizing behaviours (Sugai, Horner, & Gresham, 2002), they are more likely to rely on community staff to address students' internalizing symptoms (Lyon et al., 2013). With multiple service delivery systems in effect within the same school, efficient implementation and provision of services may be affected (McIntosh, Ty, & Miller, 2014). More importantly, multiple service delivery models may appear to ignore the high degree of co-occurrence between externalizing behaviours and internalizing symptoms (Angold & Costello, 1999).

In Singapore, most schools are now staffed with a full-time counsellor who is supported by part-time counsellors and teacher–counsellors with basic training in counselling. For children and adolescents with mental health conditions, school counsellors consult and work closely with REACH to help students access services (Choon et al., 2015). Assessment of needs by REACH is conducted in schools and homes to minimize disruption to academic learning and reduce the stigma of seeking help. In this model, school counsellors function as liaison persons to facilitate referral to more specialized services from the community.

An alternative to School Mental Health model is to integrate services for internalizing symptoms into existing school-wide multitier system of support. This model is adapted from the public health care model, which provides the population a continuum of services to address different intensity of needs (Strein, Hoagwood, & Cohn, 2003; Thompson et al., 2017). In the public health model, prevention is conceptualized at three levels—primary, secondary, and tertiary prevention. These levels of intervention differ in terms of service intensity and degree of treatment individualization. In the school system, this prevention model translates to Tier 1, 2, and 3 levels of intervention. Tier 1 intervention programmes are offered to the whole school population. Universal screening conducted for all students identifies those who may be at risk of developing more symptoms. At-risk students are subsequently provided with Tier 2 intervention, which is considered an additional dosage of support. Tier 2 intervention is typically small-group skills-building programmes that target specific problems, whether externalizing behaviours or internalizing symptoms. The goals at Tier 2 are to alleviate early symptoms, prevent further deterioration of functioning, and mitigate risk factors. At the Tier 3 level, interventions are designed to be more individualized and intensive, such as Individual Education Plans (IEPs), behavioural intervention plans, or individual counselling plans. Hence, across the three levels of intervention, at-risk students can experience a diverse array of programmes to meet the intensity of their social-emotional needs.

In recent years, schools have gained much experience and expertise in implementing Tier 1 universal programmes such as school-wide positive behaviour support strategies and social–emotional learning curriculum (Chong & Lee, 2015). School-wide positive behaviour support comprises a set of intervention practices based on principles of applied behaviour analysis to support the acquisition and use of socially appropriate behaviours in a positive and predictable school environment (Horner, Sugai, & Anderson, 2010; Sugai & Horner, 2006). Intervention practices include critical features that are implemented school wide, such as clear behavioural expectations, active instructions on prosocial behaviours, consistent positive reinforcement, data-based decision-making, progress monitoring, and outcome evaluation (Horner et al., 2010). Similarly, school-wide implementation of evidence-based, social–emotional learning curriculum helps students develop emotion regulation skills, perspective-taking skills, and various self-management skills. The aim is to cultivate positive attitudes and behaviours, as well as help students make progress in learning (Durlak, Weissberg, Dymnicki, Taylor, & Schellinger, 2011).

With regard to addressing the needs of students with internalizing symptoms, a social–emotional learning curriculum implemented school wide at the Tier 1 level can provide a foundational basis for students to develop self-awareness, self-management skills, social awareness, relationship skills, and responsible decision-making (Durlak et al., 2011). However, universal programmes have not been found to be as effective as secondary prevention programmes for students with internalizing symptoms (Werner-Seidler, Perry, Calear, Newby, & Christensen, 2017). Students with internalizing symptoms require more targeted programming to show sustained improvement.

12.5 Tier 2 Intervention Programmes

While schools continue to gain expertise in implementing universal Tier 1 programmes, they are less familiar with implementing Tier 2 programmes that are integrated within a multitier system of support. This may be due to fewer evidence-based Tier 2 programmes available for schools to choose from, challenges with integrating programmes into a multitier system of support, and limited manpower and resources to sustain additional programmes beyond Tier 1 intervention (Bruhn, Lane, & Hirsch, 2014; McCarty, Violette, & McCauley, 2011; Werner-Seidler et al., 2017; Yong & Cheney, 2013).

A distinction is made between Tier 2 versus secondary prevention programmes. Secondary prevention programmes cannot be considered Tier 2 programmes because secondary prevention programmes are not integrated with Tier 1 level support nor are they integrated with school referral systems for the provision of special services. Many small-group school-based programmes for at-risk students are considered stand-alone secondary prevention programmes. To be considered Tier 2 programmes, secondary prevention programmes will need to be adapted for implementation within schools' multitier system. With this in mind, the following sections will identify features of effective secondary prevention programmes for students with internalizing symptoms and importantly, consider ways to adapt these programmes for school implementation.

Given that Tier 2 programmes may address different areas of needs, a distinction is made between programmes designed to target externalizing behaviours versus those designed to target internalizing symptoms. The former group of programmes is typically referred to as social–behavioural programmes while the latter, social–emotional programmes. Social–behavioural programmes aim to increase students' prosocial behaviours and reduce challenging behaviours that impede learning in the school environment. On the other hand, social–emotional programmes are focused on enhancing students' emotional, self-regulation, and perspective-taking skills. Needless to say, there are considerable overlaps in the goals in these programmes such as developing students' social skills and social problem-solving skills. Furthermore, some researchers have also found positive intervention effects of social–behaviour programmes on students' internalizing symptoms despite the symptoms not being the target of the intervention (Cheney et al., 2009). As it is beyond the scope of this chapter to discuss Tier 2 social–behavioural programmes in detail, interested readers may review articles such as Bruhn et al. (2014) and Yong and Cheney (2013).

12.6 Features of Social–Emotional Secondary Prevention Programmes

In a recent systematic review and meta-analysis of school-based depression and anxiety prevention programmes for youth, Werner-Seidler, Perry, Calear, Newby, and Christensen (2017) identified about 81 empirical studies investigating primary and secondary prevention programmes. These studies were categorized under depression-, anxiety-, and both depression/anxiety-focused programmes. For the purpose of this chapter, studies investigating the same programmes were grouped together, resulting in 48 unique programmes. Subsequently, primary prevention programmes implemented universally for all students were excluded. As the focus is on students aged 12 years and above, programmes developed for younger students were also excluded as developmental differences mean that curriculum for elementary students will not be suitable or relevant for secondary level students. Furthermore, three programmes were excluded because information about participant age was not available. Another programme was excluded as it was implemented for adolescents with symptoms, possibly attributable to trauma. At the end of this process, nine unique programmes were identified. Based on descriptions provided in representative studies, main programme features are listed in Table 12.1. Given that research articles vary in the details they provide about the programmes, it should be noted that Table 12.1 is thus not comprehensive. However, for the general purpose of identifying the main features of secondary prevention programmes, the current level of analysis should suffice.

Except for FRIENDS (Shortt, Barrett, & Fox, 2001), the other eight programmes are focused on depressive symptoms. This reflects the difference in the general prevalence rates of depression and anxiety, with anxiety symptoms being more common in childhood and depressive symptoms being more common during adolescence (Costello et al., 2003). Hence, interventions for children are more likely to focus on anxiety symptoms while those for adolescents are more likely to focus on depressive symptoms. Programme lengths range from 2 to 16 sessions with most programmes having more the 10 sessions. Not surprisingly, longer programmes tend to be more comprehensive and include components such as psychoeducation, motivational strategies such as goal-setting, behaviour activation strategies, emotion–regulation skills, cognitive coping, social and interpersonal skills, a more comprehensive focus on application of skills, and/or parental intervention and involvement (Gillham et al., 2007; Kindt, 2014; McCarty, Violette, Duong, Cruz, & McCauley, 2013; Young et al., 2016).

All the programmes in Table 12.1 are conducted with small groups of students with group sizes ranging from 2 to 15. Given the group setting, programme staff will need to attend to group processes to ensure that group environment is conducive and therapeutic for participants. Positive Thoughts and Actions and Interpersonal Psychotherapy also provide individual sessions and joint sessions with parents. In Positive Thoughts and Actions, programme staff conduct two home visits per student and two workshops for parents. In Interpersonal Psychotherapy, joint sessions with parents provide opportunities for students to practice using interpersonal skills with support from programme staff.

In the programmes, psychoeducation provides specific information about depressive symptoms and the intervention approach. It also provides general information about adolescent development, family relations, and positive peer relationships. In Positive Thoughts and Actions and FRIENDS, psychoeducation is also provided to parents to help them understand their teenager's needs.

Table 12.1 Features of nine school-based secondary prevention programs for adolescents based on Werner-Seidler et al. (2017)

Programme name	Secondary prevention programmes for internalizing symptoms		
	-	Personality matched cognitive behavioural intervention	Penn resilience program
Example of study	Arnarson and Craighead (2011)	Castellanos (2006)	Gillham et al. (2007)
Duration	14 sessions	2 sessions	12 sessions
Size of group	6–8	2–9	6–4
Intervention components			
Group processes	*	*	*
Psychoeducation	*	Identify personality variable and how coping behaviours may be associated with personality style	*
Motivational strategies	*	Consider short- and long-term positive and negative consequences of behaviours associated with personality	*
Behaviour activation	*	*	*
Emotion regulation	*	*	Relaxation strategies
Cognitive coping	Enhance self-esteem	Identify and challenge personality-specific cognitive distortions using case examples	Flexible thinking, identify challenges and problems, challenge negative thinking and generate alternative helpful interpretations
Social and interpersonal skills	Develop interpersonal and problem-solving skills	*	Problem-solving and decision-making, assertiveness, and negotiation
Applications	*	*	Apply skills during group discussions and weekly HW assignment
Maintenance	*	*	*
Parent involvement and intervention	None	None	None

(continued)

Table 12.1 (continued)

Programme name	Secondary prevention programmes for internalizing symptoms		
	Teaching kids to cope	Positive thoughts and actions	FRIENDS
Example of study	Lamb et al. (1998)	McCarty et al. (2013)	Shortt et al. (2001)
Duration	8 sessions	14 sessions	10+2 sessions
Size of group	10–12	4–6	5–13
Intervention components			
Group processes	*	Cohesion, confidentiality, and rules	Normalized anxiety experiences
Psychoeducation	Common teen stresses, self-image, coping, family relationships, and communication contributing to challenges	Purpose of programme and importance of being positive	Awareness of anxiety symptoms and program
Motivational strategies	Identify individual issues	Identify individual goals	*
Behaviour activation	*	Positive actions	Graded exposure to overcome avoidance
Emotion regulation	*	Self-instructions	Relaxation
Cognitive coping	*	Connections between feelings, behaviours, and thoughts; identify maladaptive thoughts and replace with positive thoughts	Challenge unhelpful thoughts
Social and interpersonal skills	Problem-solving	Problem-solving, assertiveness, negotiation, conflict resolution and anger management	Problem-solving
Applications	HW assignments	Apply to academic learning, interpersonal relationships, and health behaviours	Apply skills during group discussions and weekly HW assignment
Maintenance	*	Planning for future	Strategies to maintain gains
Parent involvement and intervention	None	Parent psychoeducation, goal setting, positive thoughts and actions, emotion-regulation, communication, planning for future	Parent sessions mirror student group sessions and also included parenting skills, development of social support

(continued)

Table 12.1 (continued)

Programme name	Secondary prevention programmes for internalizing symptoms		
	Blues group	Op Volle Kracht	Interpersonal psychotherapy
Example of study	Stice (2007)	Wijnhoven et al. (2014)	Young et al. (2010)
Duration	4 sessions	16 sessions	11+4 sessions
Size of group	4–10	12–15	3–7
Intervention components			
Group processes	Build group rapport	Group cohesion	*
Psychoeducation	*	*	Awareness of depressive symptoms, relationship between feelings and interpersonal interactions, impact of communication on others
Motivational strategies	*	*	Review individual's current relationships to identify interpersonal goals for group
Behaviour activation	Increase involvement in pleasant activities	*	*
Emotion regulation	*	Relaxation strategies	*
Cognitive coping	Identify, track, and challenge negative thoughts, increase positive thinking	Connections between situations, thoughts, feelings, and cognitions, cognitive biases versus optimistic explanatory styles; self-esteem	*
Social and interpersonal skills	*	Problem-solving, decision-making, social skills, assertiveness, negotiation	Communication and interpersonal strategies, e.g. I-statements, right time for conversations, practice skills
Applications	Track thoughts and activities as homework	*	Use skills in relationships to reduce conflicts and build support from others
Maintenance	Develop response plans for future life stressors	*	Review skills and future application. Parent session to practice skills in specific relationship
Parent involvement and intervention	None	None	(See above)

*Details not provided in identified studies. Programmes may or may not include the relevant features

Except for Interpersonal Psychotherapy that emphasizes learning and application of interpersonal skills to improve relationships and increase social support, most programmes in Table 12.1 have a strong cognitive–behavioural focus to help participants engage in cognitive restructuring. This involves identifying and challenging maladaptive cognitive thoughts and generating alternative positive thoughts. While emotion regulation is not a prioritized treatment component for most programmes, Op Volle Kracht and FRIENDS include the topic of relaxation. Positive Thoughts and Actions also uses a self-instruction strategy to help students recognize their emotional reactions and in turn, regulate their affect.

The various programmes also aim to develop students' social and interpersonal skills, such as problem-solving, conflict resolution, negotiation, decision-making, communication, assertiveness, and other interpersonal skills. The practice and application of cognitive, emotion–regulation, and social interpersonal skills are often promoted through guided discussion, demonstration and modelling, role-plays, structured activities, and homework assignments. In addition, Positive Thoughts and Actions also includes a more specific and in-depth application component where separate individual sessions focus on the application of skills in the domains of academic learning, interpersonal relationships, and health behaviours.

Even though information may not be available, all programmes are likely to incorporate strategies for maintaining improvements made by students. Many programmes encourage planning for the future and coping with future stressors. Interpersonal Psychotherapy programme provides four individual booster sessions, 6 months after the group has ended. In programmes with parental involvement, parents are also encouraged to engage in future planning. Positive Thoughts and Actions actively involves parents in two home visits and two parent workshops. Their goals are to help parents set goals for themselves and their children, acquire skills to manage their emotions, communicate effectively with their children, as well as model positive thoughts and actions. In FRIENDS, parents learn a variety of skills to support their children, including parenting skills, affect management, social and communication skills.

While all the nine programmes are evidence-based, they are not readily integrated into school systems. Hence, their implementation in schools risks discontinuation and reduced efficacy as they are not sensitive to setting conditions of schools. In the long-term, programmes should be adapted to fit within school organizational structure and processes so as to remain implementable and sustainable. An example of such a setting-specific adaptation is described by Weeland, Nijhof, Vermaes, Engels, & Buitelaar (2015). The Op Volle Kracht programme (adapted from the Penn Resilience Programme in the USA) was implemented the Netherlands and it was adapted for use with adolescents with mild intellectual disability living in group residential treatment settings. To meet the needs of this special group of adolescents, multiple changes were made, such as reducing treatment duration and verbal content while increasing visual elements and hands-on practice opportunities. The programme was also integrated into existing treatment plans such as matching programme goals to individual goals. Hence, Weeland et al. (2015) not only adapted the programme to address the needs of the participants, they also ensured that the programme matches up with the requirements of the system.

12.7 Adapting Secondary Prevention Programmes to Become Tier 2 Programmes

Even if schools do not have a formal multitier system of support that includes Tier 1, 2, and 3 levels of intervention, many of them are already implementing universal Tier 1 programmes to target social–behavioural and social–emotional outcomes. Hence, it is proposed that a secondary prevention programme targeting internalizing symptoms be linked to a school's universal social–emotional learning curriculum to become a Tier 2 programme. Making linkages between concepts and skills taught in the social–emotional curriculum and the Tier 2 programme will ensure that at-risk students receive additional dosage of intervention and more diverse learning opportunities. Resilience-promoting concepts and adaptive coping skills are reinforced at Tier 1 and again, at Tier 2, thus supporting maintenance and generalization of skills. For example, social–emotional learning curriculum typically includes recognizing and identifying emotions as one of the first few topics of instructions. This topic can be related to the psychoeducation component of secondary prevention programmes. Feelings identification and interpretation are also relevant for the emotion regulation component of Tier 2 programmes. Social–emotional learning curriculum often includes teaching problem-solving skill, which is also an important treatment component.

Additionally, a Tier 2 programme can become part of the school's assessment, identification, referral, and intervention framework for the provision of support services. For a student to access Tier 2 intervention, the student must have been screened to have elevated symptoms (Renshaw & Cook, 2018). Screening for elevated social–emotional problems should be conducted universally for all students on a 6-monthly basis. Those found at-risk of externalizing behaviours can be referred for Tier 2 social–behavioural intervention while students found at-risk of internalizing symptoms can be referred for Tier 2 social–emotional interventions. Similar to accessing other special educational services, other common referral routes may be direct referral from teachers, counsellors, or parents. In the case of internalizing symptoms, self-referral may also be common. Progress monitoring is an integral part of a multitier system of support (Horner et al., 2010). Tier 2 programmes are required to develop assessment procedures to monitor progress in terms of levels of internalizing symptoms and skill acquisition. Assessment procedures may include ratings by students and programme staff in skill areas targeted in the programmes, as well as ratings by teachers and parents based on observations of students outside of the programmes.

As internalizing symptoms are less likely to have a disruptive impact in the classroom, teacher involvement in Tier 2 intervention may not be critical. Instead, parental involvement may be more common. Still, it is recommended that a Tier 2 social–emotional programme includes a teacher involvement component so that teachers can be another source of supportive interpersonal relationship that can help students develop positive self-esteem. Teachers can also offer students opportunities to practice interpersonal skills. They can also support progress monitoring efforts in terms of providing feedback regarding students' participation in class and engagement with peers (Cook et al., 2011).

12.8 Contextual Considerations When Adapting Secondary Prevention Programmes

As all the programmes in Table 12.1 are developed overseas for adolescents from different populations, cultural and linguistic considerations will be important when adapting programmes for use with our local student population (Bernal, Bonilla, & Bellido, 1995; Saulsberry et al., 2013). Scenarios and examples used in the programmes should reflect common stressors and situations experienced by teenagers here. Culturally appropriate language should be used, including symbols and concepts that are shared within the local context. Intervention goals can be framed to fit with the local values, customs, and traditions, such as those in Singapore (Griner & Smith, 2006; Saulsberry et al., 2013). Targeted social and interpersonal skills such as problem-solving, decision-making, communication, negotiation, and assertiveness should also be made applicable to the relevant (e.g. Asian) context. In a culture where family interests may be prioritized above individual goals, the impact of family relations on students' adjustment and coping will be important topics for discussion during parent psychoeducation and parenting components of adapted programmes (Hwang et al., 2015; Rossello, Bernal, & Rivera-Medina, 2008; Saulsberry et al., 2013). Overall, careful contextual considerations will be important to ensure that evidence-based secondary prevention programmes can remain effective in treating the underlying vulnerabilities of adolescents with internalizing symptoms.

12.9 Conclusion

Students with internalizing symptoms are receiving increasing attention in our school system. These students not only struggle with social–emotional and behavioural functioning, they may also experience adverse educational outcomes. These negative effects are additive and cumulative and may become pervasive and chronic, causing disruption to normal developmental processes. Challenges faced by students with internalizing symptoms have become more salient due to increasing knowledge about the negative impact of mental and behavioural health issues across the life span. Hence, it is no longer enough for schools to focus on remediating academic deficits and building academic competence for these students; educators also need to address students' social–emotional needs in a proactive manner that includes early identification and intervention.

For schools to play an effective preventive role, they will need to implement a multitier system of support that can provide a continuum of services to address students' individual needs. A multitier system can flexibly address a variety of students' challenges while at the same time, providing them with a diversification of experiences. Identifying effective evidence-based programmes to fit within multitier systems is a priority. Even though many programmes are found to be effective for students at-risk of internalizing symptoms, many of them are not adapted to fit within school systems, thus impacting their long-term effectiveness and sustainability.

As a starting point, this chapter provides the theoretical and empirical bases for adapting secondary prevention programmes for Tier 2 level intervention to address the needs of students with internalizing symptoms. The intervention programmes provided across the three tiers of intervention also ensure that at-risk students can access diverse learning experiences. This chapter also provides recommendations about critical treatment components for Tier 2 programmes, as well as important contextual considerations for school implementation by researchers and school practitioners.

Acknowledgement We wish to thank Sarah Soon for her research contributions to this chapter.

References

Ang, R. P., & Yeo, L. S. (2004). Asian secondary school students' help-seeking behaviour and preferences for counsellor characteristics. *Pastoral Care in Education, 22*(1), 10–18. https://doi.org/10.1111/j.0264-3944.2004.00312.x.

Angold, A., & Costello, E. J. (1993). Depressive comorbidity in children and adolescents: empirical, theoretical, and methodological issues. *The American Journal Of Psychiatry, 150*(12), 1779–1791.

Angold, A., & Costello, E. J. (1999). Comorbidity. *Journal of Child Psychology and Psychiatry and Allied Disciplines, 40*(1), 57.

Arnarson, E. O., & Craighead, W. E. (2011). Prevention of depression among Icelandic adolescents: A 12-month follow-up. *Behaviour Research and Therapy, 49*, 170–174.

Avenevoli, S., Knight, E., Kessler, R. C., & Merikangas, K. R. (2008). Epidemiology of depression in children and adolescents. In J. R. Z. Abela & B. L. Hankin (Eds.), *Handbook of depression in children and adolescents* (pp. 6–32). New York, NY: Guilford Press.

Avenevoli, S., Swendsen, J., He, J.-P., Burstein, M., & Merikangas, K. R. (2015). Major depression in the national comorbidity survey–adolescent supplement: Prevalence, correlates, and treatment. *Journal of the American Academy of Child and Adolescent Psychiatry, 54*(1), 37–44. https://doi.org/10.1016/j.jaac.2014.10.010.

Bernal, G., Bonilla, J., & Bellido, C. (1995). Ecological validity and cultural sensitivity for outcome research: Issues for the cultural adaptation and development of psychosocial treatments with Hispanics. *Journal of Abnormal Child Psychology, 23*(1), 67–82. https://doi.org/10.1007/BF01447045.

Bruhn, A. L., Lane, K. L., & Hirsch, S. E. (2014). A review of Tier 2 interventions conducted within multitiered models of behavioral prevention. *Journal of Emotional and Behavioral Disorders, 22*(3), 171–189. https://doi.org/10.1177/1063426613476092.

Capaldi, D. M., & Stoolmiller, M. (1999). Co-occurrence of conduct problems and depressive symptoms in early adolescent boys: III. Prediction to young-adult adjustment. *Development And Psychopathology, 11*(1), 59–84.

Cheney, D. A., Stage, S. A., Hawken, L. S., Lynass, L., Christine, M., & Waugh, M. (2009). A 2-year outcome study of the check, connect, and expect intervention for students at risk for severe behavior problems. *Journal of Emotional & Behavioral Disorders, 17*(4), 226–243.

Chong, S. A., Abdin, E., Vaingankar, J. A., Heng, D., Sherbourne, C., Yap, M., et al. (2012). A population-based survey of mental disorders in Singapore. *Annals Academy of Medicine Singapore, 41*(2), 49–66.

Chong, W. H., & Lee, B. O. (2015). Social-emotional learning: Promotion of youth wellbeing in Singapore schools. In K. Wright & J. McLeod (Eds.), *Rethinking youth wellbeing: Critical perspectives* (pp. 161–177). New York, NY: Springer Science+Business Media.

Choon, G. L., Loh, H., Renjan, V., Tan, J., & Fung, D. (2017). Child community mental health services in Asia Pacific and Singapore's REACH Model. *Brain Sciences (2076–3425), 7*(10), 126. https://doi.org/10.3390/brainsci7100126.

Choon, G. L., Ong, S. H., Chin, C. H., & Fung, D. (2015). Child and adolescent psychiatry services in Singapore. *Child & Adolescent Psychiatry & Mental Health, 9*(1), 1–7. https://doi.org/10.1186/s13034-015-0037-8.

Cook, C. R., Rasetshwane, K. B., Truelson, E., Grant, S., Dart, E. H., Collins, T. A., et al. (2011). Development and validation of the student internalizing behavior screener: Examination of reliability, validity, and classification accuracy. *Assessment for Effective Intervention, 36*(2), 71–79. https://doi.org/10.1177/1534508410390486.

Coplan, J. D., Aaronson, C. J., Panthangi, V., & Kim, Y. (2015). Treating comorbid anxiety and depression: Psychosocial and pharmacological approaches. *World Journal of Psychiatry, 5*(4), 366–378. https://doi.org/10.5498/wjp.v5.i4.366.

Costello, E. J., Mustillo, S., Erkanli, A., Keeler, G., & Angold, A. (2003). Prevalence and development of psychiatric disorders in childhood and adolescence. *Archives of General Psychiatry, 60*(8), 837–844.

Crowe, M., Beaglehole, B., Wells, H., & Porter, R. (2015). Non-pharmacological strategies for treatment of inpatient depression. *Australian and New Zealand Journal of Psychiatry, 49*(3), 215–226. https://doi.org/10.1177/0004867415569799.

Dere, J., Sun, J., Zhao, Y., Persson, T. J., Zhu, X., Yao, S., … Ryder, A. G. (2013). Beyond 'somatization' and 'psychologization': Symptom-level variation in depressed Han Chinese and Euro-Canadian outpatients. *Frontiers in Psychology, 4*.

Dowdy, E., Doane, K., Eklund, K., & Dever, B. V. (2013). A comparison of teacher nomination and screening to identify behavioral and emotional risk within a sample of underrepresented students. *Journal of Emotional and Behavioral Disorders, 21*(2), 127–137. https://doi.org/10.1177/1063426611417627.

Durlak, J. A., Weissberg, R. P., Dymnicki, A. B., Taylor, R. D., & Schellinger, K. B. (2011). The impact of enhancing students' social and emotional learning: A meta-analysis of school-based universal interventions. *Child Development, 82*(1), 405–432. https://doi.org/10.1111/j.1467-8624.2010.01564.x.

Fergusson, D. M., & Woodward, L. J. (2002). Mental health, educational, and social role outcomes of adolescents with depression. *Archives of General Psychiatry, 59*(3), 225–231. https://doi.org/10.1001/archpsyc.59.3.225.

Flaherty, L. T., & Weist, M. D. (1999). School-based mental health services: The baltimore models. *Psychology in the Schools, 36*(5), 379. https://doi.org/10.1002/(SICI)1520-6807(199909)36:5%3c379:AID-PITS2%3e3.0.CO;2-D.

Gillham, J. E., Reivich, K. J., Freres, D. R., Chaplin, T. M., Shatté, A. J., Samuels, B., et al. (2007). School-based prevention of depressive symptoms: A randomized controlled study of the effectiveness and specificity of the penn resiliency programme. *Journal of Consulting and Clinical Psychology, 75*(1), 9–19. https://doi.org/10.1037/0022-006X.75.1.9.

Griner, D., & Smith, T. B. (2006). Culturally adapted mental health intervention: A meta-analytic review. *Psychotherapy: Theory, Research, Practice, Training, 43*(4), 531–548. https://doi.org/10.1037/0033-3204.43.4.531.

Grohol, J. (2018, 8 October 2018). Mental Health Professionals: US Statistics 2011. Retrieved from https://psychcentral.com/lib/mental-health-professionals-us-statistics/.

Hammen, C. (2009). Adolescent depression: Stressful interpersonal contexts and risk for recurrence. *Current Directions in Psychological Science, 18*(4), 200–204. https://doi.org/10.1111/j.1467-8721.2009.01636.x.

Hammen, C., Rudolph, K. D., & Abaied, J. L. (2014). Child and adolescent depression. In E. J. Mash & R. A. Barkley (Eds.), *Child psychopathology, 3rd ed.* (pp. 225–263). New York, NY: Guilford Press.

Hausmann, A., Hortnagl, C., Muller, M., Waack, J., Walpoth, M., & Conca, A. (2007). Psychotherapeutic interventions in bipolar disorder: A review. *Neuropsychiatrie, 21*(2), 102–109.

Heary, C., Hennessy, E., Swords, L., & Corrigan, P. (2017). Stigma towards mental health problems during childhood and adolescence: Theory, research and intervention approaches. *Journal of Child and Family Studies, 26*(11), 2949–2959. https://doi.org/10.1007/s10826-017-0829-y.

Heisler, E. J. (2018). *The mental health workforce: A primer.* Retrieved from https://fas.org/sgp/crs/misc/R43255.pdf.

Horner, R. H., Sugai, G., & Anderson, C. M. (2010). Examining the evidence base for school-wide positive behavior support. *Focus on Exceptional Children, 42*(8), 1–14.

Huang, C. (2015). Academic achievement and subsequent depression: A meta-analysis of longitudinal studies. *Journal of Child and Family Studies, 24*(2), 434–442. https://doi.org/10.1007/s10826-013-9855-6.

Hwang, W.-C., Myers, H. F., Chiu, E., Mak, E., Butner, J. E., Fujimoto, K., et al. (2015). Culturally adapted cognitive-behavioral therapy for Chinese Americans with depression: A randomized controlled trial. *Psychiatric Services, 66*(10), 1035–1042. https://doi.org/10.1176/appi.ps.201400358.

Kataoka, S. H., Zhang, L., & Wells, K. B. (2002). Unmet need for mental health care among US children: Variation by ethnicity and insurance status. *The American Journal Of Psychiatry, 159*(9), 1548–1555. https://doi.org/10.1176/appi.ajp.159.9.1548.

Kessler, R. C., Berglund, P., Demler, O., Jin, R., Merikangas, K. R., & Walters, E. E. (2005). Lifetime prevalence and age-of-onset distributions of DSM-IV disorders in the national comorbidity survey replication. *Archives of General Psychiatry, 62*(6), 593–602.

Kindt, K. C. M. (2014). Evaluation of a school-based depression prevention programme among adolescents from low-income areas: a randomized controlled effectiveness trial. *International Journal of Environmental Research and Public Health, 11*(5), 5273–5293. https://doi.org/10.3390/ijerph110505273.

Kolch, M., & Plener, P. L. (2016). Pharmacotherapy in psychiatric disorders of children: Current evidence and trends. *Pharmacopsychiatry, 49*(6), 219–225. https://doi.org/10.1055/s-0042-117644.

Lamb, J. M., Puskar, K. R., Sereika, S.M., & Corcoran, M. (1998). School-based intervention to promote coping in rural teens. *MCN: The American Journal of Maternal/Child Nursing, 23,* 187–194.

Lee, B.-O. (2009). Relationships between adolescents' preferred sources of help and emotional distress, ambivalence over emotional expression, and causal attribution of symptoms: A Singapore study. *British Journal of Guidance and Counselling, 37*(4), 435–457. https://doi.org/10.1080/03069880903161393.

Lee, B.-O. (2013). Ambivalence over emotional expression and symptom attribution are associated with self-reported somatic symptoms in Singaporean school adolescents. *Asian Journal of Social Psychology, 16*(3), 169–180. https://doi.org/10.1111/ajsp.12005.

Lee, S. P., Sagayadevan, V., Vaingankar, J. A., Chong, S. A., & Subramaniam, M. (2015). Subthreshold and threshold DSM-IV generalized anxiety disorder in Singapore: Results from a nationally representative sample. *Journal of Anxiety Disorders, 32,* 73–80. https://doi.org/10.1016/j.janxdis.2015.03.008.

Lewinsohn, P. M., & Hops, H. (1993). Adolescent psychopathology: I. Prevalence and incidence of depression and other DSM-III-R. *Journal of Abnormal Psychology, 102*(1), 133.

Lyon, A. R., Ludwig, K. A., Stoep, A. V., Gudmundsen, G., & McCauley, E. (2013). Patterns and predictors of mental healthcare utilization in schools and other service sectors among adolescents at risk for depression. *School Mental Health: A Multidisciplinary Research and Practice Journal, 5*(3), 155–165. https://doi.org/10.1007/s12310-012-9097-6.

McCarty, C. A., Mason, W. A., Kosterman, R., Hawkins, J. D., Lengua, L. J., & McCauley, E. (2008). Adolescent school failure predicts later depression among girls. *The Journal Of Adolescent Health: Official Publication of the Society for Adolescent Medicine, 43*(2), 180–187.

McCarty, C. A., Violette, H. D., Duong, M. T., Cruz, R. A., & McCauley, E. (2013). A randomized trial of the positive thoughts and action programme for depression among early adolescents. *Journal of Clinical Child and Adolescent Psychology, 42*(4), 554–563. 10.1080/15374416.2013.782817.

McCarty, C. A., Violette, H. D., & McCauley, E. (2011). Feasibility of the positive thoughts and actions prevention programme for middle schoolers at risk for depression. *Depression Research & Treatment,* 1–9. 10.1155/2011/241386.

McIntosh, K., Ty, S. V., & Miller, L. D. (2014). Effects of school-wide positive behavioral interventions and supports on internalizing problems: Current evidence and future directions. *Journal of Positive Behavior Interventions, 16*(4), 209–218. https://doi.org/10.1177/1098300713491980.

Merikangas, K. R., He, J.-P., Burstein, M., Swanson, S. A., Avenevoli, S., Cui, L., … Swendsen, J. (2010). Lifetime prevalence of mental disorders in U.S. adolescents: Results from the National Comorbidity Survey Replication-Adolescent Supplement (NCS-A). *Journal of the American Academy of Child & Adolescent Psychiatry, 49*(10), 980–989. https://doi.org/10.1016/j.jaac.2010.05.017.

Nearchou, F. A., Bird, N., Costello, A., Duggan, S., Gilroy, J., Long, R., et al. (2018). Personal and perceived public mental-health stigma as predictors of help-seeking intentions in adolescents. *Journal Of Adolescence, 66,* 83–90. https://doi.org/10.1016/j.adolescence.2018.05.003.

Ng, T. P., Fones, C. S. L., & Kua, E. H. (2003). Preference, need and utilization of mental health services, Singapore National Mental Health Survey. *Australian and New Zealand Journal of Psychiatry, 37*(5), 613–619. https://doi.org/10.1046/j.1440-1614.2003.01233.x.

Quiroga, C. V., Janosz, M., Bisset, S., & Morin, A. J. S. (2013). Early adolescent depression symptoms and school dropout: mediating processes involving self-reported academic competence and achievement. *Journal of Educational Psychology, 105*(2), 552–560. https://doi.org/10.1037/a0031524.

Quiroga, C. V., Janosz, M., Lyons, J. S., & Morin, A. J. S. (2012). Grade retention and seventh-grade depression symptoms in the course of school dropout among high-risk adolescents. *Psychology, 3*(9A), 749–755. https://doi.org/10.4236/psych.2012.329113.

Renshaw, T. L., & Cook, C. R. (2018). Initial development and validation of the youth internalizing problems screener. *Journal of Psychoeducational Assessment, 36*(4), 366–378. https://doi.org/10.1177/0734282916679757.

Rossello, J., Bernal, G., & Rivera-Medina, C. (2008). Individual and group CBT and IPT for Puerto Rican adolescents with depressive symptoms. *Cultural Diversity & Ethnic Minority Psychology, 14*(3), 234–245. https://doi.org/10.1037/1099-9809.14.3.234.

Saulsberry, A., Corden, M. E., Taylor-Crawford, K., Crawford, T. J., Johnson, M., Froemel, J., et al. (2013). Chicago Urban Resiliency Building (CURB): An internet-based depression-prevention intervention for urban African-American and Latino adolescents. *Journal of Child and Family Studies, 22*(1), 150–160. https://doi.org/10.1007/s10826-012-9627-8.

Shortt, A. L., Barrett, P. M., & Fox, T. L. (2001). Evaluating the FRIENDS programme: A cognitive-behavioral group treatment for anxious children and their parents. *Journal Of Clinical Child Psychology, 30*(4), 525–535. https://doi.org/10.1207/S15374424JCCP3004_09.

Stice, E., Burton, E., Bearman, S. K., & Rohde, P. (2007). Randomized trial of a brief depression prevention program: An elusive search for a psychosocial placebo control condition. *Behaviour Research and Therapy, 45,* 863–876.

Strein, W., Hoagwood, K., & Cohn, A. (2003). School psychology: A public health perspective: I. Prevention, populations, and systems change. *Journal of School Psychology, 41*(1), 23.

Subramaniam, M., Abdin, E., Picco, L., Pang, S., Shafie, S., Vaingankar, J. A., et al. (2017). Stigma towards people with mental disorders and its components—A perspective from multi-ethnic Singapore. *Epidemiology and Psychiatric Sciences, 26*(4), 371–382. https://doi.org/10.1017/S2045796016000159.

Sugai, G., Horner, R. H., & Gresham, F. M. (2002). Behaviorally effective school environments. In M. R. Shinn, H. M. Walker, & G. Stoner (Eds.), *Interventions for academic and behavior problems II: Preventive and remedial approaches* (pp. 315–350). Washington, DC US: National Association of School Psychologists.

Sugai, G., & Horner, R. R. (2006). A promising approach for expanding and sustaining school-wide positive behavior support. *School Psychology Review, 35*(2), 245–259.

Thompson, A. M., Reinke, W., Holmes, S., Danforth, L., & Herman, K. (2017). County schools mental health coalition: A model for a systematic approach to supporting youths. *Children & Schools, 39*(4), 209–218.

Thorpe, J., Kamphaus, R. W., & Reynolds, C. R. (2003). The behavior assessment system for children. In C. R. Reynolds & R. W. Kamphaus (Eds.), *Handbook of psychological and educational assessment of children: Personality, behavior, and context* (2nd ed., pp. 387–405). New York, NY US: Guilford Press.

Vander Stoep, A., Adrian, M. C., Rhew, I. C., McCauley, E., Herting, J. R., & Kraemer, H. C. (2012). Identifying comorbid depression and disruptive behavior disorders: Comparison of two approaches used in adolescent studies. *Journal of Psychiatric Research, 46*(7), 873–881. https://doi.org/10.1016/j.jpsychires.2012.03.022.

Weeland, M. M., Nijhof, K. S., Vermaes, I., Engels, R. C. M. E., & Buitelaar, J. K. (2015). Study protocol: a randomised controlled trial testing the effectiveness of 'Op Volle Kracht' in Dutch residential care. *BMC Psychiatry, 15*(1), 1–9. https://doi.org/10.1186/s12888-015-0498-6.

Weidman, A. C., Augustine, A. A., Murayama, K., & Elliot, A. J. (2015). Internalizing symptomatology and academic achievement: Bi-directional prospective relations in adolescence. *Journal of Research in Personality, 58,* 106–114. https://doi.org/10.1016/j.jrp.2015.07.005.

Weist, M. D., Bruns, E. J., Whitaker, K., Wei, Y., Kutcher, S., Larsen, T., et al. (2017). School mental health promotion and intervention: Experiences from four nations. *School Psychology International, 38*(4), 343–362. https://doi.org/10.1177/0143034317695379.

Weist, M. D., Eber, L., Horner, R., Splett, J., Putnam, R., Barrett, S., et al. (2018). Improving multitiered systems of support for students With "Internalizing" emotional/behavioral problems. *Journal of Positive Behavior Interventions, 20*(3), 172–184. https://doi.org/10.1177/1098300717753832.

Werner-Seidler, A., Perry, Y., Calear, A. L., Newby, J. M., & Christensen, H. (2017). School-based depression and anxiety prevention programmes for young people: A systematic review and meta-analysis. *Clinical Psychology Review, 51,* 30–47. https://doi.org/10.1016/j.cpr.2016.10.005.

Wijnhoven, L. A., Creemers, D. H., Vermulst, A. A., Scholte, R. H., & Engels, R. C. (2014). Randomized controlled trial testing the effectiveness of a depression prevention program ('Op Volle Kracht') among adolescent girls with elevated depressive symptoms. *Journal of Abnormal Child Psychology, 42,* 217–228.

Yong, M., & Cheney, D. A. (2013). Essential features of tier 2 social–behavioral interventions. *Psychology in the Schools, 50*(8), 844–861. https://doi.org/10.1002/pits.21710.

Young, J. F., Mufson, L., & Gallop, R. (2010). Preventing depression: A randomized trial of interpersonal psychotherapy-adolescent skills training. *Depression and Anxiety, 27*(5), 426–433.

Young, J. F., Benas, J. S., Schueler, C. M., Gallop, R., Gillham, J. E., & Mufson, L. (2016). A randomized depression prevention trial comparing interpersonal psychotherapy—Adolescent skills training to group counseling in schools. *Prevention Science, 17*(3), 314–324. https://doi.org/10.1007/s11121-015-0620-5.

Chapter 13
The Benefits of Video Instruction as a Pedagogical Tool for Students with Moderate to Severe Autism Spectrum Disorder

Adeline M. Y. Yeong and Anuradha S. K. Dutt

Abstract Teaching in today's mainstream and special education classrooms seems to be a daunting task for teachers, considering the complexity of academic and behavioural challenges experienced by students with diverse learning needs. Research within the behavioural literature indicates the growing popularity of video-based technology to improve the learning experience for students with Autism Spectrum Disorder (ASD). Video instruction refers to the creation of videos that a teacher makes specifically to teach a concept or a specific content area. This method of instruction provides the teacher with control over the exact content to be presented in the videos, and different videos can be made at various levels, catering to diverse student needs, especially visual learners such as students with ASD. This chapter describes (a) the challenges experienced by children with moderate to severe ASD while providing a brief overview of the growing prevalence of ASD in Singapore, (b) a brief description of video instruction and its various types, (c) the benefits of video instructions for students with moderate to severe ASD, and (d) using video instructions via various handheld/mobile platforms to enhance independence and self-reliance with performing tasks across various domains among children with moderate to severe ASD.

Keywords Autism spectrum disorder · Video instruction · Disability · Pedagogy

13.1 Introduction

Autism Spectrum Disorder (ASD) is a neurodevelopmental disorder that is characterized by persistent deficits and impairments in both verbal and non-verbal communication, interaction and behaviours (Allen, Wallace, Renes, Bowen, & Burke, 2010).

A. M. Y. Yeong
Rainbow Centre, Singapore, Singapore
e-mail: adelineyeong@rainbowcentre.org.sg

A. S. K. Dutt (✉)
Nanyang Technological University, National Institute of Education, Singapore, Singapore
e-mail: anuradha.dutt@nie.edu.sg

Due to these deficits, the difficulties faced by students with ASD often extend to and affect various aspects of their daily lives (Hendricks & Wehman, 2009). Individuals with comorbid ASD and intellectual disability (ID) often experience greater limitations and deficits in their environment (Cannella-Malone et al., 2011) and are found to be less likely to pursue education, vocational, and even employment tracks, as compared to individuals with other disabilities (Shattuck et al., 2012). The difficulties faced in these pursuits often result in decreased independence, and overall poorer quality of living (Billstedt, Gillberg, & Gillberg, 2005).

To provide sufficient support to individuals with ASD and ID; educators, parents, and/or caregivers often have to resource additional interventions and environmental provisions for them. This can come in the form of prompts to help them in the performance of various tasks (including academic ones). At times, they even carry out the tasks entirely for their charges. According to a survey administered by Giangreco and Broer (2005) on 700 school personnel, individuals with ASD and other disabilities reportedly spent 86% of their day with a paraprofessional and/or caregiver who remain within a proximity of about three feet from them. The reliance on external agents often results in even greater difficulties for individuals with ASD and ID across the various environmental settings (e.g. school, home, training centre, employment, etc.) particularly when the supports are either withdrawn or no longer readily available (Hume, Loftin, & Lantz, 2009).

13.2   Prevalence of ASD in Singapore and Worldwide

The number of people diagnosed with ASD appears to be steadily increasing and it is estimated that the worldwide median prevalence of ASD in individuals is about 62 in 10,000 (Elsabbagh et al., 2012). The United States Centre for Disease Control and Prevention (CDC), through their Autism and Developmental Disabilities Monitoring Network (ADDMN), estimated that in 2012, 1 in 68 or 1.5% of 8-year-old children have been identified with ASD across multiple communities. It is estimated that currently, in the USA, there are 500,000 to 1 million children with ASD between the ages of 6 and 17 years (Community Report on Autism, 2016).

Similarly, Singapore has experienced a growing prevalence of children diagnosed with ASD and other developmental issues such as global developmental delay, or speech and language delays. Based on statistics from KK Women's and Children's Hospital (KKH) and the National University Hospital (NUH), the number of children diagnosed with developmental issues showed a 76% jump in cases between the year 2010 and 2014 (The Straits Times, 2016). Although, definitive data on prevalence rates for ASD in Singapore are not available, it is estimated that 1 in 150 children is diagnosed with ASD. This is a higher rate than the World Health Organization's global figure of one in 160 children (The Straits Times, 2016). Overall, it has been estimated that over 200 children are diagnosed with ASD every year (Autism Resource Centre, Singapore, 2016). Considering the increase in prevalence of ASD in Singapore and the reliance on external agents for support, there is an increased need for trained professionals to care for these individuals, particularly for those with moderate to severe ASD. Therefore, to better address the issue of a manpower shortage against the growing population of individuals with ASD in the school systems, there is a need for more innovative instructional methods and alternatives that are less reliant on the physical presence of professionals to improve the outcomes for individuals with moderate to severe ASD.

13.3   Video Instruction Method

The use of video instruction as a teaching method to improve learning has received good results, particularly for individuals with ASD, across various domains such as education (e.g., Burton, Anderson, Prater, & Dyches, 2013; Yakubova, Hughes, & Hornberger, 2015), social communication (e.g., Macpherson, Charlop, & Miltenberger, 2015; Wilson, 2013), social initiation (e.g., Nikopoulos & Keenan, 2007), and daily life (e.g., Allen et al., 2010; Bereznak, Ayres, Mechling, & Alexander, 2012; Cannella-Malone et al., 2011; Shipley-Benamou, Lutzker, & Taubman, 2002).

With the current pervasiveness of Information and Communication Technology (ICT) tools in varied contexts, the use of video instruction has been increasing in popularity. The use of video instruction enables the diversification of learning experiences for students with ASD and provides a means of improving their academic, social, emotional, recreational, vocational and functional/daily living outcomes. Video instruction, in this case, is a form of visual, non-static, instructional material that has been found to be effective in teaching individuals with ASD (Ayres & Langone, 2005; Bellini & Akullian, 2007; Bereznak et al., 2012). This can come in the form of video prompting or video modelling, both of which are instructional, behavioural techniques that involve the use of videos for individuals to engage in observational learning of a targeted behaviour. The principles of observational learning in these two types of video instruction stems from Albert Bandura's (1977) social learning theory, where he posited that children learn through the observation of successful learning targets, regardless of the presence or absence of positive reinforcement. The use of videos, in this case, acts as a means by which successful skill sets are observed.

13.3.1   Video Prompting

In video prompting, the individual watches a video of each specific step of a process or procedure and performs that step before moving on to the next video of the next step (Cihak, Alberto, Taber-Doughty, & Gama, 2006). The number of video clips necessary in video prompted instructions, therefore, matches the number of steps required by each complex skill. For example, a task of 10 steps would require the creation and use of 10 video clips. This could prove to be less taxing on the individual watching the clips, as they will be short, allowing fewer demands on attention and memory (Cannella-Malone et al., 2011). However, video prompting could also prove to be more resource intensive as it requires the filming of, for example, 10 different videos clips, as opposed to the production of a single video clip of the entire process. The latter was perceived as more convenient for the teachers or trainers in terms of creation of instructional materials (Cannella-Malone et al., 2006).

Research in the use of video prompting as an instructional method has shown effectiveness in teaching various functional skills. Edrisinha, O'Reilly, Choi, Sigafoos, and Lancioni (2011) provided evidence on the use of video prompting in the teaching of photography and photo printing as recreational activities. Findings showed that participants were able to visually discriminate between the various buttons and functions of the printer and were able to use sight recognition to identify the correct cables for the printer. In a similar study, Bereznak et al. (2012) examined the use of video prompting to increase daily living and vocational independence in adolescents with moderate to mild ASD. Their results found video prompting to be favourable and effective across all participants and across all the tasks used in the study. All participants were able to learn the steps required. Additionally, Johnson, Blood, Freeman, and Simmons (2013) evaluated the effectiveness of video prompting to teach food preparation skills to students with moderate ASD. Their results found favour in using video prompting as an effective instructional method in increasing the number of steps completed in the tasks, and subsequently allowed for skill acquisition and performance of the entire task.

The success of the various studies can be attributed to the fact that video prompting requires lower attentional loading on individuals, thereby requiring them to retain less information at one go (Wu, Cannella-Malone, Wheaton, & Tullis, 2016). Similarly, the use of video prompting is also considered non-intrusive and allows the individuals to learn at their own pace using a step-by-step sequence (Edrisinha et al., 2011).

13.3.2   Video Modelling

In video modelling, the individual is primarily tasked to watch a video of a desired set of skills, before he or she is required to replicate and engage in the task itself (Van Laarhoven, Johnsen, Van Laarhoven-Myres, Grider, & Grider, 2009). This means that a video model instruction of the same task of 10 steps, for example, would only require the creation of one video. The length of this video clip in video modelling, as compared with the short videos of each step in video prompting, would be longer, and would require more attention and memory from the individual. However, the amount of resources necessary would be less as only one video clip would be produced. This form of instruction would be appropriate for higher functioning students with ASD, hence further diversifying the experiences of these learners.

Research has indicated that video modelling has been successful as an instructional tool for children with ASD across various domains (Buggey & Ogle, 2012).

For instance, Burton et al. (2013) found that the use of video modelling was effective in improving the performance of functional math skills for students with ASD. Similarly, Hine and Wolery (2006) indicated that the use of video modelling helped in teaching and generalizing play actions in the classroom. In fact, their results showed success in helping young children with ASD acquire new behaviours, even in the absence of reinforcement. In the domain of social communication and initiation, Cihak, Smith, Cornett, and Coleman (2012) found that video modelling was effective in helping students learn a communication system, which resulted in a rapid increase in the number of communicative initiations, thus expanding and diversifying the experiences of the learners. Nikopoulos and Keenan (2007) also found increments in the total amount of time each participant engaged in reciprocal play when using video modelling for children with ASD, in an intervention lasting over 2 months. Shipley-Benamou et al. (2002) examined the effectiveness of instructional video modelling to enhance learning and performance of daily tasks. Results indicated that the participants independently performed the selected daily tasks and could maintain this performance after a month, even in the absence of the video model.

13.4   Benefits of Video Instruction as a Pedagogical Tool

Tapping on the preferences of individuals with ASD, research suggests that using visually cued instructions is increasingly effective in interventions for this population (Ganz & Sigafoos, 2005; Parker & Kamps, 2011). Individuals with ASD seem to perform well and respond better to tasks that involve visual stimuli (Bellini & Akullian, 2007; O'Riordan, Plaisted, Driver, & Baron-Cohen, 2001; Shipley-Benamou et al., 2002). While the use of traditional paper and print methods are still widely employed by practitioners today, the benefits of using video models are plentiful. In addition to offering a different experience to learners, the advantages of this approach include the appeal of video instructions, reduced attentional requirements from the individual, adaptation of instructional materials, reduction of face-to-face interactions, increased independence and reduced stigmatization, low costs, and instructional consistency. The following section discusses each of these benefits in more detail.

13.4.1   Appeal of Video Instructions

Children with ASD have been found to show a vested interest and inclination for learning from technology, through media such as videos or computer games (Mineo, Ziegler, Gill, & Salkin, 2009). This preference for electronic screen media (Shane & Albert, 2008), thereby acts as a natural reinforcer in learning targeted behaviours for children with ASD (Nikopoulos & Keenan, 2004; Spriggs, Knight, & Sherrow, 2015).

13.4.2 Reduction of Attentional Requirements

The use of visuals in classroom settings and home settings often requires the development and production of visual materials for teaching purposes. These can be in the form of printed pictures, symbols or texts in various teaching materials, or pasted on walls in classrooms and homes. The use of tangible materials (e.g. toys, physical objects, etc.) or step- by-step written or pictorial instructions on various tasks are also commonly employed as visuals in environments that support individuals with ASD. Despite this accommodation, however, learning could still be difficult for an individual who may potentially fail to recognize the importance and relevance of educational cues required in their learning process (Shipley-Benamou et al., 2002). The use of video materials in the classroom can hence allow for the creation and development of materials that are specific and relevant to a learning situation (McCoy & Hermansen, 2007), by highlighting specific cues or behaviours or featuring them strongly in videos, without all other irrelevant stimuli. This can help to increase focus on the main stimuli required for observational learning to take place.

For example, an individual learning from step-by-step instructional visuals on the whiteboard may potentially get distracted by other information or details on the board, items near the board, or other details in the periphery of the visual material that may be insignificant to others, but significant to the individual using the material. The use of point-of-view (POV) models, where videos show tasks according to the individual's visual view (McCoy & Hermansen, 2007), can therefore help to decrease distractions and increase the individual's focus on the relevant stimuli and cues needed to learn the desired skills (Ayres & Langone, 2005; Nikopoulos, Canavan, & Nikopoulos-Smyrni, 2008; Sherer et al., 2001; Shipley-Benamou et al., 2002).

13.4.3 Adaptation of Instructional Materials

The use of video instruction also allows for various adaptations of an instructional material, to help cater to a student's unique learning styles or behavioural characteristics (Corbett & Abdullah, 2005). A child who is sensitive to sounds can opt to adjust the volume of the sound emitted from the device to suit his or her own individual needs. Video colours in the videos can be muted in the instructional video for a child who is sensitive to bright colours. Words, sentences and audio sound clips can be included and incorporated into each video instruction presented to the individual. Overall, video instruction can be designed and created to include an individual's preferences, interests and level of functioning, as opposed to the provision of a one-size-fits-all type of instruction (Wilson, 2013; Yakubova et al., 2015). This helps to ensure reduction in the potential challenges experienced by students in learning new tasks and helps to enhance the instructional value of the teaching material for the individual. Hence, learner experiences can be diversified according to the needs and preferences of the individual.

13.4.4 Reduction of Face-to-Face Interactions

The use of physical, printed visual materials in the classroom often comes together with face-to-face interactions with teachers, trainers, parents or caregivers; a situation that is often difficult for most individuals with ASD (Charlop-Christy, Le, & Freeman, 2000). The use of video instruction (by means of handheld devices, computers or other technological tools) as an instructional method, therefore helps to reduce the unpredictability involved in face-to-face interactions required in the long run. As the individuals engage with video-based instructional tools for self-teaching and independent learning, the use of video instruction could help to reduce unwarranted, unpredictable attention that is usually necessary for traditional, static interventions (Charlop-Christy et al., 2000; Ploog, 2010).

13.4.5 Increased Independence and Reduced Stigmatization

While acquisition of a wide variety of skills is highly sought after in every environment, the challenge of being able to learn the targeted skill and independently perform it is often encountered by individuals with ASD (Hume et al., 2009). As they grow and interact in their environments, caregivers and teachers frequently worry that their charges will not be able to perform the desired skills in their absence, or that the individuals with ASD will encounter new tasks that they will not be able to carry out on their own. Training these individuals to independently learn through the use of available technological tools can therefore increase their ability to learn and cope when presented with new and novel tasks (Smith et al., 2016). The availability of technological teaching tools therefore helps to reduce the challenge of prompt dependence, supports and increase self-sufficiency in learning (Blood, Johnson, Ridenour, Simmons, & Crouch, 2011; Van Laarhoven et al., 2009). It allows an individual with ASD to play a more active role in controlling his/her learning situation (Knight, McKissick, & Saunders, 2013).

Additionally, with technology and handheld devices being commonly adopted in today's society, the stigmatization associated with using support materials also decreases. First, video watching is commonly linked to leisure or recreational activities, and the use of handheld devices has been found to be naturally motivating and reinforcing to individuals with ASD (Corbett, 2003; Corbett & Abdullah, 2005). Similarly, self-instruction on technological devices is commonly carried out by individuals with or without disability (Newton & Dell, 2011; Smith et al., 2016). For example, the use of instructional tools, such as online recipe books or video recipes to cook a dish, is quite common in current times. The popular video-sharing website, 'YouTube', hosts a plethora of various instructional videos, ranging from fixing car batteries to baking cakes or even dancing lessons or carpentry lessons. The use of these technological tools as a counterpart to traditional print methods can therefore help to decrease stigmatization faced by individuals with disability, who may require additional support in their everyday lives.

13.4.6 Low Costs

With advancements in technology and widespread availability of technological devices and tools today, the sharing of media files and information has been made extremely easy. Videos can be easily shared across electronic mail (email), thumb drives, external hard drives, or simply over Wi-Fi connections. One video file can be shared among multiple handheld devices, across multiple classrooms, and even across multiple destinations globally. This can be done in mere seconds, as opposed to the need for the creation of, for example, five different sets of printed visual instructions to be made and used across five different classrooms. This therefore increases cost-effectiveness (Mason et al., 2013), as only one video is required to be constructed, as opposed to five different sets of printed materials. The creation of video models, in the long run, is therefore seen as less time consuming and more cost-effective, due to its sharing capability (Alberto, Cihak, & Gama, 2005).

13.4.7 Instructional Consistency

The sharing of video materials also allows for consistency in the implementation of interventions across various settings. This means that while caregivers and teachers may change over time, the instructional material remains predictable and consistent to the individual. There is also a reduction in the need for training and involvement of live models. When using video instruction modelling, only one model is required to be filmed, decreasing the challenge of individual differences in the teaching process. Overall, this sharing of media instructions with teachers, caregivers and parents allows consistency in what is being taught to the individual, regardless of the individual's environmental setting (Ayres & Langone, 2005; Wilson, 2013). This consistency may come in the form of visual material, language used, instruction provided, or a sequence of instructions (Yakubova et al., 2015). The utilization of consistent, visual learning, therefore, helps to increase the predictability of the learning material to the individual (Ploog, 2010), and hence allows the targeted skills to be better generalized across various environmental settings. This helps to reduce teacher or professional errors and inconsistencies that may occur in systematic teaching (Bereznak et al., 2012). Hence, learner experiences can be diversified and made accessible and affordable across wider contexts.

13.5 Future Directions: Technology and Self-instruction

Self-determination is a term used to describe the ability to be a primary agent of his or her own life and having the ability to make decisions and choices without the interference of external agents or influences (Ayres, Mechling, & Sansosti, 2013). This includes components such as choice-making, self-instruction, self-awareness, self-advocacy and independent problem-solving skills. Compared with behavioural in-vivo procedures, audio cueing, visual cueing and Cognitive Behavioural Therapy (CBT) procedures, the use of video-instruction, regardless of type, has allowed individuals to be active agents of their own learning, tapping into aspects of self-determination.

In fact, one standout feature of the use of video-based technology is the ability to increase various aspects of self-instruction, whereby individuals are able to seek various tools to help them complete and independently engage in a desired task. For this to happen, however, it is important for individuals to first learn how to use the technology before learning from the device itself (Ayres et al., 2013). The use of video-based instructions is therefore a promising option for the instruction and teaching of various skills for individuals with moderate to severe ASD (Hong et al., 2016).

Overall, as technological advancements occur, many research studies use hand-held devices such as the Apple iPad (e.g. Macpherson et al., 2015; Spriggs, Knight, & Sherrow, 2015; Yakubova et al., 2015) or the iPhone (e.g. Bereznak et al., 2012) as a platform to present videos. This could be because these devices are widely available, and commonly used across both school and home settings. Additionally, more applications have been increasingly available to host these videos, using host applications such as YouTube or Wisteria, or applications that allow you to customize videos, books or presentations with the inclusion of videos (e.g. Book Creator, Book Writer, StoryBuddy 2, Story Creator, etc.). With these available technological resources, video instruction seems to be a viable instructional method for students with moderate to severe ASD to achieve skills in various domains pertaining to education, leisure and daily living.

13.6 Conclusion

The need for increased independence and self-sufficiency is evident, particularly for individuals with moderate to severe ASD. There is a need for current research within the Singaporean context to focus on teaching individuals with moderate to severe ASD skills pertaining to self-instruction to help them play a more active role in their learning. As previously mentioned, the increase in the prevalence of children diagnosed with ASD in Singapore and world-wide each year warrants concern, given the amount of manpower needed to help support them across mainstream and special education school settings. To enhance the quality of education and learning for individuals with moderate to severe ASD, more focus is needed on combining the availability of resources with the needs of the individuals. This is extremely important considering that these individuals spend a limited, finite amount of time in schools or training settings. There is therefore a need to match effective strategies with the targeted skills to be taught (Smith et al., 2016) in a manner that increases self-reliance in learning for individuals with ASD.

The use of technology, moreover, is not an alien concept in the educational landscape of Singapore. In 2012, the Ministry of Education (MOE) Singapore launched the Special Education (SPED) framework and curriculum, with the theme, 'Living, Learning and Working in the 21st Century' (Ministry of Education, 2018). This was launched across the 19 special education schools in Singapore, with the underlying basis of using ICT to enable teaching of various domains (e.g. vocational, daily living, academic, physical education, etc.). Students with moderate to severe ASD could be coached to independently use a handheld device such as an iPad to access instructional materials via an electronic book or ebook installed within the device. Video instructional methods could be used to teach students with ASD on how to operate handheld devices and ebooks. Subsequently, when students with ASD have learned to independently operate the ebook/iPad, they could generalize the use of this self-instructional tool to learn and perform other novel daily living skills with least dependence or support from external agents (e.g., ebooks could be created to learn to make a sandwich or fold clothes, etc.).

The research literature has evidenced video instructional methods as being an effective, feasible, and ideal option to facilitate the use of existing resources and technological tools to assist individuals with moderate to severe ASD gain independence in the performance of various tasks. Aside from its advantages, the use of technology and handheld devices enables the diversification of instructional experiences for students with ASD and helps reduce stigmatization faced by them in their learning environments. This could further assist with tackling challenges related to growing manpower needs and resource allocation while simultaneously encouraging self-sufficiency and independence in individuals with moderate to severe ASD.

References

Alberto, P. A., Cihak, D. F., & Gama, R. I. (2005). Use of static picture prompts versus video modeling during simulation instruction. *Research in Developmental Disabilities, 26*(4), 327–339. https://doi.org/10.1016/j.ridd.2004.11.002.

Allen, K. D., Wallace, D. P., Renes, D., Bowen S. L., & Burke, R. V. (2010). Use of video modeling to teach vocational skills to adolescents and young adults with autism spectrum disorders. *Education and Treatment of Children, 33*(3), 339–349. https://doi.org/10.1353/etc.0.0101.

Autism Resource Centre, Singapore. (2016, January 16). *Prevalence of autism in Singapore.* Retrieved September 21, 2016, from https://www.autism.org.sg/living-with-autism/prevalence-of-autism-in-singapore.

Ayres, K. M., & Langone, J. (2005). Intervention and instruction with video for students with autism: A review of the literature. *Education and Training in Developmental Disabilities, 40*(2), 183–196. Retrieved from https://citeseerx.ist.psu.edu/viewdoc/download?doi=10.1.1.455.4526&rep=rep1&type=pdf.

Ayres, K. M., Mechling, L., & Sansosti, F. J. (2013). The use of mobile technologies to assist with life skills/independence of students with moderate/severe intellectual disability and/or autism spectrum disorders: Considerations for the future of school psychology. *Psychology of Schools, 50*(3), 259–271. https://doi.org/10.1002/pits.21673.

Bandura, A. (1977). *Social learning theory.* Englewood Cliffs, NJ: Prentice Hall.

Bellini, S., & Akullian, J. (2007). A meta-analysis of video modeling and video self-modeling interventions for children and adolescents with autism spectrum disorders. *Exceptional Children, 73*(3), 264–287. Retrieved from https://doi.org/10.1177/001440290707300301.

Bereznak, S., Ayres, K. M., Mechling, L. C., & Alexander, J. L. (2012). Video self-prompting and mobile technology to increase daily living and vocational independence for students with autism spectrum disorders. *Journal of Developmental and Physical Disabilities, 24*(3), 269–285. https://doi.org/10.1007/s10882-012-9270-8.

Billstedt, E., Gillberg, C., & Gillberg, C. (2005). Autism after adolescence: Population-based 13- to 22-year follow-up study of 120 individuals with autism diagnosed in childhood. *Journal of Autism and Developmental Disorders, 35*(3), 351–360. https://doi.org/10.1007/s10803-005-3302-5.

Blood, E., Johnson, J. W., Ridenour, L., Simmons, K., & Crouch, S. (2011). Using an iPod touch to teach social and self-management skills to an elementary student with emotion/behavioral disorders. *Education and Treatment of Children, 34*(3), 299–321. Retrieved from https://www.learntechlib.org/p/109610/.

Buggey, T., & Ogle, L. (2012). The use of self-modeling to promote social interactions among young children. *Focus on Autism and Other Developmental Disabilities, 28*(4), 202–211. https://doi.org/10.1177/1088357612464518.

Burton, C. E., Anderson, D. H., Prater, M. A., & Dyches, T. T. (2013). Video self modeling on an iPad to teach functional math skills to adolescents with autism and intellectual disability. *Focus on Autism and Other Developmental Disabilities, 28*(2), 67–77. https://doi.org/10.1177/108835 7613478829.

Cannella-Malone, H., Sigafoos, J., O'Reilly, M., de la Cruz, B., Edrisinha, C., & Lancioni, G. E. (2006). Comparing video prompting to video modeling for teaching daily living skills to six adults with developmental disabilities. *Education and Training in Developmental Disabilities, 41*(4), 344–356. Retrieved from https://www.jstor.org/stable/23879661.

Cannella-Malone, H., Fleming, C., Chung, Y. C., Wheeler, G., Basbagill, A., & Singh, A. H. (2011). Teaching daily living skills to seven individuals with severe intellectual disabilities: A comparison of video prompting to video modeling. *Journal of Positive Behavior Interventions, 13*(3), 144–153. https://doi.org/10.1177/1098300710366593.

Charlop-Christy, M. H., Le, L., & Freeman, K. A. (2000). A comparison of video modeling with in vivo modeling for teaching children with autism. *Journal of Autism and Developmental Disorders, 30*(6), 537–552. https://doi.org/10.1023/A:1005635326276.

Cihak, D. F., Alberto, P. A., Taber-Doughty, T., & Gama, R. I. (2006). A comparison of static picture prompting and video prompting simulation strategies using group instructional procedures. *Focus on Autism and Other Developmental Disabilities, 21*(2), 89–99. https://doi.org/10.1177/108835 76060210020601.

Cihak, D. F., Smith, C. C., Cornett, A., & Coleman, M. B. (2012). The use of video modeling with the picture exchange communication system to increase independent communicative initiations in preschoolers with autism and developmental delays. *Focus on Autism and Other Developmental Disabilities, 27*(1), 3–11. https://doi.org/10.1177/1088357611428426.

Community Report on Autism. (2016). Retrieved from https://www.cdc.gov/ncbddd/autism/documents/comm-report-autism-deeper-dive.pdf.

Corbett, B. A. (2003). Video modeling: a window into the world of autism. *The Behavior Analyst Today, 4*(3), 367–377. Retrieved from https://psycnet.apa.org/doi/10.1037/h0100025.

Corbett, B. A., & Abdullah, M. (2005). Video modeling: Why does it work for children with autism? *Journal of Early and Intensive Behavior Intervention, 2*(1), 2–8. https://doi.org/10.1037/h0100294.

Edrisinha, C., O'Reilly, M. F., Choi, H. T., Sigafoos, J., & Lancioni, G. E. (2011). "Say cheese": Teaching photography skills to adults with developmental disabilities. *Research in Developmental Disabilities, 32*, 636–642. https://doi.org/10.1177/1088357614533594.

Elsabbagh, M., Divan, G., Koh, Y. J., Kim, Y. S., Kauchali, S., Marcín, C., … Fombonne, E. (2012). Global prevalence of autism and other pervasive developmental disorders. *Autism Research, 5*, 160–179. https://doi.org/10.1002/aur.239.

Ganz, J. B., & Sigafoos, J. (2005). Self-monitoring: are young adults with MR and autism able to utilize cognitive strategies independently? *Education and Training in Developmental Disabilities, 40*(1), 24–33. Retrieved from https://www.jstor.org/stable/23879769.

Giangreco, M., & Broer, S. (2005). Questionable utilization of paraprofessionals in inclusive schools: Are we addressing symptoms or causes? *Focus on Autism and Other Developmental Disabilities, 20*, 10–26. https://doi.org/10.1177/10883576050200010201.

Hendricks, D. R., & Wehman, P. (2009). Transition from school to adulthood for youth with autism spectrum disorders: Review and recommendations. *Focus on Autism and Other Developmental Disabilities, 24*(2), 77–88. https://doi.org/10.1177/1088357608329827.

Hine, J. F., & Wolery, M. (2006). Using point-of-view video modeling to teach play to preschoolers with autism. *Topics in Early Childhood Special Education, 26*(2), 83–93. https://doi.org/10.1177/02711214060260020301.

Hong, E. R., Ganz, J. B., Mason, R., Morin, K., Davis, J. L., Ninci, J., … Gilliland, W. D. (2016). The effects of video modeling in teaching functional living skills to persons with ASD: A meta-analysis of single-case studies. *Research in Developmental Disabilities, 57*, 158–169. https://doi.org/10.1016/j.ridd.2016.07.001.

Hume, K., Loftin, R., & Lantz, J. (2009). Increasing independence in autism spectrum disorders: A review of three focused interventions. *Journal of Autism and Developmental Disorders, 39*, 1329–1338. https://doi.org/10.1007/s10803-009-0751-2.

Johnson, J. W., Blood, E., Freeman, A, & Simmons, K. (2013). Evaluating the effectiveness of teacher-implemented video prompting on an iPod touch to teach food-preparation skills to high school students with autism spectrum disorders. *Focus on Autism and Other Developmental Disabilities, 28*(3), 147–158. https://doi.org/10.1177/1088357613476344.

Knight, V., McKissick, B. R., & Saunders, A. (2013). A review of technology-based interventions to teach academic skills to students with autism spectrum disorder. *Journal of Autism and Developmental Disorders, 43*(11), 2628–2648. https://doi.org/10.1007/s10803-013-1814-y.

Macpherson, K., Charlop, M. H., & Miltenberger, C. A. (2015). Using portable video modelling technology to increase the compliment behaviors of children with autism during athletic group play. *Journal of Autism and Developmental Disorders, 45*, 3836–3845. https://doi.org/10.1007/s10803-014-2072-3.

Mason, R. A., Ganz, J. B., Parker, R. I., Boles, M. B., Davis, H. S., & Rispoli, M. J. (2013). Video-based modeling: Differential effects due to treatment protocol. *Research in Autism Spectrum Disorders, 7*(1), 120–131. https://doi.org/10.1016/j.rasd.2012.08.003.

McCoy, K., & Hermansen, E. (2007). Video modeling for individuals with autism: A review of model types and effects. *Education and Treatment of Children, 30*(4), 183–213. Retrieved from https://www.jstor.org/stable/42899952.

Mineo, B. A., Ziegler, W., Gill, S., & Salkin, D. (2009). Engagement with electronic screen media among students with autism spectrum disorders. *Journal of Autism and Developmental Disorders, 39*(1), 172–187. https://doi.org/10.1007/s10803-008-0616-0.

Ministry of Education. (2018). *Which school for my child? A parent's guide for children with special education needs.* Retrieved February 27, 2019, from https://www.moe.gov.sg/docs/default-source/document/education/special-education/files/parents-guide-children-special-educational-needs.pdf.

Newton, D. A., & Dell, A. G. (2011). Mobile devices and students with disabilities: What do best practices tell us? *Journal of Special Education Technology, 26*(3), 47–49. https://doi.org/10.1177/016264341102600305.

Nikopoulos, C. K., & Keenan, M. (2004). Effects of video modeling on social initiations by children with autism. *Journal of Applied Behavior Analysis, 37*(1), 93–96. https://doi.org/10.1901/jaba.2004.37-93.

Nikopoulos, C. K., & Keenan, M. (2007). Using video modeling to teach complex social sequences to children with autism. *Journal of Autism and Developmental Disorders, 37,* 678–693. https://doi.org/10.1007/s10803-006-0195-x.

Nikopoulos, C. K., Canavan, C., & Nikopoulou-Smryni, P. (2008). Generalized effects of video modeling on establishing instructional stimulus control in children with autism. *Journal of Positive Behavior Interventions, 11*(4), 198–207. https://doi.org/10.1177/1098300708325263.

O'Riordan, M. A., Plaisted, K. C., Driver, J., & Baron-Cohen, S. (2001). Superior visual search in autism. *Journal of Experimental Psychology: Human Perception and Performance, 27*(3), 719–730. Retrieved from https://www.ncbi.nlm.nih.gov/pubmed/11424657.

Parker, D., & Kamps, D. (2011). Effects of task analysis and self-monitoring for children with autism in multiple social settings. *Focus on Autism and Other Developmental Disabilities, 26*(3), 131–142. Retrieved from https://doi.org/10.1177/1088357610376945.

Ploog, B. O. (2010). Stimulus overselectivity four decades later: A review of the literature and its implications for current research in autism spectrum disorder. *Journal of Autism and Developmental Disorders, 40*(11), 1332–1349. https://doi.org/10.1007/s10803-010-0990-2.

Shane, H. C., & Albert, P. D. (2008). Electronic screen media for persons with autism spectrum disorders: Results of a survey. *Journal of Autism and Developmental Disorders, 38*(8), 1499–1508. https://doi.org/10.1007/s10803-007-0527-5.

Shattuck, P. T., Narendorf, S. C., Cooper, B., Sterzing, P. R., Wagner, M., & Taylor, J. L. (2012). Post-secondary education and employment among youth with autism spectrum disorder. *Pediatrics, 129*(6), 1042–1049. https://doi.org/10.1542/peds.2011-2864.

Sherer, M., Pierce, K. L., Paredes, S., Kisacky, K. L., Ingersoll, B., & Schreibman, L. (2001). Enhancing conversation skills in children with autism via video technology, which is better, "self" or "other" as a model? *Behavior Modification, 25*(1), 140–158. https://doi.org/10.1177/0145445501251008.

Shipley-Benamou, R., Lutzker, J. R., & Taubman, M. (2002). Teaching daily living skills to children with autism through instructional video modeling. *Journal of Positive Behavior Interventions, 4*(3), 166–177. https://doi.org/10.1177/10983007020040030501.

Smith, K. A., Ayres, K. A., Alexander, J., Ledford, J. R., Shepley, C., & Shepley, S. B. (2016). Initiation and generalization of self-instructional skills to adolescents with autism and intellectual disability. *Journal of Autism and Developmental Disorders, 46,* 1196–1209. https://doi.org/10.1007/s10803-015-2654-8.

Spriggs, A. D., Knight, V., & Sherrow, L. (2015). Talking picture schedules: Embedding video models into visual activity schedules to increase independence for students with ASD. *Journal of Autism and Developmental Disorders, 45,* 3846–3861. https://doi.org/10.1007/s10803-014-2315-3.

The Straits Times, Singapore. (2016, December 24). *1 in 150 children in Singapore has autism.* Retrieved February 27, 2019, from https://www.straitstimes.com/singapore/health/1-in-150-children-in-singapore-has-autism.

Van Laarhoven, T., Johnsen, J. W., Van Laarhoven-Myres, T., Grider, K. L., & Grider, K. M. (2009). The effectiveness of using a video iPod as a prompting device in employment settings. *Journal of Behavioral Education, 18*(2), 119–141. https://doi.org/10.1007/s10864-009-9077-6.

Wilson, K. P. (2013). Incorporating video modeling into a school-based intervention for students with autism spectrum disorders. *Language, Speech, and Hearing Services in Schools, 44*(1), 105–117. https://doi.org/10.1044/0161-1461(2012/11-0098).

Wu, P. F., Cannella-Malone, H. I., Wheaton, J. E. & Tullis, C. A. (2016). Using video prompting with different fading procedures to teach daily living skills: A preliminary examination. *Focus on*

Autism and Other Developmental Disabilities, 31(2), 129–139. https://doi.org/10.1177/108835 7614533594.

Yakubova, G., Hughes, E. M., & Hornberger, E. (2015). Video-based intervention in teaching fraction problem-solving to students with autism spectrum disorder. *Journal of Autism and Developmental Disorders, 45,* 2865–2875. https://doi.org/10.1007/s10803-015-2449-y.

Chapter 14
Using Serious Games to Support Learners with Mobility and Sensory Impairments

Caroline Koh

Abstract This chapter provides a review of the literature on the use of serious games to assist learners with visual, hearing and mobility impairments. Its objective is to identify the trends in research and findings, with the aim of providing some recommendations for translating research outcomes into daily practice and applications. A preliminary online search for relevant articles revealed no fewer than 16,000 results within the last 3 years. Of these, a sample of articles were selected for detailed analysis, based on their relevance, year of publication and representation of the studies carried out in this field. Most of the studies identified in the search dealt with the use of serious games in conjunction with or used to assist therapy and rehabilitation of patients with impaired mobility, motor function or control. Generally, the feedback from the hearing-impaired users has been positive, although recent publications on the use of serious games for the visually impaired have been mostly conjectural and dialogic, rather than empirical. Overall, the new technologies have been well received by both patients and health care providers and the controlled trials have generated promising results, showing improvement in patient motivation and performance.

Keywords Serious games · Mobility · visual and hearing impairments · Therapy · Rehabilitation · New technologies

14.1 Introduction

Internet use and online activities have become staple fixtures of life in the twenty-first century. A survey on the popularity of online categories showed that online search and navigation ranked highest in terms of global penetration, with 88.5% reach of internet audiences (Statista, 2015). However, the survey also identified online games as a rapidly expanding category with 48.1% global penetration. Whereas early video games required game consoles or computers for operation, the widespread use of smartphones and other mobile devices such as tablets, have made online games

C. Koh (✉)
National Institute of Education, Nanyang Technological University, Singapore, Singapore
e-mail: caroline.koh@nie.edu.sg

© Springer Nature Singapore Pte Ltd. 2020   241
C. Koh (ed.), *Diversifying Learner Experience*,
https://doi.org/10.1007/978-981-15-9861-6_14

accessible to all users. Anyone with a smartphone can now download a game and play it anytime and anywhere.

A recent report on the 'State of Online Gaming' (Limelight networks, 2019) involving responses from 4,500 participants, aged 18 and above, from France, Germany, India, Italy, Japan, Singapore, South Korea, the UK, and the USA, showed that 9.2% of the participants played online games for more than 20 h weekly, whereas only about 14.9% were casual gamers who played for less than 1 h per week. Likewise, Giunti and colleagues (2015) found that digital game players form a large but diverse group, with a gaming experience of an average of 10 years, although there were youths between 8 and 18 years who spent between 30 and 60 min on gameplay on a daily basis. Whereas the original purpose of digital games was to provide entertainment to the player, there has been a growing interest in exploring the use of games for more 'serious' objectives, such as the provision of education, health, defence, policy and training (Alvarez & Djaouti, 2011). Whereas games with 'serious' objectives have been widely used in mainstream education, their application in special needs education and for learners with disabilities has gained traction only in the last decade. The spike in the literature on the use of digital games to support learners with special needs indicates that a review of the research in this domain is timely.

14.2   Serious Games

A gamut of names, such as digital games, video games, computer games, have been used to denote games that are played on or operated by a digital device. More recently, the term 'serious game' has been added to the plethora of terms, to distinguish between games used for instructional purposes and those designed primarily for leisure and entertainment. According to Zyda (quoted in Alvarez & Djaouti, 2011, p. 11), a serious game is 'a mental contest, played with a computer in accordance with specific rules, that uses entertainment to further government or corporate training, education, health, public policy, and strategic communication objectives'. Other authors, such as Alvarez and Djaouti (2011, p. 11), believed that a serious game should still retain some element of 'pleasure and play' and thus defined it as a 'computer application, for which the original intention is to combine with consistency, both serious aspects such as non-exhaustive and non-exclusive, teaching, learning, communication, or the information, with *playful springs* from the video game'. Combining elements of both definitions, one can thus describe a serious game as a mental contest, played on a digital platform using a computer or mobile device, and serving a utilitarian purpose other than leisure, but with affordances of a pleasurable outcome.

Whereas both serious game design and the gamification of learning ultimately have the objective of improving learning outcomes, they differ significantly in their approach. Landers (2015, p. 752) proposed, in his theory of gamified learning, that gamification be defined as 'the use of game attributes, outside the context of a game with the purpose of affecting learning-related behaviours or attitudes...' which in turn, 'influence learning by one or two processes: by strengthening the relationship between instructional design quality and outcomes ... and/or by influencing learning directly'. In contrast, serious games, through their instructional content, are designed to have a direct effect on learning. In supporting sensory and mobility-impaired learners, most researchers tend to adopt the use of serious games rather than gamification of learning. Their purpose is to allow for greater inclusivity and to ensure that the persons with impairments are not denied the experience of learning through games despite the challenges that they face. As such, this chapter focuses on the use of serious games as learning tools, rather than gamification of learning.

14.3 Impairments and Disabilities

The terms 'impairment' and 'disability' have been the subject of much confusion, with people often taking one as being synonymous to the other. Further contradictions have arisen due to the conflicting views of the two schools of thought leading the debate on the issue. The traditional medical model advocated by the World Health Organization (WHO), defines 'impairment' as 'an anomaly, defect, loss or other significant deviation in body structures' (WHO, 2001, p. 10). It defines 'disability' as any restriction or lack of ability to perform or function normally, as a result of an impairment. The opposing school of thought supported by the Disabled People's International (DPI) proposed a social model whereby 'impairment' is defined as a limitation to physical, mental or sensory function within the individual. 'Disability', on the other hand, is perceived as the limitation or loss of ability to lead a normal life at a comparable level with others as a result of physical or social barriers imposed within the community or environment. The concept of the social model was first introduced by Oliver (2013), following a publication by the Union of the Physically Impaired Against Segregation (UPIAS, 1976), claiming that 'it is society that disables physically impaired people' (UPIAS, 1976, p. 4), and that disability is a condition imposed on individuals with impairment rather than a condition that arises from the impairment. The aim of the social model was to remove societal and environmental barriers that would impede people with disabilities from leading an inclusive and emancipated life.

Both the medical and the social models are generally in agreement with regards to defining 'impairment', but they differ in their interpretation of the meaning of 'disability'. Whereas the medical model attributes disability causation to internal factors/impairments within the individual, the social model considers disability as an entirely social phenomenon, whereby the environment fails to provide adequate support for the impaired person to lead a normal life. Most recently, in its latest version of ICF, the WHO (2013, p. 8) has attempted to integrate the salient elements of both models, emphasizing on both the role of individual and that of the environment in its definition of 'disability', which it presently defines as 'an umbrella term for impairments, activity limitations and participation restrictions. It denotes the negative aspects of the interaction between an individual (with a health condition) and that individual's contextual factors (environmental and personal factors)'. While the causal link between impairment and disability does exist, one needs to acknowledge that more could be done to enable the impaired person to lead as close to a normal life as possible. In this respect, serious games have the potential to provide an even field in the virtual world for the impaired individuals to acquire the relevant skill sets that enable them to live as independently as possible in the real world.

This chapter attempts to present a review of extant research and literature on the use of serious games with people with impairments in sensory and mobility functions. It attempts to provide answers to the following:

> In what ways have serious games diversified learning for people with sensory and mobility impairments?
> How effective were serious games in supporting sensory and mobility impaired persons' learning?

14.4 Sensory Impairments

Although sensory impairments include reduction or limitation in functional ability in any of the five senses, the literature on serious games and learners with sensory disabilities seems to be confined to visual and hearing impairments. This is partly due to what is perceived as a limited market by game developers and producers, who are thus reluctant to invest in the creation of a digital product which would remain on the shelves (Kirkpatrick, 2016). Second, digital games rely heavily on both visuals and sound effects and it is a challenge to develop a game that retains its appeal even without these sensory inputs. Nevertheless, those with sensory impairments would still be able to profit from gameplay as long as there are appropriate cues or instructions displayed onscreen or voiced over to enable learner engagement. Brown, Standen, Evett, Battersby, and Shopland (2010) highlighted the benefits of computer-based learning to people with disabilities, namely in providing access to educational opportunities and immersion into life experiences that would otherwise have been beyond their reach. Through their virtual environments, serious games enable learners to gain exposure to and interact with combinations of visuals, animations, words that enrich learning and broaden their understanding of real-world contexts.

14.4.1 Diversifying Learning for the Hearing Impaired

Approximately 466 million people suffer from disabling hearing loss globally, of which 34 million are children (World Health Organisation, 2018). Literacy achievement remains one of the greatest challenges for the hearing impaired, with the World Federation of Deaf reporting at least 80% of the world population of deaf or hearing-impaired people being below normative literacy standard (Bouzid, Khenissi, Essalmi,

& Jemni, 2016). Research on serious games for the hearing impaired focused on three main areas: game design and models, literacy and sign language learning, and speech therapy. Park (2011) highlighted the importance of giving due consideration to the individual learner differences in the course of designing and developing serious games for the hearing-impaired. He stressed the need to assess personal attributes such as level of residual hearing, intellectual capacity and academic achievement, such that the training and game design can be customized to cater to the personal needs of the hearing-impaired learner. Along this line, a group of researchers from Tunisia, Bouzid, Khenissi, and Jemni (2015), proposed the design for an interactive game generator aimed at enabling teachers and parents to produce, without any need for complex programming, multiple versions of a game that could be adjusted to suit the needs of a hearing-impaired learner, thus diversifying learning as he/she progresses through the training.

Sign language learning. A number of authors have described serious games designed and developed to diversify learning for the hearing impaired. Khenissi, Bouzid, Essalmi, and Jemni (2015) developed the Learning version of Memory Match Game for Deaf Learners (LMMGDL), a serious game consisting of a combination of the traditional version of the Memory Match Game and elements of SignWriting, the written form of sign language, whereby a sign is represented graphically. The game includes a virtual human avatar demonstrating the sign gestures and interpreting their meanings. This visualization is of particular usefulnes, not only to the hearing-impaired learners but also to non-impaired people attempting to learn sign language in order to communicate with those with hearing loss. Gameiro, Cardoso, and Rybarczyk (2013) developed another serious game 'Kinect-Sign' that served a similar purpose. The latter allows the non-impaired 'listener' to first learn the sign letters and then to apply them in a virtual environment, such as a TV Show scenario.

There are ample benefits derived from using this type of serious game, which uses an avatar as demonstrator. First, the diversification of the learning experience brings about an element of novelty in sign language acquisition—this would pique the interest of both the hearing impaired as well as non-impaired persons attempting to learn the language. Heightened interest and enjoyment would lead to an enhancement in intrinsic motivation. Likewise, perceived satisfaction of the needs for competence and autonomy leads to improved learner motivation (Deci & Ryan, 2000). In this respect, an avatar has 'infinite patience' and 'never tires' of repeating the same instruction or demonstration over and over again. Thus, the learner has no fear of negative judgment from the instructor or therapist and is able to learn at his/her own pace and acquire greater self-efficacy and competence in the process. Third, the learner has greater ownership of his/her learning and, as in Kinect-Sign, has the autonomy to make decisions on his/her learning progression.

Speech and verbal expression. Yet other researchers have concentrated their effort in developing serious games to support verbal expression among the hearing impaired. An international team of researchers from Columbia and Saudi Arabia, Cano, Peñeñory, Collazos, Fardoun, and Alghazzawi (2015) introduced 'Phonak', a serious game supporting auditory-verbal therapy for rehabilitating children treated with cochlear implants. The purpose of the game is to promote speech acquisition by training children to learn to listen. The five stages in the game allow the hearing-impaired child to follow the adventures of a character by the name of Phonak, and in so doing, to master skills related to the levels of speech therapy learning such as detection, discrimination, identification, recognition and listening comprehension. Along the same line, Malaysian researchers, Nasiri, Shirmohammadi, and Rashed (2017) developed and implemented a serious game that was used for speech therapy intervention and also served as an instrument to measure the performance of children with speech and hearing impairments. The game had three stages, beginning with the identification of children in need of speech therapy, followed by the identified participants learning specific words while playing the game(s). In the third and last phase, the children's performances are assessed, and their learning is evaluated.

In this instance, the game structure involves a number of stages of increasing task complexity or difficulty. Typically, the game starts with the diagnosis of the learner's needs, followed by the learning or skills acquisition phase and concludes with an assessment of the progress made. In addition to diversifying the experiences of the hearing-impaired learner, Phonak's adventures provide the necessary scaffold to learning as the player progresses through these stages, and this helps to keep him/her on task while levelling up his/her competence.

Impact of serious games on the hearing-impaired learner. How effective then were serious games in supporting learning among the hearing impaired? In designing their Sign Language and Sign Writing learning game, Khenissi et al. (2015, p. 5) aimed to 'foster vocabulary acquisition for DL [Deaf Learners] in both spoken and sign languages, to render the learning experience with more fun, to engage DL and to keep them motivated'. A pilot study conducted by the team showed that in general, the participating hearing-impaired children were satisfied with the game and found it useful, easy to use and enjoyable. The observations on the behaviour of the children while playing the game showed that they were actively mimicking the avatar as it was carrying out the hand gestures. Most of the participants felt that the game helped them improve in their vocabulary since it allowed for repetition of the tasks until attainment of mastery. The older participants were however unsure about whether the game actually improved their vocabulary learning. This suggests that future games should provide opportunities for players to level up in terms of their language competency or literacy. Players could progress through stages of increasing competence, e.g. from beginner to intermediate, advanced and finally expert status. In this way, participants could enter the game at any point depending on their baseline knowledge.

14.4.2 Diversifying Learning for the Visually Impaired

According to the World Health Organization (2018), globally, about 1.3 billion people live with some form of visual impairment. These include 217 million who have moderate to severe impairment and 36 million who are blind. Whereas the feedback from the hearing-impaired users has been positive, recent publications on the use of serious games for the visually impaired have been mostly conjectural and dialogic, rather than empirical. For the visually impaired, the customization of serious games is more complex and challenging, as game developers are not able to make use of interactive displays to engage players, hence their reluctance to invest in the development of technologies specifically for this group. Accessibility of technologies to the visually impaired is thus an issue that remains to be resolved.

Nevertheless, in recent years, a few researchers have explored the development and use of serious games to support learning in the visually impaired. Prompted by the doggedness of hard core fighting game players such as Blind Warrior and Sightless Kombat, who are both blind, software engineers have begun to explore accessibility factors that would enable serious games to be used by the visually impaired, notwithstanding the extent of their disability. Thus, Jaramillo-Alcázar and Luján-Mora (2017) have proposed a list of guidelines for assessing the accessibility of serious games to the visually impaired. Thus, accessibility is enhanced if games can be operated without the need for images or visuals, or if the gameplay incorporates voice-over screen-reading technology, focusing on what can be heard rather than what can be seen. The serious games that have been developed for the visually impaired fall into two categories: (i) those focusing on literacy and language learning and (ii) those focusing on the diagnosis of the impairment and rehabilitative processes.

Literacy and language learning. Milne, Bennett, Ladner, and Azenkot (2014) presented a rare report of an actual experimental piece on the use of BraillePlay, a series of serious games for teaching Braille character encodings and promoting Braille literacy among the visually impaired. BraillePlay consist of four games, which vary in difficulty levels, enabling users to learn and memorize the Braille character encodings, and then to identify and recall them in word games, hence enabling an increase in competency level in the process. Since BraillePlay games can be played on smartphones, they are easily accessible to blind players in much the same way as other smartphone games are presented to people with normal eyesight. This longitudinal study, carried out with eight blind children, had promising results, with anecdotal evidence that BraillePlay games increased the children's motivation to learn Braille. Although one of the games proved too challenging for the children, most of them enjoyed the novel experience of being able to play games on a smartphone in the way that other children do. Except for one of the children who had cerebral palsy, most of them were able to play the games independently, displaying a sense of autonomy in the process. When interviewed, some children and their parents shared that the games helped them learn Braille letters, hence increasing their competence in Braille literacy.

Rehabilitation of the visually impaired. On their part, Ciman et al. (2013) and Gaggi, Sgaramella, Nota, Bortoluzzi, and Santilli (2016) focused on game-based rehabilitation in the design of '*HelpMe*!', a serious game developed for the early diagnosis and rehabilitation of patients affected by Cerebral Visual Impairment (CVI), a visual deficit arising from brain damage, whereby the affected person shows symptoms such as ocular delay and a reduced field of view. In these instances, the diagnostic and/or rehabilitative elements are presented under the guise of gameplay. This has the effect of engaging the visually impaired child who then perceives the rehabilitative activity as fun and enjoyable rather than daunting. As such, the child is motivated to stay on course with the therapy session and the likelihood of him/her dropping out of the program is reduced.

Leisure experiences. Video games are primarily designed for entertainment. Hence, although serious games have an educational purpose, they should still provide a fun experience to the user. Some game developers have attempted to design games that enable visually impaired people to experience leisure activities. Kirkpatrick (2016) described the development of Eyes-Free Yoga, a software application designed to assist blind or visually impaired people in the practice of six yoga positions, while other researchers developed VI Tennis, a game that uses a modified Nintendo Wii remote control that provides haptic feedback, coupled with audio and speech effects, enabling visually impaired players to locate the ball and engage in game play.

14.5   Mobility Impairments

Generally, persons with mobility impairments experience partial or total loss of function of upper or lower limb(s), reduction in manual dexterity and/or coordination. Impairments in mobility may be congenital or due to the ageing process or arising as a consequence of disease or injuries. A search using the terms 'serious games, rehabilitation, motor impairment' for the year 2017 alone yielded no less than 1,970 results, showing that research in this area is thriving, especially in the domain of Health Sciences and Medicine.

14.5.1   *Diversifying Learning for Persons with Mobility Impairments*

Most of the studies surfaced in the search dealt with the use of serious games in conjunction with or to assist therapy and rehabilitation of patents disabled by loss or impairment of mobility, motor function or control. Studies prior to 2017 tended to focus on adult or elderly patients and on dilapidating conditions such as strokes (Bower et al., 2015), Parkinson's disease (Paraskevopoulos, Tsekleves, Craig, Whyatt, & Cosmas, 2014), Alzheimer's disease (Robert et al., 2014) and multiple sclerosis.

Rehabilitation for persons with mobility impairments. Physical therapy is often prescribed for individuals who have lost partial or complete mobility through strokes, accidents or other causes (Langhorne, Bernhardt, & Kwakkel, 2011; Van Peppen et al., 2004). While this form of therapy has been shown to be beneficial to patients, adherence to the exercise regime has proven to be a challenge due to poor access to therapy, safety concerns and low motivation on the part of the patient.

Bower et al. (2015) explored the use of a suite of four specifically designed motion-controlled games for rehabilitation of stroke patients, involving 40 participants for pre-test and 16 for the intervention. The games aimed to improve upper limb activities and dynamic balance such as weight-shifting torso movements. They were designed such that participants can start playing at an early stage of rehabilitation, progressing through 10 levels of difficulty, determined on the basis of the user's response speed to moving objects on the virtual screen. This helped to build the participants' self-perception of accomplishment and competence. In addition, the participants were able to choose the type and number of games, their difficulty levels and the time spent on each game. This gave them a sense of autonomy and control over their predicament and enabled them to be challenged at their optimal levels, without fear of any safety concerns or serious adverse effects such as accidental falls or injuries. As a result, the majority of the participants enjoyed the novel experience and felt that the games injected fun in the exercise and contributed to their recovery. The findings revealed improvement over time and high acceptability among participants who found the sessions enjoyable and helpful.

On their part, Paraskevopoulos et al. (2014) introduced a set of guidelines and design framework for serious games to assist mobility rehabilitation for people affected by Parkinson's disease. The findings from their pilot studies showed that translating rehabilitative exercises into serious games could potentially improve participants' level of engagement and effort in physical activity during therapy sessions. Likewise, Robert et al. (2014) conducted a SWOT (Strengths, Weaknesses, Opportunities, Threats) analysis to assess the feasibility of using serious games for the rehabilitation of persons with Alzheimer's disease and concluded that serious games could potentially be useful tools for rehabilitation, provided that these are customized specifically to address the needs of people with this condition and more research is done to ascertain the feasibility and effectiveness of the games.

Use of artificial intelligence. Recent publications show a shift towards motor impairments affecting children such as cerebral palsy (Bonnechere, Omelina, Jansen, & Van Sint Jan, 2017) and the use of robotics in conjunction with serious games (Dehem et al., 2017). Bonnechere and colleagues (2017) investigated the effectiveness of serious games for the physical rehabilitation of children with cerebral palsy. They found that the children showed significant improvement in their trunk control and balance. On their part, Dehem et al. (2017) explored the application of a serious game on a rehabilitation robot. In that study, the serious game allowed the rehabilitation to be adapted to the specific impairments of a sample of 49 healthy children and 20 children affected by cerebral palsy. The findings showed that the participants were motivated to generate higher forces on a target ahead of them during their attempts at upper limb mobilization. In the same vein, Sucar et al. (2013) found preliminary evidence for the feasibility of Gesture Therapy, a virtual reality-based platform for rehabilitation of the upper limb impairments. However, each of these studies involved small to moderate samples of participants, with the intervention conducted over a short period of time. Hence, further research is needed, with larger participant samples and longer implementation periods, to establish the validity of these approaches.

In general, the new technologies have been well received by both patients and health care providers and the controlled trials have generated promising results, showing improvement in patient motivation and performance. Nevertheless, as with the use of serious games in other domains, the recommendations for future research on serious games and motor disabilities involve further investigations into the feasibility of long-term adherence, the validity, acceptability, safety and efficacy of the procedures, well as establishing the reliability and generalizability of the findings.

14.6 Discussion and Conclusion

The aims of this chapter are twofold—first, to provide an overview of the ways in which serious games have diversified learning for people with sensory and mobility impairments and, second, to explore how effective serious games are in supporting sensory and mobility impaired persons' learning. The literature discussed earlier revealed that serious games have diversified the experiences of sensory and mobility impaired learners by making available opportunities that would otherwise have been inaccessible to them. Moreover, with the help of interactive game generators, software developers have worked towards customizing learning tools to suit the nature and degree of impairment of their disabled clientele. In addition, the sensory or mobility impaired game players are able to explore their virtual environments, undertake tasks or perform activities with help and guidance from virtual avatars. For persons with sensory impairments, the emphasis was on literacy and language learning, with games designed to motivate and improve mastery in sign language and speech therapy for those with hearing impairments, and for the mastery of Braille for the visually impaired. For those with mobility impairment, the focus of the games was to offer an alternative form of therapy and rehabilitation, with the objective of enabling them to regain mobility, in part if not in full.

In terms of effectiveness, the response from participants in the various studies has been generally positive, with reports of improved performance as well as task engagement and motivation. However, although the more recent studies involved larger participant numbers, the earlier interventions were limited by their small sample size, and thus the validation of the studies and generalizability of the outcomes remain to be established. One has to acknowledge, however, that getting consent from the parents or guardians for under-aged participants is often not easy, with the former declining to be involved due to work commitments, lack of time and resources to ferry their children, or inability to accompany them during the intervention (Chuang & Kuo, 2016).

The literature on the use of serious games to support sensory and mobility-impaired learners is gleaned from studies conducted on a global scale, showing that research in this domain is not confined to Western contexts. There is a high degree of universality in the needs of learners with impairments. Thus, irrespective of their origins, digital tools are applicable and adaptable to diverse contexts. Just as avatars can be programmed to teach hearing-impaired learners to use sign gestures for any language, BraillePlay games may be adapted to allow visually impaired users to learn Braille character encodings for any language.

Nonetheless, there were challenges with regards to the design and development of games for persons with sensory and/or mobility impairments. These difficulties arise from the relatively small market size for games designed for specific impairments. As such, most hardware developers would hesitate to invest in the production of such games, given the uncertainty as to whether they will be able recover costs, let alone make a profit, since they are unable to gauge the size of the market. For the visually impaired, game developers also face the additional challenge of designing games that retain their appeal, despite the removal of the all-encompassing visual components.

Nonetheless, such challenges should not be allowed to deter the use of technology-enabled tools, such as serious games, to promote learning amongst people with sensory and mobility impairments. The fourth industrial revolution with its slew of the latest electronic gadgetry, has the potential of, not only resolving existing issues but also opening doors to new ideas on how to improve accessibility and inclusivity for persons with diverse types of impairments.

References

Alvarez, I., & Djaouti, D. (2011). An introduction to serious game—Definitions and concepts. *Serious Games & Simulation for Risks Management, 11*, 11–15.

Bonnechere, B., Omelina, L., Jansen, B., & Van Sint Jan, S. (2017). Balance improvement after physical therapy training using specially developed serious games for cerebral palsy children: Preliminary results. *Disability and Rehabilitation, 39*(1), 403–406.

Bouzid, Y., Khenissi, M. A., & Jemni, M. (2015, December). Designing a game generator as an educational technology for the deaf learners. In *2015 5th International Conference on Information & Communication Technology and Accessibility (ICTA)* (pp. 1–6). IEEE.

Bouzid, Y., Khenissi, M. A., Essalmi, F., & Jemni, M. (2016). Using educational games for sign language learning—a signwriting learning game: Case study. *Journal of Educational Technology & Society, 19*(1), 129–141.

Bower, K. J., Louie, J., Landesrocha, Y., Seedy, P., Gorelik, A., & Bernhardt, J. (2015). Clinical feasibility of interactive motion-controlled games for stroke rehabilitation. *Journal of Neuroengineering and Rehabilitation, 12*(1), 63.

Brown, D. J., Standen, P., Evett, L., Battersby, S., & Shopland, N. (2010). Designing serious games for people with dual diagnosis: learning disabilities and sensory impairments. In *Design and implementation of educational games: theoretical and practical perspectives* (pp. 424–439). IGI Global.

Cano, S. P., Peñeñory, V., Collazos, C. A., Fardoun, H. M., & Alghazzawi, D. M. (2015). Training with Phonak: Serious game as support in auditory-verbal therapy for children with cochlear implants. *REHAB, 15*, 22–25.

Chuang, T. Y., & Kuo, M. S. (2016). A Motion-sensing game-based therapy to foster the learning of children with sensory integration dysfunction. *Journal of Educational Technology & Society, 19*(1), 4.

Ciman, M., Gaggi, O., Nota, L., Pinello, L., Riparelli, N., & Sgaramella, T. M. (2013, May). HelpMe!: A serious game for rehabilitation of children affected by CVI. In *WEBIST* (pp. 257–262).

Deci, E. L., & Ryan, R. M. (2000). The "what" and "why" of goal pursuits: Human needs and the self-determination of behavior. *Psychological Inquiry, 11*(4), 227–268.

Dehem, S., Stoquart, G., Lejeune, T., Brouwers, I., Montedoro, V., Edwards, M., ... Dehez, B. (2017). Assessment of upper limb motor impairments in children with cerebral palsy using a rehabilitation robot and serious game exercise. In *The 5th IEEE Conference on Serious Games and Applications for Health*.

Gaggi, O., Sgaramella, T. M., Nota, L., Bortoluzzi, M., & Santilli, S. (2016, November). A serious games system for the analysis and the development of visual skills in children with CVI. In *International Conference on Smart Objects and Technologies for Social Good* (pp. 155–165). Cham: Springer.

Gameiro, J., Cardoso, T., & Rybarczyk, Y. (2013, July). Kinect-sign: Teaching sign language to "listeners" through a game. In *International Summer Workshop on Multimodal Interfaces* (pp. 141–159). Berlin, Heidelberg: Springer.

Giunti, G., Baum, A., Giunta, D., Plazzotta, F., Benitez, S. E., Gómez, A. R., & de Quiros, F. G. B. (2015, August). Serious games: A concise overview on what they are and their potential applications to healthcare. In *MedInfo* (pp. 386–390).

Jaramillo-Alcázar, A., & Luján-Mora, S. (2017, October). Mobile serious games: An accessibility assessment for people with visual impairments. In *Proceedings of the 5th International Conference on Technological Ecosystems for Enhancing Multiculturality* (p. 66). ACM.

Khenissi, M. A., Bouzid, Y., Essalmi, F., & Jemni, M. (2015, July). A learning game for deaf learners. In *2015 IEEE 15th International Conference on Advanced Learning Technologies* (pp. 418–422). IEEE.

Kirkpatrick, K. (2016). Existing technologies can assist the disabled. *Communications of the ACM, 59*(4), 16–18.

Landers, R. N. (2015). Developing a theory of gamified learning: Linking serious games and gamification of learning. *Simulation & Gaming, 45*(6), 752–768.

Langhorne, P., Bernhardt, J., & Kwakkel, G. (2011). Stroke rehabilitation. *Lancet, 377,* 1693–1702.

Limelight networks. (2019). The state of online gaming—2019. Retrieved from https://www.limelight.com/resources/white-paper/state-of-online-gaming-2019/#spend.

Milne, L. R., Bennett, C. L., Ladner, R. E., & Azenkot, S. (2014, October). BraillePlay: Educational smartphone games for blind children. In *Proceedings of the 16th International ACM SIGACCESS Conference on Computers & Accessibility*(pp. 137–144). ACM.

Nasiri, N., Shirmohammadi, S., & Rashed, A. (2017, April). A serious game for children with speech disorders and hearing problems. In *2017 IEEE 5th International Conference on Serious Games and Applications for Health (SeGAH)* (pp. 1–7). IEEE.

Oliver, M. (2013). The social model of disability: Thirty years on. *Disability & Society, 28*(7), 1024–1026.

Paraskevopoulos, I. T., Tsekleves, E., Craig, C., Whyatt, C., & Cosmas, J. (2014). Design guidelines for developing customised serious games for Parkinson's Disease rehabilitation using bespoke game sensors. *Entertainment Computing, 5*(4), 413–424.

Park, H. J. (2011). Auditory and language training service model and serious game contents Design for the hearing-impaired. *Journal of Digital Contents Society, 12*(4), 467–474.

Robert, P., König, A., Amieva, H., Andrieu, S., Bremond, F., Bullock, R., ... Nave, S. (2014). Recommendations for the use of Serious Games in people with Alzheimer's Disease, related disorders and frailty. *Frontiers in Aging Neuroscience, 6,* 54.

Statista. (2015). *Most popular online categories worldwide as of May 2015, by reach of internet audience*. Retrieved from https://www.statista.com/statistics/276074/reach-of-most-popular-online-categories-worldwide/.

Sucar, L. E., Orihuela-Espina, F., Velazquez, R. L., Reinkensmeyer, D. J., Leder, R., & Hernández-Franco, J. (2013). Gesture therapy: An upper limb virtual reality-based motor rehabilitation platform. *IEEE Transactions on Neural Systems and Rehabilitation Engineering, 22*(3), 634–643.

Union of the Physically Impaired Against Segregation, UPIAS. (1976). *Fundamental principles of disability*. London: UPIAS. Retrieved from https://disability-studies.leeds.ac.uk/files/library/UPIAS-fundamental-principles.pdf.

Van Peppen, R. P. S., Kwakkel, G., Wood-Dauphinee, S., Hendriks, H. J. M., Van der Wees, P. J., & Dekker, J. (2004). The impact of physical therapy on functional outcomes after stroke: What's the evidence? *Clinical Rehabilitation, 18,* 833–862.

World Health Organization. (2001). *ICIDH-2: International classification of functioning, disability and health*. Retrieved from https://unstats.un.org/unsd/disability/pdfs/ac.81-b4.pdf.

World Health Organization. (2013). *How to use the ICF: A practical manual for using the international classification of functioning, disability and health (ICF)*. Retrieved from https://www.who.int/classifications/drafticfpracticalmanual2.pdf?ua=1.

World Health Organization. (2018). *Blindness and vision impairment*. Retrieved from https://www.who.int/news-room/fact-sheets/detail/blindness-and-visual-impairment.

Epilogue

Abstract This chapter encapsulates the essence of what has been discussed in this book, reflecting on the diversity of learning contexts and experiences that can lead to better learner engagement. These include approaches, strategies and practices that could be applied in schools as well as other educational settings. In addition, the chapter opens a window into how learners' experiences could be further diversified to cater to their needs in an uncertain and rapidly evolving future.

Introduction

We began this book with a discussion on the concept of learner *diversity*, the need to *differentiate* between their varied needs and to *develop* a variety of instructional strategies and approaches that would be engaging to them and relevant to their distinct contexts. The current chapter gathers the views of the various authors in response to the questions set out in the introductory chapter, namely with regards to the ways in which learners show diversity in the context of their study, the approaches and technological support that could be deployed to cater to their diverse needs, and the ways in which learner experiences could thus be diversified.

Summary

The chapters in this book present a good reflection of the diversity in learning contexts that underpin the basis of our current exploration. Whereas Chaps. 1 and 7 focus mainly on elementary/primary school contexts, Chaps. 3–5 present strategies that were applied in high/secondary school settings and with older students. Chapters 8 and 9 discuss initiatives that pertained to adult learners, while Chaps. 10, 11 and 14 explore applications or interventions that were applicable to all age groups. In addition, Chaps. 6, 12, 13 and 14 describe the diversification of experiences for learners with special educational needs.

With regards to the approaches and strategies used for diversifying learner experiences, several studies were targeted at using new pedagogical practices to enhance learning. For instance, in Chap. 2, Michael Hast used Tacit Knowledge Assessment that required learners to tap into their underlying conceptions to recognize scientific phenomena and to predict outcomes, following which they had the opportunity to revisit the concepts and improve their understanding. Likewise, in Chap. 3, Kah Loong Chue discussed how diversifying learner experiences through the adoption of a Team-Based Learning approach influenced learners' achievement emotions, thereby impacting learner cognitive processes, academic motivation and performance.

Other authors chose to discuss how diversifying learner experiences through innovative, and at times, unconventional approaches could influence learner attributes. Thus, in Chap. 4, Nasyita Mohtar described the use of Positive Psychology Interventions to improve students' peer acceptance and subjective well-being. In the same vein, Hester Oh (Chap. 5) explored the use of a collaborative process to improve student motivation in art class. In Chap. 8, Isabelle Ong discussed the use of play activities to diversify the experiences of adult learners and to optimize their learning. Several authors focused on new technologies to diversify and enhance learning through virtual experiences, especially when the actual, real-life experiences were not accessible to learners. Hence, David Bell and Jeffrey Smith described, in Chap. 7, how learner experiences can be diversified using *Virtual Excursion* online visitation programmes offered by The Museum of New Zealand Te Papa Tongarewa. Along the same line, Syazlin Sazali and colleagues described an initiative that enabled students from remote locations in Australia to learn through interactive online learning activities. This allowed students at a locational disadvantage to have access to and participate in activities that were traditionally classroom-based.

Four chapters in this book describe strategies or tools aimed at diversifying the learning experiences and catering to the exigencies of learners with special educational needs. In Chap. 12, Minglee Yong and Boon Ooi Lee found that a multitier system of support was effective for learners with emotional and behavioural disorders, while in Chap. 6, this author reviewed a variety of strategies put in place to provide diversity in gifted students' learning experiences. The two other chapters discussed how learners with special needs could have their experiences diversified and enriched with the use of new technological tools. Thus, in Chap. 13, Adeline Yeong and Anuradha Dutt discussed the suitability of video modelling as a tool to teach autistic students daily-life skills, and in Chap. 14, this author found that serious games could be designed to accommodate sensory and mobility impaired learners, for whom gameplay could enable them to enjoy and benefit from a whole new learning experience.

Finally, two of the chapters discussed policies and processes that were put in place to offer greater inclusivity to marginalized learners. In Chap. 9, Steven Sexton and Sandra Williamson-Leadley described New Zealand's ministerial directive to support Aotearoa New Zealand's 'priority' learners, through a master's level ITE programme that allowed student–teachers to be exposed to diverse experiences. On their part, in

Chap. 11, Miriam Mason, David Galloway and Andrew Joyce-Gibbons reviewed the work of EducAid, a small NGO in Sierra Leone, which runs residential schools offering a personalised learning system with appropriate teaching and learning methods for a diverse group of students who grew up in an impoverished, war-torn country.

Conclusion

Although this book has attempted to offer a comprehensive view of approaches and trends in the diversification of learner experiences across multiple contexts, the learning environment and needs of learners are never static, but constantly evolving. For instance, in a matter of months, the COVID-19 pandemic that has taken hold of the world, has forced educators and educational researchers to rethink and reassess the way teaching and learning can be carried out. Home-Based Learning (HBL), hitherto confined to those who, for various reasons, are unable to attend school, has become pervasive overnight as schools are forced to shut to curb disease transmission. However, what remains to be done are investigations on its effectiveness, as well as explorations on how home-based learner experiences can be further diversified and improved.

Peace activist, Coffin (2004, p. 34), once said 'Diversity may be the hardest thing for a society to live with, and perhaps the most dangerous thing for a society to be without'. What we have offered in this book is a variety of ideas for society to live with diversity, and not be without it.

Caroline Koh

Reference
Coffin, W. S. (2004). *Credo*. Westminster John Knox Press.

CPI Antony Rowe
Eastbourne, UK
January 13, 2021